A Future for Astyanax

Character and Desire in Literature

Ferguson

A Future for Astyanax

Character and Desire in Literature

by Leo Bersani

Columbia University Press
New York   1984

Columbia University Press
New York
Columbia University Press Morningside Edition 1984

This edition published by arrangement
with Little, Brown & Co.

The author is grateful to the *New York Times,* for permission to reprint his review of Jean Genet's book *Funeral Rites* as published in the *New York Times Book Review,* June 15, 1969. Copyright © 1969 by The New York Times Company.

Acknowledgment is also made to the journal *Novel: A Forum on Fiction,* for permission to reprint the author's essay "Flaubert and Emma Bovary: The Hazards of Literary Fusion," as published in the Fall 1974 issue. Copyright © 1974 by Novel Corp.

Library of Congress Cataloging in Publication Data

Bersani, Leo.
    A future for Astyanax.

    Bibliography: p.
    Includes index.
    1. Psychoanalysis in literature.   2. Characters and characteristics in literature.   3. Literature, Modern — History and criticism.   I. Title.
PN56.P92B37 1984   809'.93353   84-1792
ISBN 0-231-05938-8 (alk. paper)
ISBN 0-231-05939-6 (pbk. : alk. paper)

PRINTED IN THE UNITED STATES OF AMERICA

Clothbound editions of
Columbia University press books are
Smyth-sewn and printed on permanent
and durable acid-free paper.

For Richard Poirier

Contents

Preface

THE READER MAY FEEL — especially in the first half of this book — that any one of several other terms might have been substituted for the word "desire." As I use that word, it obviously has affinities with the eighteenth-century notion of enthusiasm, with the concept of vision in Milton and Blake as well as in English romantic criticism, and also with the idea of freedom and images of the frontier in American literature. I freely admit to a certain blurring of conceptual boundaries. All the words just mentioned suggest an area of human projection going beyond the limits of a centered, socially defined, time-bound self, and also beyond the recognized resources of language and confines of literary form.

Formulated in this way, the ambitions and constraints described in this book have been discussed before. In general, the best of these discussions have been corrective readings of other readings of, for example, romantic speculations about the visionary self or the numerous versions, in nineteenth-century American literature, of the theme of freedom. The earlier readings tended to credit the writers being studied with a somewhat naïve confidence in the viability of the most radical possibilities expressed in their work. Later critics have pointed out a more sophisticated attitude toward these possibilities even in writers whose apocalyptic stance might seem to leave little space for qualifying skepticism. For instance, it's especially striking to find in Emerson and Lawrence an awareness of the ways in which the very act of expressing a radical imagination in language and literature limits its realization, perhaps even erases what is radical in imagination. There are particularly good discussions of these issues in Lionel Trilling's *Beyond Culture*, Richard Poirier's *A World Elsewhere*, and Geoffrey Hartman's *Beyond Formalism*.

My own emphasis will be on certain bizarre developments in modern literature of the problems just outlined. The confrontation in nineteenth-century works between a structured, socially viable and verbally analyzable self and the wish to shatter psychic and social structures produces considerable stress and conflict. But the stresses are frequently resolved in certain accommodations, accommodations which realistic fiction has been especially apt at devising. Or else the writer may mock the very enterprise of committing to writing anti-structural intentions which the structures of both verbal consciousness and literary history inevitably defeat. We then have a literature of self-parody exhibiting, as its main subject, its undermining of the literary work's most ambitious project. There is another alternative which (especially in Anglo-American criticism) we are less familiar with. It's possible to locate, from Emily Brontë and Lautréamont to some contemporary theater, an attempt to dismiss defined structures of personality which, however, does not include any faith or even interest in a "higher" or "truer" self, or in fact any transcendent reality "beyond" the known self. Much visionary literature ends up by being elegiac: it expresses the anguish of unfulfilled desire, but that anguish carries within it the stubborn belief that visionary desires *could* be fulfilled, or, to put the problem in other terms, that the vision, although frustrated, was *of something*. We will be moving toward a literature quite different from this, toward what might even be called a celebratory sense of the failure of idealistic vision.

As an alternative to both the socially defined self and the free or universal or transcendent self, there are marginal or partial selves or, perhaps most interestingly, a scattered or disseminated self. The interest in these possibilities often takes strange, even ghoulish forms. As the title of my last chapter indicates, a radical psychic mobility can even involve, at least in fantasy, brutally dehumanizing activities. The delights of self-scattering may include putting "persons in pieces," an enterprise which, in certain pornographic writing, becomes an appropriate image for the process of violently deconstructing the self.

These are difficult notions to describe, largely because of the problematic relation between psychic marginality or self-scattering and verbal expression. It has seemed to me that a psychoanalytically oriented use of the term "desire" would be more useful to us than terms such as "vision" or "freedom," terms almost inseparable from idealistic associations and contexts. Hopefully, "desire" will both clarify adventures in psychic mobility and throw some new light on the comforts and the dangers of the structured self in realistic fiction and French classical theater. (Even from a psychoanalytic perspective, however, I have not undertaken a rigorous technical study of desire. The ways in which I use, modify, and even frequently drop psychoanalytic definitions of desire will be determined by the particular requirements of particular works.) Freudian theory serves the most constraining cultural enterprises in its statements about the history and nature of human desire, at the same time that it outlines the operations of desiring fantasy in ways which explode its own narrow views of the "natural" shapes and rhythms of desire.

I recognize that the disadvantages of what I have undertaken are that I begin by going over some familiar ground which may strike some readers as having already been sufficiently treated, and that the new territory we reach in Part Two evokes analyses which at times may seem not only unfamiliar but perhaps even a bit zany. Students of literature familiar with recent French criticism will be less disoriented than others in my sections on Lautréamont and Rimbaud, but, as far as I know, no one else has attempted to give to the theatrical work of Joe Chaikin and of Robert Wilson, or to the sado-masochistic feasts of *Histoire d'O* and *L'Image*, the kind of serious scrutiny to which I submit them here. Part Two is tougher going than Part One, but it will probably strike many people as more exciting, and so I invite the reader — if he feels so disposed — to reverse my own order and to begin reading, perhaps after the introductory chapter on "Murderous Lovers," with the section on Lautréamont and Emily Brontë.

Richard Poirier's suggestions concerning the entire manuscript have been immensely useful to me, and Eléonore Zimmermann's comments helped very much in the reworking of my section on Rimbaud. I am grateful to the Rutgers University Research Council for offering me a grant during 1971–72 to begin work on this book. A few sections have appeared as articles in *Partisan Review, The Yale Review, The New York Times Book Review, Novel: A Forum on Fiction,* and the French review *Poétique*; I appreciate the permission which these publications have given to reprint parts of the present study. Finally, I wish to thank Coe Senour and Debra Zaller for the consistently cheerful competence with which they prepared the manuscript.

Berkeley, September 1975

A Future for Astyanax

Character and Desire in Literature

Murderous Lovers

THE CRITICAL ARGUMENTS, demonstrations and interpretations of this book could be located in an interval between two scenes of erotic violence — one from Racinian tragedy and the other from "Jean de Berg's" pornographic novel *L'Image*.

In Racine's *Andromaque*, Ménélas has sent Oreste into the province of Epire in order to demand that Pyrrhus surrender Hector's son Astyanax to the Greeks. Fearful lest Astyanax one day attempt to avenge the massacre of his family and the defeat of his people at Troy, the Greeks insist that the child must die. For Pyrrhus, Oreste's mission is, in part, an opportunity for sexual blackmail. He is in love with Astyanax's mother, Andromaque, and in Scene Seven of Act Three Pyrrhus's threats to Hector's widow become brutally explicit. Marry me, he tells her, or watch me condemn your son to death by handing him over to the Greeks. When Andromaque's confidante urges her, in the following scene, to marry Pyrrhus in order to save Astyanax, Andromaque, in a famous passage, evokes her first vision of Pyrrhus on that "cruel night" at Troy when he led the Greeks in the slaughter of her countrymen:

> Songe, songe, Céphise, à cette nuit cruelle
> Qui fut pour tout un peuple une nuit éternelle;

Figure-toi Pyrrhus, les yeux étincelants,
Entrant à la lueur de nos palais brûlants,
Sur tous mes frères morts se faisant un passage,
Et, de sang tout couvert, échauffant le carnage;
Songe aux cris des vainqueurs, songe aux cris des mourants
Dans la flamme étouffés, sous le fer expirants;
Peins-toi dans ces horreurs Andromaque éperdue:
Voilà comme Pyrrhus vint s'offrir à ma vue;
Voilà par quels exploits il sut se couronner;
Enfin, voilà l'époux que tu me veux donner.[1]

Luridly illuminated nights of violence (or of potential violence) are not uncommon in Racine. They indicate a traumatic break in the time and in the meanings of Racinian tragedy. Under the fitful light of torches and in the midst of a crowd's confused shouting, the hero's life is fragmented; its continuity is broken, something abruptly ends and something else abruptly begins. Titus the lover dies and Titus the emperor is born on the "nuit enflammée" when the people of Rome and the royal ambassadors from abroad acclaim him as their leader in *Bérénice*. In *Bajazet*, the chaotic spectacle of terrified soldiers, slaves and women wandering in the seraglio marks the end of Roxane's reign, and Mithridate's career as leader of the world's resistance to Roman tyranny comes to a close in the "désordre partout" and the "horreur d'un combat ténébreux" in which Pompée defeats an army of half-naked soldiers hiding in the night's shadows. In *Andromaque*, the nocturnal scene described in the passage I quoted a moment ago is catastrophic, but, as in the scene of carnage evoked by Josabet early in *Athalie*, a child is saved.

These traumatizing nocturnal tableaux indicate the death of the old and the birth of the new, a violent passage from one psychological and social order to another. I think that they are also dramatic metaphors for a fragmentation of meaning which is the Racinian hero's only hope of escape from the continuities and the coherent patterns of desire which condemn him to a life of repetition. Of course, what is repeated in Racine is a certain scheme of sexual passion, and it's true that Pyrrhus's spectacularly dramatic encounter with Andromaque imprisons him within the structures of Racinian passion. But his relation to Andromaque includes the possibility of feelings mostly undefined in the play but which are, I think, alien to those structures. In Racine's claustrophobic theater there are the outlines, however blurred, of a theater of freedom. And by that I mean a theater in which the self would be liberated from the unhappy and limiting coherence in which a psychology of sexual passion entraps it. Even when the consequences of those nocturnal traumatic scenes monotonously repeat a mode of feeling or of desiring which preceded them, the scenes themselves suggest an intention more radical than anything Racine imagines for his characters' sustained relations with one another. Only violence, in any case, could destroy the structure of those relations; and for Racine the question seems to be whether anything at all would survive what is fundamentally an explosion of being.

For criticism, literary scenes such as the one from Racine which we have been looking at have a dangerously elusive density. They seem to be charged with meaning, and yet they resist interpretation with the interrogative stillness of nondiscursive art. With our speculations, we wander around their enigmatic shapes, in the same way as the characters in James's *The Golden Bowl* helplessly wander, with their endless critical appreciations, around Maggie Verver's enigmatic, sculptural and silent presence. These scenes, which appear to condense passionate intentions into coercive images, can (and probably should) be the object of the critic's fascination; they can't, however, be taken as substitutes for his arguments. Even within these introductory remarks, we should perhaps put some distance between the two scenes being evoked, unfold their meanings, in our first interval of critical argument and reasoned interpretation.

This book will be a study of the correlations between different ways of conceiving desire and different ways of conceiving character in literature. From Racine to contemporary theater and some recent erotic fiction, I will be following stages in the *deconstruction of the self* in modern literature. My general organization will be in terms of a polarity between structured desires and fragmented desires. By structured desires I mean desiring impulses sublimated into emotional "faculties" or passions and thereby providing the basis for the notion of a distinct and coherently unified personality. We probably first experience desire in our lives as a naïve confusion of the self with the world. In the scenic (and hallucinatory) mode of desire which will be most effectively represented for us in Rimbaud's *Illuminations*, the theatricalized self *is* a series of pictures of

the world. But our desires are of course also — and perhaps primarily
— repressed. A sense both of the forbidden nature of certain desires
and of the incompatibility of reality with our desiring imagination
makes the negation of desire inevitable. But to deny desire is not to
eliminate it; in fact, such denials multiply the appearances of each
desire in the self's history. In denying a desire, we condemn ourselves to finding it everywhere. Repressed desire is repeated, disguised and sublimated. Its reappearances in various forms at different
levels of mental life create the intelligible structures, the psychic
continuities which can be formulated as an individual's personality
or character. The disguised repetitions of inhibited desires constitute
the coherent self.

But, as we shall see principally in the discussions of Racine and
of realistic fiction in the first half of our study, this psychic coherence involves a serious crippling of desire. The viability of the
structured self depends on an impoverishment of desire. The desiring imagination's contacts with the world are limited by the need
for preserving the intelligibility of a psychic structure. Even more
dangerously, the renunciation of desire, as Freud suggested, may
increase our sense of guilt instead of assuaging it. And heightened
guilt welcomes the potentially ferocious punishments of conscience
and of external moral authority. An important psychological consequence of sublimated (civilized) desire may be a suicidal melancholy. In our sublimations, our desires never die. But the endless
repetition of desires suppressed by guilt and angry frustration ultimately leads to the fantasy of death as the absolute pleasure. (D. H.
Lawrence's *Women in Love* will provide us with a novelistic version
of this equivalence between death and unending repetition.) The
repeated refusal to confess our desires gives them a kind of crim-
inally immortal activity from which only the definitive immobility
of death might rescue us.

The political implications of suicidal melancholy in a culture of
repression and sublimation would in themselves adequately justify
our asking about the possibility of reversing the process which I've
just outlined — that is, the possibility of desublimating desire (and,
correlatively, of deconstructing the self). Can a psychology of fragmentary and *dis*continuous desires be reinstated? What are the
strategies by which the self might be once again theatricalized? How
might desire recover its original capacity for projecting nonstruc-

turable *scenes?* Questions similar to these have been asked by other writers. Freud's remarkable disciple Sándor Ferenczi spoke of human character as an abnormality, as a mechanization of a particular mode of reaction. Post-Oedipal character-formations would involve the centralizing (and the spiritualizing) of pre-Oedipal fetishistic attachments. More recently, critiques of Freudianism have enjoyed a certain notoriety in our culture. I'm of course thinking of Norman O. Brown, Herbert Marcuse, R. D. Laing and the "anti-psychiatry" movement, and in France, Gilles Deleuze and Félix Guattari's impressive and intensely polemical *L'Anti-Oedipe*.[2] In different ways, all these writers are interested in helping us to reinstate a heterogeneity of our desiring impulses; and this project involves — especially in Brown and Deleuze — a militant intellectual campaign against the sublimating processes of mental life and a hyperbolic defense of the desublimated desire. With only a modest injustice to both works, *Life Against Death* and *L'Anti-Oedipe* could be read as philosophical pastorals of pre-Oedipal desire; they sketch the outlines of an Arcadia of polymorphous perversity. More interestingly, they suggest that a new emphasis on the *peripheries* of our desiring attention would not only diversify desire but would also keep it mobile. Peripheral seductions would no longer be discarded because they can't be related to a dominant interest; even our dominant interest — our "centers" of desire — would have merely a provisional, peripheral appeal. *The* desiring self might even disappear as we learn to multiply our discontinuous and partial desiring selves.

I want to raise these issues again for three reasons. First of all, I think that the thought of the men I've just mentioned is weakened by their tendency to politicize psychology somewhat glibly. Obviously, no psychology is apolitical;[3] every theory of the mind has a *strategic* value for the culture in which it is developed. But the implication of many recent critiques of Freudian thought is that an analysis of the social orders which psychological theory serves makes unnecessary any further argument about the epistemological validity of the theory. Unfortunately, however, even the most abhorrent system of thought is never adequately refuted by an exposure of the political manipulations which it either inspires or rationalizes; it must also be approached as an argument about "truth." This double approach would, ideally, make for a continuous moving back and forth between an analysis of certain logical weaknesses or contradictions in a psychological theory (for example, the attempt to repress the discovery of repression in Freud himself and especially in post-Freudian ego psychologists), and a study of the hidden political assumptions which may explain the need or the convenience of such contradictions.

Political action alone will never invalidate a philosophical argument about truth. It may make the argument seem superfluous, and it may almost fully discredit the historical use to which that argument has been put. But even in a society which realizes our brightest, most exaltingly generous dreams of the human community, we may find ourselves haunted by the impulses of a self which we had too easily dismissed as an outmoded superstructure of a rejected form of social organization. The history of a human being's desiring impulses includes modes of exchange between the self and the world, or between consciousness and the unconscious, which would probably reappear and would therefore have to be taken into account in *any* society. If, for instance, we were violently to break free from the forms of social organization which institutionalize the Oedipal structure and its conflicts, would this free us from the necessity of passing through the complexities of Oedipal love, hate, guilt and renunciation in the history of individual desires? The mere fact that every living organism has to accommodate itself to a field of reality in which its needs can never be entirely fulfilled suggests that the self, far from being only an ideological construct, would always have to go through a difficult negotiating process between its own appetitive energies and both a world *and* an internal economy which limit the possibilities of performing our energies and satisfying our appetites.

My own ambivalent attitude toward psychoanalytic thought in this book can be explained by my feeling that certain aspects of psychoanalysis are more resistant to ideological analyses than others. It will be clear from the first half of this study — especially Chapters One and Two — that I agree with Deleuze and Guattari's emphasis on the tactical purposes served by the importance which psychoanalysis gives to the Oedipal triangle. The tracing of all desires back to familial patterns of desire, coupled with the insistence on a certain pattern of normal psychic growth, neglects some crucial and highly visible psychological evidence (as we shall see in Racine) in order to enclose desire within social structures based on family structures and held together by our guilt about incestuous impulses.

The Freud of the Oedipus complex is of course the best-known Freud. There is, however, another Freud, a much more difficult and ambiguous thinker who has been brought to our attention by contemporary French psychoanalytic theory.[4] My second major reason for reopening the discussion of sublimation and desublimation in this book is that this other Freud — the Freud of *Beyond the Pleasure Principle*, or of the essays "Instincts and Their Vicissitudes," "A Child Is Being Beaten" and "From the History of an Infantile Neurosis" (the "Wolf Man" case) should help us to reformulate the terms of that discussion and to make our arguments more sophisticated. The contrasts which I've been proposing — between sublimated and desublimated desires, between the structured self and the fragmented self — are, I think, valid, but they are nonetheless rather crudely schematic. The deconstruction of the self involves much more than a happy return to the polymorphous pleasures of sensual intensities not yet petrified (as a result of being denied) into fixed and partial character structures. Our thought about this process of deconstruction should engage us in a problematic reflection about different forms of psychic mobility. In Lautréamont and Emily Brontë, for instance, we will find the phenomenon of a mysterious scattering of the self (a phenomenon far more subversive of stable psychic identities than the diffusions of the self along the narrative surfaces of Proust's *A la Recherche du temps perdu*). With *Les Chants de Maldoror* and *Wuthering Heights*, we will be confronting metamorphoses of the self, as well as the possibility of an almost unthinkable and yet compelling identity between the self and the other. And, inspired by a particularly dense and rich passage of Freud's "Instincts and Their Vicissitudes," I will be considering, at the end of this study, both the menace and the strangely humanizing potential of a sado-masochistic sexuality which shatters the self out of a dangerous security about its own sexual identity. There is a post-Oedipal security which, as we shall see in *Histoire d'O*, may divide the world into two hostile camps and condemn each sex to a panicky wish to annihilate the irreducible difference of the other sex.

Finally, I think that there is a special profit to be gained from a study of character and desire *in literature*. First of all, literature is a privileged area for a study of an oscillation between thought and sensation. By virtue of its purely verbal mode of existence, literature inevitably defends the abstract and the highly structured. Because language is a system, and because words may be, as Freud argued, compromise-formations for nonverbal scenes and satisfactions, literature is, in part, always a sublimating activity. It gives structure and continuity to what may be fragmented and discontinuous in the history of our desires. On the other side, there is a strong desublimating tendency in literature, an attempt perhaps to revive, through verbal stimulation, memories of intense bodily pleasures. As in other modes of fantasy, the writer, in the privacy and leisure of composition, may be engaged in inventing repetitions of sensual intensities. Furthermore, in the act of writing, the word itself seems to be experienced partly as an insubstantial sign referring to meanings beyond itself, and partly as a sensuous object referring to nothing but its own shape, sound and position in a design of numerous word-objects. The profound connection between literature and sensation is suggested in testimony as diverse as Proust's use of his body's involuntary memories as a principle of narrative organization in the novel, Nietzsche's suggestion that in the "esthetic state" sensuality doesn't disappear but is simply transfigured and no longer enters consciousness as sexual excitement, and Flaubert's demonstration in *Madame Bovary* of literature's paradoxical (and treacherous) status as an abstract guarantee of sensual ecstasy.

Literature has an even more profound relevance to the subject of these essays. It is not merely instructive *about* desire; in a sense, desire *is* a phenomenon of the literary imagination. Desire is an activity within a lack; it is an appetite stimulated by an absence. But it is never only a lack. Desire is a hallucinated satisfaction in the absence of the source of satisfaction. In other words, it is an appetite of the imagination. Indeed, the infant is already an artist of sorts in the sense that he invents and is excited by imaginary equivalents of remembered satisfactions. The activity of desiring is inseparable from the activity of fantasizing. There is no scene of desire which is not an elaboration, a kind of visual interpretation, of other scenes. In the same way that literary works are always critical revisions of other literary works, our desires reformulate both other desires and the pleasures which are at the source of all desire.

Like literature, desire is inseparable from repetition, but they are both modes of repetition which produce difference. The desublimation of desire will never eliminate repetition from desire; a desiring fantasy has, at the very least, an allusive relation both to other desiring fantasies and to the absent sensual intensities conjured up by the scenarios of desire. But we will come across attempts to abolish repetition entirely from literature, from desire and from the self. In Rimbaud and Artaud, the allusive repetitions of art and of desire are rejected — with a panicky violence — because they are condemned as proof of the self's dependence on enslaving origins or sources. For these writers, repetition is merely derivative; it simply proves our incapacity to produce new scenes of desire. Our fate, from this perspective, is to perpetuate the same: the son can only reenact the father, the present can only reproduce the past, and an individual's behavior in time is doomed to be nothing more than the obsessive if disguised performances of a repressed but all-pervasive inner "text." To what extent can repetition be enacted in a non-derivative mode? Or, in other terms, can repetition be separated from repression and sublimation?

This question is crucial to the topic which interests us, for the deconstruction of the self and the diversification of our desires depend on our finding ways to repeat ourselves which don't point to hidden, permanent and central truths about the self. Some contemporary theatrical experiments, as we shall see in Chapter Ten, impressively propose an allusive mode of repetition as an alternative to both the violent denial of all repetition and the inability to conceive of it except as a triumph of paternal authority (a triumph of the "parent" desires behind the symptoms produced by repression and even the ideals produced in sublimation). It would be difficult to overemphasize the importance of such an alternative. For the psychic deconstruction which I will be speaking of is far from being the kind of peaceful return to the unrepressed pleasures of the body dreamed of by contemporary theoretical pastoralists. It is much more likely to be an enterprise of great violence, a triumph of fantasies of patricide and deocide. And even without the literal realization of these fantasies, even when they have been modulated and processed for our real behavior in the world, their profound violence would affect every aspect of the cultural life in which they are represented. Is the best emblematic image of desublimated desire

Andromaque's horrified memory of Pyrrhus covered with the blood of her countrymen and her family? Pyrrhus has led the massacre of Andromaque's past. And his body, bespattered with blood, is, after all, an invitation to Andromaque to forget brothers, father, husband and country, and to raise her child on the ruins of her past. This murderous lover implicitly asks Andromaque to help him invent a future for Astyanax.

Our discussion has returned us to our first scene of violence, and the logic inspired by that image of violence will allow us to complete the scenic enclosure of these introductory remarks by presenting a second scene of erotic violence. I have just been speaking of the patricidal project which may be implicit in desublimated desire. There is perhaps an even more fundamental violence intrinsic to all desire by virtue of the lack without which desire is inconceivable. I want to consider a melodramatic, perhaps mad, sexual version of the devastations of reality to which the emptiness of desire invites the desiring imagination. I will be discussing "Jean de Berg's" *L'Image* in some detail in Chapter Eleven. For the moment, let's look at a scene from Jean's dream on the night before Claire comes to offer herself to him in the role of the masochistic victim which, until now, has been played for both Jean and Claire by Anne: "A nude girl is tied to each of the two columns, one with her front toward me, the other her back. I come closer. I realize that they are both dead, but still warm. Their bodies are pierced by many triangular stilettos in the most propitious areas." It's possible to see in the triangular wounds made by these stilettos an image of the female genitals *as* a wound. This is a man's dream in a story of violently sadistic sex with women. And it suggests, I think, that each wound inflicted on the woman re-creates the "wound" of her genitals. With each stab, another bloody vagina appears on the victim's body (and there is a sweet-tasting blood on all the wounds in the dream). It's as if the man's sadism created, or more accurately multiplied, the woman's sexuality, at the same time that it gave a physical reality both to male fantasies about the violent origin of the vagina and to male fury at the female genitals for being only an "absence." The sex of women would be the result of the violence of men. The latter ravage what they perceive as an emptiness; in the male imagination which produces this dream, violence toward women would thus be a *mutilation of a lack.*

But desire itself is an activity within a certain lack, and the logic of our desiring fantasies leads ultimately to the annihilation of all otherness. In order for plenitude to replace absence, the world we desire must replace the world we perceive. Desire is intrinsically violent both because it spontaneously assumes this annihilation of everything alien to it, and because its fantasies include a rageful recognition of the world's capacity to resist and survive our desires. But the world also offers images of desire itself. Objects of perception which can be interpreted as a lack easily become metaphors for desire; and our vision (and/or manipulation) of these objects may include a violence analogous to that associated with the activity of desiring. When this image of desire is also an object of our desires, it accumulates, so to speak, a double dose of violence. The triangular stab wounds all over the dead bodies of the two girls in Jean's dream — the girls *as* vaginal wounds — simultaneously express a hallucinated desire *for* women and a projection onto female sexuality of the intrinsically murderous nature of all desire. The logic implicit in this suggestively murderous dream in *L'Image* is that the victimization of women is the inevitable consequence of their double role as objects and analogues of desire. In the latter role, the brutalization of women represents a truth about the ontology of desire ordinarily repressed from our desiring fantasies. That truth comes back to us in the form of a mutilated lack in the world. The woman is also wounded because desire always includes some measure of the angry frustration without which desire is inconceivable. Desire depends on the withdrawal of a satisfaction; even though our desiring fantasies include certain pleasures, they also dramatize a spontaneous fury at those invincible forces (both in the world and in ourselves) which have condemned us to the loss of ecstasy, to experiencing pleasure as part of a lack.

It is perhaps the role of sublimation, conscience and character-formation to modify the potentially limitless aggressiveness of desire. In pornographic literature, the characters use one another's bodies with the same freedom from any constraining resistances or consequences as the fantasies of desire naturally tend to use the world. A more realistic sense of the extent to which reality can accommodate our desires produces a literature which, on the one hand, too frequently argues for a petrification of our desires within the character structures least threatening to established psychological and social orders. But what we call realism in art can also be an exercise in the beneficently unsettling interpretation of desire. Much of the *art* of realistic fiction consists of critical arguments, demonstrations and interpretations. And the discursively problematic chatter of criticism breaks up the sculptural finality of scenic desire and invites us to a certain skepticism about *any* fixed forms of desire or of the self. Criticism is a type of agitated thought; at best it can dislocate the obsessive desire and promote mobility in our self-definitions.

Strangely enough, we can find the promise of a similar mobility in the violence of desire itself. Pyrrhus — "les yeux étincelants" and "de sang tout couvert, échauffant le carnage" — is *carried away* by sadistic excitement on the night of Troy's destruction. It is this image of shaken cruelty that he presents to Andromaque as a possible source of erotic stimulation. Pyrrhus "outside of himself" is Andromaque's first image of the man who, later on, will threaten her in a far more calculated — and sinister — fashion. Nothing is more curious than this suggestion (which *L'Image* and *Histoire d'O* will document for us) that the activity of desiring may include a pleasure intense enough to shatter the desiring self. If this is the case, then the fantasies of both criticism *and* art could take place in those oddly mobile intervals of mental life which, at the beginning of these remarks, I had mistakenly reserved for the touchingly insecure (if proud) procedures of rational critical thought.

PART ONE

Structures of Desire

CHAPTER ONE

Racine, Psychoanalysis and Oedipus

FOR TRADITIONAL, non-Freudian criticism, psychological repetitious-ness in Racine is generally something to be "corrected" (if not denied) by the critic's demonstration of psychological variety in Racinian tragedy. An obsessively repeated diagram of sexual passion is somewhat obscured — to the relief of most admirers of Racine — by an impressive range of psychological nuances. For psychoanalytic criticism, on the other hand, thematic monotony in literature is, if only implicitly, an esthetic virtue. Taking repetition into account is perhaps the fundamental operation in the psychoanalytic reading of a literary text. Repetition provides the psychoanalytically oriented critic with his most important clue to meaningful psychological structures in a writer's work. As we shall see in the case of Racine, it makes characters intelligible within designs of meaning which transcend any single realization of character. And, most interest-ingly, it invites the critic to revise the very notion of what a literary character is.

Now the type of personal identity arrived at in traditional psy-chological analyses of literature is somewhat paradoxical. On the one hand, these analyses depend on our respecting the text's literal detail: we must be sensitive to particular uses of language, especially to those subtleties of tone which, in Racine's *Andromaque* for example, distinguish Pyrrhus's moral energy from Oreste's defeated passivity, or Hermione's impulsiveness from Andromaque's cooler temperament. On the other hand, we can describe personality only in a chain of abstractions: in Hermione, we find wounded vanity, tenderness, jealousy, rage, remorse, etc. Personality in traditional psychological analysis is an allegorical myth. In medieval allegory, an attempt is made to articulate conflicting impulses in mental life by making separate, objective entities of these impulses. Faculties are abstracted from the flux of mind and embodied in "characters" who really represent ideas *about* character. Shame and Reason in *Le Roman de la rose* are in themselves not exactly abstractions, but are rather objectifications of abstract thinking about concrete mental processes. Some of the problems involved in this technique for making sense of the mind become evident when we move to a more sophisticated art which groups the various abstract faculties within a single figure — an operation which gives us personality in literature. There is no fundamental discontinuity between characters in Racine — as well as in most nineteenth-century fiction — and the figures of medieval allegory. In writers as different as Racine, Balzac and Dickens, the mental faculties dramatized in allegory are concealed behind behavior which *represents* those faculties. And the critical method appropriate to this literary strategy is one which treats the words and acts of literary characters as signs of the allegorical entities which make up these characters. The sort of critical analysis most frequently applied to classical texts is itself a literary genre akin to forms of literature more primitive than the classical or realistic texts being analyzed. Criticism, through the psychological categories it uses to explicate a Racinian or Balzacian character, thus "helps" Racinian tragedy and Balzacian fiction to regress to their sources.

In what sense do the mental faculties which this critical exercise abstracts from behavior constitute an individual? The danger, after all, is that Hermione may seem to be merely the incoherent sum of qualitative abstractions which of course don't necessarily add up to any "total" at all: jealousy + vanity + rage + remorse = ? Furthermore, most of the psychological categories we use to describe her can be used to describe the other characters in *Andromaque*. Does Oreste become Oreste through, say, a substitution of despair for vanity in this addition? In part, the individualities described by psychological criticism are in effect both brought into a shared human nature and distinguished from one another by just such variations in the way elements from a common store of analytical tokens are distributed among various figures in a play or a novel. Even slight differences between one column of mental states and another can make the difference between two names, that is, between two personalities. Of course, both Racinian tragedy and realistic fiction resist such purely abstract characterizations on the part of criticism. Mental states are, so to speak, clothed in a variety of physical and social appearances which obscure the abstract nature of characters' psychological identities and make it easy for us to differentiate among characters. It is, for example, strikingly the case in Balzac that a mass of concrete detail helps us to visualize characters who otherwise might fade into a monotonous repetition of gestures illustrating the trait which defines their essential being (Paternity in Goriot, Avarice in Grandet). In Balzac and especially in Dickens, language is one of those particularizing appearances. The repetition of extremely idiosyncratic speech operates as a sign of a character's unchangeable psychological makeup, at the same time that such speech gives to a psychological abstraction the appearance of an individual invention. Even in Racine, where there is practically no physical description at all and where a more generalized language communicates mental states, certain particularities of situation serve to individualize figures who belong, psychologically, to a single community of passion. Several of the verses attributed to Hermione could easily be said by Roxane or Phèdre, but the different evocations of an adolescent princess, of a reigning concubine in a Turkish harem, and of the no-longer-young daughter of Minos and Pasiphaë give local variations to a psychology of abstract universals.

Both criticism and literature participate, in different ways and in varying degrees, in assumptions about personality which always play a dominant role in the makeup of an entire culture's "personality." Racinian monologues are frequently model-demonstrations of the psychology I've just briefly described. They are particularly revealing of what could be called the additive bias in this view of mental life. Different states of mind communicate with one another in the sense that the expression of state number one includes something which makes the appearance of state number two plausible.

These associative connections don't threaten the essential structure of the monologue, in which each mental state is clearly delimited, and restricted to an allotted number of verses. Hermione's famous monologue at the beginning of Act Five of *Andromaque* can be divided into five distinct moods: confusion, self-pity, anger at herself, jealousy and desire for revenge, and tenderness for Pyrrhus. Some flexibility is possible in the label we attach to each mental "figure" in the addition; but the monologue is an excellent example of the encouragement which literature itself can give to the abstractions and allegorizations of psychological criticism. Significantly, the analysis of Racinian monologues has always been a favorite classroom exercise; to the extent that it teaches us to equate human particularities with complex but manageable intellectual abstractions, it provides useful training in the more or less official psychological language of our culture.

Individuality in classical, pre-Freudian psychology tends to be a sum of abstract psychological states. However, this in no way decreases the emphasis on individuality itself, which is of course a major value of Western psychology. Indeed, most psychological discussions of literature have been exercises in differentiating among characters, in providing for each character a distinct, recognizable identity. Psychological repetition in a writer is thus likely to be looked at as a defect, as a sign of the limited and obsessive nature of his imagination. The importance of such repetition for psychoanalytic thought points to a subversion of the cult of individuality. As we shall have occasion to see several times in the course of this book, psychoanalysis both invites us to seek an alternative to a psychology of the person or the individual and discourages such a search by its own mythology of individual growth and of the healthily constituted personality. In literary studies, the psychoanalytically oriented critic is comparatively indifferent to the individual integrity of characters. In studying Racine, for example, he will pay less attention to Néron's personality within the context of *Britannicus* than to Néron's "position" in a pattern which links all Racine's plays in a single structure of significance. He will not be primarily interested in the particularities which, added up, define Néron's character; rather, he may even allow some of these particularities to be blurred in order to see how, along with several other Racinian heroes, Néron fulfills a major structural function in Racinian tragedy. In psychoanalytic criticism, "different works by a writer are merged into a single work; situations and characters lose their clear outlines, their forms disappear and then return, like the figures in a body of moving water. We are no longer working with distinct objects, in the light of consciousness, but in a field of inner forces at once obsessive and fluid." In this "field of inner forces," psychic energies move from one dramatic image to another, irrespective of age or of sex. Various characters serve the same function, and the identity of each character is overdetermined.

The quotation in the previous paragraph comes from an excellent psychoanalytic study of Racine: Charles Mauron's *L'Inconscient dans l'oeuvre et la vie de Racine.*[1] Mauron has written the best psychoanalytically inspired literary criticism I know of. In recent years, he has been overshadowed in France by the more dazzling theoretical work of Jacques Lacan and his group, but none of these psychoanalytic theorists has given us anything like Mauron's thorough, persuasive and tactful studies of literature. Mauron's position is Freudian, and among post-Freudian psychoanalysts he is influenced principally by Melanie Klein and the English school of psychoanalysts inspired by her work. As precursors for his psychoanalytic literary studies, he names, among others, Otto Rank, Edmund Bergler, Roger Fry and W. Ronald Fairbairn. I want to look at Mauron's study of Racine rather closely as part of a more general appraisal of the cultural significance of a psychoanalytic interest in literature. What follows will be a continual seesawing between Mauron's analyses and my own ideas about Racine; I'll try to keep the responsibilities for the various points clear as we move along.

How does Mauron "retell" Racinian tragedy? The most stable dramatic situation in Racine's theater is, Mauron writes, an obsessive relation with the mother. Along with this fixed element, there are two principal "factors of movement," that is, factors which undergo important changes from *Andromaque* to *Athalie*: (1) the attempt to realize a love distinct from an attachment to the mother, and (2) the transformation of characters who at first play the role of the hero's double into the father. Since there is no "real" mother or father in three of the plays Mauron concentrates on (*Andromaque, Bérénice* and *Bajazet*), what does he mean in giving them this central role in Racine's tragedies? He begins by offering schematic résumés of eight plays, admittedly oversimplified plot summaries which nevertheless reveal a significant pattern of continuity and development. In *Andromaque, Britannicus, Bérénice* and *Bajazet*, the character whom Mauron designates as "the self" oscillates between a virile aggressive woman and a tender, loved one. In each case, the self has an emotional or moral obligation toward the aggressive woman, who may also have the power to punish him if he doesn't fulfill that obligation. Pyrrhus rejects Hermione for Andromaque; Néron tries to free himself from his mother's domination and pursues Junie; Titus is faced with a dual Bérénice, who is both the woman he is rejecting and the woman he loves;[2] Bajazet would like to escape from Roxane's dangerous love and be free to love Atalide. With *Mithridate*, the picture changes: a father-judge appears who menaces his woman and his children with death. Mithridate considers punishing his sons and Monime; Agamemnon (in *Iphigénie*) is going to sacrifice his daughter to the gods; Thésée (in *Phèdre*) actually has Hippolyte killed by Neptune; and in Racine's last play, the divinely inspired Joad sends Athalie to her death, thus protecting her grandson, whom Athalie had almost taken from the temple by force.

Now Mauron is obviously put on the track of the scheme he proposes by the presence in Racine's plays of some indisputable family situations: Néron's desperate attempt to become independent of his mother, Mithridate's inclination to punish his sons for declaring their love to a woman he considers as his wife, and Phèdre's love for her husband's son. What Mauron does is to reformulate in terms of family relationships situations from other plays where the configurations of relationships repeat those we find in the literally familial plots. Thus, since Hermione's attempt to prevent Pyrrhus from marrying Andromaque (like Agrippine's trying to draw Néron away from Junie) includes an appeal to obligations contracted in the past, and since both Hermione and Agrippine accuse Pyrrhus and Néron of ingratitude and infidelity, Mauron proceeds from this similarity of function to a similarity of identity in the unconscious structure of the plays. Racine's unconscious uses Hermione in the same way it uses Agrippine. This seems to mean that, under the psychoanalytic x-ray, Hermione becomes Pyrrhus's mother. More precisely, we should of course say that Pyrrhus's function in the play is that of the ego, and the other characters represent "his temptations or his defenses, his desires or his fears." Hermione, like

Agrippine, Roxane and Phèdre, embodies the fantasy of a frightening, lascivious and powerful mother from whose fascination the child's ego — dramatized in Pyrrhus, Néron, Bajazet and Hippolyte — tries, more or less successfully from one play to the next, to liberate itself.

Essentially, Mauron interprets Racine's theater as a failed attempt to pass from an obsessional relation with the mother to a normal Oedipal situation which would in turn be resolved, thus allowing for the emergence of an adult heterosexual self. In an interesting chapter on the "doubles" in Racine's theater, Mauron traces the development, from Créon (in *La Thébaïde*) to Acomat (in *Bajazet*) of a series of characters — including Oreste, Antiochus, and Burrhus — who are either unloved or indifferent to love, who enjoy a certain authority which the other characters manage to dismiss rather easily, and who may also play the role of a desexualized witness of the hero's love. In Acomat, these traits come together. The older minister, ready to assume power and to marry Atalide for political reasons rather than for reasons of passion, creates the dim outlines of an Oedipal structure in *Bajazet* (Acomat-Atalide-Bajazet) which coexists with the earlier psychic structure (of the hero between two women: Roxane-Bajazet-Atalide), and which replaces the earlier structure in the frankly Oedipal pattern of Racine's next play, *Mithridate*. Thus the figure of the father derives from a double of the son, a double who had witnessed the son's tragic love and who transforms sexual energy into political or military energy. The father is the son's opening onto the world; he provides the impetus and the example for an impatient wish — expressed by Titus, Bajazet, Xipharès and Hippolyte — to substitute a life of action for the monotonous recitation of basically incestuous fears and desires. If this wish were realized, Racine's plays would of course be profoundly changed, and the mode in which family life itself is lived would undergo important transformations. But has the dilemma of the early plays really been solved?

With *Phèdre*, we suddenly find ourselves back to tragedy, and the most somber, unrelieved tragedy — a fact we might find inexplicable if we hadn't noticed how ambiguous the "relief" is which the father brings to the Racinian hero. First of all, if, as Mauron claims, the father's nature is derived from the conflict between mother and son, there is always the risk that his harshness will become as dangerous for the son as the mother's fierce passion. He is a kind of desexualized union of mother and son, which of course means that he has kept the other component of that union, which was a potentially murderous aggressiveness reinforced on the mother's side by an appeal to conscience. Indeed, we see the monstrous development of the paternal superego in Thésée's punishment of Hippolyte, and especially in *Athalie*. After being the impotent witness of the son's love (Burrhus), and the *entremetteur* for that love (Antiochus), the double becomes a political personality seeking power (Acomat), then attains power and uses it to judge the son (Thésée), and finally, in *Athalie*, possesses a religious power which controls and dethrones secular rulers. The final development of the paternal superego in Racine is the Old Testament God of *Athalie*, and the ruthless vengeance of that God, even though it is directed against the guilty mother, includes an oral sadism derived from the mother (the temple in *Athalie* is, as Mauron subtly points out, like an enormous open mouth "bristling with spikes," ready to swallow up God's prey).

Furthermore, the son pays a heavy price for the father's approval. With the appearance of the father, the child becomes innocent: Xipharès, Iphigénie-Achille, Hippolyte, Esther and Eliacin-Joas. He (occasionally she) gives up that criminal aggressiveness which Pyrrhus and Néron seem to have borrowed from Hermione and Agrippine. But a partial identification with the mother in violence actually served the cause of the son's rebellion. As Mauron puts it, by taking their energy from a relation they wish to escape from, the early sons found "the strength to liberate themselves and to reach a new state." This productive sadism is replaced, beginning with Bajazet's vague death wish, by a masochism which finally destroys the son. The son submits to the father; in order to be vindicated, he sacrifices his independence, his project of selfhood. His most urgent need is to flee from the mother; unable to do this on his own (that is, to assume the guilt of Pyrrhus's and Néron's crimes), the son, so to speak, buys the father off with his passivity, and the father takes over the job of killing the mother. *Phèdre* and *Athalie* are dramas of matricide. The major difficulty with this convenient solution is that the son, essentially unable to conceive of himself as distinct from the mother, *dies with her*.

At first, Racine imagines a guilty double who will play the scapegoat in the son's salvation. In *Mithridate* and *Iphigénie*, to have Pharnace and Eriphile slaughtered is to destroy criminal impulses, and their deaths purify the family atmosphere and consecrate the innocence of Xipharès and of Iphigénie. But if we consider Phèdre herself as Hippolyte's double, it becomes clear that the guilty impulses are not so easily disposed of. The idea of an identification of Phèdre with Hippolyte would appear absurd from the perspective of traditional psychological criticism, but, from our present point of view, this identification is a natural extension of the guilty double in *Mithridate* and *Iphigénie*, and it is also amply supported by the text of *Phèdre*. Mauron aptly points out, for example, that Hippolyte's confession of love to Aricie could be given, word for word, as Phèdre's confession of love to Hippolyte.[3] Furthermore, Hippolyte, Phèdre and Aricie are all terrorized by the mere thought of sexual passion. By the end of the first scene of Act Two, Racine has, in striking fashion, established a community of sexual terror among these three characters. All three are in love; they find love fearful or repugnant; each one, by loving, violates some sort of prohibition against love. In *Phèdre*, one desires only when there is a promise of desire being thwarted; a threat of love is the condition for love. The appearance of desire is a potentially suicidal choice on the part of the human organism. It is this severe law which *Phèdre* documents more explicitly than any of Racine's other plays, and which Mauron formulates in somewhat different terms when he writes that with Eriphile and Phèdre the very desire to love is judged as guilty. From Xipharès and Pharnace to Iphigénie and Eriphile, and finally to Hippolyte and Phèdre, the son's guilty double, as Mauron puts it, is feminized and then fused with an image of the masochistic mother.

The rebellions of Pyrrhus and Néron have been left behind. Far from providing an escape from the mother, the father in *Phèdre* absolves the son of guilt only after the son has already been condemned and destroyed for the guilty mother's crimes. The masochism which accompanies the relegating of aggressive impulses to the father defeats the original purpose of an appeal to the father. Since the son is unable or unwilling to accept the guilt of rejecting the mother on his own, and even more profoundly unable to imagine himself as distinct from her, to judge the mother is also to judge a son who has, in effect, already mutilated himself in donating his "immoral" virility to the father. Matricide in *Phèdre* is indistinguish-able from infanticide. And Phèdre herself is an extraordinary con-densation of roles which are also distributed among her, Hippolyte and Thésée: she is, as Mauron writes, "simultaneously the guilty impulse, the self which confesses and gives in to that impulse, and the conscience which condemns and punishes it." In *Phèdre*, we see most clearly what appears to be the bedrock of Racinian uncon-scious fantasy: love is death. Love in Racine ultimately comes back to our first love, that is, to love of the mother. And that first love is fidelity to a past in which the self was suffocated both by satis-faction and by helpless frustration, and in which the very birth of a self was made problematic by an ecstatic and terrifying fusion with the mother.

Whatever other reasons influenced Racine's renunciation of the theater after *Phèdre*, our analysis of his plays at least offers a psychologically plausible — if, for obvious reasons, biographically unverifiable — account of his much discussed "silence." Mauron suggests an analogy between the roles Andromaque and Junie play in Pyrrhus's and Néron's lives and the role of the theater in Racine's life. As Pyrrhus and Néron imagine a love which would save them from the erotic and moral demands represented by Hermione and Agrippine, so Racine finds in his writing a kind of pleasure con-demned by Port Royal, and which might save him from the terrify-ingly passionate superego which seems to be identified with his Jansenist background. But, at the same time, in his theater he is the manipulative spectator of his own unconscious life in somewhat the same way as Pyrrhus and the voyeuristic Néron prepare the spectacles (spectacles both painful and enjoyable) of Andromaque sobbing over Astyanax, and of Junie being mistreated by the soldiers or having to hide her love from Britannicus. And with *Phèdre*, as Mauron writes, "the theater ceases being a self-analysis and becomes a hallucinatory participation." *Phèdre*, Mauron profoundly sug-gests, is "Port Royal retrouvé." "When he abandons the theater, Racine is like a man who wakes up because his dream was getting too close to the fulfillment of his desire." From this perspective, Racine's "return" to Port Royal is extremely ambiguous. His last play, *Athalie*, written about fourteen years after *Phèdre*, dramatizes once again the fantasy of matricide. The victim, as in *Phèdre*, is the passionate, guilty mother, and, to the extent that Port Royal *is* passion in Racine's unconscious, the victim is also Jansenism. But we are far from Pyrrhus's rejection of Hermione in the name of an active, independent life with a new love. The self in *Athalie* has practically no existence at all; it is now embodied in Eliacin, a helpless child caught between a guilty, violent mother (Athalie) and a sadistic superego (Joad). The self has at last found life and moral approval, but only at the price of being a vengeful God's mouthpiece. The only "freedom" in Joas's future lies in the uncertainty about whether he will continue to be Joad's puppet or whether, faithful in spite of himself to the blood of Achab, he will betray his God in order to avenge the furious Athalie.

In the concluding chapter to *Des Métaphores obsédantes au mythe personnel/Introduction à la psychocritique* (1963), Mauron is careful to point out the limitations of his method: "Even when it has reached full maturity, psychocriticism would constitute only one wing — symmetrical to literary history — of criticism. But the study of creative language would occupy the center." I quoted this remark approvingly in my book on Proust, but I'm inclined now to disagree with the view that Mauron's method should be sharply differentiated from a "study of creative language." The psychoanalytic categories which Mauron brings to his work don't prevent the first half of *L'Inconscient dans l'oeuvre et la vie de Racine* from being an extremely close reading of Racine's plays — which, in a sense, obviously means a close reading of Racine's "creative language." It's unnecessary and misleading to relegate the sort of analysis we have just been applying to Racine to the sidelines of criticism. Mauron's modesty is a concession not to the creativity of art, but to certain cultural agreements about appropriate and inappropriate types of critical discourse. As Freud demonstrated (especially in *The Interpretation of Dreams, Jokes and Their Relation to the Unconscious* and *The Psychopathology of Everyday Life*), the procedures of the unconscious have much in common with those of art. In the mechanisms which Freud discovered in dreams, puns and jokes, we recognize many of the syntactic and rhetorical features characteristic of poetic language. The method Mauron applies to Racine's characters is analogous to methods of close textual analysis. Overdetermination, the poising of contradictory meanings, the paradoxes, the metaphorical condensations which another critic might find in the analysis of specific verbal strategies are exactly what Mauron finds in a structural analysis which appears to neglect verbal particularities. His "psychocritical" method reveals a type of logic governing relations among characters which, however, we have usually found more credible when that logic is said to govern relations within a group of images in a metaphysical sonnet. The psychoanalytic rearrangements of characters' identities could be thought of as exposing those mental operations from which perhaps all the major uses of "creative language" derive.

The peculiar intensity of literary figures such as Hermione, Eriphile and Phèdre is never adequately accounted for by traditional psychological analysis or even by the most sensitive study of how stylistic and dramatic originality is sustained in their speech. The mystery of Phèdre's resonance persists when we have paid tribute to her psychological richness (she is sensual, pathetic, maternal, violent, tender, remorseful), to the mythic dimensions of her fate (her family is cursed by Venus; the story of Pasiphaë is a legend of cosmic sexuality, of a kind of biological prehistory when men mated with animals and gods), and to the visual imagery which Racine skillfully uses to condense that fate into obsessive images of seeing and of being seen. And the mystery persists not just because *any* discursive analysis, however inclusive, necessarily destroys the dramatic immediacy of literary characters. There is something else in Phèdre, something elusive in her very identity which perhaps provides the deepest justification for Racine's reminding us that, according to legend, she is only one generation away from a sexuality "floating" among the human, the bestial and the divine. In part, the fantastic story of Pasiphaë operates in Racine's play as a metaphor for a depersonalization of Phèdre herself at the level of unconscious desires. The mother's cosmic promiscuity provides Racine with a mythic "objective correlative" for the daughter's wavering among different sexual impulses and identities. Phèdre the distinct person is a psychological superstructure for a simultaneous presentation, as I quoted from Mauron, of "the guilty impulse, the self which confesses and gives in to that impulse, and the conscience which condemns and punishes it."

In the same way, Eriphile in *Iphigénie* is "anguish over the crime, fear of punishment and the wish to be punished, the throwing off of responsibility onto the mother, and the certainty that the persecuted child will be punished." A character entirely invented by Racine, Eriphile is an orphan:

> Je reçus et je vois le jour que je respire,
> Sans que père ni mère ait daigné me sourire,
> J'ignore qui je suis . . . .
>
> Neither at birth nor later have I seen
> Mother or father ever smile on me.
> I know not who I am . . . .

Eriphile is an orphan in several senses. She is the progeny of no myth; she doesn't know who her parents were; and her ontological status in the play is to embody a network of impulses too complex to be derived from the "parent" impulse of her love for Achille. Indeed, Eriphile exists *only* by the ambiguous grace of her indeterminate being. When Calchas names her parents, he dooms her both within the plot of *Iphigénie* and as a dramatic creation, and she appropriately kills herself at the moment she becomes able to identify herself. Not to know who I am: this is the condition for the thriving of those impulses not yet sublimated and rationalized into the coherent identity of a person.

Racine's characters, seen from the psychoanalytic perspective, enjoy the freedom of simultaneously being different partial impulses. Personality gives a secure and deadening parenthood to desires. The power embodied in Phèdre and Eriphile is prior to the richness of a "settled" personality. And the pleasure which such literary representations give to us may be equivalent to a liberating participation in the dissolving of fixed identities. Perhaps even stronger than the anguish of returning to frightening desires and murderous conflicts is — at least in the experience of art — the delight of returning to the multiple identities among which those desires allow us to move. The psychological content uncovered by Mauron is largely composed of violence, suffering and death. Formally, however, his analysis frees Racine's characters from the constraints of their named identities, and it makes explicit a level of mental activity where relations aren't governed by the laws of conscious logic. It is this other level which gives to Racinian heroes not just psychological depth but also their esthetic power, even though the analysis of their hidden identities appears to violate all the rules for a study of esthetic effects in a literary text. Considered in this way, psycho-analytic criticism is not a reductive exposé of a writer's "secrets" or "problems"; rather, it exposes those patterns of desire which may be the affective basis for the formal organizations of art in general.

Nonetheless, I must confess to a lingering sense of reductiveness in this sort of psychoanalytic approach. Mauron himself, while he certainly doesn't mean his analysis to be reductive, never considers the psychological and esthetic *advantages* of the unconscious de-signs he finds in Racine's plays — advantages we have briefly looked at in the last few pages. Consequently, while we may feel that he has convincingly demonstrated the presence of these designs in Racine, we may not be convinced that they make a good argument for the quality or value of Racine's theater. It's not enough to say that the best artists are somehow capable of representing uncon-scious impulses and conflicts. If, after all, those conflicts are pre-cisely what the mature person is capable of resolving as he moves on to higher stages of mental development, the ambiguous talent of the artist lies mainly in his aptitude for regression. Great writers would then be neurotics with a gift for transforming their conscious experience into verbal representations of the unconscious dramas which sustain their neuroses. I should say that Mauron is reluctant to label Racine as "neurotic," but given the gravity and the primitive nature of the conflicts dramatized in Racine's plays, it's difficult not to feel that Racine must be admired principally for his unsuccessful effort, in his work, to save himself from his wish to die.

Indeed, Mauron writes: "Racine appears to us then as the hero of a silent and difficult struggle requiring souls of steel, I mean the struggle which civilization must maintain against instinct and partic-ularly against the most powerful instinct of all, the death instinct, masochism." One is reminded of Freud's moving (and inadequate) attempt to define the greatness of Michelangelo's *Moses:* ". . . the giant frame with its tremendous physical power becomes only a concrete expression of the highest mental achievement that is pos-sible in a man, that of struggling successfully against an inward passion for the sake of a cause to which he has devoted himself." Psychoanalysis, in order to save art from what it discovers in art, is obliged to admire the artist for his attempt to escape from those very impulses which nourish his art and which may in fact be responsible for his being an artist at all. The major value to be saved is always "civilization," and the rather peculiar essence of art turns out to be a rejection of the passions which it is the nature of art to indulge in. Most Freudian analyses of art exist only on the assumption that there is no such thing as a nonregressive, mature art; art becomes a *value* of civilized life only if it is considered as an ascetic exercise. It is a heroic demonstration of pleasure being transformed into morality; that is, art is a sublimation which instructively allows us to see the anticivilized passions which must be sublimated as well as the culturalized product itself, the sublime-sublimated work of art.

Mauron does seem anxious to avoid this view of art as a kind of hybrid of psychological beast and ethical angel. He ingeniously distinguishes between the hypnotic and destructive passion represented by the mother, and some milder happiness, which is both another type of love (Bajazet's love for Atalide, Xipharès' love for Monime) and the pleasure of writing tragedies. I find this distinction interesting because it at least suggests that the pleasures of artistic activity are not simply regressive pleasures; "the peaceful, sensual and literary pleasure" Mauron speaks of is invented by Racine as a *way out* of a dread-filled fascination with the past and with the mother, with what seems to be the fantasy of her passionately and murderously embracing the child. A certain form of adult play (Racine's plays) doesn't merely repeat the forbidden play of childhood; it is actually a sign of a successful moving out of childhood fantasy, and so Racine's renunciation of the theater indicates a failure of independent, mature desires and a definitive victory for regressive impulses.

Mauron would like to have pleasure on the side of civilization, but this rather daring move — from the point of view of orthodox Freudianism — gets him into deep, and I think significant, trouble. First of all, he is sufficiently orthodox in his psychoanalytic thinking to consider new pleasures as sublimations of old ones. As he suggests, the playwright's pleasure at being the spectator and manipulator of his own psychic life seems to be a sublimated form of Néron's cruel pleasure as he watches Junie suffer. I'm not arguing for the improbability of any continuity at all between the pleasure of writing and the pleasure of sadistic voyeurism, but the reductive tendency in psychoanalytic criticism is the inevitable consequence of a theory of sublimation. A radical particularity or originality of desire is impossible as long as we posit a family of psychological continuities in which each new desire can be shown to be derived from earlier desires. It's not exactly a question of deciding if the psychoanalysts are "right" in emphasizing the continuities of mental life. We can admit the existence of such continuities and at the same time investigate the possibilities of a psychology of the discontinuous, of the nonsublimating desire. Mauron may indeed be right to see the pleasures of writing in Racine's case as a sublimation of violently aggressive passions. But it could be argued that precisely because it is a sublimation, writing is a fragile defense. Indeed, in *Phèdre*, destructive passions erupt with a power which overwhelms the form meant to contain them and which destroys the alternative but related pleasure of writing tragedies.

The prejudice of continuity in psychoanalysis works in two directions: present desires are interpreted back to their "source desires" in the past, and our earliest desires are seen as destined for a certain "natural" development. Freud's formalization of the child's desires into oral, anal and phallic stages, and his conviction that a healthy libido is a genitally oriented libido, have been subjected to a variety of critiques. But, as Gilles Deleuze and Félix Guattari have recently emphasized in *L'Anti-Oedipe*, most of the objections have really done very little in the way of subverting the fundamental dogma of normal psychic development — and the scarcely less fundamental one of genital sexuality as mature sexuality. Mauron is a good example of the persistence of these dogmas in the psychoanalytic criticism of art. For all his admiration of Racine, he emphasizes more than once that we mustn't expect to find "higher values" in Racinian tragedy. "Higher values" depend on a successful resolution of the Oedipus complex, and since Racine, at his psychological best (in *Mithridate*) shows only a feeble Oedipal structure, his work, unlike Corneille's, can't be said to be concerned with adult questions of ethics.

Mauron's example is all the more instructive in that he has a special view of the relation between the healthy psyche and society. There is an interesting if confused suggestion in the Racine book that "civilized" can be distinguished from "social." Toward the end of his study, Mauron recognizes that "even a psychoanalyst" might not go along with his labeling as a regression a renunciation of the theater which, after all, had the result of making Racine "a very distinguished *honnête homme*, the King's historiographer and the best of fathers." Nonetheless, Mauron sticks to his unorthodox position: "In my opinion, the artist tears himself away from the realm of the social, attempts to go beyond it, exactly as the adolescent breaks away from the family home to look for a new love, or as the three-year-old child tears himself away from the mother as nourishment in order to reach toward the genital mother." Although we are still in a psychology dominated by the notion of stages, these analogies interestingly suggest that social integration doesn't have to be viewed as a goal of human development. But since Mauron also tells us that Racine chose art "for his own protection and the defense of human civilization in 1665," we also need to know what Mauron means by what would apparently be a nonsocial civilization. The idea, however, remains undeveloped, and we have little more than the implied assertion that art is a civilized transcendence of society. . . .

Most strikingly, Mauron insists that a priority given to art over social duties is also a victory for genitality. Now while Freud didn't place the beginnings of social consciousness at the Oedipal stage, he did think that the internalization of the father as conscience is a crucial factor in the formation of the social self. Oedipal hatred *and* love of the father serve the cause of life in society. The moral watchdog which acts as society's internal police agent is derived from the child's suppressed aggressiveness toward the father; and the homosexual love for the rival in the Oedipal triangle is sublimated into altruistic feelings which make social cohesion seem desirable and not merely a mandate of conscience. In fact, because Freud attached such great importance to the link between the social personality and the fear of castration which leads to the renunciation of the Oedipal rivalry, and since he saw the fear of castration as preceding (rather than dissolving) the Oedipus complex in girls, he was skeptical about the reliability of women as social creatures. If the Oedipus complex is a haven from the anxiety of castration for girls, the formation of their superego will suffer from their staying in the Oedipal situation longer than boys; this, Freud explains, is the reason for women's underdeveloped sense of justice.[4] I mention this only to suggest with what rigorous consistency Freud maintained the link between man as a social creature on the one hand and, on the other, the Oedipus complex and the mode of its renunciation. It's therefore all the more interesting that Mauron's

Freudian position doesn't prevent him from separating the social from the genital, at the same time that he sticks to the orthodox view which proclaims the genital as the goal of psychosexual development.

He recognizes that his position requires him to establish two sets of correspondences:

A. — Between the sado-masochistic stage, its sublimations, its reaction formations, its neurotic fixations on the one hand, and on the other hand, social structures: consumption and production, war, justice, finances, rites.

B. — Between the flight toward the phallic stage on the one hand, and, on the other hand, the flight toward pleasure [la jouissance] and esthetic creation.

We might note in passing that the enumeration of "social structures" is ideologically loaded: it is a rather unengaging résumé of life in society, and it skirts the question of whether or not more appealing forms of social solidarity might also be considered as corresponding to "the sado-masochistic stage." Since Mauron is proposing a general psychosocial theory and not one applicable only to the social options available in seventeenth-century France, and since the positive value of "civilization" must obviously include some social cohesion, it would be useful to know how he conceives of a healthy community. (Would it, for example, be a community without "consumption and production," without "justice"? . . . Is "civilization" an esthetic utopia in which everyone would be an artist?) What interests me more particularly is the alliance of the phallic with pleasure and esthetic creation. To use the astonishingly successful social integration of Racine as an example of psychological regressiveness is an original move;[5] to affirm "a correspondence between the effort toward the genital and the effort toward art" is perhaps only a desperate effort to preserve the authority of a developmental prejudice which makes a final goal of genitality. And, from our point of view, such an effort has an invalidating effect on the psychoanalytic approach. It undercuts the psychological freedom which Mauron's redefinition of literary character seemed to promise, and it unfortunately documents our sense of a reductive tendency in his criticism. How?

Let's look again at the role of the Oedipal conflict (and of an implied genitality) in Racine's tragedies. Mauron's case for a correspondence between art and genitality depends on the falling back from the Oedipal level to the obsessional level in *Phèdre*. We have seen that in *Phèdre* the haunting, aggressive, sexually terrifying mother makes a spectacular return. She is gotten rid of by the end of the play, but, given the son's regressive identification of his being with hers, a potentially liberating matricide is also the death of the child. And it's just at this moment that Racine stops writing tragedies and "is no longer interested in anything but social duties"; therefore, Mauron concludes, the obvious correspondence between social structures and pre-Oedipal structures. But, as we have seen from Mauron's own analyses, the unconscious structures displayed in *Phèdre* are more complicated than these simple equivalences would suggest. There is a crucial difference between the pre-Oedipal situation in *Phèdre* and the pre-Oedipal dramas of *Andromaque* and *Britannicus*. Since *Mithridate*, as Mauron emphasizes, the father has been an important presence in Racine's plays; it is after all the outraged Oedipal father who acts as the agent of the son's destruction in *Phèdre*. Admittedly, the Oedipal position is always weak in Racine, but even in *Phèdre*, where the Oedipal "gains" of *Mithridate* and *Iphigénie* are undercut by the son's masochistic identification with the mother, the Oedipal triangle is at least visible in a way it is not in *Andromaque, Britannicus,* and *Bérénice.*

The earlier plays offer much purer versions of "obsessional structures," and if we accept Mauron's thesis concerning the correspondence of those structures with nonliterary social duties, we should expect Racine to have given up tragedy almost at the start of his theatrical career. In the early tragedies, the self seems to be testing possibilities of independence from the mother which the matricides of *Phèdre* and *Athalie* are far from realizing. It's true that these projects for an independent life fail in Pyrrhus and in Néron (and Titus's freedom from Bérénice is accompanied by almost suicidal melancholy), and yet repeated failures of an effort to break free of a pre-Oedipal attachment to the mother didn't discourage Racine from continuing to indulge in the pleasures of writing. On the contrary: *Andromaque, Britannicus, Bérénice* and *Bajazet* are written at approximately one-year intervals, while the creative pace slows down somewhat after *Mithridate*, and there is even a premonitory halt in productivity of almost two and a half years following *Iphigénie*. The correspondences between literature and what Mauron calls the Oedipal "ascension" are far from clear. Finally, it can hardly be said that Oedipal structures are insignificant in the two plays Racine wrote after *Phèdre*. The apotheosis of the father-king in *Esther* and of the father-god in *Athalie* — whatever these fathers' secret links with the pre-Oedipal mother may be — certainly represents a dramatic triumph for an awesome, omnipotent paternal superego.

The emergence of a clear Oedipal design in Racine's plays is anything but a psychological "ascension" for his heroes. It is the sign of their permanent abdication of freedom and prefigures the playwright's return to more respectable "social duties." Significantly, the two plays in which that design is most evident — *Mithridate* and *Iphigénie* — are the only Racinian tragedies which end with happy marriages. (Since marriage presumably crowns "the effort toward the genital," wouldn't Mauron be logically obliged to say that it is not a "social structure"? But then what is it?) *Mithridate* and *Iphigénie* are also the least tragic of Racine's tragedies, and not simply because of their comparatively happy endings. In them, characters are rationally deliberative and show an occasionally comic domestic irritability, both of which point to the bourgeois dramas which begin to flourish in the eighteenth century.[6] Now Mauron *could* have said that bourgeois drama provides a creditable alternative to the destructive passions of tragedy. For the very existence of such drama presupposes that certain psychological and social accommodations have been imagined as attractive enough to dissolve the more dangerous appeals of both sado-masochistic passions and of a revolutionary freedom. Throughout Racine's works, the confidants represent this spirit of accommodation. Whether they are arguing for or against the heroes' passions, their advice assumes the superfluity of tragedy in a world where things can always be "arranged" in one way or another. Tragic passion in Racine is unavailable to argument; considerations of honor or of self-interest or even threats of death are unable to divert it from its object. To the inflexible necessity of passion, the confidants oppose a kind of cynical common sense which sees all reality as an easy fix. It's folly to bother with a woman who only humiliates you (Phoenix to Pyrrhus);

Bérénice won't mind being sent away because you've given her "cent peuples nouveaux" to rule over (Paulin to Titus); now that your husband is dead, it's no longer a crime to be in love with his son (Oenone to Phèdre: "Votre flamme devient une flamme ordinaire").

In *Mithridate* and *Iphigénie*, where we find Racine's noblest genital couples (Xipharès and Monime, Achille and Iphigénie), the world of the heroes themselves is not too different from the confidants' antitragic world. Xipharès is capable of controlling his passion for Monime out of respect for his father, Mithridate is able to forgive his son's betrayal, Agamemnon is a calculating politician, and respectable family life is preserved in *Iphigénie* thanks to the convenient presence in Eriphile of a sacrificial scapegoat who spares the others the necessity of a tragic fate. There are considerable hypocrisy and moral smugness in the two plays. As Roland Barthes points out, Xipharès is quite willing to lie to his father about his love for Monime, but only Pharnace has to pay for the crime against the father, and the guilty son's death seems to wash Xipharès and Monime clean of some devious maneuvering. Even Achille in *Iphigénie* strikes a curiously vulgar note when, in what sounds like a parody of Cornelian *gloire*, he complains to Iphigénie that if she doesn't allow him to save her, he'll lose his reputation as a hero:

> Et qui de ma faveur se voudrait honorer,
> Si mon hymen prochain ne peut vous assurer?
> Ma gloire, mon amour, vous ordonnent de vivre.

> And who would sue for my protection when
> My promised marriage cannot make you safe?
> My love, my glory order you to live.

Now while Mauron admires the maturity of Xipharès and Monime's love, as well as of the love between Iphigénie and Achille, I think he would like to dissociate their nearly adult psychology from the atmosphere of bourgeois drama in which, after all, such loves appear to flourish in Racine. Indeed, this connection has to be ignored if the positive value of the genital stage is to be maintained. The Oedipal pattern and mature genitality are naturally linked to marriage and the family, and Racine shows marriage and the family as moral alibis which prevent the self from transcending "the social" and institutionalize its immaturity.

Even more: the appeal to familial, social and religious duties can provide a kind of ideological superstructure for the most archaic desires. The alliance between conscience and cruel, possessive passion in Racine nicely illustrates Freud's view of the superego as deriving its energy from the id. The Oedipal stage provides a reinforcement for archaic pre-Oedipal passions. It is the basis not of a psychic "ascension," but rather of a legalization of emotional rigidities and moral tyrannies.

In *Phèdre*, Racine gives us his most powerful image of the pre-Oedipal mother (in a play which is, as we have seen, such a spectacular triumph of a suicidal identification with the mother that Racine immediately afterwards commits literary suicide) — and that image is also Racine's most impressive representation of conscience. A comparison between Phèdre and Racine's earlier heroines is instructive. Racine's most passionate protagonists have always had a strong view of what the loved one or the victim owes them. (Pyrrhus owes it to Hermione to marry her; Néron owes his throne to Agrippine; Bajazet owes his very life to Roxane.) But for all their appeals to *devoir*, these earlier figures in Racine's theater don't seem to take the moral argument too seriously themselves, and occasionally they even display a healthy cynical detachment from their own moral imperatives. This detachment at least suggests a certain "purity" in their desire to possess the loved one or the son. Consequently, the self is still able to strip away the moral façade from passion (as we see most clearly in Néron's answer to Agrippine's accusations in Act Four, Scene Two of *Britannicus*), and at least recognize — and therefore to flee from — the impulses to devour and to be devoured.

But in *Phèdre* the impulse itself is dignified by the fact that it is now inseparable from the moral revulsion which it inspires. There is of course the difference that Hermione uses morality to serve her passion, while Phèdre invokes it to blame her passion. But this difference loses much of its apparent significance once we realize that Phèdre's self-blame, far from effectively combating the passionate impulses she represents, merely reinforces the suicidal melancholy latent in those impulses. From the point of view of a nonpsychoanalytic approach, she of course appears morally ennobled by her resistance to passion. From a psychoanalytic point of view, however, the substitution of self-revulsion for a more frankly amoral aggressiveness seems to make it more difficult for the ego to differentiate itself from the destructive energy of the mother's desires. If, as in *Andromaque* and *Britannicus*, the mother is fantasized as a more purely aggressive figure, the son can use his inevitable identification with the mother as an instrument of rebellion against her. Pyrrhus and Néron can imitate Hermione's and Agrippine's violence in order to break away from them and also to energize their pursuit of other goals. But, as *Phèdre* illustrates, the mother's *melancholy* possessiveness is more dangerous to the child than a more active, unashamed aggressiveness. To imitate the mother's horror of passion (Hippolyte, we remember, shares Phèdre's terror of love) is to draw closer to her; even her pursuit of the son provides no model for the son's imagination of other pursuits.

It's perhaps a willingness to die, derived from the pre-Oedipal stage, which makes possible the "ascension" to the Oedipal. An earlier renunciation creates the proper conditions for the entire Oedipal situation. In Racine, the melancholy, vaguely suicidal hero Bajazet precedes the appearance of a clear Oedipal design in *Mithridate*. And the Oedipal situation itself seems to repeat the sequence of an indifference to life (to desire) followed by a condemnation of life (and of desire). Freud said that the price we pay for civilization is the heightening of our sense of guilt. But when we remember that he also came to think that civilization depends on our ability to renounce instinctual satisfactions, we come to the paradoxical conclusion that the *suppression of desire, rather than its satisfaction, heightens guilt*. Toward the end of *Civilization and Its Discontents*, Freud indeed asks whether *any* thwarted instinctual satisfaction aggravates the sense of guilt. In the so-called successful resolution of the Oedipal conflict, we renounce our incestuous desire for the mother, capitulate to a more powerful rival, and incorporate that rival's condemnation of our desires in the form of a conscience which makes civilized social life possible. It's not entirely clear why, having renounced our guilty desires, we must continue to travel with the castrating judge of those desires — unless, as I've just suggested, all such renunciations increase our need for punishment. I don't mean to suggest that the satisfaction of all desires would eradicate the phenomenon of guilt, but it does seem as if the suppression of desire excites a hatred for the real or imagined agent requiring this suppression. Consequently, we feel guilty not only about desires we may still be secretly attached to, but also about our aggressive fantasies toward whoever has made us give up our pleasures. In a sense, the most lasting and positive consequence of the Oedipus complex is conscience — that is, a permanent readiness to pronounce ourselves guilty. We become guilty as a result of having renounced our incestuous desires.

To sum up: for all the links between Racine's plays before *Mithridate* and those from *Mithridate* on, three factors in the latter group seem causally related to the emergence of an Oedipal design. They are: (1) a spirit of accommodation which tends to dissipate tragic intensity in *Mithridate* and *Iphigénie*, (2) a genuinely public-minded orientation (ranging from Xipharès' championship of national freedom against imperialistic Rome to Clytemnestre's concern with social respectability and Agamemnon's political ambitions), which also works against the tragic mode, and (3) the submission to moral judgments which steadily become more severe and unattackable (we move from the forgiving, somewhat silly fathers of *Mithridate* and *Iphigénie* to Phèdre's conscience, and then to the irreproachable king of *Esther* and finally to the righteous and vengeful God of *Athalie*). My point has been that none of these new factors, associated with what Mauron and most psychoanalysts would consider as a psychic "ascension," in any way helps the Racinian hero to find satisfactory alternative desires to the smothering passion of Racinian mothers from Hermione to Athalie. At the very best, successful genitality in Racine's work makes for two rather "nice" couples. But Xipharès and Monime combine a certain goody-goody quality with a talent for graceful lying and a willingness to let Pharnace take on their guilt in addition to his own. And Achille and Iphigénie have considerable vanity and squabble nastily when each one thinks the other is wounding his or her public image. At the worst, we have that combination of social, moral and metaphysical self-righteousness in Joad which makes the Christian tragedy *Athalie* perhaps Racine's most brutal play.

The point of view I'm taking is not a denial of the psychological reality of the Oedipus complex or of the phallic and the genital organizations of human desires. Rather, I want to suggest that a psychological theory which adopts the Freudian bias of "lower" and "higher" stages of development, and which emphasizes both the biological necessity and the desirability of a definite scheme of human growth, works to stifle the diversification and the originality of desire. Such a theory is also a *social* psychology, and Freud provided Western civilization with both a theoretical justification of the structures in which it socializes human desires and a therapeutic technique for making individuals adapt more easily to those structures. I think that one can show the complicity of literature (and not just of Racine) with this larger cultural project, as well as the possibilities in literature of a subversion of that project. My fundamental objection to psychoanalytic criticism is that it upsets conventional psychological categories only to provide a powerful reinforcement of the cultural imperatives regarding personality from which those categories derive. The traditional (non-Freudian) psychological approach to Racine is grounded in a psychology of coherent individual identities. This psychology tolerates considerable diversity and complexity, provided that the latter can be unified or totalized in a coherent portrait. It is a psychology of names, of individual persons. *Mauron erases the names, but he replaces them with roles.* He shows the freedom of unconscious relations from the constraints of individual identities, but he subverts that freedom by defining all unconscious relations in terms of a fixed evolution of familial sexuality. The names Eriphile and Phèdre disintegrate into juxtaposed partial identities, but each part fits no less coherently into a systematized history of the child's desires only as they relate to his family. Psychoanalytic criticism ignores secondary conscious traits in Racine's characters and reformulates those characters in terms of fundamental sexual energies. But it immediately *structures* those energies; as a result, desires lose their dynamic unpredictability and have, as it were, the responsibility of serving the coherence of the structure.

Ultimately, the reductiveness of psychoanalytic thought doesn't consist in its continuous references to childhood sexuality. It lies rather in its particular organization of childhood desires, or, more exactly, in its very commitment to the notion of an organized history of desire. The psychoanalytic emphasis on sex itself both limits the range of human desire and devalues the child's sexuality. The child's multiple and discontinuous points of contact with the world are reduced to the structures of familial sexual fantasies. Each stage of development is conceived of as an act in a drama of fantasized family sexuality. Psychoanalysis defines the satisfaction and the inhibition of desire in terms of interpenetrations between the parents' and the child's bodies. Those aspects of psychoanalysis which appear most sacrilegious to a popular, sentimental view of family life actually consecrate the imprisonment of human desire in a family circle. From the infant's sucking and biting of its mother's nipples to the baby's fantasy of being penetrated anally by the father's penis, and "ultimately" to a desire for genital satisfaction with the parent of the opposite sex, the child's imagination tries out different combinations of its own and its parents' apertures and protuberances until it hits on the "right" genital combination. The reference to childhood thus becomes a reductive strategy when it is combined with a certain teleology of desire: anything but successful heterosexual genitality is only a deviation from or a partial fulfillment of the natural goal of human sexuality. If desire is primarily sex, and if sex is originally and fundamentally incestuous, then the primacy which psychoanalysis accords to sex is equivalent to the apotheosis of the familial triangle as the underlying structure of all the variations of human desire.

It would nevertheless be a mistake, I think, to argue that Mauron's psychoanalytic perspective distorts the "real" text of Racine's work. His book seems to me to stand up very well under the only test to which we can fairly submit the bias of a particular critical approach (and all criticism naturally has its bias). I mean that Mauron's specific references to Racine's tragedies almost always strike me as confirming his argument about them instead of invalidating that argument. His critical solutions enrich the text by simultaneously discovering and dissipating textual problems which previous analyses had not even suspected. In fact, classical literature — and especially Racinian tragedy — is the ideal testing ground for Freudian psychology. I've just been speaking of psychoanalysis' habit of reading back from present behavior to past behavior or fantasies. Pushed to the logical extreme of his method, the psychoanalytic interpreter becomes justly impatient of the material he must interpret. The diversity of present experience makes for a frequently muddled accumulation of signs which have to be reorganized and deciphered in order for their real significance to emerge.[7] Present behavior is significant but ultimately superfluous;

it points back to those origins or causes which already contain the fundamental meanings of subsequent behavior.

Racine's characters share the psychoanalysts' interpretive suspicion about what is being said or done now. They are of course right to be suspicious: they know that almost everyone in the Racinian world is constantly either trying to disguise his passion or to find respectable reasons for it. The apparent significance of an extraordinary amount of dialogue is canceled out by the emergence of a real significance that gives the lie to what has been said. A long speech by one character is often followed by a "Je vous entends" from a second character, who then proceeds to interpret what he or she has just heard, to demolish a verbal disguise and expose the truth it concealed. But lying in Racinian tragedy is merely a secondary manifestation of a more general classical conviction: truth is never *in* language but is *behind* it. French classical language is abstract, decorous and ornamental; its peculiar resonance is due to the pressure, along its surfaces, of those turbulent feelings which it both masks and points to. The *litote* is not simply a technique of understatement; it trains us always to expect a distance between language and truth.

Psychoanalytic interpretation exposes and closes this gap. Psychoanalysis can give us an articulate formulation of the laws governing the relation between the said and the unsaid. It has a theory about the nature of the unsaid, and about how and why much of mental life is repressed; it has also developed an interpretive method designed to lead us from the manifest symbol to the hidden truth. A sense of the inadequacy of language to reality (and of the signifier to the signified) informs both Freudian psychology and the classical esthetic. The surfaces of behavior — what people seem to be saying and doing — are to be looked at with great attention and with great suspicion. Classical language invites the kind of rapid interpretation which Melanie Klein recommended for the psychoanalysis of children. The therapist interrupts the child's diversionary play with a statement of the truth which has been unintentionally illuminated in that play. Psychoanalytic theory is the ultimate form of what we can recognize as a skepticism about phenomena which has profoundly marked Western thought at least since Plato's Allegory of the Cave. From Plato to Freud, the act of interpretation is a devaluation of immediate experience. Appearances rightly yield to essences;

symptoms are replaced by the illuminating causes; discontinuous acts find their way into a historically continuous structure; Racine's theater is scrutinized so that it may be erased or at least suspended, and replaced with the affective patterns of the unexpressed but all-determining Racinian unconscious.

Are there any signs of resistance in Racine's work to the psychological assumptions which I have just discussed, any points of opposition to those limiting structures which are admittedly the main source of dramatic intensity in his plays? The signs of a rebellion in Racine against the dominant Racinian psychology are most clearly visible in *Andromaque* and *Britannicus*. Like Mauron, I would locate the psychologically progressive elements in these plays in Pyrrhus and Néron, but I don't find it necessary to limit Pyrrhus's and Néron's efforts at self-liberation to an attempted progress from a pre-Oedipal pattern to an Oedipal pattern. As I have argued, Oedipal and genital structures constitute a maturing of desires *within* a psychology already limited to familial definitions of desire. And when Racine imagines a radical liberation of desire, he dramatizes a fantasy of *orphaned desire*. The unhappy fate of the orphan Jean Racine could be thought of as the ideally liberated condition of the Racinian hero.

Néron is Racine's most extreme version of the attempt to free desire by disinheriting it. Nowhere in Racine's theater is the hero's rebellion against his past more anguished and more catastrophic than in *Britannicus*. Certainly no other Racinian protagonist is more amply advised: everyone in the play tells Néron what he ought to be doing. Agrippine tells him to be a good son; Junie tells him to be a good husband; Burrhus tells him to be a good emperor; Narcisse tells him, in effect, to be the good slave of his fantasies of omnipotence. And from the point of view of past constraints on action in the present, there is no opposition in the play between regressive dependence on the mother and the fulfillment of social duties. In a sense, though, it's irrelevant that Néron has been a good emperor until now; the conflict between good and evil in *Britannicus* is a melodramatic vehicle for a more profound conflict between a psychology of repetition and a psychology capable of inaugurating new desires. Néron discovers what seems to be his capacity for independent desires the night he sees the half-naked Junie whose tears "were shining" in the midst of the torches and the weapons of the guards Néron has sent to abduct her. As is frequently the case in Racine, a nocturnal scene of confusion and potential violence is the dramatic metaphor for the disintegration of established structures, for a certain fragmentation of meaning. And the latter is the Racinian hero's only hope of escape from the continuities and the coherent patterns which condemn him to a life of repetition. What other Néron is born on this night to replace the obedient Néron?

In his attempt to break away from those loyalties which enclose his being within definitions proposed by others, Néron merely shifts the source of his imitative inspiration. Significantly, Néron himself proposes the brutal aspect of the guards who abduct Junie — "le farouche aspect de ses fiers ravisseurs" — as one of the reasons for his excited fascination with the scene of Junie's arrival. That remark prepares us for what is perhaps the most striking aspect of his love for Junie: his curiosity about the love between her and Britannicus. Néron's voyeurism is his only resource as a lover; unable to originate desires within himself, he is the Peeping Tom of other people's desires. It's accordingly a stroke of genius on his part *to let Junie know* that he will be watching and listening to her talk with Britannicus in Act Two. Under such pressures, the lovers' passion will be expressed in a particularly concentrated form. Indeed, a vision of distilled passion is exactly what Néron gets from the scene; as he says to Narcisse, now he has a proof of the "violence" of a love which appeared even in Junie's silence. From the very beginning of his love, Néron has been as curious about Britannicus as about Junie. He asks Narcisse:

> Si jeune encore, se connaît-il lui-même?
> D'un regard enchanteur connaît-il le poison?

> So young still — does he know himself?
> Does he know the fatal sorcery of a look?

And after the scene which he has witnessed between the lovers, Néron speaks of the "joy" he will have in making Britannicus despair of Junie's love, and he even suggests that his excitement is shifting from Junie to the imagined spectacle of Britannicus's suffering: "Je me fais de sa peine une image charmante." ("I find the image of his grief enchanting.") If any justification is needed for Racine's having given the honor of his play's title to an apparently minor character, Néron's exasperated dependence on Britannicus provides it. Junie loves Britannicus, Agrippine protects him; he is the hated brother who has known how to make himself be loved, and he must be both imitated and destroyed. If there is a suggestion of homosexuality in Néron's voyeuristic jealousy of Britannicus, homosexual desire itself in this case would be simply the technique for possessing knowledge of his brother's desires and of how he makes himself desired by others. Néron's abortive rebellion is a failed attempt to substitute himself for Britannicus. He is incapable of inventing desires; he can only either betray those who would imprison him in their own wills (Agrippine and Burrhus) or do violence to those — like Junie and Britannicus — whose desires he can't possess (in the double sense of being loved by them and of imitating what makes them desirable).

The pathos of Néron — and this also accounts for his cruelty — is his awareness that he can't ever really escape from his dependence on others. They resist, and finally it is always they who win. It's Narcisse who lacks this sense of reality as resistant to desire. He is the embodiment of those masturbatory fantasies of omnipotence which we see at work in Néron himself when, on the night Junie is brought to his apartments, the sexually aroused emperor spends a sleepless night alone playing different roles with the "trop belle image" of Junie (he makes her cry, he asks her forgiveness, he sighs like a lover, he threatens her). When Néron angrily worries that Junie may love Britannicus, Narcisse says: "Commandez qu'on vous aime, et vous serez aimé." ("Command that love shall follow. You will be loved.") Narcisse (and his name is an obvious enough indication of this) has the calm and profoundly stupid self-absorption of inauthentic desire — that is, of desires supported by no imagination about the world in which they must be realized. Néron, on the other hand, really has little confidence in what might be called the masturbatory mode of freedom. His new desires are as dependent on others as his old desires, and when other people refuse to take their roles in his fantasy play, Néron destroys them or is destroyed by them. The murder of Britannicus and Junie's flight to the temple of the Vestal Virgins exhaust Néron's resources of self-definition. The action of *Britannicus* is framed by two scenes of possibly violent confusion: the soldiers' abduction of Junie, and Néron's dazed and desperate wandering through the palace at the end. The second scene confirms the illusory nature of what Néron had excitedly interpreted in the first scene as the birth of free desires. At the end of the play, only the murmured name of Junie separates Néron from his return to the familial orbit, from renewed pledges of loyalty to the waiting Agrippine.

Andromaque is a curious parody of family relationships. Three of the four main characters are children of heroes; and Andromaque is a hero's widow. The *un*heroic nature of the play's action is underlined by references to a recent past which the characters can remember but are unable to imitate. *Andromaque* takes place after the great war between Greece and Troy, and its action is a kind of sordid footnote to an epic tale of confrontation between two peoples. The great heroic acts which will nourish myth and legend have already taken place; Racine's subject is a peacetime sexual imbroglio in a Greek province. The presence at Buthrote of so many heroes' relatives merely widens the gap between the memories evoked by Racine's protagonists and their own roles. They are conscious of that gap and are embarrassed by it. Agamemnon, Helen, Achilles: the parents of Racine's characters made history, while their children try — unsuccessfully at that — to make love.

For this post-heroic generation, the choice is a simple if radical one: it can accept the crushing authority of a past it can't imitate, or it can repudiate the past. The enslavement of Racine's characters to their sexual passions could be thought of as a metaphor for a more fundamental enslavement to parental and social models of behavior. It is, I think, from this perspective that Roland Barthes' desexualization of Racinian tragedy can best be justified. In *Andromaque*, Barthes writes, ". . . Racine asks for the third time the same question: how to go from an old order [which is the order of "the Father, the Past, the Homeland and Religion"] to a new order?" The conflict in the play is not between love and hate, but rather "between what has been and what wants to be"; love is "only a sign of a totality which includes it." From the point of view of the psychologies of desire which we have been discussing, I would rather say that love and hate *belong to* the order of "what has been." That is, "what wants to be" must struggle against the very definition of desire which Racinian sex imposes (for the most part successfully) on desire. The Racinian hero's betrayal of the past would be not simply the ethical gesture which seems to appeal to Barthes. The rejection of the family would also be a rejection of those psychological structures which the Racinian unconscious has inherited from the family, and, more particularly, of that psychology of jealous love which is merely the present version of pre-Oedipal and Oedipal passions. For the most part, sexual love is not the "sign" of the larger conflict between the old and the new orders; it is rather the *antagonist* of a new psychological order. And this is because, as Mauron has shown, conscious passion in Racine can always be read as a transparent symbol of unconscious passions which are familial in nature.

Barthes' formulation of the primary Racinian conflict — "between what has been and what wants to be" — becomes fully apt only if we de-emphasize those metaphysical components of "what has been" which Barthes himself tends to stress, and if we clearly see that the basis of *all* that "has been" (in Racine, but also in general) is a concrete order of familial desire which lies behind every adult sublimation from romantic passion to the worship of God. The weakness in Barthes' impressive essay could be expressed as his failure to recognize how antagonistic his thesis is to Mauron's argument. As long as he continues to see sexual psychology as a part or a sign of a larger struggle between the past and the future, he will of course not see that there is no psychological future for Racine's heroes outside of a struggle against these psychological categories themselves. Barthes pays tribute to Mauron for placing Pyrrhus at the center of *Andromaque*'s significance, but there is an enormous difference between Mauron's sense of Pyrrhus struggling from the pregenital to a more mature genital love and Barthes' notion of a radical break with "what has been." The latter has made an important and necessary change in Mauron's argument by suggesting that Pyrrhus can be saved from Hermione only by a kind of ontological and moral "leap," and not by a normal process of psychic maturing. As Mauron describes it, there is no discontinuity in Pyrrhus's revolt; there are only the shocks of a difficult process of naturally continuous development. On the other hand, Mauron never downgrades the importance of sex and the family, whereas Barthes, by talking so much about God and so little about the real or fantasized bodies of real or fantasized mothers and fathers, makes the Racinian hero's rebellion metaphysically glamorous but emotionally empty, and thereby weakens his own notion of a radical break with the past. For unless we first of all stress the absolutely irreducible power of sexual passion in the play *and* the power of that familial psychology from which it derives and back to which it can be interpreted, we can't consider revolt as a possible reinvention of desire but only — as indeed Barthes significantly puts it — as the prelude to a new legality and a new paternity. Sexual passion is a "sign" only of that in which it is grounded: exciting and fearful fantasies of incest. It is not subordinate to a conflict between the future and the past; it *is* a past from which a certain kind of future might free us.

Andromaque gives us Racine's purest image of a liberating betrayal of the past; but the play brings us only to the threshold of a new order for which no content is imagined. The role of Pyrrhus and Andromaque in the preparation for this new order is an essentially sacrificial one. As long as Pyrrhus was alive, he might ask Andromaque to help him betray his past by betraying hers, but he could find no terms for his offer other than those of a cruel, imprisoning desire which made him a rather shallow prophet of a new order. Pyrrhus in his cruel pursuit of Andromaque, and Andromaque in her obsessive attachment to Hector's memory, have both participated too fully in the Racinian world of desperate passion to represent, in their own persons, a radically new mode of desire. But the founding of something new is at least left, after Pyrrhus's death, as a possibility for Astyanax. Andromaque, Barthes writes, takes over from Pyrrhus after the latter's death; we might also say that Astyanax will take over from *both* Pyrrhus and Andromaque.

But who is Astyanax? In a sense, he is himself *no one*, and everyone else's alibi. For the Greeks, he is a way of testing Pyrrhus's loyalty to the state and his respect for Ménélas (who gave him Hermione); for Andromaque, he has mostly been both a reminder of Hector and an obstacle to her fidelity to Hector; for Pyrrhus, he has often seemed to be nothing more than the commodity that will buy Andromaque's love. Nevertheless, when Pyrrhus is capable of thinking of Astyanax apart from his convenience as bait for Andromaque, it's clear that, as Barthes says, he wants the child to live. The survival of Astyanax is the only clear sign of a new order in *Andromaque*, and Pyrrhus and Andromaque finally identify themselves unreservedly with Astyanax's safety. But we have never seen

Astyanax; he is the child, the future, the blank page of the play, the invisible character who finally replaces the oppressive Hector as the absent dominating force of the other characters' lives. Astyanax is nothing less and nothing more than the value of pure possibility. He has lost two fathers; he is the twice-orphaned child. His life is all that has survived a history of great destructions, but he is responsible to and for nothing. He is all that remains of Troy's heroes, but he will have no obligation to avenge Troy; he is Hector's son, but it's possible that his mother will no longer speak to him of Hector; he owes his life to Pyrrhus, but Andromaque had never promised Pyrrhus that Astyanax would live *for* any particular purpose.

Astyanax, whom we never hear and never see, is the escape from tragedy — not an escape into the sensible and verbose compromises with passion and society of *Mithridate* or *Iphigénie*, or even into the rational good faith of Pyrrhus, but rather into an order evoked but unlived in Racine's theater. He is the clean blankness of being toward which Pyrrhus and Andromaque confusedly struggle, and which they are unable to attain themselves. It is to Astyanax that they delegate the possibility of being neither Greek nor Trojan, of having no father to imitate — and therefore the possibility of a new order for desire which would save the Racinian imagination from repeating its own narrow formulas of desire.[8]

CHAPTER TWO

Realism and the Fear of Desire

SOME YEARS AGO, Roland Barthes spoke of the "rigorously equal pressure" along the surface of a Robbe-Grillet narrative. With the traditional novel, we skip from crisis to crisis, as if the rhythms of our eyes' movements while we read "were meant to reproduce the very hierarchy of the classical universe, endowed with alternately pathetic and insignificant moments." In Robbe-Grillet, on the other hand — at least in Robbe-Grillet as Barthes saw him in 1955 — no one moment of writing has more value or weight than any other moment. More recently, Richard Poirier aptly defined the difficulty which some highly "literary" readers might have with Thomas Pynchon's *Gravity's Rainbow*. Pynchon (more successfully than Robbe-Grillet, I should add) would deprive us of that secure sense of general design which allows us to relax over specific passages. The sense of meaning which we bring to each sentence from our reading of previous sentences doesn't help us, so to speak, to get done more quickly with the sentence at hand. The extraordinary density of Pynchon's novel is due less to its dazzling multiplicity of characters, episodes and allusions than to a lack of "predictable direction" which, as Poirier says, makes any summary of the novel's meaning "pretty much the product of whatever creative paranoia the book induces in a reader."[1]

What Barthes calls the "insignificant moments" of traditional fiction belong to a universe saturated with significance. The classical fictional narrative may seem to shift back and forth between the meaningful and the meaningless, but meaning is potentially present everywhere. What happens is that at certain moments in the story the narrative engine puffs a little more strenuously than at other moments, and the rest of the time we can, as it were, glide along on the extra steam. The more leisurely stretches in realistic fiction also convey the immersion of meaning in time. Duration partially erodes dramatic significance, although, with rare exceptions — Flaubert is one of them — a certain staleness of meaning in time doesn't cast a radical doubt on meaning itself. The well-trained reader of novels knows when to look and listen with special care; certain meanings which inform the entire narrative are dramatized more starkly, or expressed more explicitly in the privileged moments of traditional fiction. The "trouble" with Robbe-Grillet and Pynchon is that even when they indulge in recognizably privileged or key passages, they seem to be defying us to take them as definitive or wholly serious statements. And this absence or parody of particularly meaningful moments corresponds to a diffusion of meaning, or, at the extreme, to the irrelevance or even lack of general meanings. In a novelistic universe deprived of some governing pattern of significance, all events may be equally important. No structure of meaning is powerful enough to collect all the fragments of significance into a single system.

I want to look at some of the ways in which the nineteenth-century novel has trained us to be compulsive pursuers of significant design in fiction. Whereas twentieth-century writers, especially since Joyce, tend to parody the great myths of Western culture, or to make those myths "de-signify," the realistic novelist seems spontaneously to make patterns of meaning from the most isolated and disparate details. The *tour de force* of realistic novelists from Jane Austen to the later Henry James is to combine a superficially loose, even sprawling narrative form with an extraordinary tightness of meaning. The degree of looseness varies, but in writers as different as Jane Austen, Balzac, Dickens and James, we find a shared commitment to the portentous detail. The most casual word, the most trifling gesture, the most tangential episode all submit easily to the discipline of being *revealing* words, gestures and episodes.

Behavior in realistic fiction is continuously expressive of character. Apparently random incidents neatly carry messages about personality; and the world is thus at least structurally congenial to character, in the sense that it is constantly proposing to our intelligence objects and events which contain human desires, which give to them an intelligible form. The realistic novelist can wander, linger and digress as much as he likes; he will absorb any material — as the Balzacian digression supremely illustrates — into a commanding structure of significance. Furthermore, because the realistic novel generally remains faithful to chronological time, the very sequence of events becomes an ordering principle. Even Proust, while he seems to be announcing in *Combray* a nonchronological narrative organized according to the discontinuous resurrections of the past in Marcel's involuntary memories, follows a conventional time sequence from Marcel's childhood to middle age. It's true that certain stretches of Marcel's life are skipped, and it's also true that the linear narrative of *A la Recherche du temps perdu* is complicated by the fact that the future of each moment is present in the account being given of it. The Proustian future is not only a time we move toward as we read; it is also the narrator's voice at each point of his return to the past. Nonetheless, given the theoretical statements in the work and the importance of subjective time in any accurate rendering of a man's life, it's striking that the linear sequences of *A la Recherche* remain so clear, and that we almost never have any doubts about what happened when in Marcel's life.

The conservative nature of the Proustian novel in this respect can best be appreciated if we compare it to Robbe-Grillet's *La Jalousie*. The real subversion of chronological time in Robbe-Grillet's novel is accomplished by the simple but radical device of eliminating any temporal reference for the telling of the story. The coherence which chronological time gives to traditional fiction should be measured against the temporally chaotic repetitiousness of *La Jalousie*, in which there is no controlling narrative voice at all to place in time the novel's various pictures. Robbe-Grillet's fictional episodes locate jealousy in space, but they tell us nothing about the historical development of jealousy. Nothing could be more different from the Proustian narrator's scrupulous tracing of different stages in, for example, his jealousy of Albertine. If there is temporal progression at all in *La Jalousie*, it can be discussed entirely in terms of esthetic strategy. We can never know when the various incidents took place (and therefore the question itself is an absurd one for criticism of the work), but we can follow the narrator's manipulation of our own developing sense of how jealousy has infected the entire universe of the novel.

Finally, time in realistic fiction is not merely chronological; it is shaped by a prior imagination of beginnings and ends.[2] Dates are enormously important in realistic fiction, and the first paragraphs of countless nineteenth-century novels give us the exact year when their stories begin. The specified year not only serves the illusion of historical authenticity; it also allows us the luxury of assigning precise beginnings to experience, and of thereby making experience more accessible to our appetite for sense-making distinctions and categories. Conclusions are of course just as important in this enterprise of adding sharper sense to life. Realistic novels tend to end with marriages or deaths, and marriage at the end of *Pride and Prejudice* and *Little Dorrit* is as significant and conclusive a *dénouement* to the novel's drama as is Ahab's death in *Moby-Dick* or Milly Theale's death in *The Wings of the Dove*.

Marriage has more than a purely formal importance in traditional fiction. In *The Theory of the Novel*, Georg Lukács emphasized the differences between the marriages which end novels and those which end neoclassical comedies. The sculptural form of comedy requires "a purely symbolic ceremony" (similar to the hero's death at the end of tragedy) which emphasizes, in an atemporal way, the contours and limits of the form itself. We might add that the marriages announced in the last acts of *L'Ecole des femmes* and *L'Avare* are essentially insignificant; a proper conjugal match simply strikes a note of bland harmony by which we recognize that the dramatist has finished his work. Marriages in the novel, on the other hand, complete the novel's sense. The happy marriage is as significant as the unhappy one, and while there may be more to say about the latter, the former is equally rich in psychological and moral implications. In Molière, the obstacles to the good lovers' marriages are simply pushed aside by happy strokes of fate. The young people's union is not the result of any growth of moral consciousness: *they* have generally been in love from the very start, and Arnolphe and Harpagon are just as foolish at the end of *L'Ecole des femmes* and *L'Avare* as they were at the beginning. But the happy marriages of Elizabeth and Darcy, of Little Dorrit and Arthur Clennam, and of Dorothea and Will Ladislaw are the just consequences and rewards of just perceptions of character. They are the reliable signs of the hero's and the heroine's matured consciousness, as well as an indication of what constitutes a "natural" social order in all these novels. And we should make no mistake about the creaky plot machinery sometimes necessary to bring these marriages about — or, more generally, to settle the moral issues of the novel in the "right" way. Molière proclaims the insignificance of his happy endings (which never really qualify the pessimism of his major plays) by the frivolous ingenuities of plot which make them possible. But in realistic fiction, the unexpected revelation or the surprising coincidence, far from being merely formal conveniences, seem almost to signify an awesome complicity of the most distant or unrelated corners of reality with the requirements of the novel's main psychological and moral structures. Reality is coerced into providing the suitable conclusion to a continuously meaningful chain of events.

The exertion toward significant form in realistic fiction serves the cause of significant, coherently structured character. The revealing incident makes personality intelligible; real beginnings and definitive endings provide a temporal frame in which individuals don't merely exist, but move purposefully from one stage of being to another. Personality is as rigorously structured in the realistic novel as it is in Racinian tragedy. Indeed, in a literary form remarkable for its variety and its concreteness, it's perhaps even more remarkable to find that tendency to allegorize the self which can be seen in Racine. Desire in realistic fiction is generally conceived of either as a ruling passion (Goriot's paternal love, Silas Marner's miserliness, Milly Theale's dovelike mildness), or in terms of that inner chemistry described by Sartre in which mental processes are depicted as syntheses of abstract faculties (in the same way that Phèdre is a certain "solution" of guilt and sexual passion, Swann's jealousy of Odette alternates with and neutralizes his tenderness for Odette). The richly detailed textures of characterization in realistic fiction seldom subvert the coherent wholeness of personality — or if they do, criticism has to deal with what we call an "interesting" esthetic failure. Psychological complexity is tolerated as long as it doesn't threaten an ideology of the self as a fundamentally intelligible structure unaffected by a history of fragmented, discontinuous desires.

The persistence (or rather the resurgence) of this ideology in nineteenth-century literature is a curious chapter in the political history of art. Classical French literature is a conservative social force not merely because its pessimism about human nature would discourage any hopeful view of what might be accomplished by changes in social conditions, but also because it helps to reinforce the hierarchical structure of seventeenth-century French society. Racinian tragedy is full of chaotic passions, but as far as ideologies of the self are concerned, the implied existential chaos is perhaps less important than the Racinian image of a permanently ordered self. Passion disrupts his characters' lives, but it also orders their personalities. Thanks to a dominant enslaving passion, all behavior in Racine can be "placed" in relation to a fixed psychological center. Words and gestures can always be referred to that passion; they can, in other words, be reliably interpreted. The literary myth of a rigidly ordered self contributes to a pervasive cultural ideology of the self which serves the established social order. Personality is shown to have the coherent, hierarchical wholeness suitable to a social system of sharply distinct ranks. A rigid social hierarchy reproduces, in political structures, the form of the self, and it is as if Racinian tragedy were certifying the psychological realism of such hierarchical political structures. True, classical psychology vindicates authoritarian rule partly by its dismal view of a human nature in dire need of discipline. From a purely structural point of view, it also vindicates authoritarianism by its images of a self whose very irrationality is part of its coherence — a coherence which lends itself ideally to psychological and social classifications (and control).

Neoclassical literature and realistic fiction belong to a single community of cultural assumptions about personality. This statement obviously involves a huge — and, in a sense, outrageous — historical jump. Artistic forms develop and thrive in particular social contexts, and the span of time I'm referring to includes, especially in France, great social upheavals. Even within the nineteenth century, the differences between English society in 1813 and England in 1872 should perhaps discourage us from speaking, as I did a few pages back, as if marriage in *Pride and Prejudice* and in *Middlemarch* had the same significance. Dorothea's aspirations are compromised by her marriage to Will, while Elizabeth's marriage to Darcy will presumably provide an ideal social context for her personal worth. In *Pride and Prejudice*, institutionalized forms can still accommodate individual superiority; *Middlemarch* documents the *in*adequacy of available social forms to heroic aspirations. In spite of these important differences, there is, I think, a commitment to a *psychological* integrity or intelligibility which has been a constant in Western culture. It is this commitment which we are trying to define here, and it can be distinguished from a more variable historical sense of the relation between social possibility and individual aspiration. Notions about the natural shape of the self create the durable "field" in which a wide range of historical judgments about the self and society can take place. Finally, however, the field limits the range of this historical variability. And such limitations are not politically neutral. Assumptions about human nature which may seem almost ahistorical (because of the persistence with which a culture has maintained them) nonetheless insure some continuity among all the social arrangements imagined throughout that culture's history. Indeed, the monotonously similar fates, in modern history, of political systems which apparently reflect the most diverse ideologies may be due to a certain politics of the self common to all these ideologies. The potential for change in any new type of social organization depends, ultimately, on ontological assumptions about what the self *is*.

To return to the historical periods from which the examples in this book are being taken, we might say that the availability of Racinian tragedy to psychoanalytic criticism is striking evidence of a continuity in Western thought about the nature of the self. For example, as we saw in the previous chapter, the psychoanalytic interpretations of Racine's theater by Charles Mauron and by Roland Barthes do away with the conscious identities of Racine's characters in order to identify these characters with a variety of roles in unconscious fantasies. But the Racinian self which these readings uncover (Barthes' *homo racianus*) is as highly structured as the one proposed by the traditional academic portraits of Racinian characters. Especially in Mauron, the traditional diagram of conscious passions is replaced by a Freudian diagram of familial sexuality which is equally unreceptive to signs of discontinuous, nonstructurable desires. Neither critical approach, however, violates the Racinian text. Racine himself, a critical vocabulary of conscious passions, and the psychoanalytic reading of unconscious impulses are different versions of a cultural commitment to the notion of structured character. The peculiarity of Freudian analysis is to propose a history of the self's structure which includes, as one of its stages, the solidifying of character structures (which are the post-Oedipal sublimations of pre-Oedipal impulses). Psychoanalysis partially demystifies the notion of such structures by explaining them historically rather than just deducing them from the concept of an ahistorical human nature. But, curiously enough, history is not contingent in Freudian thought, or rather, contingency is restricted to individual variations on permanent structural themes. The stages of human desire described by psychoanalysis happen in time, but this doesn't prevent them from being considered as *necessary* stages. And Freud's recourse to myths in a presumably clinical terminology suggests his wish to avoid arguments about historical conditions and particularities. We no longer have supernatural sanctions for the shape of human character, but biology and psychoanalytic logic can provide those sanctions and vindicate the claim to universal validity for a particular developmental view of the self.

Now even at times when literature appears to collaborate most closely with a view of character as a readable, coherent structure, we can find literature which contests that view. Indeed, in seventeenth-century France, the classical period is partly a reaction in the name of this coherence against images of a fractured or even empty self. Corneille's heroes, for example, have only a prospective self; their freedom consists in the very emptiness of a consciousness always ready to try out new heroic roles, a consciousness continuously throwing off definitions and projecting itself toward future acts. Baroque poetry offers another image of a kind of unanchored self. The loose organization of poetic narrative, the poet's availability to discontinuous and random associations, and his fascination with those aspects of nature which tend to blur shapes and play tricks on the identifying intelligence all express a uniquely relaxed willingness to perform the self as fragmented perceptions and desires. And in fiction, the eighteenth century offers numerous examples of a playful subversion of psychological intelligibility, or at least of an indifference to the dramatization of "serious" character structures.[3] Novelistic character is largely a pretext for episodic variety and diverting changes of locale, as well as the often tenuous thread holding together unrelated subplots and digressive anecdotes in Smollett and Lesage. And the quickly boring reminders, in Diderot and Sterne, of the author's manipulative presence become interesting as a sign of an extraordinary *indifference* to character. We are used to indifference or hostility to character in our own willfully antipsychological literature, but it is astonishing to find a similar phenomenon as a kind of parenthesis between the psychological density of neoclassical literature and the at least equal psychological density of realistic fiction.

I don't mean to suggest either that eighteenth-century novels are "better" than nineteenth-century novels, or that the former constitute the greater challenge to social order. It could be argued that the very fragmentation of the self discourages us from taking literary character seriously; it is therefore easy to ignore the potentially disruptive aspect of works which seem to embody nothing more than a culture's marginal fantasies about human nature. But the dismissal of the marginal is in itself an ideologically significant gesture within a culture which uses the notion of centrality as a criterion of value in its attempts to classify and to judge experience. In the second half of this book, I will be looking at alternatives to a psychology of stable centers of desire, centers which allow us to construct an intelligible self. What is the appeal, the power, and the danger of a psychology of the marginal or the peripheral — which would also be a psychology (if the word still applies) of the deconstructed self? To return to nineteenth-century fiction, it could of course be said that it is precisely by working within a certain field of agreement about the shape of the self that the realistic novelist questions existing orders more seriously than his psychologically playful, even irresponsible eighteenth-century predecessors. The realistic novelist's effort to make us believe in his characters may be the precondition for any challenge to the order of things: Huck Finn, to take a striking example, is socially dangerous to the extent that we do find him believable or "real." But it's also true that realistic novelists dramatize the *failure* of all such challenges, and I would suggest that a reluctance to take certain psychological risks with character at least partly explains these novelists' moral and social pessimism. It is not just the nature of nineteenth-century society which defeats the realistic hero. His defeat is also the result of his imprisonment within a psychology which his creator has adopted from the society being contested, a psychology of the coherently structured and significantly expressive self.

The belief in psychic structure and significance is so pervasive in Western culture that it may seem superfluous to assert its influence on a few works of literature. But a confidence in psychological order is an interesting phenomenon in nineteenth-century fiction because social history would seem to have made such a confidence exceedingly difficult to sustain. The realistic novelist is intensely aware of writing in a context of social fragmentation. Jane Austen already sounds the alarm in her second group of novels, and with Dickens and Balzac we have an obsessive concern with chaotically fierce human energies in the jungle of a chaotically "open" society. On the one hand — and critics have frequently emphasized this — nineteenth-century novelists tend to take a sharply critical view of this society. Even when, as in the case of Balzac, they are fascinated by the mere mass of energies exploding in this social jungle, they also document the dehumanizing brutality of a society in which "order" is always a mockery of moral orders. Those who have made it in the competitive scramble for power become the standard-bearers of a conservatism concerned with the preserving not of values or traditions, but rather of their acquired power. And, as René Girard has shown, the great nineteenth-century novelists expose a kind of inauthentic community of desire in this society. Social harmony extends no further than the imitation of other people's desires; one needs others to know what is desirable, at the same time that one needs to eliminate others in order to possess the objects which they have designated to the individual's parasitic appetites.

But the critical judgments passed on society in nineteenth-century fiction are qualified by a form which provides this society with a reassuring myth about itself. The realistic novel gives us an image of social fragmentation contained within the order of significant form — and it thereby suggests that the chaotic fragments are somehow socially viable and morally redeemable. The novel makes esthetic sense out of social anarchy. And the society being judged subtly profits from this novelistic order, even though the order includes a great deal of social criticism. A good part of the realistic novelist's imaginative energies — whatever his intentions may be — is devoted to sparing his society the pain of confronting the shallowness of its order and the destructiveness of its appetites. The ordered significances of realistic fiction are presented as immanent to society, whereas in fact they are the mythical denial of that society's fragmented nature. In a sense, then, the realistic novelist desperately tries to hold together what he recognizes quite well is falling apart. The looseness or elasticity of novelistic form is a sign of that recognition. The ordering myth of nineteenth-century society can obviously not be given within the narrow formal discipline of classical tragedy. There are too many disparate elements to take into account. The novel welcomes the disparate, it generously gives space to a great variety of experience; but it is essentially an exercise in *containing* the looseness to which it often appears to be casually abandoning itself. And even when novelists seem to become more skeptical about their ability to find a saving form for the disconnected, fragmented lives they represent, they make a last-ditch stand for the redemptive pattern rather than simply abandon the whole pattern-making enterprise.

What alternatives were available to nineteenth-century novelists? To avoid the sort of complicity I'm discussing is an enormously difficult enterprise. It would seem to involve not only a revolution in literary form, but — as a precondition for that — a successful revolt against a culture's most fundamental ways of making sense out of its experience. And surely we should respect the realistic novelist's poignant effort to provide his society with some image of a viable and morally decent order, especially since the work of almost all the most interesting writers of fiction in the nineteenth century amounts to a confession of their failure to find such an order. At the level of visible social organization, the realistic novelist courageously confronts what are after all terrifying images of destructive fragmentation. In the face of these images, the novelist tries and fails to believe in myths of social order. But, once again, I think we have to distinguish between a pessimistic view of moral and social fragmentariness, and a reassuring belief in psychological unity and intelligibility. The latter blinds both the novelist and his society to the psychic discontinuities and incoherence from which all our fragmented experience ultimately derives. A myth about psychic order and structure helps to contain, and to limit, all critiques of disorder. It also makes it practically impossible to begin experimenting with nondestructive versions of fragmented desires. There are models of such experiments in nineteenth-century poetry — in, for example, Wordsworth, Hölderlin, Baudelaire, and as we shall see, Rimbaud. True, the dismissal of psychological order would threaten the character structures without which realistic fiction, unlike lyric poetry, could no longer survive. But, as much nonrealistic fiction since the eighteenth century demonstrates, the psychological resources of fictional prose narratives are by no means exhausted by the realistic novelist's commitment to character structures which depend on the sublimation of desire — and therefore on a negation of both the sensual intensities and the fragmented variety of human desires.

Even without abandoning his character portraits, the realistic novelist might have drawn our attention more willingly to aspects of his own artfulness as an alternative to the sort of intelligibility dramatized in his characters. But in general he is anxious to make us forget his own presence in his work, and he thereby disguises a narrative performance of desiring fantasy which might have contested that organization of desire into coherent personalities which, so to speak, the novelist argues for through his characters. Perhaps only Flaubert is willing to take the risk of drawing our attention to a kind of nonstructurable randomness in his own writing, to give stylistic emphasis to dramatically "unnecessary" passages, passages which gratuitously supplement the novel's sense. And this narrative waste in Flaubert affects the integrity of the characters whom Flaubert nevertheless takes the trouble to construct — not only their moral integrity (or pretensions), but also their very credibility as full, rounded, coherent personalities of realistic fiction. From *Madame Bovary* to *Bouvard et Pécuchet*, the failure of significance spreads to the characters themselves. Under the pressures of what appears to be a skepticism about the very idea of personality, the Flaubertian character almost ceases to be. Flaubert reacts pessimistically to this potential absence of self (as a consequence of psychic randomness and self-fragmentation), but his work does suggest the futility, or at least the innocuous nature, of all social criticism which is not included within questions about the nature of the self. The formal and psychological reticence of most realistic fiction makes for a secret complicity between the novelist and his society's illusions about its own order. Realistic fiction serves nineteenth-century society by providing it with strategies for containing (and repressing) its disorder within significantly structured stories about itself.

War and Peace and *Middlemarch* will provide us with two images of this containment. Tolstoy argues in *War and Peace* against all the systematizations by which men try to simplify and make sense of history, but the most positive value in the novel is an institutional simplification of desire. The two most expansive characters in the novel — Pierre and Natasha — presumably realize a Tolstoyan ideal of nature by agreeing to be defined almost exclusively as husband and wife. Lukács spoke of the "profoundly desperate" state of mind described by Tolstoy in the "peaceful nursery atmosphere" at the end of *War and Peace*. A love meant to be the victory of nature over the false subtleties of culture is lived, Lukács wrote, as an adaptation to the lowest level of convention. Indeed, as an adequate conclusion to the immense spiritual quest of *War and Peace*, Tolstoy aggressively apotheosizes a slatternly housewife in constant anguish about the state of her babies' diapers. "Natasha needed a husband. A husband was given her. And her husband gave her a family. And she not only saw no need of any other or better husband but as all her spiritual energies were devoted to serving that husband and family she could not imagine, and found no interest in imagining, how it would be if things were different." No amount of cant about the great biological community of the family can hide the brutal reductiveness of this passage. Far from being the universalizing of love which is spoken of elsewhere in the novel, Tolstoyan marriage tends to make for an exclusive, self-contained social unit smugly indifferent to the rest of the world. The end of *War and Peace* would propose an authentic image of historic order: not the false intellectual order of historians, but the natural order of the family. But the obvious foundation of the family in nature allows Tolstoy to obscure its social conventionality. The transcendence of culture into nature turns out to be an obedient retreat into a given social form — a retreat which conveniently provides a biological alibi for social conformity.

Middlemarch is a striking example of an ambivalent attitude toward the prospect of establishing significant connections in experience. On the one hand, it is a novel about connecting enterprises which fail. Casaubon's *Key to All Mythologies* is nothing but scattered, unrelated notes. Lydgate has to abandon his medical research into "the primitive tissue," the "common basis" from which he might be able to articulate "the intimate relations of living structure." Finally, there is no social medium in which Dorothea's heroism might be adequately enacted, and we are invited to think of her as a modern "Saint Theresa, foundress of nothing, whose loving heartbeats and sobs after an unattained goodness tremble off and are dispersed among hindrances instead of centering in some long-recognizable deed." On the other hand, *Middlemarch* is about the power of connections in life — connections between ideals and the social conditions in which they must be tested; between one man's moral choices and the consequences of those choices on other people's lives; between, as George Eliot put it in a letter, "character" and "the medium in which a character moves." Eliot speaks of her story as her "particular web"; she is engaged in "unravelling certain human lots and seeing how they were woven and interwoven." Now the real connections in *Middlemarch* are ironic commentaries on the ideal connections. The "embroiled medium" in which George Eliot's characters move is a mockery of the structures they dream of, although Eliot does find some basis for a qualified optimism in the thought that that medium receives and is modified not only by the acts of a Bulstrode, but also by the life of someone like Dorothea. ". . . The growing good of the world is partly dependent on unhistoric acts . . ." and ". . . the effect of [Dorothea's] being on those around her was incalculably diffusive." We must learn to settle for the "incalculably diffusive" effect — and, if we do, we will perhaps begin to see innumerable examples of how inextricably involved human lives are with one another.

George Eliot is scarcely happy with the kinds of connections she is able to propose as a substitute for epic life. Nonetheless, like her characters, she does draw some moral comfort from the "embroiled" and strained relations which are the only connections she can realistically conceive of. She won't abandon the dream of structured significance, even if she has to sustain it by the vague doctrine of individual goodness finally, in some way, affecting the course of history, or by the more desperate move of showing how the very subversion of her protagonists' dreams is itself a proof of the interconnectedness in life. Even modern experience is a significantly structured web, although it is no longer structured for the idealism of a Saint Theresa. Nothing is more terrifying than to have behavior and environment break up into frequently discontinuous, fragmented moves and contexts. Dorothea is jarred "as with an electric shock" by "the gigantic broken revelations" of Rome, by the "vast wreck" of ancient ideals and modern "forgetfulness and degradation" in the city; "all her life" the red drapery being hung in Saint Peter's for Christmas (juxtaposed with the "excited intention" of the figures in the mosaic) will haunt her memory as "a disease of the retina" spreading itself everywhere.

Finally, George Eliot's very imagination for plot perhaps testifies to a nervous, strained determination to connect the many threads of experience which she has allowed into her work. Of course, literature is always something of an exercise in inventing a dramatic logic for unexpected relations among things. Its nature is to coerce experience into making sense. But each period or genre establishes its own criteria of acceptability for those ingenuities which fit deceptively random lines of action into a single structure. *Oedipus Rex* expresses an unlimited tolerance for coincidence. In a sense, Oedipus's presumption is, precisely, to think that events can ever be safely counted on to remain disconnected; Sophocles' work dramatizes the tragedy of inescapably significant structures. Realistic fiction, on the other hand, prides itself on a more empirical sense of probability. But the *dénouements* in realistic fiction make havoc of the verisimilitudes which the novelist has appeared to be so scrupulously observing. *Middlemarch* ends in structural fireworks; the unexpected link between Bulstrode and Will is a piece of novelistic weaving done with the coarsest, most visible threads. We were perhaps ready to think that Dorothea and Lydgate could be justly reproached for their solipsistic notions of structural harmonies in life. Their moral and scientific idealisms took no account of how those notions might be affected by experiences alien to them. But George Eliot's own indulgence in an ideally unified novelistic structure may make us view with irony *her* irony about her heroes' early views of their relation to the social medium in which they must live. By the end of *Middlemarch*, George Eliot's presence in the novel has become anything but "incalculably diffusive." She is making connections which the rest of the novel has trained us to see as naïve, unworkable novelistic connections. The subtle, almost indefinable

influence of one life on other lives has been replaced by melodramatic connections of crime and rare coincidence. Thus fiction
unexpectedly — and, I think, unintentionally — points to its own
status as purely verbal artifice by the ways in which it demonstrates
the persistence of significant structures in modern life.

Desire is a threat to the form of realistic fiction. Desire can subvert
social order; it can also disrupt novelistic order. The nineteenth-
century novel is haunted by the possibility of these subversive
moments, and it suppresses them with a brutality both shocking and
eminently logical. In formal terms, disruptive desire could be thought
of as a disease of disconnectedness in a part of the structure which
rejects being defined by its relations to other parts and asserts, as
it were, a scandalous affinity with elements alien to the structure.
Such desires resist being structured as part of a realistic character
portrait. Realistic fiction seems to give an enormous importance to
disruptive desires by embodying them in its heroes. Indeed, the
most frequent confrontation in the realistic novel is between society
and a hero who refuses to accept the definitions which society proposes of his duties and satisfactions. Since these definitions are
grounded in an established view of the self, the hero's rebellion is
fundamentally against the idea of his own nature implicit in the
opportunities being offered to him.

But this centrality of disruptive desire in the novel is very ambiguous. First of all, it is a curious fact that the central figures in many
nineteenth-century novels are the vaguest or the most mystifying
presences of the works in which they appear. It's not a question of
their being psychologically richer — and therefore more difficult to
enclose within critical definitions — than other characters. Rather,
we could, in many cases, justifiably complain that these heroes and
heroines are *less* interesting psychologically than the novelist's other
characters, or that they have a kind of density dangerously close to
unintelligibility. Many readers have found Milly Theale and Maggie
Verver flat, insubstantial heroines; critics have complained that
Marcel in *A la Recherche du temps perdu* is insufficiently realized
for the amount of moral and esthetic significance he is meant to
carry in the novel; Fabrice and Clélia in *La Chartreuse de Parme*
are said to be less interesting than Gina and Mosca; the qualities
which separate Ahab and Prince Myshkin from the other characters

of *Moby-Dick* and *The Idiot* have the ambiguity of intentions for which these novels can provide no clarifying contexts, no field or medium in which they might be distinctly seen. Not only does society in realistic fiction fail to provide occasions for the enactment of exceptional passions; the novelist also indicates in formal terms his own inability (or unwillingness) to imagine these passions in real life. As desire becomes more radically disruptive of established orders, the novel tends to become less realistic, more allegorical: the characters of *Moby-Dick* are frankly emblematic, and Balzac rightly placed the works which dramatize the most extravagant desiring imagination — *La Peau de chagrin, La Recherche de l'absolu,* and *Séraphita* — among his "philosophical novels" and not with the more realistic *Scènes de la vie parisienne* or *Scènes de la vie de province.*

Realistic fiction admits heroes of desire in order to submit them to ceremonies of expulsion. This literary form depends, for its very existence, on the annihilation or, at the very least, the immobilizing containment of anarchic impulses.[4] The hero is an intruder in a world of significantly related structures, of unambiguous beginnings and definitive conclusions. He is alien to the world of realistic fiction — but not because that world is the "real" world which the novelist objectively shows to be incompatible with quixotic idealisms. That incompatibility is largely an *a priori* choice on the part of the novelist in favor of a particular kind of world which, as I've been suggesting, he severely judges but also (perhaps unintentionally) supports. The technical premises of realistic fiction — the commitment to intelligible, "full" characters, to historical verisimilitude, to the revealing gesture or episode, to a closed temporal frame — *already* dooms any adventure in the stimulating improbabilities of behavior which would resist being "placed" and interpreted in a general psychological or formal structure. (It could be said, for example, that the very nature of the novel she appears in determines Isabel's return to Osmond at the end of *The Portrait of a Lady*; her dream of freedom has been defeated by the limited range of possibilities for being free available to the realistic imagination. Isabel *and* James can no longer imagine to what concrete use her desire to be free might be put.) The strange vagueness of certain novelistic heroes and heroines is not so strange at that: in a sense, the realistic novel makes no provision for such figures. It has very little to say about them, although the demonstration of this negative truth frequently generates a sense of the tragedy of limited forms (both social and esthetic) in the novelist, and can therefore constitute a very complex novelistic enterprise.

These heroes are of course also often very glamorous. They seem to embody an enterprise of subversion which the novelist rejects but to which he keeps returning. The model for this ambivalence is *Don Quixote.* Cervantes' novel also provides the model for the structural confrontation of the exceptional individual in an unexceptional society. Significantly, as Cervantes' complicity with his hero's madness seems to increase, his work tends to violate the realistic conventions which, in the history of fiction, it was more influential in establishing than any other single novel. The dreamlike ambiguity of certain episodes in the second part of *Don Quixote* blurs the boundaries between illusion and reality. Realistic fiction depends on the distinctness of those boundaries, and yet the first great realistic novel takes curious risks in an occasionally indecisive play with the elements meant to stand for the real and those meant to stand for delusion. Also, Cervantes allows the fate of his novel to intrude into the novel itself; *Don Quixote's* real popularity becomes an influence in the lives of *Don Quixote's* characters in the second part. The novel starts out by being a satire of literature in the name of reality, but it also demonstrates the irresistibly contagious nature of literary fantasy. First of all, the don's delusions affect even Sancho Panza; secondly, the infatuation of Cervantes' public with stories of chivalry is simply replaced by an infatuation with a satire of stories of chivalry; and finally, the prestige of Cervantes' novel comes to affect the substance of the novel itself, which turns from a naïve representation of what "real" life is like (when it is not tampered with by literature) to more complex images of the inevitable seduction of life *and* literature by literary extravagances.

The nineteenth-century realistic novelist has a more fearful sympathy with his hero's socially disruptive ideals or desires. On the one hand, the novelist would have good reason to look yearningly to his condemned hero: *he* at least, perhaps at the cost of his life, has refused to offer society anything but the assertion of his own originality. On the other hand, given the contexts in which such assertions take place, they can only be judged as dangerous. The figures of nineteenth-century novels who refuse to cooperate with social definitions of the self and of the nature and range of the self's desires are the literary scapegoats of nineteenth-century society. The glamor of many such figures seems to result from the extra lighting they receive by virtue of embodying appealing but guilty impulses; they glow more brightly at the moment of sacrifice. René Girard has argued in *La Violence et le sacré* that the expulsion of the scapegoat has a culturally stabilizing function; to sacrifice him may be the way of ending what Girard calls a vicious circle of violence in the community and to make possible structuring processes and social differentiations. From the point of view which I've been adopting in this chapter, the particular violence of novelistic heroes — a violence characteristic of such diverse figures as Ahab, Isabel Archer and Fabrice del Dongo — is to contest the very categories in which the novel encloses and defines character. Perhaps the surest guarantee of social order is psychological coherence, and the nineteenth-century novelist, in his commitment to significant structures of character, is providing his readers with more than just an intellectual satisfaction with well-drawn patterns. In spite of his troubling heroes and heroines, he has opted for, he is in fact insisting on, the readability of the human personality. The apparent chaos of social life is a relatively harmless illusion, and the writer thus sends his society a comforting message about its fundamental stability and order. There are predictable continuities among different people's desires as well as among the desires of each individual; behavior can be interpreted, structured, "plotted."

The heroes of fiction are frequently the flaws in that text, its menacing moments of illegibility. They constitute an enormous, and an enormously diversified, family; among them, we might mention Chateaubriand's René, Cooper's Deerslayer, Balzac's Vautrin and Balthazar Claës, Julien Sorel and Fabrice del Dongo, Captain Ahab, Hester Prynne and Zenobia in Hawthorne, Huck Finn, Dorothea Brooke, Heathcliff, Emma Bovary, Milly Theale and Maggie Verver, Tonio Kruger, and Prince Myshkin. Without these characters, the novels in which they appear would have no *raison d'être*; but the life they bring to the novels is almost invariably defeated by a world whose victory we are invited to find both dispiriting and inescapable. The hero of realistic fiction supports a novelistic structure which includes *his* expulsion from the viable structures of fiction and of life. The novelist glamorizes a figure who exposes the factitious nature of the social and esthetic orders in the name of which the novelist will sacrifice that figure. Realistic prudence therefore does coexist with a certain riskiness: how can we help but *prefer* the heroic victim? Both the reader and the society within the novel stand in fascinated awe of those figures who embody that secret excess or violence which perhaps prefigures a structural explosion but which also awakens the self-preserving energies of a stable order. The hero is simultaneously an invitation and a warning. The invitation could hardly be more guarded or oblique. An energetic excess of being in realistic fiction is inevitably compromised or punished in its heroes; it is tolerated only in the minor figures of fiction, in the degraded form of amusing eccentricities.[5]

The terror of desire in nineteenth-century fiction is often dramatized in the heroes themselves. The latter are by no means always the rebellious scapegoats I've just described, and perhaps nothing is more astonishing in the realistic novel than the central position frequently given to characters whose main function seems to be to smother desire, to stifle all movement. I would like to end this general (and partial) survey of nineteenth-century fiction with a study of what we may designate as a heroic stillness in fiction. The immobile hero or heroine is a complex phenomenon. He is occasionally an unambiguous warning about the dangers of desire, but he may also use his stillness as a strategy of retreat from the order which he seems to be defending, and into a realm of being where he will no longer owe anything at all to that order.

The clearest warning I know is sounded by Balzac in *La Peau de chagrin*. The novel obviously violates realistic criteria of probability, but it does provide an exceptionally clear model for the role of desire in Balzac's more realistic work, as well as in much non-Balzacian fiction. The message in *La Peau de chagrin* is simple: desire disintegrates society, the self and the novel. The ass-skein has the magic power to fulfill all Raphaël's desires, but with each desire the talisman shrinks and Raphaël's life grows shorter. Balzac's hero must therefore choose between paying for the immediate satisfaction of all his desires with his life, or prolonging his life by refusing to desire. The novel is skillfully polarized into images of disintegration and images of rigid order. It begins with a nightmare of fragmentation. The antique shop Raphaël wanders into is a chaos of historical reminiscences. "All the countries of the earth seemed to have brought there some debris from their sciences, a model of their arts."[6] The fictions of continuous historical time and of coherently organized civilizations are undermined by a mass of unrelated objects from different periods and different places. The spectacle sets off a hallucinated vision in Raphaël, one in which ". . . the universe appeared to him in snatches and in streaks of fire." Human history is an endless, disconnected poem: "Forms, colors, thought, everything came back to life; but nothing complete was offered to the soul." Raphaël's first wish when he takes the ass-skein is for a "bacchanalian" banquet. His wish is immediately granted, and the banquet begins with an orgy of disconnected conversation among the men during dinner, followed by a sexual orgy with the women brought in by the banker Taillefer. As Raphaël himself points out, he has moved from the spectacle of "the most poetic ruins of the material world" to "the debris of all the intellectual treasures which we pillaged" during the banquet, and finally to the courtesans Aquilina and Euphrasie, "lively and original images of madness." We of course recognize here the typically rigorous order of a Balzacian narrative scheme. The evidence of fragmentation is somewhat discredited by an obvious concern for thematic continuity. The orgies of disconnectedness are contained within and by a highly structured narrative progress. Nevertheless, the novel does begin with some ominous images of fragmented human energies: the ruins of history in the antique shop, the ruins of thought at the banquet, the sexual anarchy at the orgy.

What are the images of order in the novel? The old antique dealer gives Raphaël the formula to which he owes "happiness and my longevity": "*Desiring* burns us up and *Having Power* destroys us; but KNOWLEDGE leaves our weak faculties in a perpetual state of calm. Thus desire or will is dead in me, killed by thought. . . ." Such distinctions are of doubtful value in Balzac, for whom thought, desire and will are really synonymous. The antique dealer's argument depends on a very theoretical separation of feeling from expression. "What men call sorrows, loves, ambitions, setbacks, sadness are for me ideas which I can change into reveries; instead of feeling them, I express them, I translate them; instead of letting them devour my life, I dramatize them, I develop them, I enjoy them like novels which I might be reading by means of an inner vision." The fact that the writing of *La Comédie humaine* virtually devoured Balzac's life would be enough to justify our finding this passage rather glib. Formal unity and stability in Balzac's fiction do seem designed to tame and contain the violently disruptive energies of his style and in his characters, but the frantic pull toward order can hardly be said to end in an unqualified victory for order. The antique dealer's confidence depends on a fantasy of desire as a separate mental organ; but the expression of "knowledge," as Balzac well knew, is inevitably an expression of desire, and the novelist *wills* his version of the world on the reader.

But I'm less interested here in questioning the argument than in considering its implications and consequences. The major lesson in Balzac is that desire destroys; the major task is consequently to castrate desire. The antique dealer has apparently saved himself by an esthetic *dédoublement*. He has become the author of his feelings, he has de-energized them by esthetically composing them. The other principal image of amputated desire in *La Peau de chagrin* is provided by Foedora, in whom the fantasy of nondesiring is made more psychologically concrete than in the antique dealer. Foedora certainly has desires, but in order to satisfy them she has killed her sexual desires. She wants social power, and her success depends on her sexual invulnerability. Raphaël undertakes the desperate enterprise of trying to make her love him, but it is he who is almost destroyed by desires he quickly loses control of. There is perhaps a richer sensuality in Balzac's fiction than in that of any other nineteenth-century novelist, and yet he has what almost amounts to a mystique of chastity. Some of the most powerful (and malevolent) creatures in his world have a peculiar sexual purity or, at the very least, an infallible technique for controlling their erotic excitements: Bette, Vautrin, Foedora, Lady Dudley. "Virginity," Balzac writes in *La Cousine Bette*, "like all unnatural phenomena, has special riches, an engrossing majesty. Since he has economized life's forces, the individual virgin's life has a quality of incalculable resistance and duration. His brain has been enriched in the cohesion of faculties held in reserve." Raphaël's survival depends on his maintaining the virginity of his faculty for desiring. "To struggle more effectively with the cruel power whose challenge he had accepted, Raphaël had made himself chaste after the manner of Origen, by castrating his imagination." He is, as it were, the victim of a double castration. There is an obvious enough sexual symbolism in the fact that both the ass-skein and Raphaël's life grow shorter each time he gives in to a desire. But the strategy by which Raphaël tries to save himself from this fate is itself a devirilizing technique, and the nondesiring Raphaël is described as having an "effeminate grace" and "hands like those of a pretty woman."

The fear of desire in Balzac can be discussed as a fear of psychological fragmentation. Desire dynamites the Balzacian view of character — the "essentialist" psychology which allows Balzac to present characters in terms of a fixed, intelligible, and organizing passion. It threatens, in short, those coherent portraits of personality which are an important part of Balzacian expositions, and which characters' subsequent behavior will mainly illustrate and confirm. Can desires be contained by the ordering strategies of a descriptive narrative? If they cannot, narrative itself risks being fragmented into the mere juxtaposition of images of energy like those which assail Raphaël in the antique shop. The parade of disconnected scenes from human history at the beginning of *La Peau de chagrin* is the rejected alternative to Balzac's usual narrative method. The Balzacian narrator is, precisely, the godlike presence who imposes a kind of providential order on his own fictional histories. And the rigid structure of a Balzac narrative is both menaced and energized by desires which may destroy characters, but which the narrative manages to contain at least formally.

Finally, the containment of desire is a triumph for social stability. "All excesses are alike," Raphaël announces in his remarkable dissection of debauchery; war, political power, artistic creation, and mystical ecstasy are "corruptions" which necessitate "an exuberant, a prompt dissipation of one's strength." The poet and the general *spend themselves* with the same extravagance as the *débauché*. And to spend oneself excessively creates debts which can't be paid. Raphaël is incapable of paying himself back the energy he loses in desiring. But hardly less important is the fact that he creates financial debts which also can't be paid. Desire ruins him economically as well as ontologically. Not only do the various kinds of excessive spending resemble one another; all the consequences of such spending are intimately linked. "A debt is a work of imagination which men don't understand." The debtor is the poetic victim of a capitalistic society. *La Peau de chagrin* is interestingly suggestive about the connection between a social economy and the imagination of desire. The orgiastic banquet early in the novel is given by the former banker Taillefer. All sorts of "debauched spending" are inherent to a capitalistic economy. It is an economy dependent on speculation and the accumulation of debts. Indeed, it even glamorizes the speculator: he is the hero of an economy which encourages real debts for the sake of imaginary profits, and which invests its money in the fate of money itself. One can only gamble on the profits of such speculations (*La Peau de chagrin* begins in a gambling casino), but the economy ruthlessly rejects the losing gambler. The gambler and the speculator stake what they have for the sake of what they dream of having, and they are in constant danger of being forced to pay for their imaginative excesses. The effect of a capitalistic economy on the psychology of desire can only be to make desire seem irresistibly lurid: desire is the dangerous condition for enormous gains, a risky willingness to spend which may end in a ruinous obligation to pay.

In his life, Balzac was an inveterate speculator, and the psychology of desire in his work faithfully reflects his reckless financial gamblings. The real fate of speculative desire in capitalistic society thus makes the naturally disruptive nature of desire all the more terrifying. The self must be saved from expenditures of energy imagined to be as ruinous as the capitalist's risky investments. Balzac exposes the melodramatizing effect on desire of a specific economic context by his own vulnerability to that context. Desire in the society of *La Comédie humaine* swings crazily back and forth between catastrophic explosion and a panicky retentiveness. Raphaël's uncontrollable expenditures in *La Peau de chagrin* are balanced by Foedora's dehumanizing capacity for holding back desire. The most successful profiteer — both psychologically and economically — is the hoarder. Foedora, Balzac tells us at the end of the novel, "is everywhere, she is, if you like, Society." Her nondesiring egoism profits from the speculative investments of others. She is the prudent saver of desires, and in a sense Balzac's story fully justifies her affective paralysis. And she makes clear what the real basis of order is in Balzacian society. To spend and to desire are to be exploited and finally devoured. The chaos which results from the "free flow" of desire and of money makes of a personal and social morality of mean economies the only effective formula for survival.

Nothing quite so melodramatic happens in Jane Austen's more

authentically realistic novel, *Mansfield Park*, but she too proposes an ethic of stillness. The shift of Jane Austen's sympathies from the lively heroine of *Pride and Prejudice* to the tremblingly still Fanny Price corresponds to her sense of the social dangers of movement. In 1814, English society is on the threshold of major changes. A traditional, stable, rural society is about to be replaced by an industrial, cosmopolitan society; the quiet, morally reflective life of Mansfield Park will be forgotten in the agitated rhythms of life in London. All forms of agitation come in for an extraordinarily severe judgment in *Mansfield Park*. Jane Austen takes a certain risk in passing those judgments: we can easily find the principal "villains" of her story the most interesting characters in the novel. In one sense, she is scrupulously fair toward Mary and Henry Crawford. They are not merely charming; both brother and sister are capable of certain moral delicacies which Jane Austen carefully underlines. But what dooms the Crawfords morally is the ease with which they move around among various, even contradictory sorts of behavior. Henry renews his flirtation with Maria in London largely because he can't stay still; his moral worthlessness is his inability to *wait* for Fanny to change her mind and agree to marry him. (Fanny, of course, does nothing in the novel but wait for Edmund's sense of the Crawfords to become as morally accurate as hers.) As for Mary, she finally does make Edmund aware of her true nature by seeing nothing intrinsically wrong in her brother's having run away with Maria. "She saw it only as folly," Edmund tells Fanny, "and that folly stamped only by exposure." The flurry of dramatic events at the end of *Mansfield Park* merely confirms anecdotally a view of the Crawfords' characters which by then we should have independently of any single episode. "I am not born to sit still and do nothing," Mary says during the card game of Speculation, and the truth of that remark is enough to condemn her. She is simply the most subtle version of the evils of agitation which we see in much cruder versions in Mrs. Norris and in the atmosphere of Fanny's parents' home in Portsmouth.

But what does it mean not to be able to sit still? Why is movement evil in *Mansfield Park*? The home theatricals episode in the novel suggests an answer. The episode is a striking example of something I discussed earlier: the economical use in realistic fiction of significant form. The fact that the Crawfords see nothing wrong in having the theatricals during Sir Thomas's absence is the clearest signal we are given of their moral deficiency. In his introduction to the Penguin edition of the novel, Tony Tanner writes that ". . . Mansfield Park is all but destroyed once 'the inclination to act was awakened.' For Mansfield Park is a place where you must be true to your best self: the theater is a place where you can explore and experiment with other selves. A person cannot live in both." And Tanner concludes: ". . . if the self is fluid, there is no limit to what it might do, no knowing how it might behave. . . . [Life] may turn into a series of improvisations suggested by the milieu of the moment." The great threat to Mansfield Park — and to the cultural values it represents — is precisely an improvised self, or the possibility that there is no "best self" to which one "must be true." The very modern Crawfords are ontological floaters. Their liveliness is the style of beings without definition, actively ready to jump from one entertaining performance to the next. Such floating threatens the moral order of *Mansfield Park*, and it threatens a novelistic order in which each episode contributes significantly to coherent portraits of personality. We might say that Mary and Henry (somewhat like Eugenia in James's *The Europeans*) are discredited morally by the mere fact of their psychological indefiniteness.

The profound crisis of being recorded in *Mansfield Park* can be measured by the rigidity necessary to keep things from falling apart. It's as if the slightest agitation of self would be enough to disintegrate the integrity of self. Austen's argument appears to be, as Lionel Trilling has put it, "that the self may destroy the self by the very energies that define its being, that the self may be preserved by the negation of its own energies." Fanny Price is rather priggish, but priggishness can be a supreme virtue in a world which anticipates the collapse of its entire structure of values at the slightest movement. Indeed, Fanny is the ideal heroine of this world. She is not merely weak; she almost *is not*. Her years at Mansfield Park have trained her to be "totally unused to have her pleasure consulted, or to have any thing take place at all in the way she could desire." Fanny's only activity in the book is to give advice to her younger sister Susan; when she becomes a subscriber to a circulating library in Portsmouth, she is "amazed at being any thing in *propria persona*, amazed at her own doings in every way; to be a renter, a chuser of books! And to be having any one's improvement in view in her choice!" Never daring to express her own desires (Fanny loves Edmund), Fanny has a kind of negative presence in the novel. She is the moral register of other people's behavior. And it's precisely the qualities we may find disagreeable which best qualify her for the role of moral heroine in the novel. She is a stable, nondesiring center of judgment. Her infallible moral eye preserves an order which even Edmund's behavior occasionally threatens. Edmund's desires lead him to make mistakes (he agrees to participate in the theatricals), while Fanny's asceticism makes her the perfect judge. Nothing is more curious in *Mansfield Park* than this identification of true being — as opposed to the theatrical self-diffusions of the Crawfords — with self-effacement. Non-being is the ultimate prudence in the world of *Mansfield Park*. Fanny is little more than an observant stillness, but because of that she is an excellent judge, and in this deceptively mild novel the structures of self and of society are so dangerously menaced that only the most vigilant judgment and sentencing of others can testify to the continued existence of moral principle.

The power of stillness is often equivalent to the power of description. We have a particularly good example of this in Hawthorne's *The Blithedale Romance*. Like Fanny Price, Miles Coverdale, the narrator of Hawthorne's story, is a center of stillness. He is nervous, which makes him superficially agitated, but, more importantly, he opposes an inert detachment to the Blithedale experiment in social reform. Coverdale goes to Blithedale, but his principal way of participating in the community is to observe it. And yet observation in *The Blithedale Romance* yields surprisingly little information. Coverdale acknowledges his taste for spying on other people's lives, but he defeats his own voyeurism by an even stronger need to envelop everything he sees in a kind of dreamlike haze. He comes back again and again to his sense of the unreality of all the episodes to which he brings a deliberately blurred attention. Through Coverdale, Hawthorne gives us a parable of the destructive effect of artistic sublimation on reality. Coverdale's most serious criticism of Blithedale is that it fails to realize its "delectable visions of the spiritualization of labor." "Our labor symbolized nothing," and "the clods of earth, which we so constantly belabored and turned over and over, were never etherealized into thought."

The alternative to such etherealizations seems to be piggishness, and in a curious passage Coverdale tells us (while admitting that he "can nowise explain what sort of whim, prank, or perversity it was") that before leaving Blithedale, he felt compelled "to go to the pigsty, and take leave of the swine!" He finds them "involved, and almost stifled and buried alive, in their own corporeal substance." They peep at him and then drop back into sleep — yet, Coverdale adds, "not so far asleep but that their unctuous bliss was still present to them, betwixt dream and reality." The description is not too different from the one Coverdale gives of his own sensual torpor in the hermitage (high among the branches of a pine tree) to which he occasionally escapes while at Blithedale. Alone, under the "sensual influence" of "the broad light of noon" beneath him and the "thousand-fold odor" of the trees, Coverdale is suddenly "possessed by a mood of disbelief in moral beauty or heroism," and Blithedale seems so ridiculous "that it was impossible not to laugh aloud."

On the one hand, a need to spiritualize flesh, to take away — as Coverdale puts it in another passage — "the grossness from what was fleshiest and fattest." On the other hand, nonspiritualized flesh which doesn't exactly sink into unconsciousness, but wallows — as the pigs do — in a half-conscious "unctuous bliss" which mocks *any* notion of "moral beauty or heroism." For Coverdale, the life of the body is not a desublimated version of ethereal thought; rather it is experienced as thought made sluggish. Coverdale's sensuality is his sublimations turned inside out. In the same way that the swine's bliss is "still present to them," Coverdale's sensual torpor includes an awareness of itself which is equivalent to a mockery of any other sort of awareness. Coverdale's teasing irony is a mild but more pervasive version of his thick laugh in the hermitage, and it could therefore be thought of as a consequence of the dreamlike atmosphere in the novel. That is, unlike irony in Voltaire and Stendhal, for example, the irony which Hawthorne gives us in Coverdale doesn't make for sharper articulations in experience between appearance or pretense and reality. On the contrary: Coverdale's irony is a way of absorbing all differences into a state of mental sluggishness the very existence of which gives the lie to all activities and all distinctions. Coverdale is all the more pious about the ennobling effect of moral and artistic sublimations in life because the alternative to them is a kind of unexciting masturbatory torpor which he describes to us but which he could hardly recommend. The dreamlike atmosphere of *The Blithedale Romance* is equivalent to a cynical sensuality. Coverdale's voyeurism and his hunger for facts about others are merely the morbid side effects of his refusal to see anything without the fundamentally similar blinders of idealizing vision and denigrating dream-vision.

In *The Blithedale Romance*, experience which resists being etherealized sinks into the torporous vagueness of dreams. Coverdale is incapable of imagining terms for the description of reality which would remove him altogether from a moralizing opposition between high dreams and low dreams. Thus Blithedale is discredited, and Zenobia, the character most closely associated with an authentic attempt to redefine the potentialities of human desire, is perhaps described most clearly only after she has drowned herself and become a grotesquely rigid corpse. Description in Hawthorne's narrative serves mainly to de-realize the world. In a sense, this is the effect which Hawthorne tells us he wanted in his preface to the work. He laments the absence, in American fiction, of a conventional "Faery Land" which would give the writer "a license with regard to every-day probability, in view of the improved effects which he is bound to produce thereby." There is, then, an ambiguous complicity between Hawthorne and his narrator. Coverdale's remoteness from others, which Hawthorne is critically aware of, serves the latter's purpose very well. A kind of psychological freakishness produces the esthetic effect necessary for the Blithedale story to qualify as a "romance." The power of description in *The Blithedale Romance* is to change the mode of fiction itself. As in *Mansfield Park*, a still center of observation controls the world being observed and confers sense upon it. But the sense conferred is that of a dream, and a certain drowsiness in Coverdale is the strategy by which the agitations of possibly new desires in *The Blithedale Romance* can be dismissed as insubstantial fancy.

The containment of desire in Hawthorne and in Jane Austen also seems to be a triumph for social stability. Coverdale's detachment from the story he tells reinforces the established comforts and traditions of a society for which Blithedale is nothing more than a dreamlike interlude. (Hawthorne referred to Brook Farm as "essentially a day-dream" in his own life.) After the Blithedale episode, Coverdale *returns* to a familiar existence. In Jane Austen's novel, Mansfield Park provides the social context most congenial to moral principle. Mrs. Norris's departure at the end of the story purifies the place of its most seriously discordant element; Fanny and Edmund will now have a community adequate to their moral worth. But we can already see in *Mansfield Park* the possibility of heroic stillness being deprived of any social context at all. If the disconnected moral style of the Crawfords undermines the traditional values of rural life, it is in perfect harmony with modern life in London. With no respect for conventional values, Mary Crawford is nonetheless extremely conventional. In her criticism of agitation, Jane Austen also imagines the kind of social "order" which accommodates it. It is an order which requires no commitments or beliefs; it asks only for a scrupulous observation of certain forms. To defend her ideas about the clergy, Mary tells Edmund: "I speak what appears to me the general opinion; and when an opinion is general, it is usually correct." This tribute to general opinion is in fact a matter of personal convenience. Mary speaks of marriage as "a maneuvering business" in which people are "taken in; . . . it is, of all transactions, the one in which people expect most from others, and are least honest themselves." But, significantly, this low view of marriage doesn't prevent Mary from recommending it: "I would have every body marry if they can do it properly; I do not like to have people throw themselves away; but every body should marry as soon as they can do it to advantage."

This lack of principle — of a psychological and moral center — is by no means an obstacle to social respectability. Far from creating chaos, the unprincipled, theatrical self lives in harmony with a social order which demands only external conformity. The danger pointed to by *Mansfield Park* is not the disintegration of order in social life; it is rather the survival of mere parodies of social order. Mary Crawford is a threat because she reinforces certain social structures without believing in them. She demonstrates that only cynicism is necessary to accommodate "floating" desires to social stability. In short, character is not necessary to maintain the structures of community life, and, far from defending a social order on the point of crumbling, Fanny and Edmund are anachronistic survivals of a culture in which external order depended on the careful cultivation of order in personality. Society no longer needs them. To be sure, Fanny's severe stillness wins out over the Crawfords' dangerous liveliness, and Jane Austen piously asserts the renewed vitality of Mansfield Park at the end of her story. But it could also be argued that the novel has demonstrated the obsolescence of Mansfield Park. And in that case, the heroically still insistence on order in the self and in society would be deprived of *any* real context — an extremity which will allow the hero to renounce his mission and make an unexpected leap out of self, society, and the novel itself.

This is exactly what happens in James's *The Wings of the Dove* and *The Golden Bowl*, both of which have interesting analogies with *Mansfield Park*. Disruptive desire in all three novels goes along with the cynical cultivation of social forms. Like Mary Crawford, Kate Croy and Charlotte Stant are immensely adept at giving lively performances of themselves. All three are opposed to silent, nontheatrical heroines; Fanny, Milly and Maggie have no talent for representing the self in the world. And in each case a man hesitates between the flashy, more or less cynically respectable performer and a woman who does little more than wait for him to recognize her spiritual superiority. But in *Mansfield Park* there are demonstrable continuities between Fanny, a certain type of life in society, and also the kind of fiction which Jane Austen is writing. Fanny's judgments give moral significance to the events of *Mansfield Park*. The Crawfords' self-dramatizations have a diffusive effect; by seeing a moral meaning in everything they say or do, Fanny discredits them but also guarantees their suitability as intelligible characters in the novel. She therefore collaborates with Jane Austen's significant form, in which an episode is always a revealing episode, a contribution to the single meaningful structure of the entire work. In James, on the other hand, the resistance to potentially disruptive characters itself disrupts the conditions of realistic fiction. The stillness of Milly Theale and of Maggie Verver doesn't operate as a magnet which finally draws the errant behavior of Densher and of Amerigo back into an ideal social and novelistic order. Rather, James's heroines draw the two men into a community of passion for which there is no place in the real world, and for which there is no language in realistic fiction.

Under Milly's influence, for example, *The Wings of the Dove* seems to become allegory as the story is being told. Characters lose their identities as "personalities" and become spiritual alternatives in a struggle between the world of the lioness and the world of the dove for Densher's soul. A realistic conflict between personal loyalties and social opportunities is resolved in a union — between Densher and the spirit of the dead Milly — the nature of which the novel either can't express or is judged unworthy of expressing. Densher will end up living for the letter which Milly sent him before she died, but we are never told what is in the letter. The ultimate justification of his conversion to Milly is thereby saved from the contamination of narrative itself. While she was alive, Milly, unlike Kate, *did* almost nothing. Her effect is most powerful when she is dead, and the nature of her effect is inexpressible. Passivity, absence, and silence in *The Wings of the Dove* are the subterfuges by which James creates an escape from both the literary form of which he was one of the greatest practitioners and the social realities which that form assumes and essentially defends.

In *The Golden Bowl*, the happy marriage which Maggie manages to reconstitute at the end of the story is in fact the experience of a passion to which both marriage and society are irrelevant. In drawing Amerigo back into their marriage (and away from his adulterous relation with Charlotte), Maggie also breaks his ties to his own tradition-laden past and settles him, somewhat ruthlessly, in her own "improvised 'post' " which, James notes, would be marked on a map of social relations only by the geography of "the fundamental passions." The conclusion of *The Golden Bowl*, unlike that of *Mansfield Park*, is therefore also a repudiation of the order which it appears to reinstate. Far from asserting the triumph of those social forms and traditions which have been menaced throughout the novel, Maggie's marriage, unlike Fanny Price's, is merely a convenient institutional context for desires which have no place at all on any map of social structures. And since *The Golden Bowl* itself has been an elaborate exercise in structural ingenuities, its ending, once again unlike that of *Mansfield Park*, implicitly dismisses the novelistic mode in which it has been plotted. As we look back on the story, it would seem that Maggie's (and James's) passionate fiction has been sustained by the hope, finally realized in the last lines of *The Golden Bowl*, that the passion can dispense with the fiction. The stillness of Maggie Verver, while it appears to coerce errant desires back into a docile obedience to given structures, also has the opposite effect of surreptitiously providing an "out" from *all* articulated structures. Without a single flaw in a strategy of "high decorum," Maggie's passion nonetheless subverts the decorums of society, of fiction, and of language.

Can realistic fiction thus accommodate insistent, disruptive desires only by designating their triumph in a region inaccessible to fiction? Perhaps only Proust and Lawrence find a place in narrative itself for the play of such desires without exploding the very foundations of realistic narrative. I would like to end this discussion with a brief consideration of Proust's work from this point of view. The resurrection of Marcel's past in *A la Recherche du temps perdu* is essentially a resurrection of lost desires. In a sense, Marcel is nothing but a succession of desires — which is to say that he constantly reenacts the experience of a lack. His retreat from the world in order to transform his past into literature is a decision to live entirely within desire. He will, of course, report on those contacts with the world which both defeated his desires and suggested possibilities of interest in the world which he hadn't imagined in his desires. Nonetheless, literature for Proust — in his own life as well as in his narrator's life — is essentially a turning away from the world where desires are seldom realized, and a permanent commitment to the solitary cultivation of desire. For the only precious things in Marcel's past are his unfulfilled longings; he writes in order to re-create the atmosphere of his desires, "the charm which [things] owed, in our minds, to the association of certain ideas."[7] Such associations are of course the fantasies of desire, the scenarios which imagination vainly proposes to reality. In art, the existential lack in desire is experienced as a plenitude of images; in the verbal world of literature, the missing reality is present in the language which declares its absence.

In Proust, writing is the dangerous "agitation" which destroys the narrator's safe but sterile stillness. His activity will be to renounce all other activity in order to remember and to reinvent his desires. And an indulgence in desire is as intimately connected with fantasies of death in Proust as it is in Balzac's *La Peau de chagrin*. The decision to write, in *Le Temps retrouvé*, causes the narrator an anxiety similar to the young Marcel's anxiety during masturbation. Furthermore, *A la Recherche du temps perdu* makes explicit the psychological logic of the connection between desire and the idea of death.

The fear of masturbatory desire in Proust is — as it is in Balzac — a fear of psychological fragmentation. *A la Recherche* is a massive documentation of this fragmenting power of desire. To a large extent, the fragmented self is an occasion for terror. Marcel has only to assert desires independent of his mother's desires in order to feel cut off not only from her but, most painfully, from himself. The anger of *maman*, as we see in the episode in Venice when Marcel defies her in order to stay on at the hotel for a possible sexual encounter, has a castrating effect on both the world and the self. Venice becomes unidentifiable heaps of stone surrounded by water reduced to its chemical elements (and thereby deprived of all personality, of all historic and artistic associations), and Marcel himself is "nothing more than a heart that throbbed." Furthermore, the desires of other people have a kind of decentering effect on their personalities which frustrates our attempts to know them. The horror of jealousy consists in the lover's ignorance of *what* to be jealous of. Desire breaks the self up into disconnected roles, and the jealous lover gets lost in the labyrinth of partial selves implied by the loved one's shifting, elusive desires. The suffering which Albertine, Rachel and Morel cause Marcel, Saint-Loup and Charlus can be summed up in a single question: *where are* these "creatures of flight" in their desires? Personality and perhaps even gender provide fragile identities which desire easily disrupts. Desire makes being problematic; the notion of a coherent and unified self is threatened by the discontinuous, logically incompatible images of a desiring imagination. When the Proustian loved one begins to "produce" desires — and he or she does that most spectacularly in sexual pursuits — the Proustian lover is no longer able to identify being. He is confronted, as the narrator says of the tormented Charlus when the latter discovers that for Léa, Morel's homosexuality consists in the young man's interest in lesbians, "with the sudden inadequacy of a definition."

But Proust is unique among the writers I've been discussing in that the self-diffusions of desire are not merely a source of anguish in his work; he also exploits them as an inexhaustible source of nourishment for his work. The theatricality of self which, as we have seen, is so terrifying in *Mansfield Park* and in *The Blithedale Romance* becomes in *A la Recherche* a principle of psychological and esthetic expansion. Even the revelations which seem to protect

Marcel from self-fragmentation also have the unexpected effect of dramatizing the *appeal* of the fragmented self. The narrator's rediscovery of his past in involuntary memory, for example, offers reassuring evidence of "an individual, identical and permanent self," but it also dislocates self-definitions by the ways in which it revises his view of the past. The experience of involuntary memory in the Guermantes library (at the end of *Le Temps retrouvé*) which "returns" Marcel to Balbec establishes continuity between the past and the present, but in bringing back forgotten desires from the day of his arrival at Balbec, it also helps to upset the coherent formulations of the past which he of course possesses all the time in his conscious, voluntary memory.

This lesson of involuntary memory is exploited throughout the work in the specifically literary strategy of using metaphor as a kind of decentering or scattering of the self. True, the network of metaphorical correspondences in *A la Recherche* also appeases Marcel's fear of psychological discontinuity; these correspondences impose on disconnected desires — and on the literary work which records them — a self-contained unity. But they are also psychologically distintegrating in the sense that they make it impossible for us to locate any fixed center of the self from which all its images might proceed. Metaphor has a therapeutically diffusive effect in *A la Recherche*; it is a frequently humorous and consistently liberating displacement of Marcel's most crippling fantasies.[8] Almost every passage in the work echoes or anticipates other passages; and in psychological terms, this means that no one version of Marcel's fantasies is more authoritative than other versions. The self is exuberantly scattered along the surfaces of its disguises; it has the freedom of *being* the variety of its disguises. Self-knowledge is always experimental, never definitive. Theoretically, both the novel and the self are infinitely expandable. We could say that the central drama in Proust's novel is a struggle between vertical transcendence and horizontal transcendence. There is of course an obsessively repetitious quality in the work which tends to undermine the diffusiveness I've been discussing, to draw all the play of the narrator's mind back to a center of easily identifiable (and pathological) desires and fears. But the compositional *work* of *A la Recherche du temps perdu* goes against this centripetal tendency. Style in Proust is an effort to prevent passages from referring to some psychological "truth" behind them, and to coerce them into pointing to *other* passages not yet written (and not yet traced in the self). Meaning is prospective and indefinite. The significance of each passage is limited only by the amount of novelistic space the narrator will have the time to fill in the process of self-enlargement which is his literary vocation.

There does, however, seem to be considerable anxiety attached to this project in *A la Recherche*. It is, so to speak, a project performed but not confessed to. The narrator tends to speak about his self-fragmentations as if they were self-containments. His explicit aims seem to be, psychologically, to construct a stable personality which can be permanently fixed in his work, and, esthetically, to impose on the fragments of his life the order and unity of an equally stable and closed literary structure. To a certain extent, Proust is as anxious as Balzac, Dickens, Austen and Eliot to wrap up the experience of his work in a meaningful totality, to smother his availability to possibly discontinuous, fragmented images of satisfied desire for the sake of an ordered significance. Proust's ambivalent attitude toward an art of incompletion keeps his work within the limits of realistic fiction. *A la Recherche du temps perdu* is instructive in the context of the ideas developed in this chapter in that it illustrates the maximal subversion of realistic premises from within these premises.

Proust's novel documents the identity between novelizing and desiring. It is even a daring assertion of the fertility of the masturbatory imagination as a resistance to our frequently sterile agreements about what constitutes reality. But *A la Recherche*, like *La Comédie humaine*, also denies its own visionary status. The Proustian narrator shares the Balzacian terror of desire. Thus, like Balzac, he would in part like to enclose the self in a fixed portrait, to de-energize desires by transforming them into mental states or faculties. A frantic if partial attachment to a recognizable continuity of self in the time of the novel gives to the Proustian narrative the unity of a personal voice which is characteristic of realistic fiction, and which Joyce will explode in a succession of frequently impersonal voices in *Ulysses*. Also, while Proust abandons the Balzacian habit of introducing characters in definitive psychological portraits, he does think of behavior as expressive of one's "real" character. In fact, the Proustian narrator can be as intent as Hawthorne's Coverdale on getting at the supposed truth about other characters. He too is a voyeur, a determined spy into the secrets of others. Coverdale would like to compel Zenobia to give him "a glimpse of something true; some nature, some passion, no matter whether right or wrong, provided it were real." Marcel is tempted to see things and people as puzzles to be solved. He stares at flowers in order to force them to reveal a truth they seem to be both proposing and concealing, and when he discovers Charlus's homosexuality he feels that the baron's personality is now as clear as a sentence in which letters arranged at random suddenly fall into wholly coherent patterns.

But the narrator's own performance in *A la Recherche* undermines the anxiety provoked in him by the spectacle of a self "floating" among desires which can't be absorbed into a single structure of character. Marcel makes *himself* irreducible to any such structure, and as a result we may even feel that he lacks definition as a character. But this happy lack allows the Proustian narrator to experiment endlessly with the metamorphoses of desire. He himself has become a "creature of flight," but without the cruelty of Morel, Rachel or Albertine. The anxious, still voyeur peeping on other people's sexual secrets belies his frightened, parsimonious nature by the energetic open-endedness of his self-diffusions. Like Fanny Price and Maggie Verver, Proust's narrator has to deal with the threat of other people's errant desires. Furthermore, there is no moral or social order in *A la Recherche* which might be successfully opposed to these desires. Unlike James's heroines in *The Wings of the Dove* and *The Golden Bowl*, however, the Proustian narrator will not escape from disorder by removing himself from *all* scenes in which desire might be articulated or represented. Maggie Verver waits for the complications which surround her to exhaust themselves. In a sense, she waits for the narrative itself to become finally silent under the pressure of her insistent passion. She is the enemy of the Jamesian tendency to allow narrative to expand on the basis of an inspired imagination of the implications of words. She puts a stop to talk, not because the world has finally been accurately analyzed, judged and corrected (as at the end of *Mansfield Park*), but rather because the only "correction" possible is a transcendence of the world.

The Golden Bowl, like most realistic fiction, has a conclusive ending, but the conclusiveness depends on the Prince's and Maggie's dismissal of any storytelling at all. The Proustian narrator, on the other hand, reacts to the evasions and deceptions of language by producing a *text* of his own. The very impossibility of locating truth and order in the world is the pre-text to which the text of *A la Recherche* returns us. And the history of an anxiously desiring self makes the anxiety somewhat unnecessary. To recall the past becomes for Marcel an occasion for inventing multiple versions of the past, and thereby confirming not the "permanence" of an "identical" self, but the energies of a prospective self. The defeat of realism in *A la Recherche du temps perdu* is perhaps brought about most decisively by the Proustian implication that the self and the work are essentially incomplete, that they never settle into those definitive meanings which reduce artistic performances to mere exposures of character.

CHAPTER THREE

Emma Bovary and the Sense of Sex

ROMANTIC LOVE HAS BEEN one of our most effective myths for making sense out of our sensations. It organizes bodily intensities around a single object of desire and it provides a more or less public theater for the enactment of the body's most private life. In love, desires and sensations are both structured and socialized. The loved one invests the world with a hierarchy of desirability. At last we have a measure of value, and even the unhappiest lover can enjoy the luxury of judging (and controlling) his experiences according to the distance at which it places him from the loved one's image or presence. Passion also makes us intelligible to others. Observers may be baffled as to why we love this person rather than that one, but such mysteries are perhaps more than compensated for by the exceptional visibility in which the passionate pursuit of another person places the otherwise secret "formulas" of individual desire.

Love is desire made visible, but it is also desire made somewhat abstract. We don't yearn merely for sensations in romantic desire; we seek the more complex satisfaction of another desiring presence. To desire persons rather than sensations is to indicate a certain pre-dominance of mind over body. The sublime-sublimating nature of love is clearly enough pointed to by the notable fact that, as we see in Racine, even the most obsessive sexual passion can be adequately described with practically no references to the body. Indeed, the more obsessive the passions, the more insignificant the body may become; sexual fascination steals some of the body's vitality, and therefore partly dissipates physical energies. Love, like art, is a *cosa mentale*; like art, it systematizes, communicates and dilutes the fragmented intensities of our senses. But this is of course too one-sided. Even in passions as diagrammatic as those of Racine's protagonists, the diagram itself is initiated by a traumatic encounter with another body ("Je le vis, je rougis, je pâlis à sa vue," Phèdre says of her first meeting with Hippolyte). And, even more decisively, the rich verbal designs which express the Racinian lover's passion never divert him from the single purpose of possessing another body. An abstract psychology of mental states constantly refers to an impossible and indescribable meeting of bodies. The dream of certain happy sensations sustains all speech, while the realization of that dream would be the end of speech. In its continuous allusiveness to both sensation and thought, love once again reminds us of art. They are both pursuits of sensual intensities through activities of sublimation. Love, then, can be considered as an ideal subject for literature; it is the most glamorous of dramatic metaphors for the "floating" of the literary work itself between the sensual and the abstract.

The various sorts of intelligibility which literature brings to the life of the body are Flaubert's subject in *Madame Bovary*. Character has an interesting superficiality in the novel. Flaubert's intention of giving a realistic and inclusive image of bourgeois provincial life — the book's subtitle is *Moeurs de province* — partly disguises a certain thinness and even disconnectedness in his psychological portraits. True, the portrait of Emma Bovary is eventually filled in with an abundance of psychological and social details, but during much of the narrative, she is nothing more than bodily surfaces and intense sensations. Emma first appears in Chapter Two; her personality begins to be analyzed in Chapter Six. For several pages, Flaubert's heroine is a patchwork of surfaces: a "blue merino dress with three flounces," excessively white fingernails, a thick mass of black hair, the moving reflections of the sun through her open parasol on her face, a tongue licking the bottom of a glass.[1] (This attention to physical detail can of course be partly explained in terms of narrative strategy: Flaubert economically conveys the desires of the men looking at Emma by describing those aspects of her presence which stimulate them.) Not only do we thus see Emma as a somewhat fragmented and strongly eroticized surface; when we move to her point of view, we have an exceptional number of passages which describe the life of her senses. Mediocre in all other respects, as Ferdinand Brunetière wrote, Madame Bovary becomes a superior creature thanks to a rare "finesse des sens." Emma's greedily sensual awareness of the world has often been noted. The dinner and ball at la Vaubyessard, for example, provide a feast of brief but intense thrills for all her senses: "certain delicate phrases of the violin" which make her smile with pleasure, the cold champagne which makes her entire body shiver, the dazzling gleam of jewelry, the warm air of the dining room which envelopes her in a "mixture of the scents of flowers and fine linen, of the fumes from the meats and the smell of the truffles."

At moments of more overpowering sensuality there even emerges a "formula" for Emma's sensual intensities, a characteristic style of sensation which, as we know from Flaubert's other works, wasn't invented for Emma alone but rather seems to be a basic formula for Flaubertian sensation in general. Sexuality in Flaubert is frequently expressed in terms of a rippling luminosity. "Here and there," Flaubert writes as part of his description of Emma's first happy sexual experience (with Rodolphe in the forest near Yonville), "all around her, in the leaves and on the ground, patches of light were trembling, as if hummingbirds, while in flight, had scattered their feathers." The moon, during Emma's last meeting with Rodolphe in the garden behind her house, "cast upon the river a large spot, which broke up into an infinity of stars, and this silvery gleam seemed to writhe to the bottom of the water like a headless serpent covered with luminous scales. It also resembled some monstrous candelabra, with drops of molten diamond streaming down its sides." While the experience of pleasure itself seems to include a vision of discreet points of light (the diamond light is perceived as distinct "drops"), the anticipation or the memory of sexual pleasure frequently diffuses these luminous points into a heavier, even slightly oppressive atmosphere. In the garden description, the brilliantly decorated serpent and the candelabra plunging into the water are hallucinated participations of the external world in Emma's sexual pleasure. At a certain distance from sex the thought of pleasure, or the images connected with it, makes for a less dazzling hallucination, and light now suffused with color becomes softer and thicker. After that first day in the forest with Rodolphe, Emma feels that "she was surrounded by vast bluish space, the heights of feeling were sparkling beneath her thought." Much later, as she lies alone in bed at night enjoying fantasies of running away with Rodolphe, Emma imagines a future in which "nothing specific stood out: the days, all of them magnificent, resembled one another like waves; and the vision [cela] swayed on the limitless horizon, harmonious, bluish, and bathed in sun." A world heavy with sensual promise (and no longer blindingly illuminated by sexual intensities) is, in Flaubert, frequently a world of many reflected lights blurred by a mist tinged with color. As the carriage draws her closer to her meetings with Léon in Rouen, the old Norman city seems to Emma like a "Babylon" of pleasure. She "pours" her love into its streets and squares; and "the leafless trees on the boulevards seemed like [faisaient] purple thickets in the midst of the houses, and the roofs, all shiny with rain, were gleaming unevenly, according to the elevation of the various districts." Purplish masses of trees against an even darker background, millions of liquid light reflections which both brighten and obscure the city's outlines: this typical Flaubertian landscape recurs frequently during Frédéric's idle walks in Paris early in *L'Education sentimentale*, and, as in the case of Emma's Rouen, it seems to be what Flaubert's "hero" finds in the world when he looks at it with sensual longing. Desire has (or rather makes) its own *atmosphere* in Flaubert.

As soon as we speak of a characteristic formula of sensation or desire we are of course giving a certain intelligibility to what at first seemed to be the discontinuous and fragmented life of the body. But the intelligibility is all *for us*; nothing in *Madame Bovary* indicates that Emma has the slightest awareness of a durable and defining style in her sensuality. Furthermore, in the passages quoted in the last paragraph, it's by no means clear whether the images are meant to express what Emma is actually seeing or hallucinating in the world, or whether they are *Flaubert's* descriptive and metaphorical equivalents for sensations or states of mind to which they allude but which in fact don't include them. Put in this way the question is unanswerable and irrelevant. I ask it partly because, irrelevant or not, it is bound to occur to us, and partly because it is one way of formulating a problem I'll soon be looking at more closely: that of the relation between literature and sensation. For the moment, we can simply note that even if Emma does see the bejeweled candelabra in the river, that doesn't seem to be of any help to her in making sense of her sensations or in locating continuities in her experience. She is inattentive even to that which makes her superior: the exceptional refinement of her senses. Emma's consciousness is intense, but it carries very little. And of course I'm not only referring to her sensual consciousness. Emma thinks in clichés, and, as far as her moral awareness goes, she is hardly less self-centered or more scrupulous than Homais. One has only to think how richly Jane Austen's and George Eliot's novels are nourished by all the ideas and principles of their heroes and heroines to appreciate the risk Flaubert takes in creating, to us a Jamesian term, such an insubstantial center of consciousness as Emma for his novel. (Indeed, James found Emma too thin a vessel to carry the weight of the novel's meaning.) But the most interesting fact about Emma may be precisely that she has so little consciousness. For in spite of the fact that she is, after all, part of a realistic fiction in which characters have names, social positions and personalities, she almost succeeds in existing without what the realistic novel generally proposes as an identity. When she is not having intense sensations she does little more than *long for* sensations. Her principal activity is that of desiring. But what exactly is there for her to desire? In what images will she recognize a promise of happy sensations?

Love sublimates and novelizes sensation. The literature of romance on which Madame Bovary gorges herself is the only spiritualizing principle in her life. The dangers of this literature are so emphatically illustrated in Flaubert's work that we may tend to overlook the service it performs for Emma's intense but random sensuality. For a moment during the performance of *Lucia di Lammermoor* at the Rouen opera house, Emma manages to smile with a "disdainful pity" as she thinks of all the lies which literature tells about life; "she now knew," Flaubert adds, "how small the passions were which art exaggerated." The next day, when Léon visits Emma at her hotel, they attempt, with the help of literary clichés, to recompose their past, to fit the quiet, uneventful love of the days in Yonville to an ideal of glamorously desperate passion. "Besides," Flaubert philo-sophically remarks, "speech is a rolling mill which always stretches out feelings." But what alternative is there to the exaggerations and the extensions of language? In this same scene at the Rouen hotel Emma and Léon finally stop talking: "They were no longer speak-ing; but they felt, as they looked at each other, a humming in their heads, as though something audible had escaped from their motion-less eyes. They had just joined hands; and the past, the future, reminiscences and dreams, everything was merged in the sweetness of this ecstasy." In the same way, Emma's sensual torpor as Rodolphe speaks to her of love on the day of the agricultural fair is a state in which "everything became confused" and the present merges with images from the past. Emma's consciousness is invaded by the odor of Rodolphe's pomade, the memory of a similar odor of vanilla and lemon which came from the viscount's beard as she waltzed with him at la Vaubyessard, the light from the chandeliers at that same ball, an image of Léon, and finally the smell of the fresh ivy coming through the open window next to which she and Rodolphe are seated. As Jean-Pierre Richard has brilliantly shown in his essay on Flaubert in *Littérature et sensation*, a fundamental theme of Flaubert's "material" imagination is that of a fusion between the self and the world, as well as among all the elements of conscious-ness. Contours are blurred, boundaries disappear, and the great danger in Flaubert's imaginary world is that of being drowned in a kind of formless liquid dough, in a sea of thick, undifferentiated matter. I'll be returning to the dangers of fusion; for the moment I want to emphasize that even at moments of great sensual pleasure, as in the passage just quoted, the intense sensation tends to break down differences in *Madame Bovary* — differences between people, between the present and the past, and between the inner and outer worlds. Thus, not only does Flaubert present Emma as a patchwork of bodily surfaces; not only does he tend to reduce her consciousness to a series of strong but disconnected sensations; he also indicates that by its very nature sensation makes a mockery of the distinctions we invent in thought.

There is, however, the rolling mill of language to rescue us. Lan-guage *de*fuses; its conceptual nature attacks the intensity of sensa-tions, and words unwrap the bundle of sensory impressions and extend them, as distinct and separate verbal units, along the "lines" of space and time. More specifically, in the case of Emma Bovary, stories of romance raise her sensations to the level of sentiment. They replace the isolated and anonymous body with couples sharply characterized socially, and they provide spatial and temporal elaborations — that is, a *story* — for the ecstatic instant. But, interestingly enough, Emma recharges literary language by retaining only its inspirations for visual fantasies. Probably every reader of *Madame Bovary* has noticed that Emma "thinks" in tableaux. Indeed, the sign of desire in the novel is the appearance of a tableau. The desire for an ecstatic honeymoon is a mental picture of driving in the mountains, to the sound of goat bells and waterfalls, toward a bay surrounded by lemon trees; the desire for an exciting existence in Paris is a group of neatly compartmentalized images of the different worlds of ambassadors, duchesses and artists in the capital; and the desire to run away with Rodolphe takes the form of an exotic travel fantasy through cities with cathedrals of white marble and finally to a picturesque fishing village. These desirable tableaux could be thought of as halfway between verbal narrative and the hallucinated scenes of intense sensations. As she indulges in them Emma enjoys a tamed version of bodily desires. There isn't a single original image in these romantic tableaux; they are all drawn from literature. But, perhaps because of that very fact, all the books which Emma has read collaborate to form a satisfyingly consistent love story, a highly intelligible cliché which imposes order on ecstasy.

Given the immensely useful function of literature in Emma's life, it is, in a sense, merely snobbish to complain about the inferior quality of the books she reads. But something does of course go wrong with the function itself. Emma is extremely demanding. She wants the intelligibility of literature *in* the ecstatic sensation. At the risk of making things overly schematic, let's say that we have followed her from disconnected sensations to the sublimating stories of art; how will she return from art to life? There wouldn't be any problem if Emma could be satisfied with transposing literature into desirable mental tableaux. She is, however, engaged in a much more complicated enterprise, one which literature itself, to a certain extent, encourages. Much popular literature gives a seductive intelligibility to the body's pleasures; but it perhaps also invites its readers to expect the body to confirm the mind's fictions. The lie of which

Emma's novels are guilty is their suggestion that the stories which in fact modulate and dilute existential intensities are equivalent to them. It is as if writers themselves were tempted to ignore the abstracting nature of language and to confuse an extended novelistic fantasy with the scenes of hallucinating desire and sensation. Emma welcomes the confusion; she waits for experience to duplicate literature, unaware of the fact that literature didn't duplicate life in the first place.

This fundamental error naturally leads Emma into considerable trouble. For example, the books she reads (like all literature) make use of a conventional system of signs. Flaubert enumerates several of the gestures and the settings which signify love in the novels Emma read when she was at the convent: "[These novels] were filled with love affairs, lovers, mistresses, persecuted ladies fainting in lonely pavilions, postriders killed at every relay, horses ridden to death on every page, dark forests, palpitating hearts, vows, sobs, tears and kisses, skiffs in the moonlight, nightingales in thickets, gentlemen brave as lions, gentle as lambs, virtuous as no one really is, always well dressed, and weeping like fountains." We could say that in this passage Flaubert gives us a list of the principal signs used in popular romantic fiction; and the referent for all these signs is love. The connection between the sign and the reality is of course arbitrary (as it is for individual words), although it is also necessary for the coherence of a specific literary system. Emma, on the other hand, sees the connection as inevitable, as a *natural* one. She consequently takes a short cut and dreams of "persecuted ladies fainting in lonely pavilions" and of "nightingales in thickets" as if they *were* romantic passion. It's as if someone expected to possess the object "chair" by pronouncing the word which designates it. Love seems impossible to Emma unless it appears with all the conventional signs which constitute a code of love in fictions of romance. Since Charles doesn't respond to the romantic clichés she tries out on him, Emma, "incapable . . . of believing in anything that didn't manifest itself in conventional forms," decides that his love for her must be diminishing. (Rodolphe, incidentally, makes the opposite mistake. Unable to see "the differences of feeling under the similarities of expression," he doubts Emma's passion because she uses formulas he has heard from so many other women.) There are particular words, costumes, gestures and settings which, so to speak, manufacture passion. As Flaubert says of Emma: "It seemed to her that certain places on the earth must produce happiness, like a plant indigenous to that soil and which would be unable to thrive anywhere else."

In a sense, however, there is a subtle rightness in Emma's confusion. We can point to a tree or a chair to indicate what we mean by those words, but where is the object "love," the definite shape we might evoke each time we say the word? Like all abstract concepts, love is a phenomenon created by its own definition. It is a synthetic product (the result of a synthesis, and existing nowhere in nature), and its only reality is on the level of the sign. (And, like all conceptual codes, it is subject to historical change: twentieth-century love is not the same as love in ancient Greece.) But if love is a certain composition of signs, is Emma so wrong to feel that she won't have found love until she assembles the signs in the right combination? "In her desire," Flaubert writes critically, "she confused the sensual pleasures of luxury with the joys of the heart, elegant habits with delicacies of feeling. Didn't love, like Indian plants, need a prepared soil, a particular temperature?" But the concept of love does in fact "grow" only in the "soil" of romantic fictions. We should therefore qualify what I said a moment ago: Emma's mistake indeed *seems* to be to confuse the literary props of passion with its reality, but more profoundly she errs in thinking that passion is a reality which can be determined *at all* outside of literature. I don't mean that she (or anyone, for that matter) is "wrong" to use abstract words to describe concrete experiences; conceptual syntheses are as necessary outside of books as in books. The dangerous confusion is between the usefulness of a synthesizing vocabulary and a preexistent reality which we often assume it contains. For if we make this confusion, our experience comes to have a crippling responsibility to our vocabulary, and people far more intelligent than Emma torture themselves with the vain question of whether or not certain relationships can "really" be called "love." Emma Bovary is an impressively rigorous if narrow thinker; having picked up certain words in literature, she refuses to use them a bit sloppily (which is the only way to use them) in life. ". . . Emma tried to find out exactly what was meant in life by the words *felicity*, *pas-*

sion and *rapture*, which had seemed so beautiful to her in books."
But nothing is meant by those words in life; they "mean" only
verbally, and especially in books.

Furthermore, in seductive (and treacherous) fashion, the books
which Emma reads attribute duration to the rapturous instant.
Romantic love in literature may end tragically, but it is not likely
to run out of emotional steam and end in boredom. Of course, all
literature not only makes sense of the instant, it also makes time
from the instant. The life of the body sublimated in time is the
history of a person. But in Emma's favorite books history is glam-
orized as a succession of intensities. Romance conceptualizes sensation; furthermore, it suggests that time never dissipates sensations.
Emma does experience sensations which seem to her to live up to
her definitions of romantic ecstasy; but she learns that romantic
ecstasy doesn't last. And we find the dramatization of this banal
fact interesting only because it is made through a character who,
quite remarkably, refuses to make any compromise at all with time.
While Flaubert gives detailed attention to the modulations of feeling in time (I'm thinking, for example, of the chapter which sum-
marizes the change in Emma between her return from la Vaubyessard
and the move from Tostes to Yonville, and of the few pages which
describe her agitated, rapidly changing feelings after she discovers
that Léon loves her), his aristocratic heroine expects each moment
to repeat the rapture of a previous moment. But Emma's thrilling
excitements are quickly submerged in ordinary time, and it is this
shattering absence of drama which wears her out, which leads her
to complain bitterly about the "instantaneous rotting away of the
things she leaned on" and to feel that "everything was a lie!"

Maurice Blanchot has suggestively said of Flaubert that he shows
us "the horror of existence deprived of a world." We might consider this remark in two different ways. On the one hand, as I've
suggested, Emma finds in literature a world in which to place and
to identify her sensations. One could say that without literature she
has existence without essence: disconnected, unidentifiable sensations on which literature will confer a romantic being or essence.
On the other hand, she returns from literature with everything
except the physical world in which the romantic existence might
be lived. And she is finally crushed by the weight of an insubstantial imagination which has been unable to discharge itself of its

fables, which has never found a world. The gap between an excessively signifying imagination and an insignificant world occasionally produces attacks of acute anxiety in Emma. Boredom is a crisis in her life because it is the lie which experience gives to the constantly interesting stories of literature. Things continue not to happen; and even the most trivial sight or sound can provoke panic simply by not corresponding to the mind's expectations, by illustrating the indifference of the world to our fictions. Jean Rousset and Gérard Genette have perceptively spoken of certain "dead moments" in Flaubert's work, of descriptive passages which seem to have no dramatic function but merely interrupt or suspend the novel's action.[2] A Balzacian description, however superficially digressive, is never dramatically irrelevant; it either provides information necessary for our understanding of the story or metaphorically characterizes the people involved in the story. In Flaubert, on the other hand, descriptive detail often seems to be given for its own sake; suddenly the story is no longer "moving," and we have an almost detachable literary *morceau*. These apparently gratuitous descriptions have a relation to the rest of the story similar to the relation between Emma's uneventful life and her action-packed imagination. They are the formal narrative equivalents of experience which fit into no design. A certain carelessness on Flaubert's part about the dramatic significance of description educates the reader into being somewhat casual about meaningful patterns. In *Bouvard et Pécuchet*, Flaubert will finally bloat his narrative with information which we can dismiss as soon as we have received it. And even in *Madame Bovary* there are signs of his wish to train us to experience literature itself as having some of that boring insignificance which Emma is so exasperated to find in life.

Of course, one could scarcely imagine a novel more likely to exasperate Madame Bovary than *Madame Bovary*. Emma's distaste for Flaubertian art can be assumed from the way she eventually turns against even non-Flaubertian art. Literature has served Emma very poorly indeed. It makes sense of experience for her, but experience doesn't confirm the sense she brings to it. And this is especially disastrous since Emma can't really return to literature. If *Madame Bovary* is a critique of the expectations imposed on life by literary romances, it is also a critique of the expectations which those same romances raise concerning literature itself. Flaubert's novel is an extraordinarily subtle dialectic between literature and sensation; the movement between the two creates a rhythm less immediately obvious but more profound than the alternation between exalted fantasies and flat realities.

Emma indicates her impatience with the literary imagination when, in answer to Léon's remark (the evening of her arrival in Yonville) that verses are much more "tender" than prose and are better for making one cry, she says: "But in the long run they're tiring . . . and now, on the contrary, I love stories in which the action doesn't let up from start to finish, and which make you frightened." It's true that as disappointments accumulate in Emma's life, books provide her with the "up" she no longer finds in love; unable to feel any "profound bliss" in her meetings with Léon, Emma turns to literature for a "quick fix." She stays up at night reading "lurid books full of orgiastic scenes and bloody deeds. Often she would be seized with terror, she would cry out." At these moments of terror Emma has, it might be said, finally achieved her ideal if unbearable equilibrium between mind and body. An organized activity of sublimation (literature) is providing her with extraordinary sensations. The intensities of a body left to itself are discontinuous and mystifying. Literature explains those sensations, but it also dilutes them in the abstract, somewhat ghostly time of verbal narrative. The explanations of literature don't work in life, and the intensities of life are lost in the endless and tiring meanings of literature. Consequently, what else is there to do but cultivate a style of reading in which the mind would excite itself out of consciousness? To get the fantastic fables of romantic literature without the words of romantic literature would be to allow imagination to act directly on the body without the cumbersome mediation of language. In her nocturnal screams, Emma — however briefly and unviably — has resolved the paradox of seeking sensations in the airy fancies of imagination.

An unbearable and an unworkable solution: in reading those wild stories, Emma is of course profiting from neither the originality of her own talent for sensations nor from the sense-making structures which literature invents for the life of the body. Now Flaubert seems more sensitive to the sin against literature than to the sin against life. Much of the force of a potential argument in *Madame Bovary* against literature's violation of experience is lost because experience hardly seems worth the trouble. The alternatives to literary romance in the novel are Homais' invulnerable self-sufficiency, the boredom and pettiness of provincial life, Charles's bovine mediocrity, Rodolphe's egoism and brutal sensuality, and Léon's pusillanimity. Indeed, even when, as in *L'Education senti-mentale*, Flaubert broadens the social context of his fiction beyond the narrow limits of dull provincial towns, he is never even mildly tempted by the "serious" activities and institutions of adult life (such as marriage, political involvements, or even ordinary sociability). And the only characters who appear to have his unqualified approval are the inaccessible and vaguely outlined Madame Arnoux, and those mute, simple-minded, virtuous creatures, Dussardier in the *Education* and Félicité in "Un Coeur simple."

Flaubert's radical critique of almost all versions of sentimental, intellectual and political "seriousness" could be thought of as expressing a profound distaste for all those sublimating activities which organize life in society. And Flaubert seems to encourage this view of his work by the attention which he gives, as we have seen, to the variety of sensual contacts which his characters have with the world. Emma Bovary is a sentimentalist, but her creator desublimates her sentimentality *for us* by presenting her both as an exciting physical presence and as having an exceptionally refined talent for sensual responses. Nevertheless, Flaubert's attitude toward this aspect of Emma is ambiguous. The natural inclination of Flaubertian sensual desire is toward dangerous fusions; in other terms, desire leads to the nightmare of a loss of form. There are, it's true, fusions as well as a kind of material and spiritual oozing which indicate ecstasy rather than panic. The "vague and prolonged cry" which Emma hears after she and Rodolphe have made love in the forest blends harmoniously "like a piece of music with the last vibrations of her throbbing nerves," and a few moments earlier ". . . something sweet seemed to emanate from the trees." But the hallucinated sense of substances breaking out of their forms is also a sign of terror in Flaubert. After Rodolphe refuses to give her money, and just before her suicide, Emma's very being seems to jump out from her body and explode in the air or sink into the moving soil:

> She stood there lost in stupor, no longer conscious of herself except through the beating of her arteries, which she thought she

could hear escaping like a deafening music that filled the country-side. The earth under her feet was softer than the sea and the furrows seemed to her like immense dark breaking waves. All the reminiscences and ideas in her head were rushing out, in a single leap, like a thousand pieces of fireworks. She saw her father, Lheureux's office, their room in the hotel, a different landscape. She was going mad, she had a moment of fright, and managed to take hold of herself. . . .

Emma regains her sanity only to kill herself; how will *Flaubert* protect himself from these "escapes" of being?

Only art is saved from Flaubert's pessimism about sensation and the sublimating mechanisms of social life. The Flaubertian cult of art explains Flaubert's severity toward inferior art. The realistic claims of Emma's favorite novels depend on their ignoring their own mediating processes, on their attempt to hide the differences between the nature of the intensities they seem to exalt and that of the exalting narrative itself. As I've said, they encourage Emma to search in life for the abstractions invented in books, and they also invite her to expect that real time, like the printed time of a novel, can be an uninterrupted succession of intense passages. Emma con-tributes to the sins of literary romance and, in a way, skillfully dismisses art by trying to separate the romance from the literature and thereby ignoring the work — the effort and the product — of the writer. She brings to these books exactly what they require: a lack of imagination. She reads literature as we might listen to a news report. Emma Bovary parodies all the pious claims which have been made by realism in Western esthetics for the relevance of art to life. Down-to-earth even in the midst of her raptures, Emma "had to be able to extract from things a kind of personal profit; and she rejected as useless everything which didn't contribute to the imme-diate gratification of her heart, — being by temperament more sentimental than artistic, seeking emotions and not landscapes."

Flaubert's writing is a continuous correction, through stylistic example, of Emma's confusions. The book we are reading constantly draws our attention to its own nature as a *composed* written docu-ment. Flaubert speaks in his correspondence of moments when he himself is, as it were, so taken in by the realism of his own writing that he begins to experience the incidents he describes: he shares both Emma's and Rodolphe's sensations in the scene of their love-making in the forest, and he writes the section on Emma's death with the taste of arsenic in his mouth. Occasionally Flaubert thus tends to draw from his own writing something like the immediate "personal profit" which Emma demands from literature. But to spend a couple of weeks shaping a single paragraph hardly seems calculated to leave the writer capable of "seeing through" his writing to the experiences it describes. The painfully slow composition of *Madame Bovary* is much more likely to leave Flaubert with the taste of verbal agonies rather than with the taste of arsenic.

More importantly, Flaubert's language, unlike Stendhal's, calls attention to its own strategies, sounds and designs. Flaubert's text has kept traces of being continuously worked over; and while this gives something awkward and heavy to his writing, we might also feel that a certain stylistic opacity is Flaubert's decisive refutation of Emma's confused argument for a literature of pure sensation. The very fact that, because of Emma's sensuality, Flaubert has so often to describe moments of intense sensation gives him frequent occasions for illustrating the "proper" literary use of sensation. And what Flaubert shows us is a detailed process of establishing intervals within sensations of fusion which seem to allow for no intervals. In the passage I quoted a while back, which describes Emma and Rodolphe's last night together, Flaubert compares the reflection of the moon in the water to a "headless serpent covered with luminous scales," and also to an enormous candelabra with drops of molten diamond flowing down its sides. The sexual suggestiveness of these images is obvious; they transpose Emma's sensual pleasure into a hallucinated scene in the external world. But also, by the very fact of being literary images, they are the sign, for us, of a certain distance from the sensations they describe. In her sexual exaltation, Emma may actually *see* the serpent and the candelabra; a much cooler novelist tells us that the moon's light "seemed to writhe to the bottom of the water like a headless serpent covered with luminous scales," and then, somewhat awkwardly, he starts the second comparison (in a new sentence) with: "It also resembled . . ." These last few words could have been eliminated; we might have had a single sentence, with the two images closer to each other. "It also resembled [cela ressemblait aussi à]" is a heavy but salutary reminder of the *work* of comparison. To make a verbal analogy is to bring together two things which may usually not go together, but at the very instant we say the second term of the analogy we establish a difference between it and the first term. We create a linguistic space which no similarity can abolish.

Writing is the creation of such intervals, spaces, and differences. To speak and to write are the sublimating activities which allow us to spread out sensations in time and in space. Flaubert, whose terror of sensual fusions seems to have made this a literally saving truth, makes the point for us in more extreme ways than most other writers. Comparisons can be particularly obtrusive in his work; a somewhat creaky machinery for making analogies almost mangles the object of comparison. In a famous and frequently derided analogy Flaubert compares Emma's memory of Léon to an abandoned campfire in the snow of a Russian steppe, and by the end of the second paragraph of an extravagantly extended comparison, there is some question of whether or not Emma's anguish is going to survive this exercise in Slavic meteorology. Proust declared that there is not a single beautiful metaphor in all Flaubert. But the presumed "real" point of departure for a Proustian comparison is, as in Flaubert (but even more frequently than in Flaubert), volatilized and absorbed into the imaginative logic of a process of composition. What is not "beautiful" in Flaubert is not the content of his metaphors but the glaring visibility of his literary strategies. He is far more concerned than Proust, perhaps because of those terrors of the sensual imagination which we have briefly looked at, with maintaining a sharp distinction between art and the rest of life. The heaviness of much of his writing could therefore be thought of as pedagogically useful: he is constantly demonstrating the extent to which literature renounces the immediacy of sensations in order to express them.

As an example of those fusions which take place in Flaubert at moments of great sensual excitement, I've spoken of the passage which describes Emma's sensual torpor in the city hall of Yonville on the day of the agricultural fair. Present and past, Rodolphe and Léon, the odor from the viscount's beard and the odor from Rodolphe's hair merge into a single swimming sensation. "The sweetness of this sensation [of smelling Rodolphe's pomade] thus penetrated her desires from the past, and like grains of sand in a gust of wind, they swirled in the subtle breath of the perfume which was spreading over her soul." Everything has merged into a single, indistinct, whirling sensation — everything, that is, except the only thing we are really given, which is this exceptionally complex sentence. And the coherence of the sentence depends on our moving carefully from one distinct unit to the other in order to follow the construction of Flaubert's metaphor. The sentence begins with a kind of abstract chemistry, suddenly switches to the concrete image of sand in the wind, which seems to authorize the verb "swirled [tourbillonnaient]" when we return, in the last part, to the penetration and dancing of past desires in a present sensation. As even these brief remarks indicate, the fusions of literature are always separations or articulations, and they invite the critic to even further articulations. The Flaubertian workshop is one in which a master craftsman — somewhat at the expense of his own craft — teaches us to read.

CHAPTER FOUR

The Paranoid Hero in Stendhal

JULIEN SOREL is a paranoid hero. ". . . He was a fine plant," the narrator writes toward the end of *Le Rouge et le noir*; had he lived longer, age would have allowed him to give in more easily to his natural goodness and "he would have been cured of an insane distrust."[1] Julien's social ambitions are both motivated and defeated by that "méfiance folle." I know of no other major novelistic character who so consistently expects to be insulted. Julien's readiness to repel insult is a characteristic worthy of a minor comic figure in realistic fiction. What does *Le Rouge et le noir* tell us about the relation between paranoia and character, between paranoia and desire in Stendhal?

Had Julien realized his ambitious projects, he might have reached a position where no one would have dared to scorn him anymore. He is certainly not ambitious because, as we would expect in a Balzacian hero, he finds the exercise of social power appealing. Indeed, he is tempted to give up his exhausting struggle to make it when he thinks of the moral stench he will have to put up with if he does make it. To succeed in society is for Julien the only way to defeat all those "enemies" who can feel they have the right to look down on him as long as he's not above them on the social ladder. But something panicky in Julien's paranoid fantasies makes it impossible for him to postpone his revenge against the enemy, and the impossibility of bearing an insult almost spoils the entire plan designed to protect him permanently from insults. Julien's ambition holds out the prospect of satisfactions much too remote for his tortured imagination; an insulting or a flattering gesture *now* destroys the carefully calculated design of his social progress. What could be more dangerous to his career than his readiness to have a duel with Amanda Binet's lover on the day he arrives at Besançon in order to become a seminarian? What could be more imprudent than to have an affair with the Marquis de La Mole's daughter at the very moment when Julien can reasonably hope to profit in tangible ways from the marquis' affection for him?

Julien's paranoid sensibility depends on his inability to distinguish between being insulted and being destroyed. Given his nature, it would be hard to imagine a greater disaster for Julien than to fall in love with Mathilde. One day she is all submission; the next day her pride revolts at the idea of "having a master," and she either ignores her puzzled lover or treats him to an outburst of rageful, insulting scorn. Stendhal treats this peculiar love affair at great length but rather lightly. A certain mocking detachment from both Julien and Mathilde is Stendhal's way of indicating the essential insignificance of their affair — an insignificance which Julien himself sees only when he is in prison. This is as far, Stendhal is saying, as an "amour de tête" can go. Mathilde is more original (certainly more imprudent) than any other Parisian "doll," but she is a spoiled if extravagantly imaginative brat whom it's best to watch, at a distance, with amused curiosity. But Stendhal's *sagesse* must be distinguished from Julien's enslavement to Mathilde; she reduces him to paroxysms of self-hatred. In what Stendhal calls a state of "*imagination renversée*," Julien, under the effect of Mathilde's scorn, comes to be "mortally disgusted with all his good qualities, with all the things he had loved with enthusiasm." When Mathilde insults him, it seems to him that she "was right, and that she wasn't saying enough." "Good God! Why am I me?" Julien cries in despair at ever having the "merit" that might make Mathilde love him. Her scorn drives everything from his mind except self-nausea, a crazy wish to expel himself from his self.

From the very beginning, Julien has been a most unlikely candidate for grand social designs. He is, first of all, too fastidious in his moral and intellectual tastes. He is repelled by the Valenods' bad manners and vulgar talk about money; the coarseness of his fellow seminarians at Besançon disgusts him (or, at best, moves him to pity); and the prudently empty talk of Parisian *salons* bores him. Alone at the top of the mountains near Vergy, early in *Le Rouge et le noir*, Julien enjoys one of his rare moments of respite from ambition, and Stendhal makes it clear that his hero wants only to be safely far away from the blows of his fellow man: "Hidden like a bird of prey, in the midst of the bare rocks which crown the great mountain, he could see from a long way off any man who might be approaching. He discovered a little cave in the middle of the almost vertical slope of one of the rocks. He went toward it, and was soon settled down in this retreat. Here, he said to himself, his eyes shining with joy, no man could do me any harm."

A little before this incident, Julien had already surveyed "twenty leagues of country" from a rock on the mountain where he could feel "sure of being separated from all men." From his protected position, Julien catches sight of a hawk in the sky, "silently tracing huge circles. Julien's eyes mechanically followed the bird of prey. He was struck by its tranquil and powerful movements, he envied such strength, he envied such isolation." And Stendhal concludes: "This was Napoleon's destiny, would it one day be his?" The appropriateness of the reference to Napoleon is somewhat questionable. The appeal of Julien's position here is its isolation, its distance from all human affairs. Was it in fact Napoleon's destiny to be as remote from other men as the circling hawk is from the earth? When Eugène de Rastignac looks down on Paris from the Père Lachaise cemetery at the end of *Le Père Goriot*, it is with a grimly exalted determination to plunge into that social jungle and become one of its princes; for Julien Sorel, worldly success would authorize his taking leave of the world. That "sense of altitude" which Proust recognized as fundamental to the Stendhalian imagination expresses not only the impulse to rise in society. It is also an impulse to rise *out* of society, into the splendid isolation of a hawk circling above mountain peaks, or even into the forced isolation of Fabrice del Dongo imprisoned high in the Farnese tower.

"His entire life had been only a long preparation for misfortune," Stendhal says of his hero when Julien is in prison; consequently, death, "which is considered as the greatest misfortune of all . . .

wasn't *horrible* in his eyes." Exhausted from his attempts to make himself invulnerable, Julien almost welcomes the punishment which, in a sense, he finally forces society to inflict upon him when he shoots Mme. de Rênal. Shocked by Julien's speech at his trial, which awakens and attacks "the petty vanity of this *bourgeois aristocracy*" (the "intérêt de caste" of Julien's jurors), the powerful M. de Frilair speaks to Mathilde of Julien's death as "a sort of *suicide*." It's as if Julien had been subverting his ambitious projects all along. Social success would never have given him the isolation we see him dreaming of early in the novel, and he often seems to be collaborating with his enemies in offering them occasions to expel him from the social arena. Julien's "insane distrust" of others could be thought of as an inverted sign of his own rejection of society. In a sense, other men would be right to feel mistrustful of *him*. And, although I recognize that nothing in the novel explicitly indicates this as part of Julien's intentions, we may also feel that Julien's extreme susceptibility to insult disguises a need to be punished. If we look somewhat schematically at the explicit psychological evidence in the novel, we have, in Julien, the desire to succeed in society and to dominate others, the fear of being persecuted by others, the inability to resist demonstrating his courage in ways which jeopardize his plans for success and practically invite others to put him down, and finally a desire to love in safe isolation from a society capable of destroying him by its scorn. We don't have to go very far beyond this evidence to suspect that Julien's paranoid sensibility includes an attack on others for which he expects to be punished. And since the punishment (in prison) includes more happiness than he has ever known before, we might even ask to what extent Julien attacks *in order to be attacked*. The attempted murder of Mme. de Rênal is Julien's way of justifying the persecution he has always dreaded. He is both the attacker and the attacked, and by striking back at him, society gives Julien the chance both to recognize his most profound desires and to make reparations for his "crimes."

   To understand the exact nature of these "crimes" we must first of all look more more closely at Stendhalian desire. I have spoken in *Balzac to Beckett* of the apparent importance of the Oedipal triangle in Stendhal. In *Armance, Le Rouge et le noir, La Chartreuse de Parme, Lucien Leuwen,* and in the autobiographical *Vie de Henri*

Brulard, we find hostility or, at best, a profound temperamental incompatibility between Stendhalian fathers and sons. Older men in Stendhal tend to be brutal and selfish, or, like M. Leuwen, they are worldly in a way which prevents them from appreciating the young hero's readiness to renounce the world for a generally forbidden and secretive love. The fathers belong to society; or, more precisely, a hostile, unimaginative society in Stendhal seems to be an extension of the father's nature, a projection into politics and history of paternal egotism and cruelty. Only a kind of impotence makes Stendhal's male characters worthy, so to speak, of loving his young heroes: the Abbés Chélan, Pirard, and Blanès are priests and, except for the Abbé Pirard, senile. Even Mosca, the most sympathetic of the middle-aged men in Stendhal's novels, belongs to the world. His sensibility has been somewhat corrupted by the years he has spent as a courtier, and at the end of *La Chartreuse de Parme* we learn that he has the ambiguous privilege of surviving and becoming "enormously rich" after the deaths of Fabrice, Clélia and Gina. The "happy few" in Stendhal are the young heroes and the loving women. They constitute a community of love which excludes the vain and hypocritical society which eventually destroys them.

But what are the activities of Stendhalian love? The happiest scenes in Stendhal's fiction are scenes of childlike play. Fabrice, his mother and sisters and Gina take boatrides on Lake Como and study astrology with the Abbé Blanès. Fabrice invents word games so that he can send messages from his prison cell to Clélia in her aviary. Julien runs after butterflies with Mme. de Rênal's children in the garden at Vergy. In these instances the hero-son enjoys an intimacy with a woman attached to (or, in Clélia's case, destined for) someone else; the woman loves the hero passionately but, as with the mother-mistress Mme. de Rênal, she may also like to think of him as a child. The role of sex in these love stories is ambiguous. Stendhal's extreme reticence about his characters' sexual experiences has often been commented on. Balzac and Flaubert refer much more explicitly to sexual desires and fulfillments than does Stendhal; the latter tends either to skip over periods of sexual happiness or to describe sex in vague and abstract terms. This sexual *pudeur* in Stendhal would be hardly worth pointing out if intense sensations didn't occupy such a central place in his imagination of happiness. I think it's less important to run after psychological explanations for sexual timidity and sexual *pudeur* in Stendhal (which are undoubtedly linked, as *Armance* suggests, to an obsession with impotence) than it is to ask how a cult of sensation can be maintained with practically no effort to describe sensations. As an alternative to the exhausting complications of life in society, Stendhal proposes the ecstatic sensations of love — but he is as secretive with the reader about the exact nature of those sensations as his heroes and heroines are with the society hostile to their love.

Stendhal's *pudeur* is, in part, a way of protecting his characters' ecstasies from a possible complicity on the part of his readers with that hostile society, just as all the smoke screens which Stendhal throws up to conceal his exact relation to his own art (pseudonyms, wrong dates of composition, ironic denials of his deepest sympathies) seem designed to protect *him* from those clever "French" readers ready to mock his tender and passionate nature. There is, however, much more to the question than this. It's not at all certain that Stendhal is reticent about sensations which *could* be described in the first place. Inasmuch as happiness in Stendhal includes sexuality at all, he seems to be interested in sex free even from stimulating complications. In *Le Rouge et le noir*, he makes an interesting comment about the effect of Mme. de Rênal's feeling of guilt, when her son is ill, on the quality of the love between her and Julien. Their happiness, he writes, was now of a superior nature, their passion more intense and even extravagant. "Their happiness would have seemed greater in the eyes of the world. But they could no longer recover the exquisite serenity, the cloudless felicity, the easy happiness of the early times of their love. . . . Their happiness would sometimes take on the aspect of a crime." Mme. de Rênal's remorse obviously creates material for drama; conflict gives a certain variety to love and helps to make it a good novelistic subject. Stendhal the novelist certainly exploits the interesting complication — of social ambition as well as of love. It is the very nourishment of his fiction, but, significantly, he also judges these elements of dramatic diversity as spiritually inferior to a kind of easy and monotonous "felicity" about which there is very little to *say*. Happiness can only be alluded to rather abstractly ("exquisite serenity, cloudless felicity"). Its presence in *Le Rouge et le noir* is felt principally in a negative way. It plays practically no role in the novel, but almost the entire story is an immense detour which Julien takes in order to return, in prison, and this time consciously and with full consent, to the happiness of merely being with Mme. de Rênal which he had thought himself ready to sacrifice to his ambition.

Stendhal does manage to propose settings and conditions for happiness, but its nature is indescribable. Isolated from a hostile society (from brutal fathers and husbands), the hero can experience ecstatic sensations with the loved one. But the very intensity which guarantees the authenticity of this happiness makes it unanalyzable. Only sensations are true, Stendhal writes as he tries to recall his past in the *Vie de Henri Brulard*, but how can they be correctly transcribed forty years later from the detached perspective of an analytic memory? Even more: not only does analysis violate sensation, but past sensations imperfectly remembered may also dim our intelligence and make it impossible for us to see clearly the events which produced these sensations. "The extreme vivacity of sensations" produces an "aureole" which hides truth. Stendhal complains in the *Vie de Henri Brulard* of being able to recall only the effects which things had on him, and not their causes. To reach the truth concerning the women he has loved, he must "destroy the charm, the *dazzling* [the English word appears in Stendhal's text] of events, by considering them thus in a military fashion." The only reliable memories are memories of sensations, but the closer we come to reliving past sensations, the less likely is it that we will be able to give an accurate account of them (either of their nature or their cause).

Indeed, we may have to *invent a story* which will make the intense sensation intelligible. If autobiography tries to work back from the remembered sensation to its causes, the novel will proceed from imagined circumstances and causes to sensations. *La Chartreuse de Parme*, for example, schematically moves from one set of circumstances to another (from military life to court life and to love) in order to try out the potentiality of each set for producing intensely happy sensations. Fabrice's love for Clélia is the best novelistic formula for producing ecstasy. It produces indescribably happy sensations in the lovers themselves, and it is also meant to cause vibrations of happiness in the reader. "A novel is like the bow of a violin, the violin case which makes the sounds is the reader's soul." Fiction plays or works on our sensibilities; the actual "sounds" of happiness, however, are made outside of fiction. The novel awakens sensations which it is unable to describe. For Stendhal, the ecstatic instant is the novelist's point of departure and the ideal effect of his novel; it is the novel's origin and purpose, although it can never be its content.

In this way, Stendhalian fiction carefully avoids the deception of which Emma Bovary's favorite novels are guilty. The inflated rhetoric of literary romance tempts readers to confuse verbal inventions with bodily intensities; to feel, as Emma does, that stories literally contain sensations and that they must therefore be exactly duplicated in life before the happiness they seem to promise can be felt. Linguistic escalations blind Emma to the suggestive, the strategic and the metaphorical nature of language; she takes the excited language used to describe certain scenes of love as a guarantee of the excitement intrinsic to the scenes themselves. Stendhal, on the other hand, will continually emphasize the distance between ecstasy and writing by a deliberate reticence and even dryness in his writing. This is of course not to deny other influences on his style. He admired the eighteenth century, and especially the *idéologues*; by training and taste, he was suspicious of exaggeration in romantic literature. We must also take into account his fear of the unsympathetic reader. To let himself go verbally would be to expose himself to the danger of ridicule, and Stendhal's profound sympathy for his passionate heroes hides behind a complicated if transparent system of ironic denials of this sympathy and anticipatory attacks on a hostile audience. None of this, however, excludes Stendhal's highly sophisticated sense of the relation between literature and sensation. Literature serves the intense sensations which alone give value to life, but it does this not by translating sensations into words, but rather by proposing a psychological and social ambiance for the privileged instant. Fiction is the middle term between the writer's unrecordable intensities and the equally unrecordable intensities to be produced in the reader. It is a way of reinventing unremembered past stimuli of joyful sensations in the hope of creating — for the novelist's hero, for the novelist and for his public — a *future* for joyful sensations.

We do find certain formulas for perceptual pleasures in Stendhal. In *Littérature et sensation*, Jean-Pierre Richard, for example, has noted that Stendhal finds the world a spectacle for happiness when a scene satisfies a need for both clarity and continuity, for sharply distinct sensations and impressions of fusion and unity. Furthermore, in *De l'Amour* we read: "The crystallization formed in each man's head must include the color of that man's pleasures." That is, since in love reality is modeled along the lines of desire, the idealized image of the loved one which "crystallizes" in the lover's mind tells us what the lover needs from the world (and this would naturally involve more than just sensations) in order to be happy. The portrait he makes of the person he loves can be read as a code of the pleasures — physical and spiritual — which he desires most intensely. The psychological dissections of *De l'Amour* are, however, irrelevant to the most exalted experiences of love in *Le Rouge et le noir*, *La Chartreuse de Parme* and *Lucien Leuwen*. All the stages and types of love can be described except its most profound and authentic version. And to the different accounts of Stendhal's reticence or *pudeur* which we have already mentioned, we can add his pursuit of a pleasure too particular to be traced to any model.

In *Le Rouge et le noir*, Stendhal is consistently satirical about desires which imitate historical or literary models. "In Paris," Stendhal writes early in the novel, "Julien's position with respect to Madame de Rênal would have been simplified very quickly; but in Paris, love is the child of novels. . . . Novels would have outlined the role they were to play, shown them the model to be imitated, and sooner or later, although without any pleasure, perhaps with grumbling reluctance, vanity would have forced Julien to follow this model." Unlike Emma Bovary, Mme. de Rênal "considered as exceptional or even as something completely unnatural, love as she had found it in the very small number of novels which chance had brought to her attention." Julien's first night with Mme. de Rênal is disappointing to him because he's too busy thinking of his "duty" to pay attention to her "transports": "He feared a frightful remorse and an eternal ridicule if he didn't live up to the ideal model which he had resolved to follow." With Mme. de Rênal, models will finally be forgotten; with Mathilde, love lives only on models, from the heroic ancestors whose destinies Mathilde desperately wishes to imitate to that comical but effective campaign for winning back Mathilde's love which Julien scrupulously carries out on the advice of the Russian prince Korasoff, his instructor in "the fundamental rules of high fatuousness." Imitations of history are always parodies of history in Stendhal: the Napoleonic tactics to seduce the timid wife of a provincial mayor, the bored star of nineteenth-century

Parisian *salons* equating her affair with a carpenter's son from the Jura with Marguerite de Navarre's passion for Boniface de La Mole, and in *Chartreuse*, Ernest IV's funny attempts to imitate Louis XIV. Stendhal's rejection of models extends even to his habits of composition, to his attitude toward the material of his fiction. ". . . The appeal to memory kills imagination (in me at any rate)"; therefore, Stendhal prefers to do an outline of a novel *after* writing the story. To follow a preconceived outline is to imitate the mind's past designs. Even the models provided by one's own imagination must be rejected. "My talent, if there is any talent, is that of an *improviser*." Ideally, improvised writing knows no responsibility to the constraints of already proposed compositional models. Having eliminated even his own literary plans as a source of imitation, the writer may be able to give to his work that quality which lovers unaware of literary romances may give to their love: the quality of being "natural." Speaking of the difference between love in Paris and love in the country, Stendhal writes: "Everything moves slowly, everything is done little by little in the provinces, things are more natural [il y a plus de naturel]." Both love and art profit from a certain indifference to given models.

It's true that the realistic novelist can hardly think of himself as working entirely without models. Whether he be improvising or following an outline, he is, theoretically at any rate, imitating the real, reporting facts which exist prior to his work. But if Stendhal likes to think of the novel as a mirror held up to reality, he can also qualify or even dismiss realism when he speaks of his heroes and heroines. Heroines, for example, don't have to exist in nature; the novelist is justified in idealizing them, in making them resemble the "beau parfait," because the reader has seen the woman he loves only by idealizing her. Reality can be violated in order to remain faithful to certain violations of reality — in reality. Even more: "Except for the hero's passion," Stendhal writes in the first preface to *Lucien Leuwen*, "a novel must be a mirror." The hero's passion reflects nothing. It seems to obey indefinable impulses analogous to those which sustain the improvising writer. Indeed, Jean Prévost noted in *La Création chez Stendhal* a similarity between the "movement of invention" in a Stendhalian novel and the "movement of passion" in the hero. There is perhaps an ecstasy of composition in Stendhal as there is an ecstasy of love. And the ultimate privilege conferred by writing and by loving is that of escaping from the laws of imitation. Or, as Georges Blin has put it in his subtle discussion of the complexities in Stendhal's realistic credo, the novelist according to Stendhal portrays nature "through a certain work of crystallization, nature as it is refracted in the lyrical soul at those moments when the soul is hyperbolically affected by completely individual traces of illusion or enthusiasm."

I referred a few pages back to the Oedipal structure in Stendal's work. In psychoanalytic terms, to love without a model could be thought of as a way of eliminating the father. The son's pleasures owe nothing to the father's pleasures. Imitation, ideally, would play no role in desire. There is no resolution of the Oedipus complex for those characters who stand for the son in Stendhal's fiction (Julien, Lucien, Fabrice). That is, the son does not renounce the mother out of fear of being punished for his desires by the father, and the punishing father is not internalized as an ideal or as a regulatory conscience for the ego. Furthermore, in the Stendhalian version of Oedipal fantasies, there appears to be an effort to eliminate dramatically ambivalent feelings toward the father. Stendhalian fathers are neither destroyed, submitted to, nor loved; the sons want merely to dismiss them.[2] Consequently, there is little basis for the development either of the superego or of social feelings. Stendhal's work supports the Freudian notion that some erotic attachment to the father is necessary to stimulate the wish to internalize him as an ego-ideal, and that social cohesion is, in part, a sublimation of homosexual desire for the father. If the child sees the father as the representative of society (and later on sees society as an extension of the father's territory), the rejection of the father as a model will also be, as indeed it is in Stendhal, a rejection of social life.

Stendhal's most profound intention is to eliminate the Oedipal stage itself. The very transparency of the Oedipal design in Stendhal is somewhat misleading. It is perhaps the *willed* insignificance of the rivalry with the father which allows it to become so obvious. The father and society are indeed enemies of the Stendhalian hero. But far from renouncing the mother, imitating (with other women) the father's attachment to the mother, and transforming love for the father into social involvements, Stendhal's heroes attempt to dismiss the father and retreat from society into a secret and blissful intimacy with the woman (or mother).

In part, the defeated father is reduced to being jealous of the son's happiness. M. de Rênal angrily sees that he is an unwanted intruder on the happiness of Julien with Mme. de Rênal and their children; Mosca suffers from feeling excluded from the joyfully animated talk of Gina and Fabrice; and in *La Chartreuse*, society itself seems intent on punishing the "happy few" in the novel simply because of their aptitude for happiness. But if the father seems never to win, he never stops being dangerous. He can be eliminated as an erotic rival and still be feared as an enemy. We begin to see some of the complications in the deceptively simple move of doing away with the father as a rival in love, as well as an object of love and a model for loving, when we realize that the father or society almost always wins in the end. Julien is put to death by society; Fabrice is the victim of social enmities which make it impossible for him to marry Clélia. In a sense, Julien's paranoid sensibility is fully justified. He has twice seduced a woman away from her most "legitimate" family ties: Mme. de Rênal recognizes that she loves him more than she loves either her husband or her children, and Mathilde betrays her father by choosing a man with neither title nor fortune. At his trial, Julien says that his jury is composed only of "indignant bourgeois" anxious to punish a young peasant who has had "the audacity to mix with what rich people's pride calls society." It could also be said that Julien has intruded on erotic territory which "belongs" to other men. And these others, as Julien has feared all along, take their revenge by sending the irresistible intruder to the guillotine.

The peculiar nature of the fathers and of society in this Stendhalian fantasy is to be both insignificant and all-powerful. This accounts, I think, for the difficulty we may have in deciding exactly how to take what happens in a Stendhalian novel. Critics have seemed particularly puzzled about *La Chartreuse de Parme*: is the novel closer to farce or to tragedy? But in Stendhal the farcical doesn't exclude the tragic, and the Oedipal fantasy which I've been discussing helps to make psychological sense out of all those characters who simultaneously announce their comic insignificance and illustrate their ominous power. Parma may be populated with *opéra bouffe* characters, but the buffoons are capable of destroying the heroes. As we have seen in Racine, to reduce the father to silliness is by no means equivalent to reducing him to impotence. In fact, the hero may expect to be punished not only for stealing the woman, but also for his refusal to acknowledge the father. The hero would initiate a new and indescribable order of desire which excludes the father and which owes nothing to his desires. And the novelist has, so to speak, collaborated with the hero by creating suitably ridiculous paternal and social figures. But it is as if the fantasy which trivializes the father included a fantasy of the father's fury at being trivialized. The Stendhalian society of older men is as justly suspicious of the Stendhalian hero (and of the Stendhalian imagination . . .) as the hero is of them. Julien is right to expect a punishment which finally does come; and a society of indignant fathers is just as "right" to strike out at him for making fools of them and for inviting Mme. de Rênal to enjoy a happiness whose existence she had never suspected and which makes this pious woman ready to accept eternal damnation.

We haven't exhausted the dangers of dismissing the father. The unprecedented and indescribable pleasures of intimacy between the hero and the woman he loves are themselves somewhat threatening. Happiness in Stendhal would be the fulfillment of a dream of uninterrupted play between the child and the mother. But at the structural level which psychoanalytic criticism seeks to make explicit, the women in Stendhal's fiction who could be thought of as representatives of the mother are somewhat ambiguous. We generally find two very different women competing for the hero's love: Mme. de Rênal and Mathilde, Clélia and Gina, Mme. de Chasteller and Mme. Grandet. A mild, unworldly woman is opposed to a frankly social creature who very much enjoys playing to the dazzled appreciation of others. These others may of course include the reader, and it's hardly surprising that many of Stendhal's readers prefer the rich colors of Gina's personality to the duller traits of Clélia's other-worldly presence, or even the complicated maneuvers of Mathilde's pride to the somewhat monotonous simplicity of Mme. de Rênal's selfless devotion. The Stendhalian narrator himself is certainly sensitive to the appeal of these agitated women of the world, but it's nonetheless important to see that for the young heroes of Stendhal's fiction they never carry the promise of happiness embodied in their less colorful, almost conventual rivals.

These female couples may embody fantasies of the "good mother" and the "bad mother." The latter's love is ominous for the son; it is undependable and violent, and it brings the hero dangerously close to his enemies in society. By withdrawing her love, Mathilde can plunge Julien into paroxysms of self-hatred; through Gina, Fabrice becomes involved in the intrigues at the court of Parma, and her jealous passion leads her to take revenge on Fabrice for his indifference by working for Clélia's marriage to the Marquis Crescenzi. Safety would seem to lie in retreating from the world with the mild, all-loving "mother." But even here there are some curiously sinister notes. For example, we find betrayal and revenge in these good loves: Julien betrays Mme. de Rênal with Mathilde, Mme. de Rênal betrays Julien by portraying him as a calculating hypocrite in her letter to the Marquis de La Mole, and to avenge himself he shoots her. Julien is therefore punished for a double crime against the mother *and* the father. I've discussed the son's crimes against the father; Julien must also make reparations for his crime against the mother.[3] (In a sense, Lucien also "betrays" Mme. de Chasteller by falling into Du Poirier's trap: he believes that she has had a child by another man.) The death of a child is also associated with the hero's love for the "good mother." In *Le Rouge et le noir*, Stanislas almost dies, and Mme. de Rênal thinks of this death as God's punishment for her affair with Julien. Sandrino dies in *La Chartreuse* as a result of Fabrice's wishing to have the child live with him.

The fantasies involved here seem to be forbiddingly complex. One could think that the son has divided himself into two distinct figures in order to express opposite feelings about a union with the mother: he enacts his happy love with her, at the same time that he (as a child now) dies as a result of that love. Does the very nature of this intimacy explain the death? Does even the good mother's embrace stifle life in the child, and/or have the worst consequences of the bad mother's nature been projected into the relation with the good mother? Or perhaps the baby's death belongs to fantasies of punishment which are dramatized more clearly in the fate of the baby's double, the young Stendhalian hero. That is, the baby may die, as the hero will, as a result of the father's anger, or perhaps because the hero must atone for having betrayed the mother. Things become even more complicated when we remember that Fabrice, for example, could represent not only the son, but, since Sandrino is his child, also the father. The violence of Oedipal revenge is enacted twice in *La Chartreuse*, once with Fabrice as the son-victim and the other time with Fabrice as the father-punisher. Society would like to punish Fabrice for being happy with Clélia; but then Fabrice becomes a father, he takes his child away from its mother, and the child dies.

I say all this tentatively because such structures are far less developed in Stendhal's fiction than they are in Racine. The unconscious drama which Mauron makes explicit in Racinian tragedy is much closer to the surface of Racinian drama than the network of unconscious fantasies which I've just outlined in Stendhal is to Stendhalian fiction. The very abstractness of personality in Racine's theater leaves an uncluttered field, so to speak, for the display of unconscious forces. Even if we speak of Racinian characters in nonpsychoanalytic terms, we tend to define them almost entirely in terms of a few passionate impulses which determine practically all their behavior. In Stendhal, on the other hand, as in most realistic fiction, the elemental dramas of unconscious passions are obscured by a field of rich appearances — that is, by the particularizing details of conscious personality as well as by the social contexts which deflect those passions and also provide new objects of desire. Psychoanalytic interpretation therefore seems to distort the texts of Stendhalian fiction much more rapidly than it does those of classical tragedy. The Oedipal triangle has a rather high visibility in Stendhal, but the anxieties and dangers in the child's relation to the mother are only dimly sketched. All my remarks on the last couple of pages concerning that relation are extrapolations from very scant evidence. They represent less what the text tells us than what Stendhal might tell under the pressure of an (impossible) psychoanalytic interrogation. Consequently, I'm not interested in testing the relative strength of my various suggestions (for instance, does the fantasy of being punished for betraying the mother have affective priority over the fantasy of maternal love as a potential carrier of death?). Rather, we can be satisfied with pointing out that the mere enumeration of these interpretive possibilities suggests that happiness with the mother may be as fraught with dangers as life in society. Not only will the father strike back; the mother has her own grievances and her very nature may, ultimately, be murderous. Such fantasies obviously widen the gap between happiness and society in Stendhal — and between happiness and novelistic invention. Stendhalian heroes and heroines would sacrifice everything else for their ecstatic love. Even before they are persecuted by society, Julien and Mme. de Rênal and Fabrice and Clélia have little use for the company of others. Love in Stendhal seeks out cloistered retreats. And in the prison towers and solitary gardens where the Stendhalian lovers come together, they enjoy ecstatic sensations of which no account can be given. Uncomplicated by sex or perhaps by any event at all, productive of sensations whose "extreme vivacity" precludes their being described, menaced by the excluded rival and perhaps even by its own nature, Stendhalian love is the purpose of Stendhal's fiction, but it also leads to the hero's death, as well as to the end of talk, the death of the hero and of fiction.

Of course, nothing could be more astonishing from such a master of talk as Stendhal. The essential problem for Stendhal the novelist will be to protect his hero's dream of happiness at the same time that he protects himself — and his work — from that dream. I think that he can do this only by *reinventing the father.* A certain opposition to ectasy is necessary to the presentation of ecstasy; it can best be described negatively, in terms of the distance which separates it from other kinds of experience. The persona of the Stendhalian narrator provides the ideal mixture of critical detachment and sympathy. He is the only loving father in Stendhal's fiction. The narrator generally tells his story from the point of view of his young hero, but their voices are not to be confused. In *La Chartreuse de Parme*, for example, the character whose style is most like that of the narrator is not Fabrice, but the older Mosca. Having eliminated the father as a loving and lovable presence in his fiction, Stendhal brings the father back in the form of a narrator tenderly protective toward his hero-son. We can describe the relation between the narrator and the hero in Stendhal's fiction as the esthetic realization of a dream of self-creation. The novelist creates, or engenders himself. More exactly, Stendhal splits himself into a narrator-father and a hero-son, thus suggesting a happier alternative to that disastrous relation between the parent and the child which is more explicitly dramatized in his novelistic plots. The Oedipal enmity is played out between Julien or Fabrice and society; the father's tenderness is enacted as narrative sympathy.

This happy narrative solution is an ingenious transformation of the hero's paranoid mistrust of society. As we have seen, the hero constantly expects to be attacked by hostile older men. We have also seen that, for various reasons, he appears to be inviting this attack. He may secretly feel that he deserves to be attacked because of his own hostility toward the father or because of his desire to possess a forbidden woman — or because, as in *Le Rouge et le noir*, society's punishment conveniently reunites him, in an imprisoned solitude, with the woman. Finally — and this remark is suggested by Freud's view of the connections between paranoia and homosexuality — to be sexually attacked by the father would be to give birth to the child, that is, to the self. Such an attack might therefore be fantasized as a desirable occasion for "re-doing" one's entrance into the world, in a less contingent, more controlled fashion.

To be a novelist is to live an even better version of this *causa sui* project. As he writes, the novelist, through the voice of a paternal narrator, gives birth to the young hero of his story. The novelist creates both father and son; an ideally sympathetic father has been impregnated with a particularly appealing and glamorous son. To be one's own father solves the problem of how to live without models and yet not violently reject the father. We have a desiring child and a possible model for the father, but they are both aspects of a single self, which has achieved autonomy through this internal division. The source of his hero's desires is the novelist's imagination; to identify with his hero is, for the novelist, a way of experiencing his debt to himself for the nature of his desires. The son's desires are the father's desires. The *causa sui* project is our most daring fantasy of desires which would originate in the self and which would meet no obstacle from competing desires external to the self.

Why, then, is it apparently so difficult for Stendhal to imagine a happy fate for his heroes? Octave, Julien and Fabrice die young; Lucien was to have married Mme. de Chasteller in the section of *Lucien Leuwen* which Stendhal never got around to writing. Stendhal is deeply mistrustful of his most exalting desires. I spoke some pages back of fiction as the middle term between the writer's unrecordable intensities and the equally unrecordable intensities to be produced in the reader. The writer invents a story which, while it can't be an exact transcription of ecstatic sensations, awakens the reader's longing to participate in the hero's undescribed happiness. We have also looked at some of the ambiguities and dangers in the Stendhalian dream of love. Fiction is not only the theater for the imagination and pursuit of happiness; it is also a *sacrificial* reenactment of the *chasse au bonheur*. In part, the work of fiction serves the fantasy of happiness by providing sensibilities and milieux congenial to happiness. But the Stendhalian novel also moves toward the death of that fantasy. The work of art promotes the repetition of remembered intensities; it also serves to exorcise and to dissipate those memories. The *causa sui* project, which is designed to eliminate the father from the son's existence, can have the effect of permanently resettling the father in the son's life. In that *dédoublement* which allows Stendhal both to give birth to an ideal version of himself and to watch over his hero-son with loving protectiveness, Stendhal borrows from the hated father's nature. For a certain imitation of the father is necessary in order to *be* both father and son, to differentiate a paternal part of the self from the filial part.

As a result, the relation between Stendhal and his heroes is, in some respects, a repetition of the relations between real or symbolic fathers and sons in his fiction, as well as a repetition of the relation between society and the hero. As I've said, the death of a child is a recurrent motif in Stendhal's fiction. Octave, Julien and Fabrice are Stendhal's "children" and through them, as it has often been suggested, Stendhal seems to enjoy the pleasure of possessing that irresistible appeal (especially in the eyes of "heavenly" creatures such as Mme. de Rênal and Clélia) about which the novelist could have no illusions as far as his own person was concerned. But these idealized offspring are also punished for their successes by a creator condemned — like Mosca — to the far less ingratiating role of a sympathetic but perhaps nonetheless jealous older man. For all his sympathy, Stendhal behaves toward his heroes in a way analogous to society's behavior toward them; that is, he plots their deaths. The novelist's imagination is a major agent of revenge for wronged fathers (and more obscurely, perhaps, wronged mothers), at the same time that he is busy imagining ways to defend the son against their charges.

This double role gives an extra dimension to the form of paranoid sensibility which we find in the Stendhalian narrator. He is as mistrustful of his readers as Julien, for example, is of society, and as society is of his heroes. Stendhal is most apparently mistrustful of our willingness to love his heroes as they deserve to be loved. But, as we have seen, the "insane distrust" of others is accompanied, in each case, by aggressive intentions toward others. Julien constantly expects to be attacked by a society which he himself wishes to invade and whose trust he betrays (with Mme. de Rênal and with Mathilde). And Stendhal's skepticism about his readers' sympathy certainly goes along with an aggressive repudiation of the reluctantly sympathetic reader. The audience he is writing for is different from the audience he is speaking to, and the "happy few" capable of loving his heroes are invited to take the place of those readers who have been dismissed by Stendhal's ironic deference to them. Finally, however, we may feel that Stendhal's mistrust of the reader is a displaced version of his aggressiveness toward his hero. Given Stendhal's identification with his heroes, it doesn't seem improbable that he should plot their tragic fates with ambivalent feelings. It is, after all, Stendhal who carries out the father's vengeance in his fiction, and the Stendhalian narrator's nervous evasiveness may express his uneasiness at having passed into the enemy's camp through tactics designed to *protect* the son from his enemies. The narrator may be the only father in Stendhal's novels who shows signs of feeling guilt about punishing the son.

Thus Stendhal partially identifies himself with a hostile father and a hostile society by taking the very role which allows him to represent the son in their midst. The narrator's protective sympathy for the Stendhalian hero presupposes a certain distance from the hero, and it is as if that distance also makes it probable that the narrator should begin to judge the hero. For example, the narrator's criticisms of Fabrice in *La Chartreuse* are by no means always to be taken as insincere, as a way of making the criticism seem ridiculous and therefore forcing the reader to love Fabrice. The ironic intelligence with which the narrator speaks to his hostile "French" readers makes it impossible for him not to recognize — and to mock — what is morally and intellectually naïve, and even dangerous, in the beautiful "Italian" sensibility of his passionate hero. The Stendhalian narrator protects himself from his hero's fate by imagining himself (as he imagines Mosca) somewhat unworthy of that fate. Unlike Fabrice and Julien, Stendhal belongs to the world.

Is a compromise possible between society and the hero, between the father and the son? Stendhal's most precious dream is perhaps the dream of a harmony between the social self and the happy self. "I thought that a man should be passionately in love," Stendhal writes in the *Vie de Henri Brulard*, "and at the same time be bringing joy and movement into all the social groups where he might find himself." Stendhal tries to imagine a congenial social medium for happiness. The importance of the *salon* in Stendhal's fiction seems to be that it does bring the lovers from their cloistered retreats into society, at the same time that it is a small chosen society which, ideally, would be a meeting place only for the "happy few." The people who meet in Paris at Mme. Leuwen's home, or in Gina's *salons* in Naples (during the period she and Mosca are in exile from Parma toward the end of *La Chartreuse*) perhaps constitute that ideal *salon*. But nothing is more difficult for Stendhal than to keep his loving heroes and heroines at these exceptionally agreeable parties. It is as if they — and he — knew only too well that too many powerful forces are drawing Stendhalian love toward prison cells, and ultimately toward death, for the *salon* to exercise any truly effective pressure in the name of society and of life. Octave and Lucien wander in their mothers' charming *salons* like unhappy exiles and Gina, the most charmingly social creature in all Stendhal's fiction, implicitly repudiates her own genius for inventing social pleasures by dying soon after Fabrice dies. The only *salon* that survives in Stendhal's fiction is maintained by the witty, sophisticated intelligence of the Stendhalian narrator. For all his nervous irony and tireless shadowboxing with a hostile audience, he works toward finding an ideal tone for the talk to which he obliquely invites the "happy few" among his readers. Poised between images of unlivable happiness and of a murderous society, Stendhal's voice creates a strictly literary *salon* in *La Chartreuse*, one in which Fabrice's spiritual beauty can be protected, imitated, and even socially articulated.

This narrative compromise is not without its ironies. On the one hand, talk in Stendhal provides material for the unfolding of personal histories. It is frequently through the improvised monologue —

with its repetitions, contradictions and discontinuities — that the Stendhalian hero discovers his desires. These desires emerge from individual verbal dialectics rather than from those imitations of historical models which, as we have seen, render authentic desire impossible and make parody of history. The Stendhalian narrator, with his refusal of the constraining outline or compositional model, similarly shapes the story he tells from those novelistic inspirations which he "meets" during the time of his writing. And yet, for all its improvised qualities, Stendhalian fiction never escapes from what seems to be an inexorable psychic fate. It returns over and over again to the sacrificial enactment of a fantasy of happiness in love, to what might be called the hero's dangerous superiority over a mean-spirited but all-powerful society. It is perhaps Stendhal's deference to this power, as well as his mistrust of the indescribable ecstasy which would be the end (both the goal and the disappearance) of his fiction, which explains why he can improvise a compromise between happiness and society but not a transcendence of the conflict itself. The most sublime desires in Stendhal can neither be spoken nor, finally, lived. Thus the Stendhalian narrator prudently chooses sociability as an alternative to ecstatic sensations. His heroes are not both "passionately in love" and bearers of "joy and movement" in the social milieu which they fear, or ignore, or scorn. They are indeed passionate lovers, but a much cooler narrator takes on the task of keeping up the pleasant agitations of social intercourse. He will even fill his work with details of political intrigues which he himself judges as deadly to a novel's rapturous spiritual music.[4]

The high visibility of Oedipal structures in Stendhal's fiction corresponds to a certain reluctant "maturity" in Stendhal himself. He is up to his neck in the father's interests and therefore in the so-called serious interests of social life—while he is just ironic enough about those interests to suggest that the only truly serious business in life is the ecstatic play in the garden at Vergy and in the Farnese tower. But then he is sufficiently ironic about his lovable children's play to be able to illustrate his own allegiance to the compromised and sublimated sensation by writing stories somewhat to the side of, or rather "around," sensations. While even Julien comes to yearn for the empty and timeless ecstatic moment, Stendhal "plays" in another and safer medium: he fills hundreds of pages with witty talk which simultaneously praises his heroes and betrays them. By his constant care in making distinctions, in establishing intervals of time and of significance, and in pointing to the distances created by ironic statement, Stendhal announces his willingness to play the games of "adult" thought.

By the same stroke, literature is advertised as essentially alien to love, and the father — the figure hostile to love in the Stendhalian Oedipal drama — is presented to us as a necessary presence in realistic fiction. He is in fact the representative, and perhaps the origin, of what fiction generally considers to be reality. But, as we have seen, the realistic novel pays a massive tribute to "the real" at the same time that it expresses, through its heroes, an enormous fatigue with given forms of life. Realistic fiction proudly advertises its fidelity to history: it documents the ways in which a particular time and a particular place determine the nature of human desires and the field in which they may be realized. But it can also glamorize a doomed effort to escape from history. It celebrates — and punishes — the rejection of established social formulas of "serious" desires. Nothing is more curious than the ambiguous allusion, at the center of realistic fiction, to an indescribable, almost religious experience. As we have seen in Stendhal and as we shall now see in James, a scrupulous attention to historical realities is frequently the pretext for proposing, and sacrificing, an ecstasy for which no history could give an adequate account.

CHAPTER FIVE

The Jamesian Lie

HENRY JAMES and Stendhal are our two most sociable novelists. They speak in different styles, but they share an immensely sophisticated talent for talk. And their sophistication lies mainly in a superficially limited view of what makes talk most interesting. They are exceptionally sensitive to those details of tone and appearance which carry the messages of major importance in social intercourse. They possess a high urbanity about what "signifies" most heavily in talk among men and women, and this includes considerable skepticism about the social power of philosophical or moral intensities. Their heroes and heroines *are* philosophically or morally intense, but the effect of this is almost always to remove the Jamesian or Stendhalian hero from society. Other novelists may be skeptical about the historical success of an idea or a moral passion, but for Balzac, George Eliot, Dostoevski and Tolstoy, ideas at least have an active social life; their characters respond seriously to one another's ideas, find one another interesting for their ideas. As a result, social life in these other novelists tends to be a confrontation of principles, whereas for James and Stendhal it consists in all the harmonies and frictions possible among numerous individuals' highly particular interests and desires. Both James and Stendhal are consistently ironic about the independent value of an idea — that is, about an idea presented apart from the desire which it both expresses and disguises. They are, we might say, willing to desublimate social life — to decipher the intellectual abstractions of an official social code in order to indicate the individual needs which the code's rhetoric obscures.

At the same time, James and Stendhal admit and enjoy the *play* of those needs along the surfaces of talk. Ideas by themselves are neither attractive nor powerful in conversation; the appeal of civilized speech comes from our recognizing those detours — of wit, of tone, of shifting rhythms and of ideas — which "being civilized" imposes on the expression of a desire. The greatest Jamesian and Stendhalian sophistication is to find a kind of sensual pleasure in following the ingenious evasions and indirections with which language deflects and serves insistent desires. James and Stendhal invite us to use those evasions as a source of entertainment rather than as a pretext for cynicism. Language and thought, as I've been suggesting, inevitably compromise desire, but the compromises themselves may offer us more than the meager satisfaction of seeing through them. The surfaces of our thought and our speech don't merely cover up the depths behind thought and speech. They have appeals of their own, and as we compose our sublimations we can discover pleasures distinct from those for the sake of which we perhaps "began" to sublimate. Stendhal and James are open to those appeals precisely because they are skeptical about the intrinsic or absolute value of ideas. They are inclined to "reduce" mental abstractions to the concrete interests which people have in one another, but then they also see that a certain abstract play of the mind doesn't simply reflect such interests but may inspire or re-create them. In the improvisations of a Stendhalian monologue, as well as in those of the ideal Stendhalian *salon*, the numerous local agitations along a line of thought or speech make for an entertaining display of energetic human desires. The Stendhalian hero and the Stendhalian narrator both expose and create themselves as they go along. To express the same idea in Jamesian terminology, we could say that, ideally, character would be equivalent to the elaboration of an interested version of character. Society would then be an exciting occasion for self-inventive behavior.

Given this optimistic view of how speech and thought can, in time, diversify desires and break up rigid structures of character, it's all the more striking to find in both Stendhal and James an ultimate rejection of their own sociability. What could be called the freedom *not* to be is threatened by the petrifying definitions of others, definitions from which even the most airily evasive talk can't escape. Thus we have the peculiar spectacle of the two most sociable talkers in realistic fiction giving the highest value in their work to the secret, inexpressible passions of unworldly heroes and heroines. Stendhal and James are exemplary versions of the ambiguous attitude of realistic fiction toward reality. It's perhaps more shocking to see them turn their backs on "the real" than it would be to see Balzac do the same thing. The latter's immense appetite for social conquests includes a hallucination of social life. And Balzac's hallucinated realism implies an impatience with the mass of social details and psychological nuances in which James and Stendhal seem to find an exciting reason for wishing to be realistic. We have just looked at Stendhal's accommodations with social reality, as well as at the fantasy of happiness which finally can make no place for itself in the life of society. We will now follow another version of this tension between social reality and individual fantasy in the Jamesian effort to coerce society into becoming an arena for the performance of the passionate fictions of James's heroes.

This enterprise takes the form, throughout James's career, of a struggle against a crippling notion of truth. There are, first of all, truths about character. As we have seen in the case of Racine, the availability of literary characters to psychoanalytic interpretation is frequently a sign of the insignificance of their present desires. Everything which characters say and do now can be traced back to a determining structure from the past which impoverishes present behavior by making it both tautological and excessively coherent. James's fiction is notoriously dense in what I suppose we have to call psychological detail, but it is remarkably resistant to an interest in psychological depth. This is especially true of the later fiction. While it's obvious, for example, in *The Bostonians* that Olive's politics idealize her lesbianism and that her lesbianism energizes her politics, and while it's at least possible to detect "behind" Isabel Archer's unfocused appetite for experience a terror of sex made fairly explicit in her scenes with Caspar Goodwood, the grounds for what we might think of as "vertical" motive (plunging down "into" personality) eventually disappear from James's fiction. There is no reason to believe that any "obscure" motives enter into Vanderbank's refusal to marry Nanda Brookenham in *The Awkward Age*, or that an inability to be active with women explains Strether's adventures in *The Ambassadors*, or that Maggie and her father have an "unhealthy" attachment to each other in *The Golden Bowl*. In James's late fiction, the narrative surface is never richly menaced by meanings it can't wholly contain. Complexity consists not in mutually subversive motives but rather in the expanding surface itself which, when most successful, finds a place in its intricate design for all the motives imaginable. We can easily be misled by the numerous passages where James's characters, burdened by their sense of the portentous, retreat into exclamation or expressive groans. What they renounce trying to express is generally not an intuition that would expose the ambiguity of all efforts to understand, but rather a richness of understanding which would expand the dialogue to monstrous proportions. This richness is in fact allowed to bloat the surrounding narrative in which an indirectly presented lucidity almost submerges the elliptical talk of James's characters.

Nothing could be further from Jamesian conversation than the classical *litote*. His characters' interjections and half-completed sentences are either a comment on analysis or an invitation to analysis, but they don't refer us to a surplus of meaning which any formulation would be bound at least partially to betray. Classical language (the best modern example is Gide — who complained of finding "no mystery" in James, "no secrets" — in *L'Immoraliste* and *La Porte étroite*) is spare not simply as a technique of mystification, but rather because of a recognized incompatibility between expressive possibilities or intentions and the sources of behavior. Whatever is said — we have seen this in Racine — can merely be designed to violate as gently as possible the necessarily unsaid, to "tremble" from the pressure of hidden desires. Psychological density in French classicism (and in certain Greek tragedies) lurks behind a language both ominously allusive and defensively decorous. In James, on the other hand, density is what we move toward. With time we will have all there is to have, whereas, say, in Euripides and Racine both time and language, instead of creating motive, merely postpone the explosion of motive into act. And that explosion could have taken place before the illusory action ever began: the work of art is a delayed time bomb, and an exquisite language both entertains and excoriates our suspense.

The essential difference is of course in the imagined relation between meaning and expression. In both classicism and the kind of realism which James seeks to move beyond, language is not strictly necessary to the subject of art. The self (in Racinian tragedy) and society (in realistic fiction) are either beyond or behind or prior to the work. And this fundamental premise can accommodate such superficially antagonistic manifestations as the art of the *litote*, the naturalist's exuberance at the prospect of making art a scientific copy of life, and the literature of suicidal silence as the ultimate deference to an ineffable or inexpressible "real." What James asks us to do in his later fiction is to detach the notions of reality and probability from all such external references — which is to say that he would encourage us to believe that our range of experience can be as great as our range of compositional resource. In short, compositional play need not be merely tangential to being; and, in the immense faith in time and language which this gamble implies, James works toward a richly superficial art in which hidden depths would never ironically undermine the life inspired by his own and his characters' "mere" ingenuities of design. By moving from causes to composition rather than from composition back to causes, James insists on the fact that fictional invention is neither evasive nor tautological; instead, it *constitutes the self.*

The recurrent Jamesian subject is only superficially the international theme, or the confrontation of innocence and experience, or the conflict of acquisitive and self-renouncing impulses. His subject is freedom — but we must understand that word in the sense of inventions so coercive that they resist any attempt to enrich — or reduce — them with meaning. James asserts that freedom much more confidently in his prefaces than in his fiction. His discussion of his books almost only in terms of their technical ingenuities, and his refusal "to go behind" technique to "meanings" which technique would merely serve, constitute a triumph of composition over depth which is more often an aspiration than an achievement in the novels themselves. The latter dramatize the difficulties of living by improvisation: the incompatibilities among different ways of composing life, the absence of determined values by which to discriminate morally among various compositions, the need to develop persuasive strategies capable of imposing personal ingenuities on the life of a community, and finally, the nostalgia for an enslaving truth which would rescue us from the strenuous responsibilities of inventive freedom.

"I see. I see." Apparently nothing is more stimulating, more exhilarating for James's characters than that act of recognition which they constantly and somewhat breathlessly confirm. But seeing can be dangerous as well as thrilling. James's fiction is full of visual shocks which constitute crucial turning points for his heroes and heroines. Isabel's "sense of accident" dies on the day she enters her drawing room and, in "a sudden flicker of light," sees her husband and Madame Merle in an attitude of "familiar silence"; the way they have of being together in private strikes her as "something detected." "Their relative positions" (Osmond seated, Madame Merle standing), "their absorbed mutual gaze" give Isabel her first glimpse into their intimacy. Hyacinth Robinson finds something "inexpressibly representative" — of the degree of Paul Muniment's intimacy with the Princess Casamassima and of the change in Hyacinth's own relation with her — in his vision, through the fog, of his two friends getting out of a cab, talking on the princess's doorstep, and then reentering her house. In "a wave of anxiety" during which Hyacinth "felt his heart beat insanely, ignobly," he has "a very exact revelation of the state of feeling of those who love in the rage of jealousy." And in *The Ambassadors*, Strether's recognition of Chad and Mme. de Vionnet in their boat, and their recognition of him, make for "a sharp, fantastic crisis that had popped up as if in a dream" and which has only to last for a few seconds to make Strether feel it "as quite *horrible*." Finally, "lighting up the front of the great black house with an expression that quite broke the monotony, that might almost have shocked the decency, of Portland Place," Charlotte and Amerigo offer their splendid and intimately conjoined presence to Maggie who, seeing them on the balcony from the street below, thinks again "of how the pair would be at work," of how securely and masterfully they have organized their betrayal.

Each of these scenes is interpreted as a betrayal, and the betrayal takes the form of an intimacy which excludes its witness. The violent, traumatic nature of these sights is not always immediately explicit (the language in the scene from *The Portrait of a Lady*, for example, is comparatively mild), but they haunt the consciousness of the Jamesian hero as images of a hidden and threatening truth from which, for what usually turn out to be sinister reasons, he has been excluded. James of course uses such scenes as an economical way of moving his heroes from one stage of awareness to another: a process of awareness is compressed into an instant of packed vision. But it would be foolish to pretend we can avoid "going behind" James's interest in these pictures. His preference for *this* technique of compositional compression makes us feel, inevitably, that composition profits here from some obsessive memory, a memory of glimpsed intimacy interpreted as both violent and treacherous. And it's perhaps an inability — or, for reasons we can naturally never know, an unwillingness — to recuperate from the impact of that vision which explains the exasperating avoidance of fact and direct statement in the late fiction. A dismissal of fact, as we shall see, can be liberating; but there is also a kind of playing with it in its absence which allows James's characters both to keep fact out of sight and yet to be constantly teased by it. James increases the power of traumatic scenes — or, more generally, of "truth" — by the fluttering verbal evasiveness which surrounds them. The absorption of his characters in the margins or the implications of facts makes the unmentioned facts all the more ominous. And perhaps nowhere is the violence of fact so complete as when the curiosity or terror of it precludes its actual appearance — as if the brutal nature of certain situations could best be shown by their blinding effect on the persons most determined, afraid and finally unable to see.

But if seeing can spell catastrophe for James's characters, it also satisfies a frequently cruel curiosity. The two sides of the visual coin may be distributed in different characters, but the intensity of suffering and the intensity of pleasure in the single act of seeing suggest a dialectical unity in the act beyond its division into various personae. Observation, Mitchy remarks to Mr. Longdon in *The Awkward Age*, is the "most exquisite form" of "pursuit," and the cruelty of Dr. Sloper in *Washington Square* consists in his curiosity about how far Catherine will go with Morris Townsend, in the entertainment he finds in spying on her character. Even Ralph Touchett, James curiously remarks, has "an almost savage desire" to make Isabel complain about Osmond so that he may directly see her suffering. A "psycho-critical" case, admittedly neglectful of qualifying contexts, could, I think, be made for a skeletal psychology of vision in James's work. There is a tortured identity and contrast between masochistic and sadistic "moments" in the act of seeing, between seeing as punishment submitted to and seeing as punishment inflicted. From this interpretive point of view, we might also detect a certain willfulness in the ostensibly imposed visual shock. The advantages of suffering betrayal (or of inviting it) perhaps lie in the peculiar sort of intimate detachment which betrayal creates. It gives the right to accuse, which we can use to break a relation while secretly continuing it. Thus, on the one hand, a kind of general snooping may constitute a desperate claim for independence, a means of breaking away from figures who threaten to engulf the self. But at the same time the evidence of betrayal assures the durability of superficially broken bonds within the protective and ambiguous terms of resentment — or forgiveness. In such a scheme, *The Golden Bowl* would represent this harmony between betrayal and the security of unbroken attachments: the intimacy between Charlotte and Amerigo is the beneficent treason which transforms the intimacy between Maggie and Amerigo from an illusion into a reality.

But let's reverse the interpretive direction, proceeding from this point of departure to more of the novelistic surface which I have been ignoring in my conjecture about psychological depths. In James's fiction the connection between vision and betrayal is less interesting as something to be explained than as a novelistic provocation. I call it a point of departure not because it's where he begins chronologically, but because, throughout James's career, it frequently recurs as that stroke in the design from which it's both most difficult and most imperative to "depart." Psychological explanations alone account poorly for the departure since they seek out the reasons for taking pleasure in the point of supposed origin. They tend, in other words, to denounce the psychological obscurantism of the text instead of repeating its psychological initiative. The availability of such criticism as a weapon against literature is made painfully clear by Maxwell Geismar's use of the obvious voyeurism in James to clinch his vindictive assault against James in *Henry James and the Jacobites*. But James exploits the frustrations of a recurrent pattern in order to compel his imagination to invent *other* pleasures. Thus we shall see James's characters exploiting — often unsuccessfully — the possibilities of what might be called a luminous blindness.

The basis for escape from the cruel shock of vision is a radical casting of doubt on the objects of vision. And James generalizes the question of what there is to see into a skeptical view of truth. The truth-seekers in his fiction are usually the betrayed Americans, but they are betrayed less because they are Americans than because they believe in the truth. James's criticism of this belief is of course hesitant; and the texture of his dialogues profits from his inability to shake off easily his own intellectual and moral commitment to truth. We see that commitment in the difficulty he has dissociating artfulness from evil. Expression itself in James often seems to be intrinsically suspect and, most melodramatically, it is equivalent to hypocrisy and betrayal. Throughout James's career (notable examples are *The Portrait of a Lady* and *The Wings of the Dove*) we find an almost necessary deduction of dishonesty from the art of appearances. The problem, we might say, is to find an alternative to Isabel Archer different from Madame Merle. Or, to put it another way, James has to recuperate Madame Merle morally by incorporating her into Isabel — that is, by creating a character whose intentions coincide exactly with his or her fictions.

The success of this project, which seems to me fundamental in James, involves taking enormous risks with the definiteness of novelistic plot and character. In the middle ground between victimization by fact and the triumph of fiction, there is only suspense. Being and acting are delayed and suspended as either unspecified possibility or uncontrolled conjecture. Eugenia in *The Europeans* lives the novelistically dangerous life of a character whose reality depends on the willingness of other characters to expand their own natures by inventing one for her. Of Eugenia James writes: "There were several ways of understanding her: there was what she said, and there was what she meant, and there was something between the two, that was neither." The essentially narrow honesty of Robert Acton — which, James suggests, would impress us like carrying an agreeably perfumed but occasionally inconvenient bunch of flowers — finally settles for the vulgar view that Eugenia "is a woman who will lie"; the other view would be that she is a woman incessantly open to interpretation. Eugenia's "dishonesty," as Richard Poirier has indicated in *The Comic Sense of Henry James*, is the margin she leaves for her own and for other people's absorbing possibilities. If she lied she would say the opposite of what she means, but· "between" her words and her meanings lies the *prospect* that the beneficently strenuous conjectures of another mind may offer some views of her meanings rich enough to make a relation seem appealing. With Eugenia, James dramatizes the possibility of an intentionality unsupported by motive, that is, of a desiring self so responsive and so indefinite that it is created entirely (but never limited) by the responses to its performances.

There is nothing "profound" about Eugenia, which perhaps explains the discomfort James clearly feels with her. The idea of her fibbing hides her psychological originality (her emptiness) in the unflattering but novelistically safer image of a character bent on deception. She exchanges, as it were, the moral benefit of not lying for the ontological benefit of having a character. James hesitates to deprive her entirely of the definiteness which a specific motive gives her; and his moral opinion of Eugenia reflects the uncertainty of his creative conception. As Poirier also says in the best discussion we have of the early novels, it's Felix who most conveniently distracts James from his unsettled opinions with regard to Eugenia. Easy, charming, open and honest, Felix provides a more conventional image of civilized urbanity which saves James the trouble of deciding just how far he will go in proposing a civilized artfulness both indifferent and superior to the Wentworths' moral sincerities. James thus manages to evade making Eugenia's dishonesty either completely irrelevant or completely sinister.

Eugenia is nonetheless central in the imaginative progression I'm speaking of. She suggests the possibility of identifying character with the appreciation of character; the possibility, ultimately, of both limiting and infinitely expanding reality by defining it only *as* (and not merely through) an interested version of it. James moves slowly and hesitantly toward an epistemological position implicit in his defense of the center-of-consciousness method in the preface to *The Princess Casamassima*: "What a man thinks and what he feels," James writes, "are the history and the character of what he does. . . ." by which James really dismisses the independent importance, and perhaps even the existence, of what he does: "I then see their 'doing,' that of the persons just mentioned, as, immensely, their feeling, their feeling as their doing. . . ." What we know we know through appreciation and not perception; knowledge is a kind of seeing which can dispense with the objects of vision. Thus the possible shock of seeing disappears when, having emphasized the obvious fact that to see creates a relation between the seer and the thing seen, James identifies the latter with the *activity* of the former and implicitly challenges us to locate the exact point at which appreciation or conjecture violates the truth. The problematical quality of the correspondence between our mental possessions of reality and reality itself makes the obsession with the latter an unnecessary restriction of freedom. The reality of a thing depends on the quality of the treatment it gets. There is no truth to tell, only, as James writes in the preface to *What Maisie Knew,* "truth diffused, distributed and, as it were, atmospheric."

The center-of-consciousness method could be used as a technique for the continuous deflection of dangerously energetic desires; passion is filtered through mental appreciations. Actually, it appears to serve a more complicated purpose in James. The philosophical position I outlined in the previous paragraph guarantees both the unlimited power of desire and the taming of desire. If truth is entirely subjective, a compositional product of the "feeling" consciousness, then the mind is liberated from the constraints of either internal (psychologically "deep") or external truths. The self would no longer be victimized by the shock of vision, and it would also be protected from the latent and appealing cruelty of its own appetite for seeing. An energetically ingenious intelligence composes the desires which it will offer as an adequate truth for the self and for others. But desires thus composed can never have the fractured, discontinuous quality of less intellectualized memories or fantasies of the body's multitudinous contacts with the world. In James, desire is always designed. He never gives us, as Flaubert does in *Madame Bovary,* an anthology of sensations or, more precisely, the hallucinatory images which are the mental signs of our experiencing or longing for sensations. Like Stendhal, as I suggested earlier, James is interested in desires freely improvised by intelligence. There is a mystique of bodily ecstasy in both writers (it's of course more explicit in Stendhal), but they are also both concerned with the liberation of those higher mental processes which, by nature, dilute and bind desires. The Stendhalian ideal of talk and the Jamesian ideal of consciousness express a dream of detaching instruments of sublimation (speech and thought) from the activity of repression. The best talk and the best thought would be the talk and the thought which resist interpretation. Language would no longer reveal character or refer to desires "behind" words; it would be the unfolding of an improvised and never completed psychological design. The avoidance of undeflected, unmodulated desire in both Stendhal and James is thus eminently social. It is at the highest level of civilized discourse that both novelists experiment with the disintegration of fixed definitions of being, of given structures of character.

The direct expression of passion is dangerous; are there any pitfalls in passion deflected and tamed by our improvising intelligence? For one thing, the position I have just outlined has important consequences for the social attitudes dramatized in *The Bostonians*, *The Princess Casamassima* and *The Tragic Muse*. James treats the energetic projects of revolutionaries and social reformers with the distrust he reserves for all forms of direct pursuit. And in a way parallel to his redefinition of "doing" as "feeling" in personal relationships, he deflects the perception of historical fact to the artistic, politically passive appreciation of history. But the invalidation of political activism implied by the Jamesian epistemology is perhaps *our* loss; for James himself the dangers seem to have been of another order. We see them most clearly in *The Turn of the Screw* and *The Awkward Age*. The former can certainly be read as James's least "psychological" story. It is, I think, a study in pathology, but the sickness depicted is one of pure consciousness, of a lucidity intense enough to create life from a violation of life's probabilities. This "excursion into chaos," as James calls *The Turn of the Screw* in his preface, is at the same time the novelist's experiment with the fairy tale, the governess's adventure, and the reader's confrontation with a story in which the very question of what is "true" is made irrelevant by the *consequences* of an agitated imagination. The questions of the ghosts' reality and of the governess's repressions are unanswerable simply because *The Turn of the Screw* raises no questions at all. Rather, it illustrates the power of questions (those which the governess asks Mrs. Grose and the children) to produce events by the very intensity and consistency with which they are asked. The governess is the Jamesian character idealized to the point of parable, that is, to the point where the essentially conventional distinction between character and author disappears and the character, released from the obligation of having to operate within a clearly and distinctly given world of fictional events, assumes the function of novelizing. The governess is in pursuit, but she is, quite literally, in pursuit of the story itself. There is nothing to know about in *The Turn of the Screw*, there are only conjectures to be imposed, conjectures which the governess makes catastrophically credible. We have no analysis of her psychology; we never "go behind" the children's behavior; no one authenticates the ghosts' appearance for us. We simply see — and this is the purity and the power of the story — a conviction about the ghosts strong enough to destroy the children.

The governess creates at Bly a tightly knit drama in which each of her moves contributes to the realization of her fears. Her imagination builds a structure of inexorable events perhaps more frightening than the "chaos" we imagine when the mind is no longer constrained by a secure perception of truth. Composition, as James demonstrates in *The Turn of the Screw*, isn't threatened when the mind is liberated from the superstition of truth (or the conventions of realistic fiction); but composition by itself is morally neutral. The ethic of fiction is thus menaced by this unqualified commitment to fictions. A world without truth accommodates anguish and cruelty just as easily as a world in which truth provides a basis for hypocrisy and betrayal. The most difficult Jamesian enterprise will be the search for the morality of a strictly structural coherence. Is composition, in short, amenable to moral discriminations?

The Awkward Age makes an even stronger case against the liberated imagination than does *The Turn of the Screw*. The latter gives us the melodrama of consciousness, and while it has been received as a model of mystification, both its simplicity and its originality are apparent, I think, once we stop assuming that such a story has to have a hidden subject, that there must be either real ghosts or real neuroses. *The Awkward Age* is a much more difficult work; in it the critique of appreciation and conjecture is made not through a sensational image of their power to destroy, but rather through the subtle display of a corrupting fineness of appreciation. *The Awkward Age* is about the naturally promiscuous nature of talk, about a taste for talk so cultivated and yet so uncontrolled that the passion for conversation has affected the capacity for passion. It's as if the interest of Mrs. Brook and her friends in intelligent chatter had revealed the impersonal nature of what makes talk *purely interesting.* Conversational discriminations are self-promoting, and, in its most refined and satisfyingly designed state, language entertains personality out of existence and, as it were, continues to chatter on its own steam. Nanda is the moving victim of that extremity in *The Awkward Age,* and Vanderbank provides a troubling image of a man nostalgic for distinctions more personal than verbal, but no longer able to find in himself a personal pressure which would limit and humanize his intelligence. He is nonexpressive, extraordinarily civilized, and spiritually dead. He is in fact nothing but talk, but the subject of *The Awkward Age* is talk, and the novel's perfection consists in precisely that scenic form which may at first strike us as so artificial. Or rather, its very artificiality is the novel's point. James has given us what he calls in the preface "really constructive dialogue, dialogue organic and dramatic, speaking for itself, representing and embodying substance and form." The world of *The Awkward Age* is one in which only artful dialogue exists, and its profound subject is the superficially non-Jamesian theme of a civilization destroyed by its superior entertainments, that is, by what might almost be taken for its art.

The Turn of the Screw and *The Awkward Age* dramatize the dangers to civilized life in fictions released from a shared if conventional belief about the nature of reality. To believe that certain things (like time and death) are absolutely resistant to the persuasive powers of fiction naturally provides a basis on which to make a moral hierarchy of fictions: we can at least begin to "place" them ethically by referring to those aspects of life which no fiction can violate. I think that James did go so far as to conceive even of time and death as merely our most privileged fictions (think, in addition to *The Turn of the Screw,* of *The Great Good Place, The Sense of the Past* and the essay "Is There a Life After Death?"); but a view of life as wholly obedient to a willed consciousness of life could hardly make for untroubled optimism. It's frivolous to see in James only a limitless faith in the civilizing powers of intelligence, or to think of his trust in consciousness as a naïvely hopeful dream of escape from the constraints of experience. Society and personality are more likely to be *victimized* by the autonomy of an intelligence responsive only to its own discriminatory logic.

In *The Ambassadors, The Wings of the Dove* and *The Golden Bowl*, James deals with this danger by making an ultimately illusory but crucial regression to a novelistic mode he had almost abandoned. The plots of these novels are neither shadowy nor improbable; they are simply inferior, corny plots compared with those of other realistic novelists intent, unlike James, on imposing plots as definitive versions of reality. But "what happens" in James's stories is nonetheless appropriately used to reinstate a necessary resistance of "reality" to pure consciousness, or, more exactly, of novelistic fact to the theoretically limitless capacity of the imagination to expand. Given, generally painful situations in the later fiction create relations for consciousness which limit its play and make its achievements socially and morally workable. However, James seems still tempted to minimize the importance of the resistances, although now in ways more complex than in the works just prior to the "major phase." *The Wings of the Dove*, for example, might lead us to believe that fictions can have the kind of power James wants them to have only when the world is reduced to a single, depersonalized consciousness. There is a merging of narrative perspectives in the novel which gives some point to Quentin Anderson's approach to James's work as moral allegory, although the specific references (derived from the Swedenborgian system of James's father) which Anderson brings to the novels tend to make them unrecognizable. In part, we have in *The Wings of the Dove* a social drama involving distinctly different individuals. But their distinctness is threatened by the resemblances among the various narrative blocks: all the principal centers — first Kate, then Milly and finally Densher — seem to be reenacting the moral choice of the mind from whose point of view the story is really being enacted. It's as if we had three images of the self confronted with the alternatives of the world of the lioness and the world of the dove. And when Kate has chosen the former and Milly the latter, they allegorically become their choice for the final and most crucial spiritual performance, which is of course Densher's.

How do we recognize this mutation of personality into allegorical function? First of all, the records of consciousness hover between what seem to be the characters' actual thoughts and the narrator's sensitivity to the compositional appeal of (his or their?) mental sequences. James's habit of giving us the consequences and the implications of a thought or a fact before giving us the thought or the fact itself shifts the organizing principle of the text from the temporal logic of a character engaged in the story's movement to the spatial perspective of a narrator who ignores his character's time for the sake of his own designs. And the design has inspirations of its own: we see it spilling over the character's consciousness in all those passages where the narrator tells us what his center "might have thought." Most important, the potential thought has as great a propelling force as the actual thought. In fact, the distinction between the potential and the actual is superficial, and the narrative hunger for meanings in *The Wings of the Dove* produces plot; speculation is not simply about events but also promotes them.

This displacement of dramatic pressure from novelistic event to the verbal surfaces of narrative does seem to mark the success of what I spoke of a few pages back as the freely improvising intelligence. But we can see the ambiguity of this triumph if we look more closely at Densher's relation to Milly, and James's attitude toward that relation. The sophistry in which Densher must strenuously indulge in order to justify his continuing to deceive Milly could strike us as exemplary proof of the Jamesian moral sense gone awry. James, whose center-of-consciousness method leaves an ample margin for ironic comment, is strikingly tolerant of Densher's self-righteous conclusion that he's behaving decently toward Milly simply by remaining perfectly still and refusing to lie with his lips (a strategy which serves Kate's plans beautifully). But, more interestingly, the tortuous moral arguments by which Densher tries to justify his failure to act dramatize an awkward transition from a novel of social relationships to an allegory of spiritual appreciations. The importance of Milly as a possibility *internal* to Densher makes James underplay the murderous implications of his hero's treatment of her as a distinct human being. Densher's flabby reasoning allows him to move from one spiritual allegiance to another without ever disturbing the perfect stillness of his being. Indeed, the very sequence of events in the novel, especially in the last books, seems to be determined by the development of Densher's surrender to the dovelike in human nature. Everyone "lets him off": Lord Mark by delivering the fatal blow to Milly, Sir Luke (who understands that Densher "had meant awfully well"), Milly, and James himself. As a result, Milly's success in redeeming Densher is partly undermined by something unconvincing in his betrayal of her. It's as if Densher's prolonged deception of Milly were nothing more than the time-filling pretext which allows his appreciation of her to mature. We are to believe that the deception kills her, but her death seems hardly to matter when she has been treated for so long merely as an appeal of consciousness.

The record of Densher's anguished shift of allegiance from Kate to Milly is one of the most moving sections in all James's writing, but we are partly moved, I think, by the creative dilemma of the center behind the center. Having made such a powerful representation of conflict in life, the Jamesian narrator underplays the tragic outcome of the conflict by inviting us to consider it not as a consequence of cruelty but rather as the ultimate novelistic convenience which rids us of Milly as a character and transforms the greedy pursuit of her fortune into the voracious desire to be identified with her spirit. But she has really disappeared before she dies, disappeared, that is, into the Palazzo Leporelli of Densher's spirit. And Densher's spirit has in turn been merged into a perspective from which the move from Lancaster Gate to the Palazzo Leporelli involves nothing more than a private change of spiritual climate. Densher's paroxysm of moral scruples therefore affects us as the creative strategy meant to veil the fact that we are no longer in the kind of novelistic world where such scruples would be relevant. In this novel in which social truth is essentially social brutality, James allows Densher, finally, to die to the world as completely as Milly has died. The image of Densher alone in his rooms with his conjectures of the "turn" Milly might have given to the letter which he has given to Kate (without reading it himself) is perhaps James's most powerful image of consciousness, once again, triumphantly and eerily self-sufficient.

Consciousness in James can use its fictions to overcome resistances and actually change relations in life only when it acts on a crucial distinction between criticism and art. It could be said that criticism implies a certain suspicion of art; it watches that performance of life which is art and attacks its finality and its peculiarity by absorbing it into an interpretive argument. And critical interpretation is intrinsically generalizing and depersonalizing; art as it exists *in* criticism, as Santayana suggested, "belongs" to the community rather than to the individual — it has gained in significance and lost in particularity. At the extreme, criticism is an exercise which needs no personal desire to sustain it; its ultimate logic is to be a kind of laborious babble, an organized form of play in which the critic renounces the performance of *his* desires in order to recapitulate the activity of a mind he must finally recognize as inaccessible. Criticism may even strike us as being between personalities, and in that unidentifiable "position" it can discover the somewhat sickening richness of disinterested conjecture. A contemporary tendency to speak of a "silence" as the origin of literature, or of the incessant murmur of an impersonal language, is accompanied, significantly, by an unprecedented prominence of critical writing and an equally unprecedented aspiration in literature itself toward the suicidal inclusion of its own criticism, toward the replacement of a personal voice by a voice which seeks to compose conjectures about what it *might* express. The menace of criticism, in short, proceeds from its very freedom of appreciation. If it liberalizes art by "respeaking" it in a less insistent, more abstract language, it also proposes a passionless indulgence in the possibilities of design. If style in art itself is, to some extent, already a more or less abstract transposition of particular ways of distributing bodily intensities, criticism is twice-removed from those intensities and indeed (as we see in the writing of Maurice Blanchot) moves toward the erasure of style itself.

James's prefaces are a résumé of the history of criticism's inevitable violations of art; they celebrate the privilege of an expression not expressive of a self. But in his novels James tests the viability of this critical freedom for the representation of life in art. And in *The Turn of the Screw* he gives us the nightmare of criticism; in *The Awkward Age*, a society appreciating itself, we might say, out of its capacity to subordinate smart talk to personal desires; and in *The Wings of the Dove*, a drama of blurred identities in which the real hero is a narrator-center responsible to other people only in his appreciations. The community of consciousness achieved in *The Wings of the Dove* is an impressive warning of the very dangers to community in the critically minded Densher's "reading" of the "text" of Milly. He literally makes her his own, destroying the real peculiarity of her presence which we feel early in the work. Densher illustrates how a language of appreciation runs the risk of generalizing the particular too successfully, thereby eliminating the unassimilable differences among individuals without which community extends no further than the reaches of one man's ingenuities.

Thus James's work dramatizes a rather bleak view of the autonomous intelligence. He manages, in works as different as *The Turn of the Screw* and *The Wings of the Dove*, to propose a language responsive almost exclusively to the inspirations of its own surfaces. The mind of the Jamesian center of consciousness is free in the sense that it invents and satisfies desires which meet only a minimal resistance from either the external world or internal depths. Language would no longer be principally a reflection or sublimation of given desires; it would promote new versions of being. But this very freedom from external and internal constraints depersonalizes and, in a sense, re-enslaves consciousness in James. Nothing impedes the play of the Jamesian "I" — but the "I" itself has become merely the neutral territory occupied by language, that is, by a system which is by nature always "outside" any particular self. The autonomous consciousness no longer thinks or desires; it is thought or desired *through*. Intelligence detached from psychology traces designs that belong to no one. The notion of human character, as I've been arguing in this book, limits the imagination of desire; but, as we see in James, the absorption of character into language can also be the dehumanization of desire.

But James finally submits the critical or speculative intelligence to a critique provided by what might be called the superior finality of art. *The Golden Bowl* affirms the triumph of fictional composition over a powerfully resistant reality, but Maggie Verver's fictions have the irresistibly coercive strength of an art which uncompromisingly rejects any attempt to tamper with its forms. She lacks that vulnerability to appreciation which makes Mme. de Vionnet in *The Ambassadors* extraordinarily but somehow imperfectly artful. (Mme. de Vionnet is finally willing to believe, with Strether, that her magnificent forms *are* deceptions; she would have liked to "be" as sublime as he has imagined her to be.) In *The Golden Bowl*, we see the action of art from the point of view of the artist. James now shifts from dramatizing a critical appreciation of art to representing directly an artistic manipulation of life's materials. And the deceptions which throughout James's fiction have allowed him to consider the idea of discrediting art are now offered as art's moral justification. Maggie is a fusion of Isabel Archer and of Madame Merle, an extraordinary fusion in which personal nobility is confirmed by a willingness to lie which makes Madame Merle's duplicity seem tamely scrupulous. In *The Golden Bowl*, James proposes a kind of sincerity absolutely divorced from truth; the fictions which Maggie rather ruthlessly imposes on everyone else in the novel leave no room for truth — they create reality instead of hiding it. She brings Eugenia of *The Europeans* to the fruition of a definite and major lie; but the lie itself leaves an even greater margin for other people's freedom than Eugenia's elaborately evasive manners. At the same time Maggie's own freedom to compose reality, unlike the governess's freedom in *The Turn of the Screw*, is disciplined by what she suffers as a result of her early efforts at composition. Reality in *The Golden Bowl* consists in the novelistic arrangements of the first half; the second half gives us the correction, the unashamed, radical revision which Maggie then makes of her own work and which James, speaking in the preface to *The Golden Bowl* of his own revisions for the New York edition of his novels, defines and defends as "re-perusal, registered," as "the particular vision of the matter itself that experience had at last made the only possible one."

We couldn't hope for a more exact summation of *The Golden Bowl*. In it human relations are seen entirely in terms of their compositional appeal. The only drama in the novel is the conflict between Amerigo's and Charlotte's defective reading of the Ververs' composition in the first half, and Maggie's successful resistance to their interpretation in the second half. As James says of himself in the preface, Maggie doesn't consider for a moment the possibility of "re-writing"; she simply "registers" the "re-perusal" of her work made imperative by the adultery which has, with some appearance of coherent appreciation, been inferred from her work. We accept the prestigious morality of Maggie's insisting on "not, by a hair's breadth, deflecting into the truth" because the only status given to the truth she denies is that of a compositional invitation which she has merely to withdraw. It's not that the facts which Maggie defeats are obscure; indeed, Maggie's success — and the success of *The Golden Bowl* — depends on a complete lack of ambiguity about how the Ververs' ingenious arrangements for keeping everyone happy have been exploited by Charlotte and the Prince. The latter engage in a strenuous "interpretation of signs" which leads them to conclude that Maggie and her father don't want their marriages to interfere with the intimacy between the parent and the child; and Charlotte and Amerigo might also be thought of as "helping" them to stay close by becoming intimate themselves. We know what's going on in *The Golden Bowl*, which is not the case in *The Turn of the Screw*, where the only clear events are those willed or at least imagined by the governess. Furthermore, there is no convenient death, as in *The Wings of the Dove*, to dissipate antagonisms in an allegory of posthumous reconciliations. Betrayal does take place in *The Golden Bowl*, and it causes great suffering. But what James suggests is that this reality — so ominously final elsewhere in his work — is not a fact prior to artfulness but, like all human activities, is rather a possible development of some artful design and can be replaced by other possible developments. This is the profound justification of James's refusal "to go behind": because experience is never without design, it's impossible to locate an original design, that is, an absolute fact or motive which could not itself be recomposed, whose nature would not be changed by changes in its relations.

In a sense, it's irrelevant in *The Golden Bowl* that Amerigo and Charlotte were in love before the story began. Their past is a concession on James's part to an order of psychological probability which the novel in fact dismisses; what's important is that they make love as a result of the arrangements contrived during the time of the novel itself. It's as if the geometry of human relations *implied* what we call human feelings into existence. The feelings are real enough, but they are, so to speak, the elaborations of surfaces — they have no depth. Conflict in James means the conflicting implications of designs; to revise life may be agonizing, but revision can remain strictly superficial. And what we may find lacking in James is the reconciliation of this compositional view of experience with a sense of depth — a reconciliation attempted by Proust, who manages to account for the unconscious not as a formless source of designs but as a kind of persistent compositional "theme" recognizable in all our compositional variations. It's therefore more difficult for James to imagine how some relations can be harder to avoid than others. He can, as we have seen, imagine the freedom of consciousness as unlimited. But when he imagines resistances to the free imagination, the resistances either take on the prestige of an implacable reality which destroys his characters' taste for life (as with Isabel and, I think, Strether) or they are overcome (as in *The Golden Bowl*) by strategies which depend on certain religious assumptions for their power.

There *is* a religion of art, overworked as the expression may be, and *The Golden Bowl* defines it very precisely: it assumes that the observation of forms is sufficient to produce a conversion of being. Charlotte and Amerigo are rather complacently considered (by Adam Verver, by Maggie, and by James) as fine pieces in an art collection. The characters in *The Golden Bowl* constitute a human museum, and conflict derives from competing views of how the different pieces of this rare collection should be "placed." It's up to Maggie to keep them at the right distances from one another, and her activity resembles the novelist's resistance, which James speaks of in the prefaces, to the tendency of his material to get out of hand and defeat his structural intentions. The material, as it were, begins to collaborate too intimately in the design; it menaces the work by being too appreciative of the work's possibilities. It's as if the creative critic were lurking within the work itself; indeed, his presence is figured in *The Golden Bowl* by Charlotte and the Prince, and by Fanny Assingham. The extraordinary section at the end of the first part in which Fanny figures out what will happen in the second part is a kind of critique *in medias res* in which the dependence of novelistic plot on critical speculation is introduced as a literal possibility within the novel itself. Fanny is James's clearest image of an interpretive promiscuity at work in art itself long before the critics submit art to *their* interpretations. Because the second half of the novel seems almost forced into being by the logic of her appreciations, Fanny appears to suggest a legitimate subordination of art to criticism. By letting us see how his intelligent *ficelle* pulls the strings of his own imagination, James would almost appear to be suggesting that critical argument creates the reality of art, that a critic's hypotheses are responsible to nothing more than their own developmental logic.

But Maggie prevents this possibility by her happily narrow insistences, by the self-sacrificial cruelty which makes her both the artist and the savior of *The Golden Bowl*. Fanny, like the adulterous lovers, has to be checked. She is willing to see everything (she even imagines an entirely different novel, one in which she would have been in love with the Prince herself) and just as willing to take nothing seriously (if she breaks the bowl, adultery ceases to exist, as if Charlotte and the Prince existed only in Fanny's mind). Maggie's speculative entertainments, on the other hand, have a very different kind of insignificance. The major difference between *The Wings of the Dove* and *The Golden Bowl* is that plot is *not* resolved by appreciative speculation in *The Golden Bowl*. Maggie is constantly imagining what people might have said or thought, but, interestingly enough, these conjectures are generally set apart from the "real" text in quotation marks, like a warning to the text not to let itself be seduced by its own suggestiveness. Maggie's speculations really produce nothing; they are simply a way of filling time while she, as we shall see in a moment, is standing outside of time. She does absolutely nothing but wait for the single fiction she promotes — that of her own and her father's happy marriages — to stifle every other way of living the story. Her art includes discriminations but it doesn't depend on them; indeed, it seems to depend on her stubbornly presenting again and again her original design. The novel — both in its events and in the style which relates them — is constantly entertaining implications and deductions (often within an extravagant metaphorical logic), but Maggie's purpose checks James's apparent complicity with the body of his work. Intelligence fills *The Golden Bowl*, but its moral value is made extremely ambiguous by the fact that Charlotte and the Prince deduce their love affair from an ingenious but authentically intelligent view of their situation. Maggie, so to speak, pays no attention to their "argument"; she receives it without accepting it. Instead of entering into a critical relationship with their logically defensible understanding of what she has intended, she defeats that understanding with the interrogative stillness of a finished work of art.

Maggie lies, and waits to see what time will do. She has the "eternity" of great art, that is, the historical persistence of objects about which nothing final can ever be said, around which conjectures multiply, compete and usually disappear. Of course, something does happen to the work of art in time, whether it be the time of the artist's creation, or of his revisions or of the revisions of criticism. The very strength of the design depends on a certain loss or erosion of some of its values; in his prefaces, James movingly evokes those sacrifices of profit which Laurence Holland, in *The Expense of Vision*, has impressively shown to be part of the enacted drama of

James's fiction. The lost profit in *The Golden Bowl* on which the triumph of the original design depends is the relation between Maggie and her father. The Ververs' departure for America is the consequence of that critical lucidity which, during the time of this composition, has discovered the contradictions and the dangers of a too-ambitious design.

But the profit gained from this loss testifies to a power in the design greater than any weakness. The coerced freedom which Maggie gives to Amerigo, analogous to the freedom which art offers to criticism, consecrates a marriage in which there is finally nothing to say or to know. Her patience requires that his appreciation of her mature to the point where his interest in interpretation will have died. The adulterous lovers' ingenious use of Maggie as a "compositional resource" yields to the pressure of the decorous fiction that she *is* a wife, that is, a "value intrinsic." (James uses these expressions to describe her in his preface to *The Golden Bowl*.) That surrender of interest in the name of a more complete surrender is of course the love for which Maggie tells Fanny Assingham that she can bear anything. And when Maggie's forms have survived every possible interpretation of them, Amerigo intimately identifies himself with her self-confident art, thus ending her performance by his unqualified participation in it.

It's here, however, that we can see the ambiguity of the passion which sustains Maggie's fictions. On the one hand, Maggie is "heroically improvising" for the sake of certain given social forms — especially, her own and her father's marriages. Maggie's strategic stillness seems designed to bring errant desires back into strict conformity with the official roles assigned to them. Indeed, Charlotte and the Prince seem tempted to blackmail Maggie into leaving them alone by appealing to her immense respect for social appearances. As a kind of warning when he first realizes that she may be on to something, the Prince manages to give his wife a "conscious reminder" of "a life tremendously ordered and fixed" which her suspicions may threaten. And at Fawns, the Ververs' country house, Maggie herself sees that she can people the family scene, "by the press of her spring, either with serenities and dignities and decencies, or with terrors and shames and ruins." Having chosen to maintain "all this high decorum," Maggie is all the more responsive to the message Charlotte subtly makes her take as they walk along the terrace at Fawns, admiring "the very look the place had of being vivid in its stillness, of having, with all its great objects as ordered and balanced as for a formal reception, been appointed for some high transaction, some real affair of state."

This sense of public responsibility seems intimately connected with the fact of marriage in *The Golden Bowl*. The Ververs' spouses bring the world into their lives, although the father and daughter continue for a while with the illusion that marriage doesn't have to change their habits, that they can continue to live in the protected and secluded community of happy intimacy between parent and child. Adultery educates Maggie into being a wife more than a daughter; to use the crude economic terminology we find so often in James, we could say that Maggie has to pay with her father in order to buy her husband. And as she affirms her marriage, she also appears to accept more of a social role for herself. *The Golden Bowl* thus seems to support a conventional view of marriage as the responsible public representation of love. Doesn't Maggie work for social representation? She separates the father from the daughter and the adulterous lovers from each other, and — so it would seem — the two married couples are now properly placed for enacting those "high transactions" of adult life in society.

But the interest of *The Golden Bowl* is that things are by no means that emblematically simple. At the end of the novel, the duties of public representation appear to be entirely relegated to Adam and Charlotte, and the fact that their marriage will be only that is underlined by the fact that they will have to practice their high social transactions in America. Ironically, Charlotte is *exiled* into a social role; she takes on the full-time job of "representing the arts and the graces to a people languishing, far off [somewhere west of the Mississippi . . .] in ignorance." The forms and duties of marriage are thus left to the couple whose marriage is without passion. Maggie and the Prince remain in Europe, but are we meant to imagine a high public visibility for their marriage from now on? The willingness of English society to accommodate its Lady Castledean and her Mr. Blint makes a mockery of the very forms which Maggie seems so determined to preserve. The society we see in *The Golden Bowl* is indifferent to marriage beyond the terms proposed to Maggie by Charlotte and the Prince, terms which Maggie unhesitatingly rejects. That is, society considers the observation of certain minor forms to be sufficient to protect the major form of marriage itself. *The Golden Bowl*, contrary to what may be our first impression, asserts the hopeless incompatibility between society and passion. There's not, it's true, a single critical word in the novel regarding "a life tremendously ordered and fixed." But Maggie saves an "order" which seems to be totally irrelevant to her passion. She makes Amerigo come back to her without sacrificing anyone's social respectability, but she draws Amerigo *out* of society in order to absorb him in the great social form of marriage.

This, however, is of course equivalent to saying that the social aspect itself of marriage is irrelevant. Indeed the forms so dutifully preserved in *The Golden Bowl* are, I think, merely the convenient social envelope for desires imagined as too original to be contained or expressed by any established forms of social life. Maggie reflects that while Amerigo has a "place" in the world made for him by "historical" facts, a place "made by ancestors, examples, traditions, habits," she has only an "improvised 'post,' " one that "would have been sought in vain in the most rudimentary map of the social relations as such. The only geography marking it would be doubtless that of the fundamental passions." Maggie's artfulness consists in her finally being able to remove the Prince from history. Her art can therefore find no place in the consciousness of a collector of art. It is, in short, an art incapable of being represented. Maggie and Amerigo stay in Europe, the origin and repository of representation in art. But their love removes them from culture and society as definitively as "happiness" separates the Stendhalian hero from life in society. As part of the very energy of their social representations, Stendhal and James thus designate privileged, nonrepresentable areas where their heroes transcend, or die to, the novels which seem to exist so that these heroes may escape from them.

The Prince's conversion in *The Golden Bowl*, like Densher's in *The Wings of the Dove*, depends on his recognition of a sacrifice so lovingly and so tyrannically devoid of specific claims that in order to accept it he must imitate it. By appearing to ask for absolutely nothing in return for their stupendous gifts, Milly and Maggie make partial reimbursements impossible. As the Prince guesses even before his marriage, he will have to pay for Maggie's love and for the Ververs' millions with his being. We of course recognize the profound Christian bias in this notion of a generosity which can be acknowledged only by a reenactment of the generous life. The freedom which Milly and Maggie give to Densher and to Amerigo has a beauty as terrifying as the spiritual luxury given to men by Christ's repudiation of the law's constraints. The convenience of the world's laws is that they allow us to fabricate a self (and its relations) from our concessions and resistances to moral or material necessity. But a gift of total freedom — in James, the gift of mildness and money from his heroines — perhaps creates no terms for a relation except those of betrayal or emulation. The conquering passivity of Milly and of Maggie, their passion of sacrificial love, doesn't make any provision for the dialogue which inevitably compromises intimacy: Densher is never closer to Milly than when he can no longer speak to her, when, after her death, he trains himself in the quality of her spirit by trying to write the letter he will never see.

Milly's death, like Christ's crucifixion, announces the spectacular power of an embodied fiction celebrating human love, but it does so at the very moment when the body of love is removed from the world of human forms. *The Golden Bowl*, unlike *The Wings of the Dove*, succeeds in eliminating the crucificial aspect from the *imitatio christi*. The success, however, depends on what might be called the novel's strained unity of composition. Its plot, it's true, does not submit to the pressures of narrative speculation (as do elements of plot in *The Wings of the Dove*), but the conflicts among characters in *The Golden Bowl* are minimized by the excessive analogies they present with James's relation to his material. What we must perhaps finally see as the necessary defect of James's compositional ethic is the very coherence and unity into which those analogies between his fictional world and the process of creating it allow him to organize life. Conflict can be resolved in *The Golden Bowl* because of the *derivation* of conflict from the design which it threatens. The novel's theological bias is profoundly connected to James's imagination of life as a product of art: the "work" of the Ververs' marriages, like human history divinely inspired and controlled, returns to the original plan of a single creator. The accidental, the inessential, and the incoherent are eliminated, and the "story" of human life finally appears secondary to the inspiration at its source. If human sin is nothing but a flaw introduced into the Creator's design, history itself, because it can never escape the logic of that design, may finally assent to stop being history and simply reenact in "eternity" the passion of the design. And if that hope is a sustaining fiction of religion, it is also, as James shows us, the truth of an artistic passion so intense that it works, most deeply, to destroy the very manifestations, the history, the text of its designs.

Maggie triumphs in *The Golden Bowl* because she has James's faith that her work will come back to her; it *depends* on her. The most intimate movement in the creation of her design is beyond its display, and it is pointed to when Amerigo, no longer the fine crystal, the *objet d'art* around which Maggie and her father can walk admiringly, participates in the *work* of art. He renounces the observation of forms in order to embrace them passionately. But *The Golden Bowl* has, of course, been all display, and the comparatively simple but poignant sacrifice of the work itself is the condition of Amerigo's redemption, of the sexual union introduced in the novel's conclusion. James's work is sustained by the hope, finally realized in the last lines of *The Golden Bowl,* that the novel itself can be discarded. Perhaps only then is fiction invulnerable to the interpretations of criticism, for it has made a definitive retreat from the interpretive medium in which art is realized. The reward of that retreat, as Amerigo says, is that there is no longer anything to see beyond a love which the heavily appreciative text of *The Golden Bowl* has naturally been unable to express directly. Thus we see the inescapable ambiguity of a fiction so utterly released from the comfortable superstition of truth. The strength of James's uncompromising ethic of fiction finally requires a renunciation of that faculty to see (to criticize and to subvert) which, after all, protects us — and not simply in relation to art — from the tyranny of any community united in its assent to a single, insistent passion.

CHAPTER SIX

Lawrentian Stillness

MATTER MOVES; the spirit is still.

In D. H. Lawrence, we have once again the opposition between agitation and stillness which we have found in novels by Jane Austen, Hawthorne, James and Proust. And in Lawrence, as in these other writers, it would seem that movement and agitation are on the side of psychological and social evil, and that only a kind of psychic immobility can successfully maintain or create stability in the self and in society. But, unlike what we have seen in *Mansfield Park*, *La Peau de chagrin* and *The Blithedale Romance*, Lawrentian stillness is not a strategy for preserving given structures from the disruptive effects of desire. The given structures of personality and of society are, for Lawrence, either false or rotten; we can only discard them. The Lawrentian hero never cultivates stillness in order to protect history. He is closer to Milly Theale than to Fanny Price. By remaining quiet, Fanny keeps various orders in place: the social order represented by Mansfield Park, the psychological and moral order of the self, and the esthetic order of Jane Austen's novel. The stillness of James's heroine, on the other hand, is a means of escape. In her dovelike passivity, Milly transcends the worldliness of Lancaster Gate *and* the novelistic document which is, finally, inadequate to her spirit. Lawrence's heroes frequently argue verbosely for quietness; but their talk is of course not to be confused with the state of stillness itself, and the latter is fundamentally incommensurable with all the dialogue apparently necessary to convince us of the insignificance of dialogue itself.

Neither society nor language provides any models for the Lawrentian goal of an integrity of being. Jane Austen still enjoys the luxury of historical references for what she calls a life of "principle"; but Lawrence, like James in his later work, takes on the burden of exalting a spiritual integrity which is *represented* nowhere in the world. But, unlike James in *The Wings of the Dove*, Lawrence refuses to exile (and to protect) his ideal from life itself. He submits fiction to the pressure of his insistence that regenerated being can be realistically portrayed. Nowhere is the pressure exerted more poignantly and perhaps more successfully than in *Women in Love*, and we can use this novel as our final test of the representability of nondesiring stillness in realistic fiction.

The Lawrentian opposition between agitation and stillness has almost the diagrammatic neatness of the Cartesian dualism between matter and mind. In *Women in Love*, a dehumanized life is identified with a mechanical life, and the mechanical is associated with "infinitely repeated motion." Like Descartes, Gerald Crich dreams of the conquest of matter by mind. But for Descartes, the conquest is made possible by intellectual procedures which systematize the mind's unique capacity for knowledge (and therefore illustrate the intrinsic opposition between mind and matter). Gerald, the industrial magnate, begins with a kind of militant Cartesian sense of mankind as "mystically contradistinguished against inanimate Matter," but his conquest of matter (specifically, his struggle "with the earth and the coal it enclosed") depends on his *imitating* certain qualities of matter. Man subjugates nature through his will, but will in Lawrence is the inhuman principle of the mind, and in constructing machines which embody his will, Gerald makes himself like matter in order to subdue it:

There were two opposites, his will and the resistant Matter of the earth. And between these he could establish the very expression of his will, the incarnation of his power, a great and perfect machine, a system, an activity of pure order, pure mechanical repetition, repetition ad infinitum, hence eternal and infinite. He found his eternal and his infinite in the pure machine-principle of perfect co-ordination into one pure, complex, infinitely repeated motion, like the spinning of a wheel; but a productive spinning, as the revolving of the universe may be called a productive spinning, a productive repetition through eternity, to infinity.

"Infinitely repeated motion" is the fundamental property — at once terrifying and desirable — of the nonhuman universe. It is terrifying because any repeated motion — from a particular compulsive ritual to the "productive spinning" of the universe itself — can, by its very nature, never be penetrated by consciousness. Pure, undifferentiated repetition is always (even when it lasts only a short time) intrinsically infinite, eternal and nonhuman.[1] We can imagine the *end* (the temporal finitude) of a series only when we can perceive differences among units of the series. The perception of differences acts for us as a guarantee of both renewal and death: to be aware of difference, in mental and physical phenomena, is to know that life exists, that is, that things appear and disappear, that there are birth and death. Even the difference between two logical propositions, or two rocks, or two rays of light can operate as an epistemologically useful metaphor for the organic processes which make of life continual change.

Nothing is more timeless than mechanical time; a clock endlessly repeats, at precisely identical intervals, the sound by which it marks what we call the passage of time but which we *hear* as the repetition of changeless intervals. In *Women in Love*, it is appropriate that Gudrun — a creature, like Gerald, of mechanical will — should express her terror of repetition in terms of the monotonous movements of a clock. Life with Gerald would be "the terrible bondage of this tick-tack of time, this twitching of the hands of the clock, this eternal repetition of hours and days"; and even in Gerald's love she finds "the same ticking, the same twitching across the dial, a horrible mechanical twitching forward over the face of the hours." All life, for Gudrun, resolves itself into a tick-tack from which there is no escape. For pure repetition can't even be thought about; it can only be borne. The clock in Gudrun's parlor has "a ruddy, round, slant-eyed, joyous-painted face" inserted in its dial; with the ticks of the clock, the face wags back and forth "with the most ridiculous ogle," giving to Gudrun (overcome by a "maddened disgust") "an obtrusive 'glad-eye' " at each movement. The image marvelously expresses a sense of helplessness in the face of mechanical repetition. A relentless, nonhuman movement is hallucinated into a kind of conniving and obscene mockery of the entrapped mind. Gudrun's horror is her intuition that one's primary experience of life may be merely one of indefinite repetition; it is the horror of a metaphysical rather than an anecdotal boredom.

But there is also something desirable in "infinitely repeated motion." It is Loerke, the industrial artist, who preaches most explicitly in the novel what almost amounts to a religion of continuous motion. The granite frieze he is doing for a granite factory in Cologne is "a representation of a fair, with peasants and artisans in an orgy of enjoyment," in "a frenzy of chaotic motion." Man at the fair, he tells Ursula and Gudrun, "is fulfilling the counterpart of labour — the machine works him instead of he the machine. He enjoys the mechanical motion in his own body." And when Gudrun asks him if there is "nothing but work — mechanical work," he answers: "No, it is nothing but this, serving a machine, or enjoying the motion of a machine — motion, that is all. You have never worked for hunger, or you would know what god governs us." The appeal of repeated motion is identical with its horror: it lies in the illusion of being an immortal machine, or inorganic matter, rather than a mortal human being. The maddening tick-tack of the clock can suddenly become a principle of liberation. The beauty of a machine is that its nature is perfectly fulfilled by its movements; it exists only within its own operations. What Lawrence calls the will is that human faculty by which we manage to function without interruption, to continue "moving" as if we had severed all connections with our own disruptive desires and anxieties as well as those of other people. "To work for hunger" is indeed an excellent apprenticeship in the skill of mechanical being, for in extreme material need the preservation of life itself depends on our ability to go on repeating the deathlike motions of a continuously efficient machine. One can stop a machine, but one can't distract it; it has no connections beyond its own system of organized motions. And for human beings, will is what allows us to continue as if nothing were happening to us apart from the process of continuing.

The perfection of Loerke's nature is precisely this inability to be distracted from his work (his operations, or functioning). And he can be "a pure, unconnected will, stoical and momentaneous" because "in the last issue he cared about nothing, he was troubled about nothing, he made not the slightest attempt to be at one with anything." Gudrun's shift of loyalty from Gerald to Loerke is a choice *against* relations, in favor of unconnected singleness.[2] She will now live perhaps entirely in the world of the tick-tack. And, as Lawrence suggests, in a world of infinite, eternal motion, the only *possibility* is death. We can see the logic of this truth in both Gerald and Gudrun. Gerald exalts the will and the machine in order to flee from the organic death which terrifies him. And in a sense, as I've suggested, "infinitely repeated motion" is indeed a form of immortality; the repetition of the same is not a process of organic matter. But since the body changes even if the mind has committed itself to what Lawrence calls indestructible matter, death is the one thing that can happen to someone committed only to "repeating himself." Gerald's life is, most profoundly, a chase after death, and Lawrence says of Gudrun at the end of the novel that "the lovely, iridescent, indefinite charm" which she finds in the notion of pure possibility ("Anything might come to pass on the morrow") is equivalent to the charm of "pure illusion. All possibility — because death was inevitable, and *nothing* was possible but death."

This rejection of life gives the illusion of immortality and of infinite possibility. But the triumph of will is essentially the triumph of the impulse to die. Death is the only interesting event — the only event to look forward to — in a life of perfectly regulated repetitions designed to save the self from unexpected changes and connections. "Infinitely repeated motion" is thus curiously linked to the end of all movement. Repetition, as Freud suggests in *Beyond the Pleasure Principle*, is the activity which brings together the pleasure principle and the death instinct. If pleasure results from the reduction of tension due to stimuli, the ultimate pleasure is the elimination of all stimuli, and the wish to die is a fantasy of ecstatic inertia. In order to conserve itself, the organism chooses to repeat rather than to change; repetition is the movement which is meant to save us from all movement. Repetition, in a deeply paradoxical way, is the *activity of inertia*. Doomed to live, we can express our urge to "return" to the peace of inanimate matter only by maintaining the tension of constantly performing identical movements.

Motion serves death; and Birkin, Lawrence's spokesman in

Women in Love, tries to teach and live the difficult lesson of a life-preserving stillness. The critique of repeated motion extends to all kinds of activity. It is perhaps most interesting — and most surprising — when it is made with respect to sexual activity. Ursula's need for agitation in love brings a discordant note into her relation with Birkin, even at moments when they seem most harmoniously at one with each other. "She wished he were passionate," Lawrence writes of Ursula in the chapter called "Excurse," "because in passion she was at home. But this [the "new heaven" of Birkin's eyes "beautiful and soft and immune from stress or excitement"] was so still and frail, as space is more frightening than force." Within sex, there is good sex and bad sex, and — in striking conformity to the argument we've been following — the best Lawrentian sex seems to involve the least movement. Or, more exactly, the villain in sex is frictional movement. Before making love with Mellors, Lady Chatterley would get her satisfaction in sex by working herself up and down on Mick's penis after he had had his orgasm. Not only was this sex frictional, but the friction, so to speak, went on twice as long as "necessary" because Connie would begin her sex when Mick had finished his. With Mellors, Connie gets beyond the sharp pleasures of rubbing and rubbed skin; he initiates her into a kind of rippling, liquefying orgasm, into an "unspeakable motion that was not really motion, but pure deepening whirlpools of sensation swirling deeper and deeper through all her tissue and consciousness, till she was one perfect concentric fluid of feeling. . . ." In the same way, Cipriano educates Kate, in *The Plumed Serpent,* out of her need for "the white ecstasy of frictional satisfaction, the throes of Aphrodite of the foam." He brings her "to the new, soft, heavy, hot flow, when she was like a fountain gushing noiseless and with urgent softness from the volcanic deeps."

There is frictional sex, and there is frictional thought. In *The Plumed Serpent,* Lawrence describes the pleasure of the former as "one final spasm of white ecstasy which was like sheer knowing." With Loerke, Gudrun enjoys a kind of frictional knowledge, "the last subtle activities of analysis and breaking down." Gerald is for Gudrun "the most crucial instance of the existing world," and when she has all but murdered him, she is finished with life and with the world, and there is only what Lawrence calls "the inner, individual darkness, sensation within the ego, the obscene religious mystery of ultimate reduction, the mystic frictional activities of diabolic·reducing down, disintegrating the vital organic body of life." Reductive analysis is the mental equivalent of frictional sex. In the same way that the ecstasy of frictional sex results from the repetition of distinct thrusting motions, "the subtle thrills" of reductive knowledge come from a kind of rubbing of experience until it breaks down into a series of distinct units. Reduction is the intellectual screwing of life through repetition and relentlessly regular thrusts of analytical understanding.

The "love" beyond love to which Birkin brings a reluctant Ursula is, in its most perfect expression, a "star-equilibrium which alone is freedom," a juxtaposition in which they connect but don't fuse. The connection described toward the end of "Excurse" is physical but nonsexual; it is mystical but within the body ("pure mystical nodality of physical being"); and it is a connection between minds without thought, one coming from "that other basic mind, the deepest physical mind." I emphasize, as Lawrence does, these apparent paradoxes partly to stress the difficulty of making logical sense of the passage in question. The second half of "Excurse" is the section in *Women in Love* where Lawrence is obviously taking the greatest novelistic risks. He must put into the "agitations" of speech, into the "movements" of thought, a state about which there may be nothing to say except that it is inaccessible to whatever might be said or thought. Nonetheless, Lawrence makes the attempt to put something of this state into words, although he has to rely on such apparently self-canceling expressions as "physical mind" and "mystical nodality of physical being" to suggest the literally unspeakable nature of his "star-equilibrium." (He also relies on a certain heightening of tone which can easily be found ridiculous. As we enter something that is "neither love nor passion," we also move from the narrative voice of a realistic, often satirical modern novel to the incantatory tone of biblical affirmations: "It was the daughters of men coming back to the sons of God, the strange inhuman sons of God who are in the beginning," and: "She had found one of the sons of God from the Beginning, and he had found one of the first most luminous daughters of men." The jolting shifts in "Excurse" between "sons of God" [or "an Egyptian Pharaoh"] and Birkin's car or his bickering with Ursula give a good idea of the difficulties, for realistic fiction, in this mingling of mystical intuition with prosaic details of modern life.)

The paradoxical expressions I mentioned a moment ago are perhaps only superficially self-canceling. They keep meaning poised between two contradictory words or expressions, they immobilize thought in an equilibrium of opposites. "Mind" is not meant to cancel out "physical" in "physical mind." Unlike Mallarméan negation, Lawrentian paradox (and paradox in general) maintains all its incompatible terms. A first term is never erased; but the thought that might use that term as a point of departure is paralyzed by the juxtaposition of another term which gives us an unthinkable phrase. In a sense, there is nothing to "understand"; we are merely asked to maintain a connection between two words. The narrative continues, but it thus manages to suggest its own arrest. An enforced stillness on the stylistic level runs parallel to the characters' spiritual stillness. True, there is apparently some movement in this state. At the back of Birkin's thighs, Ursula feels "the strange mystery of his life-motion," and "a rich new circuit, a new current of passional electric energy" floods them both with a new and rich peace. "There were strange fountains in his body," and "deeper, further in mystery than the phallic source [the source of friction], came the floods of ineffable darkness and ineffable riches." But Lawrence suggests that even this movement is compatible with, perhaps even equivalent to, stillness: "the strange and magical current of force in [Birkin's] back and loins, and down his legs" is "so perfect that it stayed him immobile." Fundamentally, there would seem to be no compromise possible between friction and stillness. *Women in Love* moves between the opposite poles of "infinitely repeated motion" and Pharaoh-like stillness. And while there are gradations from one extreme to the other, the polarity between the two is anything but a "star-equilibrium"; it is polarity of pure antagonism.

To what extent does the Lawrentian contrast between agitation and stillness accommodate novelistic characters? In a well-known letter to Edward Garnett, Lawrence spoke of his indifference to the psychology of traditional fiction: "You mustn't look in my novel for the old stable *ego* of the character. There is another ego, according to whose action the individual is unrecognizable, and passes through, as it were, allotropic states which it needs a deeper sense than any other we've been used to exercise, to discover are states of the same single radically unchanged element." And in one of the essays of *The Reality of Peace* (published in the summer of 1917, shortly after Lawrence finished his rewriting of *Women in Love*), Lawrence seems to be explicitly defining what the content of that other ego might be: "For there are ultimately only two desires, the desire of life and the desire of death. Beyond these is pure being, where I am absolved from desire and made perfect." The fact which most interests Lawrence about human beings is the extent to which they are being carried along by either currents of life energy or currents of death energy.

Now the impulse to live and the impulse to die are not exactly attributes of personality; rather, they are attempts to enlarge on or to obliterate the very field in which the anecdotes of personality are possible. Personality must therefore be read as a system of signs or of choices which can be deciphered back to a primary choice of life or of death. And the deciphering takes almost no time at all in Lawrence. Interpretation is immediate, and tends to bypass the mediating and distorting vehicle of language. There are flashes of recognition instead of an interpretive process. Lawrentian desire has to be extricated from language, for life and death energies *in* language are already tamed or derived energies. Or, to put it another way, they are desires already on display, both showing and hiding themselves in an essentially social theater. In the kind of simplifying vision which Lawrence's characters have of one another, individuality in the usual sense is disregarded and only the organism's inclination to destroy or to survive and grow is registered. Perhaps Lawrence asks us really to accept only one assumption about human beings: that it is possible to know at once (although it may not be formulated at once) if people's impulse to live is stronger than their impulse to die, or vice versa.

These intuitions account for the sudden shifts of language in *Women in Love* — shifts which may puzzle or irritate us — from the prosaic to the extravagant. When the connection is made between two life currents or two death currents, minds "go," people "lapse out" and "swoon," they have "transports" and "keen paroxysms," and the "veil" of "ultimate consciousness" is "torn." Nothing is more disorienting in *Women in Love* than the use of such expressions as descriptive narrative accompaniments to the most banal action or the most controlled, unremarkable dialogue. Hermione enters the church for Laura Crich's wedding, sees that Birkin isn't there, and, apparently without the slightest change in her behavior, "A terrible storm came over her, as if she were drowning. . . . It was beyond death, so utterly null, desert." The first time Gudrun sees Gerald, she is immediately "magnetised" by the appearance of a man "so new, unbroached, pure as an arctic thing." She has "a keen paroxysm, a transport . . . all her veins were in a paroxysm of violent sensation," and she feels herself already enveloped, alone with him, in "some pale gold, arctic light."

These sudden crises of "swooning" or "lapsing out" can make a Lawrentian narrative seem both quite mad and quite monotonous. The variety of social encounters and the richness of psychological textures are constantly being dismissed by unrelentingly repetitious references to those currents of life and death energies which underlie both social history and the nuances of individual psychology. What is involved here is nonetheless a radical redefinition of character and desire in fiction. Proust — who might be used as an instructive point of comparison — is much more hesitant than Lawrence in his subversion of what Lawrence calls in *The Plumed Serpent* the "assembled self." Literature for the Proustian narrator is in part a resolution of crises in which he feels emptied of all being. The literary work provides him with reassuring evidence of "an individual, identical and permanent self." It is a document of ontological security; literature can give to Marcel the stable and fixed image of an identity he finds neither in introspection (to turn inward is to find only "an empty apparatus") nor in the anguishing otherness of the external world. Writing fixes the writer's self in an external self-portrait which never escapes from the writer's control. So while stable and unified portraits of personality are radically subverted in *A la Recherche du temps perdu*, the self-fragmentations of Proust's novel are nonetheless enacted within a rigorously unified composition. Personality in Proust begins to disintegrate as a result of excesses of verbal inspiration. The Proustian narrator exuberantly attacks his own coherence and allows himself the luxury of *being* the multiple desiring perspectives on the world which he discovers while writing. Such self-multiplication is, explicitly, the work of literature, and the narrator can perhaps afford to indulge in it because he knows that the excesses of literature are always contained within the coherent system of a language. Being is exploded, made discontinuous and multiplied in Proust within a field of great compositional security.

Proust eludes the more fundamental impulse to live or to die by the identification he makes between life-producing processes and the productive resources of literary metaphor. There is in fact a very powerful impulse to freeze life, to kill being, in *A la Recherche*, but it can be made to appear almost irrelevant in a work which, from the very start, takes for granted that the primary energies of life are the essentially secondary, social energies of language. What interests Lawrence most in novelistic character — the life and death energies which break through the appearances of character — is beyond the language of fiction. And yet Lawrence never renounced his efforts to represent in literature the wordless energies which produce life or death. What are the risks involved in this enterprise of deliberately superimposing on realistic character a view of the individual as a kind of nonindividualized, or a-psychological, mass of life and death energies?

The first — and far from inconsiderable — danger for Lawrentian fiction is that life and death energies may lend themselves to some complicated psychological interpretations. Such interpretations are encouraged by the allowance which Lawrence himself makes for conventional psychological complexities in his characters alongside of their elemental drives toward life and death. Personality has just enough content in *Women in Love* to make us suspicious of the simplicity of those drives, and it's often difficult to resist speculating on reasons unconfessed to by Lawrence himself for a character's sudden click from one level of consciousness to another. For example, the chapter called "Rabbit" can be discussed in terms of Gerald and Gudrun's desire for a frenzied release into chaotic whirling from their mechanically controlled wills. Lawrence would probably approve of this reading, but the chapter also lends itself to psychoanalytic interpretation. The rabbit scratches Gerald and Gudrun, and Gerald feels "as if he had knowledge of her in the long red rent of her forearm, so silken and soft." And "the long, shallow red rip" seems to tear "the surface of his ultimate consciousness, letting through the forever unconscious, unthinkable red ether of the beyond, the obscene beyond." It's obvious that the wound inflicted by the rabbit awakens in both characters an anticipatory sexual excitement. And brutal, wounding sex is another version of frantic and destructive motion. But the language goes too far for this reading to be enough, and in going too far it invites a psychologically more reductive interpretation. What can this "obscene beyond" be? Given the emphasis on a "long red rent" in soft skin, it's tempting to feel that Gudrun's arm has been hallucinated into the fantasy of a bloodily castrated vagina. The escalated language of the passage — "unthinkable red ether of the beyond" — may be a verbal mystification designed to hide a terror of or disgust at the female genitals. It's not necessary to say exactly who has this terror: at the psychoanalytic level of interpretation (as we have seen in Mauron's reading of Racine), the narrator, Gerald, and even Gudrun are merely conscious, personified aspects of a fascinated unconscious horror, on the part of the male, at the mystery of a "lack" in the female genitalia. We can assume that this is not what Lawrence intends to reveal about Gerald (or about himself) in this passage. But how can we resist being suspicious of the language here?

Applied to Lawrence, such suspicion is necessarily reductive. We have a very different situation from the one we encountered in Racine. The psychoanalytic interpretation of Racinian characters emphasizes and elucidates a psychology of monolithic passions. What is usually taken for psychological subtlety in Racine — his characters' conscious conflicts between anger and tenderness, or between sexual passion and remorse — is essentially the realistic disguise which masks a psychology of depersonalizing impulses. Self-conscious analysis civilizes and individualizes desires to absorb or destroy others which are prior to our social personalities. The very analytical system which dissects passion in Racine is a denial of the power of passion: as a result of such analysis, we see that desire can be made a subject of social discourse. Monolithic passion tends to simplify, to de-individualize the self, and it is against this tendency that Racinian psychology, as it is usually defined, works. The care with which Racine establishes numerous distinct identities, from Etéocle and Polinice to Athalie, for a single passional impulse suggests a highly sophisticated denial of his own intuitions about desire. The desiring impulse is diluted in the "interesting" complexities of personality. But the diluting process is never entirely successful in Racine, and we feel that his characters' passions are simpler and stronger than the individualities toward which his super-subtle analyses strive. A psychoanalytic interpretation reasserts the level of nonpersonal desire: as we have seen, it redefines individual characters in terms of certain fantasies of possession and rejection of the other (especially, of the mother) which "inhabit" all Racine's heroes and heroines. The self in psychoanalytic interpretation is not a personality; it is a succession, or the simultaneous presence, of experimental, partial identities. The self may thus *be* the roles of the murderous mother, the rebellious son, and the punishing father — and these roles are distributed among Racine's characters regardless of their sex or their social personalities. Thus a psychoanalytic awareness adds density to Racine's theater in the very operation by which it tends to disparage what has generally been praised as Racinian complexity.

But in *Women in Love,* Lawrence himself is attempting to destroy the superstructure of personality in order to redefine human beings in terms of their primary desires to live and to die. The continuous shifts in the novel between familiar social identities and currents of life or death energy train us to recognize the latter in the midst of the former; they are designed to reawaken us to the constant, if momentary, demolitions of the "assembled self" by energies which the self has been assembled largely in order to deny. A psychoanalytic reading can defeat this enterprise by giving too precise a sexual content to these energies. And it does this merely by interpreting them — that is, by questioning their finality. It treats both the conscious personality and the life and death energies as signs of specific repressed fantasies. The hyperbolic language used to designate the will to live or to die thus loses its *merely* melodramatic quality, and it takes on a symbolic density which only psychological interpretation can penetrate.

A Freudian reading of Racine's plays demonstrates that personality can never have the final word about itself: its very nature is to be a sublimated fixation and elaboration of infantile fantasies. But Lawrence is generally impatient of personality. And, with the freedom of analytic comment which the narrative form of the novel allows him, he claims to substitute a more central reading of his characters' natures for the superficial and flattering readings which they themselves propose. Nothing could therefore be more fatally ironic for his work than for his narrative comment to be exposed as having the same status as his characters' speech. A psychoanalytic interpretation of Racine helps to locate the otherwise unlocated rich vagueness of Racinian language; a psychoanalytic interpretation of a Lawrentian novel merely suggests that Lawrence himself has failed to locate his characters' central motivations.

From this same interpretive point of view, the Lawrentian ideal of stillness itself risks being discredited. I've discussed the relation finally achieved by Birkin and Ursula at the end of "Excurse" in terms of the "star-polarity" — the nonfusing connectedness — which Lawrence proposes as an alternative to destructive sexual passion. But even the most sympathetic discussion of stillness and singleness in Lawrence is bound to raise questions which his novels tend to evade. First of all, there seems to be a profound tendency in Lawrence to get rid of sex altogether. In part, this tendency is not only confessed to but argued for. Sex is more often than not simply a physical version of wills in frictional, antagonistic tension; therefore, Birkin argues with Ursula for a relation beyond sex ("not meeting and mingling . . . but an equilibrium, a pure balance of two single beings: — as the stars balance each other"). In "Water-Party," Birkin gives in to Ursula's "hard, fierce kisses of passion" and becomes "a perfect hard flame of passionate desire for her." But this desire means giving up a "perfect mood of softness and sleep-liveliness," and after sex Birkin goes home, as Lawrence says in impressively balanced phrases, "satisfied and shattered, fulfilled and destroyed." Almost the last word in *Lady Chatterley's Lover* is given to the praise of chastity. Mellors, in the letter to Connie which ends the novel, speaks of living his enforced chastity, "which is the pause of peace in our fucking," and which he describes as "a river of cool water in my soul." We might also remember that one of the titles Lawrence considered for this epoch-making document of sexual fulfillment was *Tenderness*. Indeed, sexuality comes to be equated with tenderness in the novel: Connie tells Mellors that his most exceptional quality is "the courage of your own tenderness," and Mellors makes no differences between "cunt-awareness" and tenderness (for ". . . sex is really only touch, the closest of all touch").

Furthermore, the exact meaning of nonfrictional sex in Lawrence is by no means clear. Precisely how does sex during the night Ursula and Birkin spend in Sherwood Forest (at the end of "Excurse") differ from the experience of sexual passion referred to in "Water-Party"? In the "Excurse" episode, Ursula "had her desire fulfilled. He had his desire fulfilled," and Ursula receives from Birkin "the maximum of unspeakable communication in touch, dark, subtle, positively silent, a magnificent gift and give again, a perfect acceptance and yielding, a mystery, the reality of that which can never be known, vital, sensual reality that can never be transmuted into mind content, but remains outside, living body of darkness and silence and subtlety, the mystic body of reality." "Unspeakable communication in touch," "silence," "subtlety," "body of darkness": the words suggest something different from the fierce "rushing of passion" of "Water-Party," a kind of physical contact in which ultimate sensuality would no longer be incompatible with peace and stillness. For the woman, this would mean a deep vaginal orgasm rather than a frictional clitoral orgasm; Kate in *The Plumed Serpent*, for example, "progresses" from "the white ecstasy of frictional satisfaction" to the "soft, heavy, hot flow" she experiences with Cipriano. But what does nonfrictional sex involve for men? What is the relation between Birkin's subtle, silent touch and the activity necessary for a man to reach orgasm? If there is actually penetration, what kind of thrusting activity makes the difference between the hard flame of passion and a sensuality which is the "living body of darkness and silence and subtlety"? Do slow, deep thrusts — rather than rapid short ones — transform sex from a tense pursuit of physical release into the extraordinary mystical experience we are asked to accept in "Excurse"?

Perhaps the male body's closest approximation to the female orgasm is in "passive" anal sex with fantasies of being a woman, and even then the physical sensation itself probably depends on some friction against the prostate gland. But such remarks raise the question of homosexuality in Lawrence, and at this level of explicit sex, homosexuality is irrelevant to *Women in Love*. At least it is irrelevant to the novel as it now stands — without the astonishing prologue (deleted by Lawrence himself) in which we are told that only male beauty is "vivid and intoxicating" to Birkin, and that "he would never acquiesce to" his "keen desire to have and to possess bodies of [certain] men, the passion to bathe in [their] very substance." In the published version of the novel, Birkin's love for Gerald certainly includes a keen physical awareness, but it has almost none of the sexual specificity suggested in the prologue. (In the chapter which describes the two men wrestling, specific sexual acts are indirectly evoked by images of sublimated penetration: "It was as if Birkin's whole physical intelligence interpenetrated into Gerald's body, as if his fine, sublimated energy entered into the flesh of the fuller man. . . .") A profound love between man and man is part of Birkin's ideal, but there is no clear indication that this would include sex, and there is certainly no suggestion that only a form of homosexual physical contact could solve the problem of frictional sex for men, and allow them to enjoy the "soft, heavy, hot flow" available to women. For the heterosexual or genitally active man, the only escape from frictional sex is chastity, or perhaps a kind of nongenital physical intimacy. The most desirable contact seems to be a peaceful touching, the nonfrictional *placing* of one bodily surface on another bodily surface.

It would hardly be a criticism of Lawrence to say this were it not for the fact that he seems anxious to avoid saying this himself. Given Lawrence's constant concern with sex, it is extraordinary that there should be so much vagueness about sex in his work. He frequently either leaves important questions unanswered, or he answers them in a confusing rhetoric which transposes erotic experience to the level of an unutterable mystic reality. The result of all this is that we may finally be tempted to ask what many of Lawrence's readers will surely condemn as irrelevant and unfair questions. What is the relation between stillness and sexual impotence in Lawrence? Does he get beyond sex, or does he have exceptional trouble getting *to* sex? Furthermore, Lawrence's disgust with female sexuality seems to me undeniable. Lawrence is repelled by the clitoral orgasm, by any activity on the part of the woman in pursuit of sexual satisfaction, as well as by the woman's expectation or insistence that the man work in order to give her spasms of pleasure. (In 1931, John Middleton Murry wrote: "A sexual marriage in which he does not have to satisfy the woman, where the sexuality, being transformed into sensuality may give him the opportunity of re-asserting the manhood he had lost — this is precisely Lawrence's dream.") In *The Plumed Serpent* and in *Lady Chatterley's Lover*, the criticism of female sexuality is cleverly entrusted to the women characters themselves. This doesn't make the criticism any less sharp, and the former novel is a particularly brutal repudiation of female desire. Kate has only to begin enjoying a clitoral orgasm for Cipriano to stop his sexual activity: "By a dark and powerful instinct he drew away from her as soon as this desire rose again in her, for the white ecstasy of frictional satisfaction, the throes of Aphrodite of the foam."[3]

Finally, there is Lawrence's curiously extreme attitude toward anal sex. He has a melodramatic view of anality worthy of Norman Mailer — but without the saving humor of *An American Dream*. It seems probable, although Lawrence doesn't say so explicitly, that Birkin, in a mood of "strange licentiousness" and "mocking brutishness" after an evening of dancing at their hotel in the Austrian Alps, introduces Ursula to anal sex. Afterwards, she at first thinks of what they have done as "degrading" and "bestial," but then exults in being able to be "really shameful. . . . She was free, when she knew everything, and no dark shameful things were denied her." A similar situation is treated in even more exaggerated terms in *Lady Chatterley's Lover*; Connie feels that the shame is burned out of her when she is (apparently) sodomized by Mellors. In a sense, the episode is an apt climax to the process of her breaking away from Clifford and all that he represents. An entire civilization's denial of sex is attacked in two ways in *Lady Chatterley's Lover*: through the Lawrentian narrator's nervously agitated sarcasm, and through Connie's shift of loyalty from Clifford to Mellors. But the angry and frustrated tone of the novel suggests some sense, on Lawrence's part, that it may be impossible to get free of the society being attacked. The unrestrained enjoyment not only of sex but of officially forbidden sex is presented — not too convincingly — as the only effective revolt, for the individual, against a culture of life-killing sublimations.

But the burning away of all shame is a rather heavy burden for anality to take on — except as a consequence of fantasies which, to begin with, attribute extraordinarily intense affective and moral values to anal pleasure. That is, the explicit value conferred on anal sex makes no sense except as the sign of a more complicated fascination with anality. We have a pseudo-tautology with which psychoanalysis has made us familiar: anality has extraordinary (conscious) value because it has extraordinary (unconscious) value.

What is represented is also *expressed* as a conscious desire, although the conscious version omits those elements of the fantasy which both condemned it to repression and determined a specific conscious preference or desire (for anal sex). The thrilling interpretation of an act of transgression suggests a secret complicity with the interdiction of the act. In the society which forbids anal sex, it is the fearful pleasures connected with such sex which are repressed; in the Lawrentian transgression, it seems to be the condemning conscience which is suppressed by the very exaltation with which the "crime" is committed. A terror of anality is suggested by the hyperbolic praise of anality as a magic key to guiltless being. Repression therefore manifests itself in the form of a repression of repression.

In "Excurse," Ursula releases a "rich new circuit, a new current of passional electric energy" from Birkin's body by "following some mysterious life-flow" at the back of his thighs, by tracing "with her hands the line of his loins and thighs, at the back." They both "seemed to faint" when Ursula, on her knees in front of Birkin, "closed her hands over the full, rounded body of his loins, as he stooped over her, she seemed to touch the quick of the mystery of darkness that was bodily him." There is a long history of critical agitation over this scene. John Middleton Murry, in his 1921 review of *Women in Love*, wrote of these "crucial pages" in "Excurse": ". . . to us they are completely and utterly unintelligible if we assume (as we must assume if we have regard for the vehemence of Mr. Lawrence's passion) that they are not the crudest sexuality." G. Wilson Knight, less reticent than Murry in a discussion which owes much to the latter's remarks, concludes that the mysterious touching in "Excurse" consists of anal caresses.[4] Knight's case is convincing, although it seems silly to argue about what's "really" going on when in fact all that's going on is some impenetrably mystifying language. It would be more legitimate, I think, to question Lawrence's assumption that we will immediately acknowledge the specific spiritual significance which he attributes to the anal caress. Why should we be expected to recognize that "the darkest, deepest, strangest life-source of the human body" is "at the back and base of the loins"?[5] What *is* a dark and deep life-source, and what exactly is "new" about the "current of passional electric energy" which, apparently, one can start up by tracing one's fingers along the line of someone's loins and thighs? The passage can easily strike us as vague and pretentious, even if we don't feel as convinced as Murry and Knight do that Ursula's fingers are giving Birkin a very specific kind of pleasure which Lawrence doesn't want to spell out, and which he dresses up in obfuscating, mystical language. If we accept Knight's reading, we of course have a devastatingly ironic situation: the passage in *Women in Love* in which a perfect stillness of spirit is finally achieved would also be the passage in which Ursula stimulates herself and Birkin into an ecstatic faint by a "massage" of his anal sphincter, that is, by working not toward a center of spiritual stillness, but rather toward the deposit of spiritual waste, the collection center for human excrement.[6]

Another central problem for Lawrence is to find a way to identify individuals within a mode of characterization which discards the usual signs of individuality. In part, he relies on the individualizing psychology of realistic fiction. His characters have distinct physical, psychological and social identities. Each one has a recognizable and separate style of being; conventional personalities make for general clarity of characterization. In a sense, the realistic character-portrait provides Lawrence with a safety valve in his risky experimentation with character as a mass of life and death energies. Furthermore, conventional characterization is especially useful since Lawrence, in his redefinition of character, doesn't discard individuality; it is, in fact, an ideal which personality prevents us from attaining. Personality is the trap in which the individual gets lost. It is the sign of the self's inability to remain alone, an alluring invitation to self-destroying fusions. But, Birkin insists, "there is a real impersonal me, that is beyond love, beyond any emotional relationship. . . . The root is beyond love, a naked kind of isolation, an isolated me, that does *not* meet and mingle, and never can." Beyond personality, "there is no speech and no terms of agreement . . . no standard for action . . . because one is outside the pale of all that is accepted, and nothing known applies." Lawrence must therefore describe or at least suggest an individuality to which the individualizing attributes of personality are irrelevant. And he must also find a way to differentiate among characters about whom the only essential thing to be said is that they wish to die or that they wish to live.

The latter enterprise is all the more difficult in that life energies and death energies are often manifested in almost identical interests and almost identical speech. There is realistic diversification of character in *Women in Love*, but there are also striking continuities among the characters. And the thematic recurrences in the novel will create considerable confusion for us if we insist on keeping doctrinal distinctions absolutely clear. The characters in Lawrence's novel seem to have been conceived as almost imperceptible variations on a few major themes. And a scale of occasionally blurred gradations among the various versions of a theme is nonetheless meant to illustrate a sharp and fundamental opposition between the will to live and the will to die. It is particularly striking that almost all the other characters repeat Birkin's ideas in one way or another. They don't merely illustrate what he says about people; they often say what he says, and even seem to live as he lives. And yet they are clearly meant to be negative embodiments of his ideas and his life.

What, for example, are we to think of the opposition between sensual spontaneity and cerebral knowledge in the novel? Hermione's attack on modern self-consciousness (the young, she says, are "burdened to death with consciousness") is a fairly good recitation of a favorite Lawrentian idea, but Rupert angrily answers that young people don't "have too much mind, but too little." But he also argues for the "dark sensual body of life." Hermione wants passion and the instincts only through her head: "You have only your will and your conceit of consciousness," Birkin brutally tells her, "and your lust for power, to *know*." On the other hand, when he tries, later in the novel, to resolve the contradictions he recognizes in his always talking about "sensual fulfillment," he concludes that "he did not want a further sensual experience." He imagines what happened in Africa thousands of years ago as a "lapse from pure integral being, from creation and liberty," a fall into "mindless progressive knowledge through the senses, knowledge arrested and ending in the senses." What he wants with Ursula is "another way, . . . the paradisal entry into pure, single being, . . . a lovely state of free proud singleness" apparently different from those frightening "sensual subtle realities" of African art. For the Africans, to go beyond the phallic is to reach "knowledge such as the beetles have, which live purely within the world of corruption and cold dissolution." For Birkin and Ursula, to go beyond the phallic is to come upon "floods of ineffable darkness and ineffable richness"; it is "to be awake and potent in that other basic mind, the deepest physical mind."

I don't think there is much to be gained from trying to figure out exactly what differences Lawrence means to establish between a bad sensuality of the mind (Hermione), a meta-phallic corrupt sensuality (Africa), and the good meta-phallic sensuality of what he calls "the deepest physical mind."[7] We can make sense of the distinctions only by being very abstract about them, and Lawrence himself — rather admirably — is at times willing to admit that he is floundering among his own concepts. It is more interesting to look at some of the effects in the novel of these blurred distinctions among characters and ideas. They make, curiously, for a tendency toward fusion: separate beings, separate cultures, and separate ideas in the novel are constantly being rubbed against one another in unharmonious friction. There are numerous examples of this not quite identical, frictional repetition. In Birkin, "singleness" is a positive term. But the word is also used to describe Loerke: Gudrun finds in him "an uncanny singleness, a quality of being by himself, not in contact with anybody else, that marked out an artist to her." There is, then, a wholly unconnected singleness, and there is also, as Birkin tells Ursula, the singleness that makes possible "an equilibrium, a pure balance of two single beings: — as the stars balance each other." It would surely be unjust to apply to Birkin Lawrence's remark that Loerke "made not the slightest attempt to be at one with anything." Nevertheless, there is a certain indifference in Birkin too, and Gerald suffers from his "consciousness of the young, animal-like spontaneity of detachment" in the other man: "He knew Birkin could do without him — could forget, and not suffer." Lawrence plays dangerously with these similarities; we are always being asked to make crucial but almost imperceptible distinctions. We must keep Birkin's singleness separate from Loerke's and Gudrun's anatomies, we mustn't confuse Gerald's idolatry of organization and Rupert's pursuit of harmony. Winifred Crich is a strange hybrid of Loerke and Birkin. Some of the terms used to describe her "nihilistic" nature will be taken up again to characterize Loerke ("she never formed vital connections . . ."), and others remind us of Gerald's judgment of Birkin (her will "was so strangely and easily free, she is like a soulless bird . . . without attachment or responsibility beyond the moment").

Finally, what does it mean to be an artist? Gudrun's art is a function of her need to murder other people spiritually by reaching some final knowledge about them. (And of course her need to know reminds us of Hermione's obsessive lust for knowledge.) Gudrun likes to place people "in their true light, give them their own surroundings, settle them forever." Thus she disposes of the guests at Laura Crich's wedding in Chapter One: "She knew them, they were finished, sealed and stamped and finished with, for her." She "loves" Gerald until she feels that she knows him completely. "She wanted to touch him and touch him and touch him, till she had him all in her hands, till she had strained him into her knowledge." And this is exactly the attitude which Gudrun brings to her painting. As she sketches water-plants, she "sees" them rising from the mud, and her seeing is a kind of knowledge untranslatable into words: ". . . she could feel their turgid fleshy structure in a sensuous vision, she *knew* how they rose out of the mud, she *knew* how they thrust out from themselves, how they stood stiff and succulent against the air." Now final knowledge about anything is deathlike. "You can only have knowledge strictly," Birkin announces in "Breadalby," "of things concluded, in the past. It's like bottling the liberty of last summer in the bottled gooseberries." But, first of all, there are similarities between Gudrun's obsessive need to know through touch and that "unspeakable comunication in touch" which Birkin and Ursula enjoy. For the latter is also a kind of knowledge, although it is knowledge of something "never to be seen with the eye, or known with the mind, only known as a palpable revelation of living otherness." Also, Birkin's notion of art includes the idea of complete knowledge. It's true that, like Ursula, he would reject Loerke's (and Gudrun's) absolute separation of art from life, but when he explains to Gerald why the carved African figure of a woman in labor is "art," he says: "It conveys a complete truth. . . . It contains the whole truth of that state, whatever you feel about it." Finally, we are by no means meant to feel that Gudrun's art is bad or uninteresting (Birkin praises it), and, more significantly, Birkin explains why he is copying a Chinese drawing of geese in almost exactly the same terms used to describe Gudrun's sensuous knowledge of the water-plants. He "gets more of China, copying this picture, than reading all the books." He satisfies a kind of ontological curiosity about other people's most intimate perceptions of reality: "I know what centers they live from — what they perceive and feel — the hot, stinging centrality of a goose in the flux of cold water and mud — the curious bitter stinging heat of a goose's blood, entering their own blood like an inoculation of corruptive fire — fire of the cold-burning mud — the lotus mystery."

From the point of view of traditional fiction, these transparent analogies subvert a desirable diversity of character and plot. Like Proust, Lawrence nonchalantly exposes what the realistic novelist seems anxious to disguise: the derivation of his work from a single creative imagination. The characters of *Women in Love*, like those of *A la Recherche du temps perdu*, repeat, with variations, a single psychology. And the clarity of the repetitions in both works tends to destroy the realistic myth of distance between the novelist and his work. There is no difference of being between the author and the world he describes; fiction is always a form of autobiography, and the writer's relation to his work is fundamentally one of paternity. But in Lawrence the psychological and thematic repetitions which I've just outlined undermine an explicit credo of singleness. The distinctions among characters are blurred by similarities of attitude and of temperament; and the mystical notion of singleness risks being compromised by a tendency toward fusion, or psychological community, on the level of realistic personality.

Such fusions are clearly not what Lawrence intends. In the foreword to *Women in Love*, Lawrence takes note of the fact that "in point of style, fault is often found with the continual, slightly modified repetition." His first answer to this criticism is that such repetitions are "natural" to him, and then he adds: ". . . every natural crisis in emotion or passion or understanding comes from this pulsing, frictional to-and-fro which works up to culmination." It is as if he found an analogous type of frictional characterization necessary in order to work toward that spiritual culmination in distinct singleness which Ursula and Birkin come close to attaining at the end of "Excurse." We have, then, a curious case of frictional movement in the service of life-creating stillness. Frictional repetition is not merely a negative quality in Lawrence's world. More precisely, we must distinguish between the mechanical, tick-tack repetition from which Gerald and Gudrun suffer (and on which Loerke thrives), and *almost* identical repetitions designed to bring out profound differences in what might be mistaken for sameness. *Women in Love* is a succession of scenes in which nearly identical points of view antagonistically confront, or rub up against, one another. All the characters repeat, with more or less subtle variations, a few principal themes. But the very blurring of points of view which results from these repetitions is meant to serve the most finely differentiating activity. In part, the Lawrentian technique of characterization expresses the tentative and experimental nature of Lawrence's fiction. Each novel tries out several possibly destructive or life-creating selves. Novelistic character is a means of testing the life and death potentialities of certain styles of being; and the fate of a specific character, as it slowly takes shape in the course of a novel, reveals the value of his or her style, its complicity with life or with death.

But the goal of frictional characterization is nonetheless stillness of being, a state beyond movement and even character. And there would be nothing to say about that state: a case of true singleness could have no point of reference, it could not even be compared to another example of what Birkin calls "an isolated me, that does *not* meet and mingle, and never can." We can now see a further significance in Lawrence's implied comparison of stylistic repetition to the pulsing to-and-fro of frictional sex. Friction in sex "works up to culmination," which means to the end of friction and of sex. The only tolerable aspect of frictional sex for Lawrence seems to be that it leads to a kind of collapse, to an at least temporary, nonsexual stillness which he finds more desirable than the agitation of sexual passion. In the same way, what makes frictional characterization acceptable may be that it points the way to a "culmination" in, say, the inexpressible Pharaoh-like stillness of Birkin in "Excurse." And if that stillness were definitive, neither sex, nor character, nor the novel would any longer be necessary. Nearly identical versions of being would finally give way to a single version of being. The gaps separating characters would be closed, and the already limited range of characterization would be reduced to the single "point" of the ideal spiritual state. As the orgasm relieves the body of tiring movement, so perfect stillness would relieve the novelist of the fatiguing obligation to move constantly back and forth among identical but antagonistic versions of the energies which produce life and death.

In exactly what way does the love between Birkin and Ursula serve life? There is a curious resemblance between Birkin's and Gerald's ideas of "perfect union" with a woman. Gerald pursues Gudrun in order to escape from the exhausting struggle of his conscious will against "the hollow void of death in his soul." When he first makes love to her, ". . . the miraculous soft effluence of her breast suffused over him, over his seared, damaged brain, like a healing lymph, like a soft, soothing flow of life itself, perfect as if he were bathed in the womb again." But this "soothing flow of life" is of course also a deathlike peace. With Gudrun, Gerald escapes not from the void of death, but rather from his resistance to his profound desire to die. Toward the end of the novel, Gudrun resentfully thinks that ". . . the secret of his passion, his forever unquenched desire for her [was] that he needed her to put him to sleep, to give him repose." In a sense, she allows him to satisfy his impulse to be murdered — an impulse which largely accounts for his sexual appeal. He has an exciting passivity; just below the surface of his active will, there is a willingness to be penetrated or violated to which even Birkin is by no means insensitive. Sex with Gudrun is a preliminary version of Gerald's final sleep in the snow; love is a seductive version of death.

How different from this is the peace which Birkin seeks? Perhaps beyond what we might call the secondary ambiguities of sex in Lawrence (lack of genital vitality, disgust at female sexuality, anal eroticism), there is the more fundamental ambiguity of love as a longing to die disguised as a formula for life. We have seen the connections between "infinitely repeated motion" and death; but there may be even more profound connections between a nondesiring stillness and death. Birkin sees the connection: he tells Ursula that he wants "love that is like sleep," and that love should be like sleep "so that it is like death," but he makes this admission respectable, so to speak, by falling back on the ancient notion that the old self must die in order for a new self to be born. But even his attempts to describe the new self brings us back to suggestions of death. In "Moony," Lawrence is careful to point out that Birkin's peace with Ursula is not sleep, but what he describes is, so to speak, a conscious sleep: "To be content in bliss, without desire or insistence anywhere, this was heaven: to be together in happy stillness." The ultimate Lawrentian goal is the death of desire.

To desire is to experience a lack or an absence; and the sign of desire is movement (actual physical movement or the mental movements of thought and fantasy). We move in order to remove the lack, to make something absent present. Such movement is also the sign of individual life. It indicates a sense of a particular existence, that is, a sense of the self as not being all reality. To begin to live psychically as an individual is to recognize, in desire, the existence of realities distinct from the self. Desires provide a kind of negative of one's individuality: they implicitly define the self by explicitly defining what it lacks. Thus individual life is inseparable from desire and movement. This is of course by no means the same thing as saying that individuality itself is desirable; there may be no reason to prefer individuality to an experience of peaceful, nondesiring fusion with the universe. But then we should realize that we are aspiring, precisely, to our death as individuals. Lawrence, however, wants to propose the peace of being without desire as the condition of true singleness or individuality. Furthermore, such peace is meant to be creative of life. It's true that the movements of desire erode life. We can escape (or think we are escaping) this erosion of life — the process of dying — only if we eliminate desire from life. And one way to do this, as I suggested at the beginning of this chapter, is to engage in a type of movement which has no history. This "solution" is the illusory immortality of "infinitely repeated motion," of which, as we have seen, Lawrence provides a brilliant critique. Exact repetition implicitly denies the desiring individual (and therefore individual life); it would make the self eternal by removing its activity from all contingencies (history doesn't affect this sort of repetition). I called such repetition the activity of inertia. And what I'm now suggesting is a secret complicity in Lawrence between "infinitely repeated motion" and the idea of still singleness. The peace of Lawrentian love is the literal inertia which "infinitely repeated motion" paradoxically achieves through purposeless agitation.

There is nothing to do in Lawrentian love but sustain it. And the novel, as an artistic form, mercilessly exposes the difficulties of such a task. Lawrence has chosen to place his characters, for better

or for worse, in the framework of a generally realistic fiction, and
it is a virtue — at once dull and impressive — of realistic fiction to
pursue the consequences of mystical ecstasy in everyday relations.
The end of *Women in Love* suggests a certain staleness in the lovers'
union, and the danger of their beginning to look merely old and
tired. Lawrence's perfect lovers would be engaged in the hopeless
task of repeating an intensity without movement, a state without
content. To a certain extent, Birkin (without of course admitting
or even knowing it) has merely found a *doctrine* to justify Gerald's
impulse to rest in the definitive sleep of death. It is a doctrine which
claims individualizing and life-creating energies for a deathlike stillness. Birkin, like Gerald, must find a way out of the exhausting
erosions of desire. Love is an escape from a desiring life which does
in fact both vitalize and kill us. It is the panacea which unites both
the death-seekers and the supposed life-seekers of Lawrence's fiction
in the peace of nonverbal, nonmoving, nondesiring spiritual death.

Finally, however, the peace of "Excurse" is by no means followed only by boredom; the lovers also return to conflict. About a
third of *Women in Love* takes place after "Excurse," and the latter
chapters are certainly not free of frictional antagonism between
Birkin and Ursula. They were happy, Lawrence says of them before
they leave Austria for Italy, "but they were never *quite* together,
at the same moment. One was always a little left out." Indeed, the
novel ends on a note of conflict between the two — about whether
or not Birkin's ideal of "eternal union with a man" is possible. We
might consider Birkin's wish for such a union abstractly, apart from
what it may "mean" psychologically. It can easily enough be interpreted in terms of the principal sexual ambiguities of *Women
in Love*: it is, as Ursula says, a "theory," and it may disguise both
Birkin's dissatisfaction with heterosexuality and the homosexual impulses to which the suppressed prologue to the novel explicitly, and
guiltily, confessed. But we can also think of Birkin's desire simply
as a desire — that is, as a sign of Birkin's inability to be satisfied with
nondesiring stillness. His exhortations to "happy stillness" may
make us forget how restless he is throughout the novel — certainly
more restless than Ursula, whom he accuses of wanting the agitations of passion rather than the quietness of the union he offers her.
I don't mean that Birkin's striving is "better" than what he says he

is striving toward, but one can't help but admire the casualness with which Lawrence allows Birkin's aims to be questioned by others and tested by time. As Frank Kermode has written: "One of the achievements of the novel is to criticise the metaphysic, both by attacking Birkin and by obscuring doctrine with narrative symbolisms capable in their nature of more general and more doubtful interpretation." There is nothing final about the peace of "Excurse." If the language of that chapter makes it clear that the episode is something crucial which the novel has been struggling to reach, it's also true that the novel's apparent goal is not its climax but merely a narrative unit somewhere in the middle of the work, and that the novel itself works beyond its most exalted achievement.

For all Birkin's insistence, the dominant mode of *Women in Love* is interrogative rather than assertive. Birkin himself admits to confusion, foolishness and self-destructiveness, and Lawrence also allows him to be mocked by the other characters in ways which inject a healthy dose of humor into frequently strident pronouncements of doctrine. Ursula serves the immensely useful purpose of forcing Birkin into a dialogue. The will to know, as it is embodied in Hermione and in Gudrun, gets some ferocious treatment in *Women in Love*, and, as we have seen, the "unspeakable communication" reached in "Excurse" is something which "can never be known . . . never transmuted into mind content." But was Lawrence himself ever really convinced by something which he couldn't transform into "mind content"? There are no authentic mystical leaps in his work. If rational speech is confused, as Birkin recognizes when Ursula catches him in a contradiction, it must nevertheless be spoken. "And to know, to give utterance, was to break a way through the walls of the prison as the infant in labour strives through the walls of the womb. There is no new movement now, without the breaking through of the old body, deliberately, in knowledge, in the struggle to get out." Thus the tremendous importance of what Lawrence calls in the foreword to *Women in Love* "verbal consciousness": "Any man of real individuality tries to know and to understand what is happening, even in himself, as he goes along. This struggle for verbal consciousness should not be left out in art. It is a very great part of life. It is not superimposition of a theory. It is the passionate struggle into conscious being."

This defense of conscious knowledge could be thought of as

Lawrence's most serious limitation (although it could of course also be said that literature itself is inconceivable outside of "verbal consciousness"). The struggle to imagine new styles of being is prejudiced from the very start by an attachment to old modes of expression. The defender of "unspeakable communication" spent his life arguing and explaining, and he used almost every *known* literary form in his "struggle for verbal consciousness": the novel, the short story, plays, poems, letters, travel books, literary, philosophical and psychological essays. Lawrence's admirable (if sometimes tedious) need always to begin explaining again is the natural consequence of his insistence on transmuting into "mind content" states of being which may be instantly betrayed by each effort "to know and to understand what is happening." The confusions of deliberate speech constantly make him skeptical about what he imagines speech is referring to. But how *could* that speech refer to something fundamentally alien to the very field of knowledge allowed or provided for by rational discourse? And yet Lawrence wants to make verbal and essentially rational sense out of what he also claims is untranslatable into words. It is of course an impossible task, one which condemns him, furthermore, to endlessly repeating, although in a variety of forms, the same effort to integrate the unspeakable into speech. Lawrence sought verbal knowledge as an authenticating guide to "new movement" in himself and in the rest of humanity, whereas the very condition for that new movement may be an attempt to explode verbal consciousness.

However, this commitment to a constantly renewed struggle for rational utterance gives to Lawrence's work its intensely dramatic quality. As I suggested a moment ago, the most strident assertion almost always turns out to be tentative and interrogative. No statement is exempt from a dramatic confrontation with a different statement; thus all statements are subject to modification and even dismissal. And, finally, Lawrence found in realistic fiction an ideal vehicle for his qualified enthusiasms and his qualified rejections. It often seems that the mental activities most congenial to Lawrence are those of passing judgment and issuing formulas for salvation, and yet the novel is always an implicit mockery of such activities. In a remarkable essay entitled "The Novel," Lawrence spoke of this literary form as a discovery "far greater than Galileo's telescope or somebody else's wireless . . . because it is so incapable of the absolute. . . . In a novel, everything is relative to everything else, if that novel is art at all."

The conservatism of realistic fiction is the inevitable consequence of this relational bias. The heroes of most realistic novels are condemned to defeat by the mere fact that they are placed in social contexts which provide no occasion for heroic projects, and therefore no congenial relations in which the exceptional desires of exceptional individuals might be enacted.[8] In Lawrence, the banal and the ordinary are not used to confirm the dangerous impracticality of the heroic imagination. Rather, they are meant to stimulate his hero to imagine adjustments and refinements which would convince us of the social workability of his desires. Lawrence perhaps never does convince us definitively, but his work is nonetheless an extraordinarily impressive attempt to use the skepticism inherent to realistic fiction as a means of promoting rather than of deflating projects designed to revolutionize the self. Lawrence gives a certain nobility and even heroism to the usually petty criterion of probability to which realism would have us submit all speculations and desires. The Lawrentian ideal of stillness might have simply dismissed Lawrentian fiction, as the dovelike stillness of Milly Theale in James's *The Wings of the Dove* is essentially a dismissal of the novelistic world in which she briefly consents to live. Instead, fiction *continues* in Lawrence both to challenge and to strengthen that which transcends it. The extraordinary thus insists — perhaps in vain — on its compatibility with the ordinary; it accepts constraints which the less scrupulous apocalyptic works of modern literature simply ignore.

PART TWO

The Deconstructed Self

CHAPTER SEVEN

Desire and Metamorphosis

It is a man or a stone or a tree about to begin the fourth canto.[1]

Is Mr. Heathcliff a man? If so, is he mad? And if not, is he a devil?

THE MYTHIC LIMIT of questions about human identity is a question about the necessity of being human at all. The two passages I've just quoted raise precisely this possibility of a human body concealing or switching to nonhuman identities. We are probably not meant to take Isabella's questions in *Wuthering Heights* literally. They express her moral horror of Heathcliff's nature rather than a serious inquiry about whether or not he incarnates a real devil. In *Les Chants de Maldoror*, on the other hand, we have ample reason to expect that the narrator's doubts about what he himself is will be fully justified. Lautréamont's "heroes" move with ease between the human and the nonhuman: Maldoror frequently has the supernatural powers of God or the devil and at times he literally is, for example, a shark or an eagle. Emily Brontë's work is, on the surface, less fantastic than Lautréamont's; she observes certain criteria of probability regarding human behavior, criteria by which the amphibious and winged Maldoror is never constrained. Nevertheless, both books violently reject — in surprisingly similar ways — those assumptions about the natural or inevitable shape of the self which all the works we have looked at so far either reflect or at least partly accommodate. In *Wuthering Heights* and *Les Chants de Maldoror* we no longer have coherent, individuated, intelligible structures of personality; in a sense, we no longer even have a locatable self. Neither Lautréamont nor Brontë is interested in particular types of being. Rather, their works dramatize a frenetic uncertainty about the very possibility of being. For Maldoror, as well as for Heathcliff and Catherine, the question is not so much what to be as how to be. And for these heroes without being, there is nothing particular to desire. They will provide us with our purest examples so far of desires to which personality is irrelevant.

Appropriately enough, we know almost nothing about the author of *Les Chants de Maldoror*. Isidore-Lucien Ducasse was born in 1846 in Montevideo, where his father was then chancellor in the French Consulate. The boy was brought to France in 1859; he studied at the Lycées of Tarbes and Pau until 1865. In 1868, Ducasse was in Paris and the first canto of *Maldoror* was published. The other five cantos were printed in Brussels in 1869, but the printer — perhaps because, as Ducasse wrote in one of the few letters we have, "he is afraid of the attorney general" — refused to let them be sold. In two letters of February and March, 1870, Ducasse spoke of preparing a new volume in which he was renouncing his own literary past and "the poetry of doubt"; having completely changed his method, he would now "sing exclusively of hope [both *l'espoir* and *l'espérance* are used in the letter], calm happiness, duty." This small — and final — volume called *Poésies*, of about thirty pages, and which consists of aphoristic prose, was published in 1870. On November 24 of the same year, Ducasse died (at the age of 24). The death certificate gives us the date and the place of his death, and adds only: "bachelor, no further information." It was only in 1890, when a second edition of *Maldoror* was published in Paris, that the reputation and legend of Ducasse began to be made. He was praised by Huysmans, Jarry, Larbaud, Maeterlinck, and Remy de Gourmont (who spoke of *Maldoror* as "a magnificent, almost inexplicable stroke of genius, which will remain unique"). But it is the surrealists who brought real fame to Ducasse; they saw in him one of the few names from the past worthy of being kept alive. They found in his work ambitions similar to theirs, and, in their infatuation, even tried to create a personality and a biography (now discredited) for their hero. From 1919 (when he published the integral text of *Poésies* after having copied it from the manuscript at the Bibliothèque Nationale) to his angry answer, in 1951, to Camus's labeling of Lautréamont's revolt as conventional and factitious, André Breton consistently saw in Ducasse the one unattackable inspiration from the past for the surrealist adventure.

The Belgian printer had good reason to fear the attorney general: in spite of its consistently "respectable" diction, *Maldoror* is a steady stream of blasphemy and obscenity. Thematically, the book is un- original and boringly adolescent. It is a long diatribe against the evil nature of God and of man, at the same time that it documents the evil of its own hero, Maldoror. Lautréamont doesn't even bother to make the moral point of view consistent. At times, man is the virtuous victim of a malevolent God; at other times, he more than deserves whatever punishments he may have to suffer. Occasionally, Maldoror is the moral martyr who defends man against the persecu- tions of an unjust Creator. But he is also (and more often) the persecutor of his fellow men (if we can call Maldoror a man), and the book is full of Maldoror's spectacularly sadistic attacks on others — preferably on adolescent boys. *Les Chants de Maldoror* could be taken as the model for a very special literary genre: the sado- masochistic comic book.

Almost at the very beginning of the first canto, the narrator an- nounces that he uses his genius "to depict the delights of cruelty!" It's true that the reader's potential terror is forestalled by the manner in which Lautréamont both ridicules his own most terrifying inven- tions and smothers them in a kind of pasty dull prose. Nonetheless, the inventions themselves are remarkably wild and gruesome. Here is the narrator's description of his first view of God:

> . . . I slowly raised my mournful eyes, ringed with great bluish circles, towards the inverted bowl of the firmament, and dared to try and penetrate, young as I was, the mysteries of heaven. Not finding what I was seeking I raised my [terrified lids] higher . . . higher yet . . . until at last I perceived a throne built of human excrement and gold upon which was enthroned with idiot pride and robed in a shroud made from unlaundered hospital sheets, that one who calls himself the Creator!
> In his hand he held the decaying trunk of a [dead] man and

he lifted it successively from his eyes to his nose and from his nose to his mouth, where one may guess what he did with it. His feet were bathed in a vast morass of boiling blood to the surface of which there suddenly arose like tapeworms in the contents of a chamber-pot, two or three cautious heads which disappeared instantly with the speed of arrows; for an accurate kick on the nose was the well-known reward for such a revolt against the law, caused by a need to breathe the air, for men are not, after all, fish!

Amphibians [at the very most], they swam between two waters in that unclean juice! And when the Creator had nothing left in his hands he would seize another swimmer by the neck with the two first claws of his foot as in a pincers and raise him up out of that ruddy slime (delicious sauce!)

We are also treated to a view of God sprawled out drunk on the road, uttering incoherent words as blood pours from His nose; a man passes by and defecates, for three days, on God's "august face." Scalping and skinning are favorite forms of torture in the book. Maldoror also likes to reach down (or up) into people's insides and rip their organs out. He is also a great bloodsucker and enjoys cutting off a young man's wrist or throwing him into a sack and flinging him against a stone wall. He has sex with a female shark; he sings the praise of filth and of fleas; and he describes with relish the "cleaning" of a prostitute's vagina by a bunch of roosters and hens, who trampled "over her body as if it were a dunghill, and [pecked] at the flaccid lips of her swollen vagina until the blood came."

But the cruelty of Maldoror is somehow insubstantial. Lautré-amont is always adding the corny comment which takes the bite out of his indignation. For example, soon after the long passage I quoted in the previous paragraph, the narrator refers to God's lower jaw (as He chews up men) moving "his beard full of brains," and adds: "O reader, doesn't this last detail make your mouth water?" It is as if he were doing a tongue-in-cheek imitation of a straight horror story. At times he seems intent on outdoing the most extravagant Gothic inventions or the most impassioned romantic monologues, and at other times he deliberately — and rather grandly — dismisses his own success by longwinded, flat comments. Lautréamont is like a student showing he can excel in a certain type of written exercise — and showing at the same time that he doesn't even care about the effects that exercise is supposed to produce. The ultimate in showing off includes a suggestion of indifference to showing off. "I have sung of evil," Lautréamont wrote in a letter, "as did Mickiewicz, Byron, Milton, Southey, A. de Musset, Baudelaire, etc." To fill in the "etc." with other appropriate names would make for an impressive anthology of literary sources. Other critics have emphasized Lautréamont's bookishness; his work invites us to a feast of literary source-hunting. What I referred to a moment ago as a certain insubstantiality in *Maldoror's* violence derives mainly from the way in which that violence is continuously being exposed as an act of literary virtuosity. *Les Chants de Maldoror* seems to be about nothing more than Lautréamont's ability to write *Les Chants de Maldoror.* But it is this very extremity of literary self-consciousness in Maldoror which gives to the book its ontological originality. It is as if Lautréamont were so immersed in literature that he could begin to conceive of identities being constrained by nothing outside of literature. He makes the easy but radical step from a *nom de plume* to an *identité de plume,* and the result is a revolutionary decentralization of self, and an extraordinary psychic mobility.

The biographical Isidore Ducasse is almost lost, both to literary history and to the works which attribute their authorship to a fictive Comte de Lautréamont. But then where is this unreal Lautréamont in his own book? The narrative "I" sometimes reports on Maldoror as if the latter were clearly distinct from the former. At times, the narrator is omniscient and insightful; at other times, he seems to be a stupefied and not particularly well-informed spectator of Maldoror's activities. But there are also moments when, without indicating that he is quoting Maldoror, the narrator speaks with Maldoror's voice, and Lautréamont, his narrator, and his hero are fused into one. Thus the identity presumably "behind" *Les Chants de Maldoror* — that of Isidore Ducasse — gets lost in its derivations. And the indeterminate voice we hear — does it belong to Ducasse? to Lautréamont? to an omniscient narrator outside of the story? to a narrator participating in the story, even if only as a spectator? or, finally, to Maldoror? — also shifts indeterminately along various attitudes. Its moral personality is sometimes sadistic, sometimes humane; it belongs to "someone" ready to defend men, and then to torture them, someone who both sings "the delights of cruelty" and sheds tears over men's cruelty to one another. The sliding of identities in *Maldoror* isn't limited to various names or various moral attitudes. Lautréamont responds to the suggestions for self-transformation in literary comparisons. Early in Canto One, he (who?) writes that he would have liked to be the "son of a female shark," and then he describes his physical appearance: "No one yet has seen the green furrows in my forehead, nor the protruding bones of my emaciated face, resembling the bones of some great fish, or the rocks which cover the seashore, or the rugged Alpine mountains which I climbed often when my hair was of a different color." What is to prevent him from becoming that which he resembles? He confesses to having lived "a half-century in the form of a shark among the submarine currents that extend along the African coast," and in one of his happiest dreams he lives in a pig's body. The capacity for metamorphoses is shared by everyone in the book. In the Mervyn short story which constitutes Canto Six, Maldoror becomes a black swan. God is a rhinoceros, and one of his archangels "had taken on the form of a hermit crab large as a vicuna." Elsseneur and Reginald are changed into a giant spider so that they may punish Maldoror for trying to kill them by sucking the blood from his neck every night for twenty years.

What makes these metamorphoses so powerful in *Maldoror* is precisely what might seem to condemn them to triviality: their purely literary derivation. They have their source in an imagination unconstrained by any sense of responsibility to the real. And the invisible Ducasse finds his peculiar liberty of self-effacement and self-transformation both frightening and exhilarating. What the isolated and bookish author of *Les Chants de Maldoror* seems to discover is that, alone with words, one experiences the extent to which language doesn't merely describe identity but actually produces moral and perhaps even physical identity. We can of course choose to be literal-minded and insist that no amount of self-comparisons will suffice to change us into sharks. But in trying to account for the originality of *Maldoror*, I think that we have to allow for a kind of dissolution or at least elasticity of being induced by an immersion in literature. Up until now we have of course been examining the opposite effect of literary activity on the imagination of character and desire. In previous chapters, we have seen literature's complicity with the rational articulations and structural coherence of language. The coherent system of language is paralleled both in the compositional coherence of traditional works of literature as well as in the coherent characters who inhabit those works. The self is a unified whole, and even its most idiosyncratic desires can be made intelligible in a personality portrait. Once literature approaches noninterpretable being, it begins to show suicidal tendencies. Even in James and Lawrence, the intuition of desires or states of being unassimilable to the structural designs of a story or a self leads to a loss of novelistic energy *and* of life energy. Original desire either becomes the secret of death (as in *The Wings of the Dove*) or creates a deathlike stillness in life which is really the renunciation of all desire (as in *Women in Love*).

With Lautréamont, we see for the first time the *destructuring* possibilities of language. There is a kind of verbal terrorism which murders sense without even disrupting legitimate verbal orders and sequences. The attack against structure in *Maldoror* is carried out in the most rigorously structured way; each sentence, each stanza, each canto, and the succession of cantos are prodigies of controlled composition. What distintegrates the composed work and the composed self in *Maldoror* is a kind of exacerbated receptiveness to the very procedure of thought which generally helps us to compose a self or a literary work: that is, to comparisons. Instead of making reality intelligible by establishing relations among distinct units of experience, comparison in Lautréamont dislocates reality by violating two conditions never stated in any specific comparison, but which guarantee the epistemological usefulness of all comparisons. First of all, Lautréamont refuses to acknowledge that there has to be any recognizable similarity of nature between the two terms of a comparison, and secondly he doesn't hesitate to convert an analogy into an identity. Lautréamont's most original comparisons are not an extension of our sense of affinities; they do not make us suddenly see, in a flash of recognition which is generally thought of as part of the poetic shock, unsuspected relations among "distant" elements of reality. Here are two examples of the much-praised "beau comme" construction which appears most frequently in Cantos Five and Six:

> Although he [the pelican being described by the narrator] possessed no human countenance, he appeared to me as beautiful as the two long tentaculiform filaments of an insect; or rather as a sudden interment; or again as the law of the restoration of mutilated organs; and especially as an eminently putrescible liquid!

> [Mervyn] is as handsome as the retractability of the claws of birds of prey; or again, as the uncertainty of the muscular movements of wounds in the soft parts of the posterior cervical region; or rather as the perpetual rat trap, re-set each time by the trapped animal, that can catch rodents indefinitely and works even when hidden beneath straw; and especially as the fortuitous encounter upon a dissecting table of a sewing machine and an umbrella!

These comparisons have no educational, no cognitive function. What they do is simply to move us away from their supposed points of departure. There is no resemblance between Mervyn's beauty and a "perpetual rat trap" or the meeting on a dissecting table of a sewing machine and an umbrella. Proust writes that "truth" in literature begins only when the writer establishes the relationship between two different objects or when, "comparing qualities shared by two sensations, he makes the essential nature common to both sensations stand out clearly by joining them in a metaphor, in order to remove them from the contingencies of time. . . ." Nothing could be more alien to the poetics of *Maldoror*. Lautréamont's comparisons are strategies for leaps of being. The word "like" does not draw disparate aspects of our experience into a single structure; instead of being a technique of enclosure (as it is in part for Proust), metaphor in *Maldoror* is an invitation to metamorphosis. The second term of a comparison doesn't illuminate the first term; rather, it proposes that we forget it, that we almost literally jump away from it.

Les Chants de Maldoror is one of literature's most daring enterprises of decentralization. It is a major document among modern efforts to break away from what Jacques Derrida has been brilliantly anatomizing as the Western cultural habit of referring all experience to centers, or beginnings, or origins of truth and being. With Lautréamont, such points of departure are authentically negligible. And every aspect of his work contributes to the dispersion or the crumbling of fixed identities. By a happy misfortune of literary history, Isidore Ducasse is as fictive a personality for us as the invented Lautréamont who takes credit for the adventures of an imaginary Maldoror, adventures told by a narrator elusively floating among various physical and moral identities. And where exactly can we locate Ducasse-Lautréamont's imagination? *Maldoror* (and this is even truer of the *Poésies*) is the work of a plagiarizing genius; or, to turn the formula around, it testifies to the genius of plagiarism, to the appeal of wandering among styles and episodes all of which could simply be designated as *other*. They belong to or come from neither Ducasse nor his presumed sources. *Maldoror* is at once so like and so unlike those sources that it transcends its own imitations and forces us to renounce the critical compulsion to make attributions.

Lautréamont's work is "about" the capacity of being to glide from one form to another. From the stylistic level of the narrator's comparisons to the "characters'" fabulous transformations, we are somewhat tauntingly put through a circus of metamorphoses. There is also Lautréamont's unrelentingly ironic self-consciousness. Always willing to destroy his effects, to deflate the pose of anguish with a trivial detail or a corny joke, to allow the melodramatic and the prosaic to cancel each other out, to make such monstrously long and boring sentences that we can't even be sure he wants to be read, Lautréamont manages to disappear from a statement at the very moment he makes it. He is the master of irony — if we take irony to be something more radical than a discrepancy between apparent significance and real significance. Irony is the style of a mind in constant metamorphosis. In Lautréamont, as Maurice Blanchot has written in *Lautréamont et Sade*, the ironic statement hides no definite meaning but merely designates the author's absence from his statements. The narrator's "person" in *Maldoror* — whoever or whatever that may be — is never where he is speaking; he is, bizarrely, perhaps nothing more than a somewhere else.

Compared to *Les Chants de Maldoror*, *Wuthering Heights* is sensibly realistic. No one changes into a shark, or even flies through the air, and the sadism in Emily Brontë's novel seems mild after Lautréamont's feasts of sexual violence. But it is almost as difficult to locate and define human identity in *Wuthering Heights* as it is in

Maldoror. Both works have a kind of ontological slipperiness; being is always somewhere else, and human utterance tends to make personality problematic rather than to express it. There are, first of all, the complications of narrative point of view in *Wuthering Heights*. Point of view in the novel is both derived and scattered. Brontë has chosen a narrative method consistent with the self-diffusive energies dramatized in her work. There is a movement *away from* the author in *Wuthering Heights* not unlike the movement away from Isidore Ducasse which we have noted in *Les Chants de Maldoror*. True, there is no confusion of points of view in the former work, whereas in *Maldoror* the narrator is at times distinct from Maldoror and at other times merged with him. The similarity between the two works lies in the system of narrative replacements which they both use. Maldoror replaces Lautréamont who replaces Ducasse; Nelly replaces Lockwood who replaces the (hypothetical) omniscient narrator standing outside the story. In *Wuthering Heights*, especially in those passages narrated from Isabella's or Heathcliff's point of view, the effect is one of little boxes within bigger boxes: Isabella's letter is inserted in Nelly Dean's story which is recorded in Lockwood's journal which, as an "event," is itself only a part of *Wuthering Heights*. These superficial complications are of course conventional narrative tricks, and in themselves they don't make for the indeterminacy of being which everything in *Maldoror* advertises more loudly and more directly. But, taken in conjunction with other elements in her work, Emily Brontë's narrative method, like Lautréamont's, works toward the disappearance of a simple identity continuously recognizable throughout the story as the creative identity at the origin of the story.

The complicated network of family relationships in *Wuthering Heights* is a more effective, but also more ambiguous, device for the subversion of individuality. Emily Brontë uses genealogy as a pretext for depersonalization at the same time that it provides her characters with a biological structure of self-perpetuation. Marriage in the novel is the legalistic sign of more mysterious psychological fusions. Catherine's marriage to Edgar Linton is the first official bond between the Earnshaws and the Lintons. Isabella's marriage brings Heathcliff into the family, and in fact creates the only "nameable" bond between him and Catherine: she becomes his sister-in-law. That connection is strengthened, and complicated, by the young Catherine's marriage to young Linton: Heathcliff's niece becomes his daughter-in-law. Finally, the projected marriage between Hareton Earnshaw and Catherine Linton-Heathcliff appears to bring all these family threads together, but it is, formally, more of a repetition of the link established between the Earnshaws and the Lintons by the first Catherine's marriage, and therefore a reconfirmation of Heathcliff's exclusion from the family circle. It is a sort of special victory for the Earnshaws, in whose household Heathcliff had been the *unrelated* intruder. The Heathcliff line disappears. And having gone from one Catherine Earnshaw to two Catherine Lintons (mother and daughter), we finally return to one Catherine Earnshaw (who brings both the Linton and the Earnshaw estates — the latter by virtue of her being Heathcliff's daughter-in-law — back to the Earnshaws). Finally, even the Lintons are somewhat squeezed out by this curiously narcissistic union of Earnshaw with itself: both Hareton and Catherine have had one Earnshaw as a parent, and each one gets half an Earnshaw for a spouse.

This can get to sound like a funny family play, but *Wuthering Heights* is, in effect, an ingenious exercise in creating family ties and resemblances. The claustrophobic inbreeding in the novel is paralleled by psychological repetitions which also draw the characters into a single family. Psychological affinities are at times superimposed, in a more or less realistic way, on family ties; at other times, they exist outside of family ties. Hindley's despair after his wife's death prefigures Heathcliff's despair after Catherine's death. The former becomes as sullenly misanthropic as the latter; and just as Heathcliff will rule over the unhappy Catherine and Linton, and then Catherine and Hareton, Hindley, after his wife's death, terrorizes Catherine and Heathcliff (as well as his son Hareton). There are obvious differences between the two situations, but in each case children are tyrannized or neglected (or both) by a man grief-stricken at the loss of a loved woman. And this similarity tends somewhat to dilute Heathcliff's originality. When we look at the novel in this way, certain configurations of characters begin to compete for our attention with the individual characters themselves. (In the same way, as we have seen, Charles Mauron's and Roland Barthes' readings of Racine draw our attention to repeated groupings in the plays rather than to individual personalities.) Heathcliff is no longer, so to speak, entirely within himself; he "occurs," in modified versions, elsewhere in the novel. The most dramatic example of this repetition of being is, as Heathcliff himself sees, in Hareton. Heathcliff has put Hindley's son in almost the same situation as the one in which Heathcliff had suffered at the hands of Hindley. In Hareton's aspect, Heathcliff sees, he tells Nelly, the ghost "of my wild endeavors to hold my right, my degradation, my pride, my happiness, and my anguish." Hareton is also "the ghost of my immortal love": to Heathcliff's exasperation, Hareton resembles Catherine rather than her hated brother Hindley. In a sense, then, Catherine and Heathcliff's union in *Wuthering Heights* is realized only in the peculiarly hybrid "person" of Hareton. Instead of merely punishing Hindley through his son, Heathcliff has managed to create himself outside himself. And he "can hardly bear" to see Hareton — which reminds us (I'll return to this) of Catherine's inability to bear seeing her own reflection in the mirror during her delirium shortly before her death.

There are other striking parallelisms in the story. Isabella's unhappy solitude at Wuthering Heights reminds us of the young Catherine as Lockwood sees her at the beginning of the novel. Occasionally Emily Brontë emphasizes the victimization of a couple of children by an unhappy and violent man (Heathcliff and Hindley); with Isabella and with Catherine after the death of Heathcliff's son, Brontë also underlines the isolation of a woman imprisoned by a man who hates her. Also, the second generation in *Wuthering Heights* has inherited certain characteristics from the parent generation. Catherine's daughter is almost as high-spirited and stubbornly independent as her mother. The young Linton is a more whining version of his mother, and Edgar Linton, before Catherine's death, curiously displays some of the traits we will find in Isabella's son: he is weak and sickly, and given over to fits of trembling and crying when Catherine and Heathcliff oppose him. Finally, and in a more general way, the second part of *Wuthering Heights* repeats the major patterns of the first part. But the marriage of Catherine and Hareton after Heathcliff's death provides a happy ending for the novel's unhappy children. The dangerous man (who, in Heathcliff's case, is also the stronger) dies, and Brontë finally coerces her literary fantasy into a form tame enough to satisfy Nelly Dean, and moral enough to put an end to Nelly's half-hearted but persistent scolding.

If these affiliations and resemblances disperse individual identities in *Wuthering Heights* (each character is, genealogically and/or psychologically, present in other characters), they also tend to enclose experience within a circle of repetitions. The world is a family in *Wuthering Heights*, and the novel examines both a threat to the family from something outside it and the familial strategies for transforming life into an uninterrupted repetition of the same. The contrast between the Grange and Wuthering Heights is a false, or at least an insignificant, one. Emily Brontë does not oppose a world of civilized moral conventions to one of untamed passions. Edgar and Isabella belong as little as the Earnshaws and Heathcliff do to "society"; they are uninterested in its pleasures (which Lockwood vaguely evokes) and indifferent to its morality (which Nelly tirelessly proposes). When Cathy and Heathcliff first go to the Grange, they come upon a scene worthy of Wuthering Heights: Isabella is screaming at one end of the room, Edgar is crying, "and in the middle of the table sat a little dog shaking its paw and yelping, which, from their mutual accusations, we understood they had nearly pulled in two between them." Edgar and Isabella's parents, the possible representatives of civilized society, practically don't exist in the novel; they conveniently die as soon as the Lintons become important in the story, and the children of both the Heights and the Grange quickly have the stage to themselves. To go from Wuthering Heights to the Grange is not to go from nature to society; it is to go from the strong children to the weak children, or, more precisely, from aggressively selfish children to whiningly selfish children.

The relation between the family and individual being is a problematic one. The family is simultaneously a source of confusion about the nature and the boundaries of the self, and a self-reflecting structure where each member provides a reassuring mirror in which the others can recognize and fix themselves. In the beginning, the mother is the world; furthermore, the reality and, subsequently, the illusion of oneness with the mother give us our brief period of immunity from the problem of individuality. But as we are forced to recognize that the world exists beyond the mother, and also that her existence is distinct from ours, we must confront a double and fundamentally terrifying puzzle: what am I? and what is it which exists beyond me? The familial fantasies of infancy and childhood are in large part a compromise solution to this puzzle: we try out *being* various parental roles, we imagine parts of our parents' bodies in our bodies, or, conversely, we fantasize being swallowed up into their being or penetrating — beneficently or destructively — their bodies.

It could thus be said that while the family is of course a natural biological structure, the child's fundamental project within that structure is, curiously enough, to create a family. That is, he has to be able to recognize people whose being is co-extensive with his own, whose individuality he can "rob" in order to give himself substance, to fill up the forlorn emptiness of his own individuality. In parents and in brothers and sisters, the child finds himself by finding himself repeated. But he doesn't know himself before the repetitions, or the repetitions wouldn't be necessary. There is not an original self he first discovers and then seeks to reproduce or perpetuate: the "original" self *is* the reproduced, reflected, repeated self which the real and imaginary resemblances, penetrations and fusions of family life provide.

Wuthering Heights documents a frenetic attempt to create family ties — or, to put it in another way, to tie the self up in an unbreakable family circle. I don't mean that any of the characters is explicitly engaged in this project. Rather, it is the project behind the novel's organization. If we think of the book in this way, the necessity of the rather boring second half of the novel begins to be evident. Emily Brontë needs the alliances of a second generation in order to bind all her characters together into a single bundle of familial repetitions and cross-references. A certain amount of genealogical confusion is a guarantee of ontological stability. Thus, the marriage of Hindley's son to Heathcliff's son's widow (who is also the daughter of Hareton's aunt and of Linton's uncle) reinforces the singleness of the novel's familial purpose: everyone is finally related to everyone else, and, in a sense, repeated in everyone else. The young Catherine's two marriages emphasize the connections between her family and those of Linton and Hareton; her marriages are, as it were, tautologies by which she merely reasserts (in new form) the familial connection already existing between her and Linton and between her and Hareton. The psychological parallelisms discussed earlier work in the same direction. Characters are like one another both in blood and in spirit, and while this may make it impossible to draw sharp boundaries separating one individuality from another, a world of identical beings makes it possible for everyone to be everywhere, even if he is nowhere in particular.

Wuthering Heights provides a familial solution to the problem of identity because it is imprisoned within the familial imagination of the problem itself. More specifically, its perspective on the family is that of neglected — and therefore free but desperate — children. The emotional register of the novel is that of hysterical children, and several scenes in the novel remind us of children's cruel play. There is, apparently, no room for the helpful parent in Brontë's familial imagination. Nelly Dean is tolerated but never looked up to; the Earnshaw father and Isabella's and Edgar's parents are insignificant and fleeting presences in the story. (This is, incidentally, especially curious since the material coziness provided by parents is never absent from the novel, even at the moments of greatest chaos in the household. Domestic routine, it has been pointed out, is always maintained; fires are tended to, food is served, great numbers of dishes are carefully arranged on shelves. But those parental routines which, so to speak, helpfully banalize a child's melodramatic imagination, merely coexist, in *Wuthering Heights*, with that imagination; they have no effect on its extravagances.) The frantic nature of the effort to create family ties in *Wuthering Heights* can in part be explained by the absence or the insignificance of parents. But even this doesn't fully explain the frenzy in the novel, and in order to provide such an explanation we must now look more closely at the threat to the family which gives such urgency to the project of enclosing the self within a narrow and inviolable circle of familial mirrors.

Three times in *Wuthering Heights* a young stranger is thrust upon the family as a member of the family. Mr. Earnshaw brings Heathcliff back from Liverpool and asks his children to accept him as a brother. Hindley returns to Wuthering Heights after his father's death almost like a stranger (he "was altered considerably in the three years of his absence"), and he brings with him a wife whose origins no one knows ("what she was, and where she was born, he never informed us . . ."). Edgar brings young Linton to the Grange after Isabella's death, and after only one night at the home of the uncle he has never known, he is carried off to live at the Heights with the father he has never known. The differences between these characters and episodes are obvious. Frances Earnshaw, for example, is hardly a Heathcliff-like figure, and the young Catherine, unlike her mother and Hindley in the earlier incident, eagerly anticipates her cousin's arrival. But there is also the similarity, and I think that it gives us the key to the most significant psychological structure of *Wuthering Heights*.

We can begin by noting that the last two episodes in the series are merely pale reflections of the first. While both Hindley's return with Frances and Linton's arrival have important consequences for the other characters, they are not comparable to the consequences of Heathcliff's appearance at Wuthering Heights. The aspect of repetition would therefore seem to indicate the obsessive nature of the pattern in Emily Brontë's imagination, while the *significance* of that pattern seems to me to be worked out only in the case of Heathcliff. And Brontë puts Heathcliff in distinct opposition to everyone else in the novel, including Catherine. I argued a few pages back against a view of the novel which opposes the Grange to the Heights; I would also maintain that the view which pits both Heathcliff and Catherine against all the other characters is just as false. Both in situation and in temperament, Catherine and Heathcliff are profoundly different from each other. She is sociable, high-spirited, indeed often manic; he is quiet, closed, and he hoards his feelings in a way dramatically opposed to Catherine's wild display of feelings. If, as we shall see in a moment, Catherine's assertion that she *is* Heathcliff is enormously important, she is by no means *like* Heathcliff. Furthermore, beyond these anecdotal differences of personality, Catherine, like all the other principal characters, belongs by blood to a family in the novel; we know her origins. It's tempting to put her — wrongly, I think — on Heathcliff's "side" because it is mainly through Catherine that Brontë examines the danger and the appeal of Heathcliff. She is, in psychoanalytic terms, the principal ego of the novel, the "I" who, while not providing the narrative eye in the technical sense of point of view, nonetheless expresses most clearly the novel's psychological point of view on familial and nonfamilial identities. It is through Catherine's relation to Heathcliff that Brontë dramatizes most powerfully her children's exhilarating and terrifying confusion about what and where the self is in and beyond the family.

Heathcliff is the Maldoror possibility of *Wuthering Heights*. We might say that Emily Brontë gives us a psychologically realistic version of Lautréamont's fantastic experiment in the decentering of personal identity. I spoke of the problematic or insignificant nature, on various levels, of points of departure in *Les Chants de Maldoror*. A floating narrator is untraceable to any definite source; Maldoror is less a fixed or consistent character than he is a prospect of metamorphoses; the second term of a comparison negates any ontological responsibility to the first term; and Lautréamont's ironic tone prevents us from using what he says as a reliable path to what he "really" thinks. In *Wuthering Heights*, Heathcliff embodies the Maldoror fantasy of existence without origins. Not only does no one know how Heathcliff had come to be on the streets of Liverpool, where Mr. Earnshaw finds him "starving and homeless, and as good as dumb"; we are not even told where he goes or what he does during the time of his absence from the Heights. He merely appears, each time without causes, without history: first as an abandoned child, then as the elegant and rich gentleman whose good fortune is as untraceable as the forlorn wandering of the child had been. The frenzy of *Wuthering Heights* is the result of Heathcliff's sudden appearance in the middle of a family whose members know who they are, where they come from, what they belong to. What can be the family's relation to this creature without relations? And, more radically, how is it even conceivable that Catherine should claim an identity with this alien intruder? What does it mean to *be* the other?

There are, of course, all the signs of a drama of sibling recognition in *Wuthering Heights*. The drama is a familiar one, and I don't suppose it would surprise anyone if we could prove (which we cannot) that it was a major unconscious "theme" in the Brontë family. To the mystification of the other children, a new child is brought home; they are expected to love him, to believe that he is as much a part of the family as they are, and to accept the division of their parents' attention between the intruder and themselves. Older children's ambivalent feelings toward their new brother or sister become, in *Wuthering Heights*, the nonambivalent feelings of two distinct characters: all the passionate attachment is enacted by Catherine, all the passionate hostility is attributed to Hindley. (In parallel fashion, Mr. Earnshaw comes to idolize Heathcliff; Mrs. Earnshaw scolds her husband for bringing the strange child home.) The novel also suggests the skepticism with which children receive the news that the sibling-stranger is part of their family. To a certain extent, Heathcliff is allowed to penetrate the family circle. He marries a Linton, and his son marries an Earnshaw's daughter. In addition to this, as I suggested earlier, Heathcliff's particularity is somewhat diluted by certain psychological analogies, and by analogies of situation, between him and Hindley, and between him and Hareton. A diffusion and repetition of Heathcliff in other characters of *Wuthering Heights* could be taken as the sign of a willingness to recognize the sibling's right to be in the family. Emily Brontë establishes continuities of being among Heathcliff and the others which partially break down the barriers between him and them. Anecdotally, he is resented and fought against, but structurally he is allowed to contribute to the complete network of familial and spiritual affinities in *Wuthering Heights*. (Also, he is the alien orphan, but the Earnshaws give him the name of a son who died in childhood.) Finally, however, the decision seems to go against Heathcliff. His death and Catherine and Hareton's marriage make of his presence at the Heights a kind of parenthetical intrusion into the Earnshaws' and the Lintons' family life. The last marriage in the novel expels Heathcliff once and for all from the two families' futures, and the stranger, now dead, has once again become the wanderer. We first heard of him roaming the streets of Liverpool, and now, according to Nelly, ". . . the country folks, if you asked them, would swear on their Bible that he *walks*."

But Heathcliff has been more than the half-wanted and half-detested sibling. Brontë subordinates the drama of sibling recognition in *Wuthering Heights* to the more fundamental ontological drama of what might be called self-distancing. Suspicion of the sibling, and ambivalent feelings toward him or her, are occasions for certain discoveries about the self and the world. If a child feels mystified about a younger sibling's origins, and yet is somehow persuaded that they have the same origins, he is confronting, in a particularly confusing form, the possibility of his being elsewhere than where he recognizes himself to be. This possibility will bring us back to *Maldoror*, but I should first say that it presents a more difficult problem than that of recognizing that the world contains spaces where we don't exist. This latter recognition is implicit in the child's game of "disappearance and return" described by Freud in a famous passage of *Beyond the Pleasure Principle*. A one-and-a-half-year-old boy has a wooden reel with a piece of string tied around it. Holding the reel by the string, he throws it over the edge of his curtained cot, so that it disappears, and he utters an "expressive 'o-o-o-o-,' " which Freud and the child's mother both see as representing the German word "fort" ("gone"). He then pulls the reel back to him by the string and greets its reappearance "with a joyful 'da' ('there')." Freud connects this game to "the child's great cultural achievement — the instinctual renunciation . . . which he had made in allowing his mother to go away without protesting. He compensated himself for this, as it were, by himself staging the disappearance and return of the objects within his reach." The game can also be looked at as evidence of the child's awareness that the world exists beyond his perception of it. The child "knows" that the world exists, and that he is not the entire world. And this awareness is the necessary condition for imagination and for desire: without a sense of realities beyond us, we would be incapable of experiencing the lack without which desire is inconceivable.

In a footnote to this passage from *Beyond the Pleasure Principle*, Freud speaks of another game in which, having been left alone for several hours one day, the same child finds "a method of making himself disappear. He had discovered his reflection in a full-length mirror which did not quite reach to the ground, so that by crouching down he could make his mirror-image 'gone.' " This new game brings us closer to *Wuthering Heights*. Freud makes almost no comment on the later development of the child's play, but it's clear that the boy has now become a victim of his own discovery. His sense of reality is, as it were, *too* developed. For whereas the wooden reel did in fact exist although it was "gone" or "away," the child's mirror-image is of course not somewhere else when the child is no longer in front of the mirror. Our reflection in a mirror cannot be present and then authentically absent; it can only be present at the same moment that it is at a certain distance from us.

As long as the child takes his self-reflection for someone else, there is no problem: the image in the mirror is just another person, and it is therefore part of a world which the child is either engaged in absorbing into himself (in order to deny his severance from his mother), or which he recognizes as existing independently of his own existence (it exists when it is "fort" as well as when it is "da"). But his realization that what he is seeing in the mirror is himself is different from both these possibilities. He knows that he is not in the mirror, and yet he must get used to the fact that he *is* that distant foreign person. I suspect that the resonance which Freud's anecdote has for the adult imagination has to do with the suitability of the mirror as a metaphor for the inaccessibility of one's possible selves to one's present consciousness. It is a spatial representation of an intuition that our being can never be adequately enclosed within any present formulation — any formulation here and now — of our being. It is as if the experience of perceiving ourselves elsewhere suggested the possibility of our becoming something else. Mirrors represent as a phenomenon of distance our capacity for unpredictable metamorphoses.

Of course, mirrors can also be used as instruments of ontological security. The world loses its threateningly alien aspect if we can continuously recognize our own image in it. This is the side of the mirror experience which Proust and Sartre have emphasized. In *A la Recherche du temps perdu*, for example, Marcel is always trying to find himself in others, to transform them into mirrors in which he can recognize a stable image of himself. But we shouldn't confuse the use to which the experience of the mirror can be put with what is the original and perhaps essential nature of that experience. The attempt to make others into stabilizing mirrors is an attempt to deny that very distance of part of the self from consciousness which the mirror originally represents. Once we have a familiar image of ourselves, we can try to plant it everywhere, thus eliminating all distance in our contacts with the world. But in fact a mirror is nothing if not a producer of an effect of distance; it even adds to our realistic sense of distance by creating a false space. Thus, although it is ourselves we see in the mirror, the experience can paradoxically be considered as a model for our imagination of being different from ourselves.

Wuthering Heights represents the danger of being haunted by alien versions of the self. We even see Catherine, during her delirium, terrorized by her own image in the mirror. She complains to Nelly that her room is "haunted," that the strange face (her own) is "behind there still" even after Nelly has covered the mirror with a shawl. Catherine would flee from this self "out there," but she is also fascinated by it, and in Heathcliff she finds an incarnation of herself as another person. It is, of course, a reciprocal discovery. "Oh God!

it is unutterable!" Heathcliff cries after her death, "I *cannot* live
without my life! I *cannot* live without my soul!" In a sense, Heathcliff is pursued by *his* life, by *his* soul, during the years between
Catherine's death and his. Catherine's spirit hovers about him, but
she seems to be unable, or to refuse, to show herself to him. Heathcliff dies simply from his sense that her appearance is imminent. He
doesn't die from the pain of losing her; he dies from the unbearable
exaltation of knowing that he is about to find himself again in her.
Nelly is struck by the "strange joyful glitter in his eyes"; he smiles
more than he ever has during the few· days before he dies. His
frame shivers "not as one shivers with a chill or weakness, but as a
tight-stretched cord vibrates — a strong thrilling, rather than trembling"; and even in death his eyes keep a "frightful, life-like gaze
of exaltation." True, Heathcliff doesn't eat for four days before his
death, but even the prosaic Nelly realizes that ". . . he did not abstain
on purpose; it was the consequence of his strange illness, not the
cause." Indeed, we see Heathcliff ready, almost anxious, to eat, but
he seems unable to touch the food, as if someone else were keeping
him from it. It is almost as if the inclination to eat were a mistake
about which form of himself he should now nourish — and the
dead Catherine corrects that mistake by forcing him to starve the
Heathcliff she finally succeeds in making him leave.

But it is of course Heathcliff himself whom we see most clearly
as a nonidentical double. Certain aspects of the famous passage in
which Catherine tells Nelly: "I *am* Heathcliff. . . ." could lead us
to underestimate the originality of that assertion. At moments it's
difficult to know exactly what sort of self-projection Catherine is
speaking of. She seems almost to be saying — quite banally — that
it's more beautiful or more moral to live beyond oneself than to be
entirely contained within oneself: ". . . Surely you and everybody,"
she says to Nelly, "have a notion that there is, or should be an
existence of forces beyond you. What was the use of my creation
if I were entirely contained here?" This could fit all sorts of presumably generous, or at least acceptably egotistical impulses: impulses to give oneself to others, to enlarge one's sphere of influence
on the world, to escape from the spiritual poverty of an isolated
individual existence, or even to immortalize oneself in a work of art.

But Catherine really cares very little about whether or not her
creation, as she puts it, has any use. Heathcliff is her "great thought

in living. . . . If all else perished, and he remained, I should still continue to be; and if all else remained and he were annihilated, the universe would turn to a mighty stranger." This, however, doesn't strike an original note either; it is a conventional cry of romantic passion. Much weirder — as Nelly sees — is the view of her connection to Heathcliff implied in Catherine's certainty that Edgar won't mind her marrying him in order to "aid Heathcliff to rise" and to escape from Hindley's power. And when Heathcliff first visits Edgar and Catherine at the Grange after his long absence, Catherine makes almost no attempt to hide "the intensity of her delight" and seems surprised that Edgar doesn't share it. (Merle Oberon's Catherine, in the movie version of *Wuthering Heights*, is guilty of no such originality: her nervousness at Heathcliff's return is the unmistakable sign of a guilty romantic passion. She and Laurence Olivier transform Emily Brontë's work into a great romantic film.) But Catherine's feelings are irrefutably logical. She appears to take literally the identification between Heathcliff and herself, and therefore expects Edgar to recognize her in Heathcliff, to love her in him. Of all her motives for marrying Edgar, the desire to help Heathcliff strikes her as the least selfish, the motive most worthy of Edgar's appreciation: "This is for the sake of one who comprehends in his person my feelings to Edgar and myself." Catherine uses the word "love" to describe her attachment to Heathcliff, but love is irrelevant to this mysterious identity of being. That love is "a source of little visible delight, but necessary"; Heathcliff is always in Catherine's mind, "not just as a pleasure, any more than I am always a pleasure to myself — but as my own being."

Heathcliff is so radically the other that he is almost the beastly or even the inanimate. The only time we see Catherine in Heathcliff's arms is more likely to remind us of Maldoror's mating with a shark than of even the most turbulent scenes of romantic passion. They embrace so fiercely that Nelly fears Catherine has fainted, but as Nelly approaches them, Heathcliff "gnashed" at her and "foamed like a mad dog. . . . I did not feel as if I were in the company of a creature of my own species; it appeared that he would not understand, though I spoke to him; so, I stood off, and held my tongue, in great perplexity." "Mad dog" is of course "merely" a comparison, and there is always a realistic "out" for the extravagances of *Wuthering Heights*. Lockwood's encounter with the dead

Catherine may be part of his nightmare, and the rumors of Heathcliff's and Catherine's spirits wandering on the moors may be, as Nelly says, the "idle tales" of superstitious "country folks." It is astonishing how, without ever frankly transgressing the boundaries of realistic probability, Emily Brontë manages to suggest, at least as powerfully as Lautréamont does, the potentially fragile nature of our distinctions between the human and the nonhuman. Significantly, it is the stranger Heathcliff who is most closely associated with the moors around Wuthering Heights. In one sense, Wuthering Heights (unlike Thrushcross Grange) represents the outside world: not the world of society, which is simply ignored in the novel, but merely the world outside the self and its comforting repetitions in the family. Heathcliff is an intruder into the household at the Heights, but he belongs to the place, which is a way of saying that he (and, only through him, Catherine) belong to the alienating possibilities of Wuthering Heights.

As his name suggests, Heathcliff is a reminder of our ties to matter. "My love for Heathcliff," Catherine tells Nelly in a comparison which we might take more literally than we are apparently meant to, "resembles the eternal rocks beneath the trees"; Catherine describes Heathcliff to Isabella as "a fierce, pitiless, wolfish man," and as "an arid wilderness of furze and whinstone." Brontë's imagination is as receptive as Lautréamont's to our potentialities — both imaginary and corporeal — for a kind of sliding back and forth along the evolutionary scale. The distinctive trait of *Wuthering Heights* is that, due to its comparatively realistic format, it examines these potentialities in an ambiguously domestic framework. On the one hand, the domestic is a defense against the alienating metamorphosis; there is the family circle at the Grange, which in fact triumphs at the end of the novel when, with both Heathcliff and Catherine dead, Hareton and the young Catherine plan to leave the Heights and live at the Grange after their marriage. On the other hand, attachment to a place becomes, in Heathcliff and Catherine at the Heights, almost a literal identification with the place, an identification which denies any human domesticity at all. *Wuthering Heights* dramatizes the potential eeriness, the dehumanization, of a closeness to the land or to nature, a closeness usually spoken about in more sentimental terms as a richly humanizing influence.

Death is the most appropriate metaphor for that radical transference of the self to another which Emily Brontë dramatizes in Heathcliff and Catherine. The protection of the Grange, as Catherine finally sees, is also a bondage; it encloses her in the oppressive security of the family, where she would be doomed to see herself reflected and reproduced in her children. The family perpetuates the same, and to escape from self-repetition Catherine dies just as another Catherine — made from her own body, perhaps destined to be like her physically and spiritually — is born. Irked by "this shattered prison," as she says just before she dies, she is "tired, tired of being enclosed here. I'm wearying to escape into that glorious world, to be always there. . . ." The "glorious world" is death, an escape from the boring immortality of familial self-reflections. And yet it is important to see that death itself condemns the protagonists of *Wuthering Heights* to another kind of unceasing life. If we are to take seriously all the rumors of the dead Catherine and the dead Heathcliff's wanderings, then we might also say that they are, apparently, unable to die. Strictly speaking, we have no right to explain the wandering of ghosts whose presence Brontë seems anxious to avoid denying or confirming. And when I say that Heathcliff and Catherine are unable to die and finally to find rest, I realize that one could just as legitimately claim that the only "rest" they want is to be together and to be able to wander freely around the Heights. But it is also in the logic of their attachment to each other not to be able to stop their wandering. The fate of all fascination with the self as the other — the fate of a radical open-endedness of being — is a kind of restless immortality.

The self as a potentiality for metamorphoses is a self which has renounced not only the closed circle of family repetitions, but also the limiting definitions of individuality. A certain "closing" of the self within some unchanging bodily and psychological attributes is the prerequisite for being an individual, and therefore for having the privilege of dying. *Wuthering Heights* does not have anything like the dizzying succession of metamorphoses which we find in *Les Chants de Maldoror*, and it's true that Catherine and Heathcliff imagine being nothing more than each other.[2] But their "love" for each other signifies a desire for self-alienation which Lautréamont's "characters" are allowed to satisfy literally — and endlessly. Catherine's mysterious sense of identity with the homeless, undefinable Heathcliff expresses a potentiality for self-distancing which the narrator of *Maldoror* expresses more simply, and more radically, when he announces: "It is a man or a stone or a tree about to begin the fourth canto." And Lautréamont's hero, like Emily Brontë's couple, is an eternally restless wanderer. There is no conclusive ending to *Les Chants de Maldoror* or to Maldoror's life. In other words, there is no reason for Ducasse-Lautréamont-Maldoror's imagination not to continue being different from itself. The imagination of metamorphoses is without beginnings or endings; and as *Wuthering Heights* suggests, only death can provide us with a myth of uninterrupted life. The visible destruction of *this* body, with its all too particular history, is the condition for being nothing in particular, the ambiguous license to roam eternally in other bodies and other histories.

Desire in *Wuthering Heights* and in *Les Chants de Maldoror* is essentially vampiristic. Brontë and Lautréamont are uninterested in desires aimed at specific pleasures; their protagonists want to devour being. Heathcliff is "always, always" in Catherine's mind, as she says, but "not as a pleasure"; to be with Heathcliff may include some pleasure, but Catherine's desire for Heathcliff is a desire for more being, and pleasure is irrelevant to it. The lack which constitutes desire in both *Wuthering Heights* and *Maldoror* couldn't be filled by particular sensations, or by particular presences and events in the world; it is a hole in being, and it can be filled up only if other being is poured into it. The activity of desire is ferocious in both works because desire is an absolute rather than a partial lack. Catherine, Heathcliff and Maldoror don't exactly ask the world to give them anything; they are rather, in the etymological sense of the adjective, an aspiring openness which sucks in and becomes other forms of being. Heathcliff's wild embrace almost kills Catherine, as if he wanted to crush her into himself. They are apparently even beyond using the pleasures of sex as an occasion for breaking down (at least in fantasy) the resistance of the other person *as* another person. These sexless lovers are both too naïve and too important to be seductive with each other; each one merely pounces on or haunts the other in order to prevent the other from escaping.

This cruel appetite for others is of course more explicit in *Les Chants de Maldoror*. We learn in Canto One that Maldoror had already been given the nickname of "the vampire" in his youth. The two preferred forms of torture in the work are to pierce a hole in

someone else's body from which the torturer drinks his or her blood
or rips out a few organs, and to stick to someone's body like a leech.
In the tenderest love scene of *Les Chants de Maldoror*, Maldoror and
the female shark come together "like two leeches"; they glue themselves to each other until they are "one glaucous mass exhaling the
odors of sea-wrack." And in curious images of purity for what he
has called their "carnal desires," the narrator describes Maldoror
and the shark "borne upon an undertow as in a cradle, and rolling
upon one another towards the [unknown] depths of the ocean's
abyss, they join together in a long, chaste and hideous coupling!"
Sex in *Maldoror* is the ultimate gluing of the self to another form,
a plunging into "unknown depths" where each viscous form of
being may slip chastely if repulsively into other forms of being.

What is the place of personality in a psychology of metamorphosis? In a sense, the figures in *Wuthering Heights* and especially
in *Maldoror* are without personality. That is, they are without that
coherent, unified, describable self which is a premise of most Western
literature from medieval allegory to early twentieth-century fiction.
Neither Brontë nor Lautréamont imagines human identity primarily
in terms of stable psychological contents. We can, it's true, say certain things about their characters: Maldoror is cruel, Heathcliff is
sullen and resentful, Catherine is stubborn and high-spirited. But
these character traits are secondary in the two works; both writers
are clearly less interested in the psychological continuities which
make personality possible than in those radical discontinuities and
transformations which explode the myth of personality.

We should, however, also recognize that both Emily Brontë and
Lautréamont have difficulty rejecting what we ordinarily think of
as subjectivity. In my section on Racine, I emphasized the connection between familial desires and the intelligibility of the self. The
personality structure elaborated in psychoanalytic thought would
collapse without the support of a theoretical history of the child's
desiring fantasies within the family circle. In literature, the escape
from a reductively interpretive criticism is inseparable from the
work's escape from familial patterns of desire. It is significant that
in both *Wuthering Heights* and *Les Chants de Maldoror*, the
possibilities of metamorphosis and of the self's otherness are con-

nected to a breaking away from the family. Also, this breaking of family ties seems to be identified with the transcendence of sexual secrets. *Wuthering Heights* is both almost embarrassingly vulnerable and astonishingly invulnerable to psychoanalytic interpretation. The familial fantasies are transparent: fantasies of sibling rivalry as well as of an incestuous attachment between brother and sister, fantasies of a paradisiac children's universe from which parents have conveniently disappeared, as well as of a hellish children's universe in which the parents are no longer there to protect the younger children from the older brother's cruelty. Thomas Moser has even proposed that we see in Heathcliff an embodiment of the characteristics which, according to Freud, belong to the id; and he uses all the references to keys, doors and windows in the novel to make a case for patterns of sexual symbolism in this deceptively sexless work.[3] But it is not enough to say that this sort of evidence exists in *Wuthering Heights*; we have to consider its *status* in the novel. Familial drama and sexual symbolism are what *Wuthering Heights* struggles against. More exactly, the family is both the self's prison and its protection against its own potential foreignness. The arrival of a sibling is not only an occasion for rivalry; it also poses the problem, for each of the other children, of an alien double of mysterious origins. The acceptance of the self's strangeness to itself depends on a rejection of those family ties in which the self is repeated in other people, as well as on a rejection of the incestuous dramas which cement family ties. *Wuthering Heights*, as we shall see more clearly in a few moments, reneges on its own commitment to the exciting prospect of metamorphosis. But to the extent that the novel does dramatize a fantasy of the self triumphantly "leaving" itself for other forms of being, both familial drama and the sexual symbolism connected to it appear almost irrelevant to a gluttonous and yet almost ascetic, an erotic and yet sexless, passion for otherness.

The status of psychic autobiography in *Les Chants de Maldoror* is more confusing. The narrator is constantly teasing us with hints of a secret crime in Maldoror's past. We can guess almost from the very beginning that the crime was one of violence toward a close friend. In setting the scene for one of the incidents in Canto One, the narrator writes that it is a stormy winter night, a night when

". . . the adolescent boy meditates some crime against one of his friends, if he is like what I was in my youth." Indeed, Maldoror's preferred victims are adolescent boys. In what may be obsessive replays of his past crime, he seduces adolescents into following him and then tortures and kills them. In a sense, the work is a slow dredging up of this badly concealed secret; at the end of Canto Five, we are finally given a long and explicit account of Maldoror's betrayals, ten years before, of his two intimate friends Elşseneur and Reginald. There are different ways of considering this crime. We may consider it as the personal secret — not only of Maldoror, but also of Isidore Ducasse — which the literary text seeks simultaneously to hide, to reenact, and to confess. It would then have the status of a psychic origin in *Les Chants de Maldoror*; it would provide the fictional and perhaps the biographically real source for the obsession with cruelty in the work, as well as for Maldoror's dual moral nature and his shifting feelings toward both God and mankind.

But the nature of the crime which might thus provide a key to both Maldoror and to Ducasse should make us suspect that its emblematic value is more significant than its possible biographical authenticity. The betrayal of a brother-friend is a self-betrayal. It is the melodramatic anecdote which best dramatizes a frantic attempt to escape from repetition, to eliminate the identical or the same. If we are tempted to think of this crime as the central secret of Lautréamont's narrative, we can also think of it as the condition for the narrator's most ambitious activity: the activity of metamorphosis. Only by smashing self-reflections can Maldoror decentralize himself, move away from any explanatory secrets and give himself up entirely to the enterprise of being always somewhere else. Significantly, the sections which are most elaborately explicit about Maldoror's crime — Cantos Five and Six — are also those in which most of the "beau comme" sentences occur, sentences in which the second term has nothing to do with the first and invites us merely to forget it. These stylistic leaps and discontinuities are indulged in most freely at the very moment when the narrator would seem to be revealing the weighty secret from which he cannot escape. Are the metaphors frantic attempts to counteract the imprisoning effects of the narrator's confession, attempts to insist on rhetorical leaps just when the ontological leap is being exposed as an illusion?

This is of course possible, but it's also possible to see the supposed confession as an anecdotal working out of a liberating self-betrayal. And this self-betrayal is implied in the stylistic virtuosity of Lautréamont's wildly disconnected comparisons.

Maldoror's victims are always virtuous little boys, and several times the virtuous victim is explicitly placed in a family setting in which he is betrayed by a brother or corrupted and betrayed by Maldoror. As in *Wuthering Heights*, the security of the family circle is opposed in *Maldoror* to the hero's dangerous but exciting adventures outside the family. Catherine is torn between her family and her sense of being a figure alien to the family, and the obedient sons in *Maldoror* are seduced by an outcast-outlaw who is also a master in the art of metamorphosis.

But the fratricidal project in Lautréamont has certain ambiguities which will help us to understand the terror and rejection of metamorphosis in both *Wuthering Heights* and *Les Chants de Maldoror*. The murder of the "good" self is accompanied by a fascination with the good self. First of all, Maldoror is sexually stimulated by his victims. In the stanza devoted to pederasts in Canto Five, he cries: "I don't like women! Not even hermaphrodites!" And, since the universe is not, as he would ideally wish it to be, "an immense celestial anus" into which he could plunge a fabulously powerful penis, he invites a boy of "not more than fifteen" to share his bed. The adolescent betrayal of a brother-companion is thus repeated, ten or fifteen years later, as the sodomizing of a teenage boy by a man of about thirty. But the crime now includes (and may have included then) an act of vampirism. In the passage just quoted, Maldoror (or the narrator) speaks of drinking blood from the throats of those who lie next to him. The good adolescent is not merely destroyed; he is also absorbed into the traitor's body. Furthermore, Maldoror specifies, immediately after announcing that he likes neither women nor hermaphrodites, that he needs creatures who resemble him, "upon whose brows human nobility is graved in deeper and more durable characters!" It is as if, even before the crime of adolescence, the good self had been expelled into the universe and lost; and Maldoror reincorporates it by drinking the blood of a virtuous boy who resembles him.

It's useless to speculate on the reasons for the original expulsion, although Lautréamont does seem to be reenacting an infantile fantasy-drama of rejection and introjection. Perhaps the only way to save the good self from the bad self was to project the former into the world and beyond the latter's reach — although, as we see, Maldoror nonetheless pursues his good double in order both to destroy him (again) and to be him (again). The very act which would seem to free Maldoror from the family and from self-reflections, and to launch him on his career of metamorphoses, is also the act by which he seeks to possess an almost exact image of himself. If *Maldoror* documents incredible leaps of being among discontinuous forms of animate and inanimate life, it also hints at a profound, and profoundly sentimental, nostalgia for the eternal repetition of the same self. "I was looking for a soul who resembled me," the narrator writes at the beginning of a section in Canto Two, "and I couldn't find one." True enough, the search seems to be mocked in the same stanza: Maldoror has found someone like himself but it is the female shark he (more or less) copulates with, and he derisively celebrates the fact that "she had the same ideas as I." However, the motif is no less recurrent, and it is a serious one despite the irony to which, like everything else in Lautréamont, it can be submitted. (We find this motif, for example, in the narrator's praise of the ocean as "the symbol of identity," and in his contrast between all the changes to which human destinies are subject and the unchangeability of mathematics: "But you [mathematics] are unchanging. No change, no envenomed wind, touches the steep rocks and wide valleys of your identity.")

Blanchot has spoken of "la hantise du semblable" in *Les Chants de Maldoror*, of a nostalgia for a mythic identity between the self and the other. Is there, the work seems to ask obsessively, a nontransforming union? In a sense, nothing could be stranger than this question from our acrobat of metamorphoses. But the peculiar strain we find in the work, its frantic nervousness, can perhaps be traced to a conflict between the desire to sever all connections with one's sources of being and to be always elsewhere (to change into a tree or a shark; to use the second term of a comparison as a leap away from rather than as an illuminating reference to the first term; to be so ironic that one's thought never coincides with the expression of one's thought), and, on the contrary, the desire to find oneself eternally in the same form and thereby to save the self from all change in its contacts with the world.

This conflict is also suggested in Maldoror's attitude toward sleep and dreams. He tells us in Canto Five (although he contradicts himself elsewhere) that he hasn't slept for more than thirty years. The reason he gives is that he refuses to have his being spied on by God. It is an unbearable torture "to see one's intellect in the hands of a sacrilegious stranger. An implacable scalpel probes into its dense underbrush . . . Humiliation! Our door is open to the ferocious curiosity of the Celestial Bandit." What can God actually see when we sleep and dream? He has the opportunity of being the "hideous spy upon my causality! If I exist, I am not someone else. I will not admit any equivocal plurality within myself. I wish to dwell alone within my intimate reason [dans mon intime raisonnement]. Autonomy . . . or let them change me into a hippopotamus." The "equivocal plurality" seems to be created by God's presence in Maldoror's brain; it might, however, also have referred to the multiple selves we become in dreams. Indeed, Maldoror seems almost as repelled by the activity of dreaming as by God's snooping. A little earlier in the passage, he admits that he sometimes dreams with his eyes open ("In order to be surer of myself I prop my swollen eyelids open with splinters"), "but without losing for an instant the lively sense of my personality." He insists that even phenomena we would associate with sleep — nightmares, fever and "every unclean beast [which raises its bloody] claws" — are controlled by his "will," for ". . . free will . . . does not include sottishness [l'abrutissement] among its sons: he who sleeps is less than an animal castrated yesterday."

The last sentence becomes particularly interesting in light of the narrator's statement, in Canto Six, that his purpose in writing is to produce a "feeling of wonderful stupefaction" in the reader; the latter's intelligence should be "stupid" or "besotted" ("abrutir" is used again), and he should be able to say of the writer, as a flattering tribute: "He has greatly stupefied me [Il m'a beaucoup crétinisé]." The ideal esthetic state resembles the state of being from which Maldoror flees in his attempt not to sleep. Les Chants de Maldoror is, as the narrator also says in Canto Six, a book designed to exhaust us to the point of paralyzing our intelligence; after reading it, we should be — like the man who gives in to sleep — "less than an animal castrated yesterday." And the castrating effect of both sleep and literature seems to be the result of the dizzying metamorphoses we experience in both. Lautréamont's work is full of the "impure animals," the "nightmares," and the personified "fears" which constitute the dreams of his willed insomnia. The orgy of metamorphoses in *Maldoror* is accompanied by the most relentless self-discipline. And we may even suspect that the virtuosity with which Ducasse-Lautréamont-Maldoror manages to be always elsewhere is essentially a strategy of aggression toward the reader. That is, it is a means of cretinizing or spiritually castrating the other, while the narrator, for all his self-transformations, secretly *remains himself*. We are warned, in the very first sentence of Canto One, to arm ourselves against the poisonous emanations of the work's swamplike atmosphere. The reader must become "ferocious like what he is reading," and he must bring to the work "a vigorous logic and a spiritual tension equal at least to his distrust." Astonishingly enough, Lautréamont's work, for all its dreamlike and a-logical extravagances, is conceived of as a contest in logic between two antagonistic wills. Whose intelligence — the author's or the reader's — will manage to escape from sinking into "the desolate morass of these gloomy and poisonous pages?"

In a sense, *Les Chants de Maldoror* is an extremely "tight" book. The narrator takes a visible pleasure, for example, in seeming to leave the point of departure in a sentence or in a stanza hopelessly behind, and in then coming back, after apparently disconnected digressions, to the original point of the sentence or the stanza. All connections seem to have disappeared, and suddenly they are re-established. The far-fetched comparison turns out to be a pertinent illustration of the main theme. No digression has the power to destroy the coherence and the unity of any narrative unit. In this extraordinary work, the authentic if frenzied pursuit of otherness, of ontological discontinuity, is played against a kind of dry, powerful compulsion to be always the same. The passion for metamorphosis is subdued by the vigilant insomniac's deep mistrust of any "equivocal plurality" in the self. No wonder, then, that Maldoror flees sleep. Not only do dreams point to psychic "causes" which make a mockery of our conscious will's autonomy; they also plunge us, without the will's consent, into a multiplicity of roles. Literature, on the other hand, is the willful manipulation of such roles, and Lautréamont could say of his literary hallucinations what he says of the nightmares he has with his eyes open: ". . . it is my will which keeps them going round and round in order to provide solid nourishment for its perpetual activity." Literature for Lautréamont is simultaneously the dissolution of fixed identities (and therefore the willing sacrifice of a controlling will) and the demonstration that nothing can dissolve the identity of an unchanging, autonomous will. The impossible Maldoror ideal is to become everything without ever losing the self: a permanent metamorphosis without change. . . .

Wuthering Heights proposes the family as a solution to the question which Blanchot finds in *Maldoror*: only familial relations realize the ideal of a nontransforming union. I am at one with someone else who is not really another; he is — in his very substance, in his blood — a repetition of myself.[4] The Earnshaws and the Lintons tighten familial bonds in opposition to Heathcliff, and Heathcliff, in his revenge against Hindley and Edgar, makes those bonds even tighter at the same time that he destroys the security they give. By becoming master of the Heights, by marrying Isabella and forcing Catherine's daughter to marry his son, Heathcliff places himself at the center of the family, which is to say that he subverts its very essence by making it revolve around an unrecognizable "other" who has no origins. His perverse strategy is to exaggerate the family's natural tendency to exclude everything foreign to itself. He transforms the familial enclosure into a familial prison, and the man to whom nothing belonged becomes the hoarder, the avaricious guardian of family properties.

The danger represented by Heathcliff is finally exorcised in Brontë's novel, or at least it is contained within the abandoned premises of the Heights, where the restless spirits of Heathcliff and Catherine are allowed harmlessly to wander. The stranger's occupation of the family territory ends because he no longer has the strength to pay attention to the family. Heathcliff stops caring about the circle which he has drawn with such elaborate care, and he dies simply because he stops holding himself *in* and lets himself at last go to that mysterious "outside" where there is neither life nor death, neither the family nor society, but merely a restless union, deprived of beginnings and ends, with an alien self. And Brontë seems to deny her own fearful if passionate interest in such a union by her willingness to dilute it in the cozy and conventional romance between the young Catherine and Hareton Earnshaw. Heathcliff's vengeful entrance into the family is enough to sustain our interest during the second half of *Wuthering Heights*, but the story is now drawn out and frequently boring. Until Catherine's death, the voices of Lockwood and of Nelly Dean have had to obey rhythms and tones with which they are deeply out of sympathy; indeed, they seem to be in the wrong novel, they are ludicrous vehicles for the story they tell. But gradually the story begins to obey them, and whereas Nelly's scolding of Heathcliff and Catherine has the effect of someone shaking her finger at wild animals on the rampage, her domestic decency and mild moralizing seem perfectly suited to the younger Catherine's playful independence and to the cute story of how antagonism changes to love between Catherine and Hareton.

That love is a conventionalized replay of the relation between Catherine Earnshaw and Heathcliff. It's as if Emily Brontë were telling the same story twice, and eliminating its originality the second time. The latter part of *Wuthering Heights* is a repudiation of its own radical difference from other novels. Brontë expresses her complicity with circles of familial self-reflections by gradually drawing her work within a circle of novelistic tradition in which it resembles or reflects other novels. Its identity — like that of each individual in a family — is now somewhat confused because it is shared, but this diffused identity is mainly a repetition of being and not a promotion of being. The discontinuity between *Wuthering Heights* and other novels is gradually erased; its nature is no longer deeply and richly problematic, but has simply been generalized and made somewhat anonymous. The difference between the first half and the second half of the novel is analogous to the difference between the two Catherines' intimacies. The first Catherine asserts her identity to someone outside the family and whose being is *incomparable* to hers, while the second Catherine loves in Hareton a kind of legitimized Heathcliff, a cousin who resembles her mother. In Hareton, Heathcliff is transformed from the other into the same.

Finally, the narrative structure itself of *Wuthering Heights* also works toward the expulsion of difference. The neat circularity of Lockwood's narrative, and the obvious parallels (in spite of the differences I've just emphasized) between Catherine and Hareton loving each other against Heathcliff's will and Catherine and Heathcliff loving each other against Hindley's will, create a structure in which events are repeated or return to their points of origin. In

the same way that the Earnshaws and the Lintons tighten familial
relations until they become an unbreakable knot of self-repetitions,
Wuthering Heights works toward a structural circularity and re-
petitiveness which only Heathcliff might disrupt but which finally
leaves no room for Heathcliff.

We find, then, in the structure of *Wuthering Heights* something
parallel to the organization of Lautréamont's sentences and stanzas.
An apparent movement away from beginnings or sources is counter-
acted by a compositional tour de force which returns us to our
point of departure and suggests that we have really not been anywhere. Peculiarly enough, Lautréamont's work also moves toward
the kind of anonymity I've just referred to in speaking of *Wuthering
Heights*. The tight construction of individual sentences and stanzas
in *Les Chants de Maldoror* is transferred to an entire canto in Canto
Six, the Mervyn story, which reads like a parody of compositional
order. Allusions to the story's numerous threads are casually and
unintelligibly made at the end of each stanza, and each allusion
appears to be unrelated to what we've read so far. But the sounding
of each motif is invariably followed, sooner or later, by its anecdotal
development as part of the story, and all the threads contribute to
a narrative design as carefully plotted as the complex machinery
which sends poor Mervyn flying from the column of the Place
Vendôme to the dome of the Panthéon.

In the first stanza of Canto Six, the narrator proclaims a fundamental difference between what we are about to read and Cantos
One through Five. The first five sections were merely "the frontis-
piece of my work, the foundation of the construction, the preliminary explanation of my future [poetics]." They were "the synthetic
section" of his work; now the narrator will be undertaking "the
analytical section." This distinction is far from clear, and the stanza
is full of difficulties and possible ironies. The narrator does, however, seem to be announcing a greater objectification of the themes
treated in the preceding cantos. In describing the earlier sections,
he speaks of "exclamations," "noisy cacklings of a cochinchina
chicken," "pure speculation," "anathemas," and "nightmares." But
now ". . . I believe I have found at last, after several feelers, my
final formula. It is the best, since it is the novel!"

Blanchot suggests that Lautréamont has gotten rid of Ducasse in
the blood which has flowed so profusely in the first five cantos. The

visceral reality of Isidore Ducasse is pushed away so that Lautré-amont may be born, and in the sixth canto "the novelist exists." I have discussed this pushing away from any biographical source in *Les Chants de Maldoror* as a movement toward a purely literary existence, as well as toward a psychology of metamorphosis to which literature is congenial. The narrator himself speaks in this same stanza in Canto Six of only now setting out "for the domains of imagination." But the Mervyn "novel" is in fact less of a departure from the rest of the work than the narrator's (and Blanchot's) comments suggest. Maldoror's pursuit of Mervyn is a variation on several earlier episodes; it reveals the central psychological motif of a crime against an adolescent boy (which, in turn, as we have seen, repeats the theme of the bad companion-brother killing the good companion-brother, the bad self destroying the good self). Neither do I find anything new stylistically in Canto Six. We simply have a more sustained narrative development of a single episode. Lautré-amont holds on longer, as it were, to the same story. As a result, Canto Six, although it appears to have a more objective literary form (as distinct from the "exclamations" and "nightmares" of more directly subjective writing), actually reinforces the self-reflective tendency in *Maldoror* which we also see in the tight coherence of Lautréamont's sentences and stanzas.

There is perhaps more dramatic representation and less "pure speculation" in the last canto than in the others, but the compositional virtuosity of Canto Six consists in the narrator's demonstrating that everything contributes to the dramatic unity of his story. The section is full of apparently extraneous or random notations, but by the end we are forced to recognize that nothing has been extraneous or random. The narrative comes back to those notations and makes sense of them; they all have a place in a story which, in serpentine fashion, slowly "refolds" itself into a perfect circular bundle. Once again, we see the ambiguous nature of literary invention. The potential for discontinuity in verbal sequences invites us to explore our potential for ontological discontinuities; the subversion of linguistic structures of meaning is a model for the subversion of structures of being. At the same time, literature provides an ideal field for self-enclosures. The very nonreferential bias of a work like *Maldoror* authorizes a perfectly closed narrative, from which the contingent and the random have been eliminated. A dazzlingly coherent narrative form refers to nothing but the logistics of its own coherence, and it thus also provides a model of self-containment for a self fearful of metamorphoses and anxious for the world to reflect or to repeat its own nature.

Lautréamont went even further than this, and in the aphoristic prose of the short work he called *Poésies* we find a curious combination of metamorphosis and sameness. Lautréamont is even more elusive in the *Poésies* than in *Maldoror*, and to do justice to the ambiguities of the later work would require a separate study. We can look at the *Poésies* only briefly here; I want to mention the extreme solution it seems to propose to the conflict between self-transformation and self-enclosure which we have been considering in *Wuthering Heights* and *Les Chants de Maldoror*. In the first half of *Poésies*, Lautréamont apparently repudiates a kind of romanticism which would include his own performance in *Maldoror*. He orders his readers "to burn . . . the [duck] of doubt," to believe in God and in virtue, and never to renounce the virtue of hope. ". . . Man should not create unhappiness in his books." Suffering is a weakness, and, having denounced "the whole clamorous series of pasteboard devils" in literature, history and myth which includes the animal divinities of ancient Egypt, Prometheus, Caligula, Iago, Faust, Don Juan, Werther, and Cain, Lautréamont announces: "I desire that my poetry may be read by a young girl of fourteen years." Down with "purulent insomnia and atrabilious nightmares. I scorn and execrate pride and the infamous voluptuousness of any irony become extinguisher which sets aside justness of thought." All literature should have a "moral conclusion"; genius must be "the supreme health and the balance of all our faculties," and "the masterpieces of the French language are prize-giving speeches for schools, and academic speeches." Camus, unbelievably enough, was taken in by what he condemned as the "choirboy morality" and "the conformity without nuances" of the *Poésies*. But Breton, Marcelin Pleynet, and Blanchot have been rightly suspicious of the goody-goody pronouncements of the *Poésies*, and, as Blanchot points out, Lautréamont celebrates virtue "so scornfully, or on the contrary, so excessively that the praise becomes denigration."

The moral farce of the *Poésies* is, in any case, secondary to the notion of "impersonal poetry." How can we guarantee that literature will see only good in the universe and praise the "external axioms" established by a just God? Lautréamont suggests that only a poetry of universal authorship ("poetry should be made by all"), without sources in individual existences, can be relied upon to repeat the maxims of official morality. An "impersonal poetry" would, by definition, not include any of the personal experiences which put to the test those maxims' truth. But, as we see in the second part of the *Poésies*, the moralizing bias behind Lautréamont's new esthetic gives way to a much more ambiguous appeal in "impersonal poetry." First of all, what exactly is "impersonal poetry"? It seems to be a "poetry" of axiomatic prose, or, more precisely, of moral maxims. And the attractiveness of the maxim is its self-containment. "An argument demands an argument. A maxim is a law which includes a collection of arguments. An argument is perfected insofar as it approaches the maxim. When it has become a maxim, its perfection rejects the proofs of . . . metamorphosis." In other words, the reasoning process is always prospective. The maxim, on the other hand, is reason solidified or essentialized into a truth. It has no future, only a past; it is the tombstone of thought, a definitive intellectual obituary.

In a sense, the maxim is the ideal literary genre: it is the best conceivable example of experience re-presented as formal perfection. And the self-contained literary formula refers only to other formulas; its sources are only in other literature. In the *Poésies*, Lautréamont seems to be moving toward a theory of literature as continuous and deliberate plagiarism. "Plagiarism is necessary. Progress implies it. It presses after an author's phrase, uses his expressions, erases a false idea, replaces it with the correct one." Now this does seem to suggest more than purely formal criteria for esthetic value. One writer would modify another writer's sentences in order to bring them in line with the truths which historical progress gradually reveals. But the next paragraph contradicts this idea: "A maxim, in order to be well constructed, doesn't require [being] corrected. It requires [being] developed." A maxim can't be changed ("its perfection rejects the proofs of metamorphosis"); it can only be added to. The issue is further confused by the fact that, in his constant plundering of other writers' formulas in the second part of the

Poésies, Lautréamont is in fact always "correcting" those formulas, but it can hardly be said that his frequently meaningless and self-contradictory revisions of Pascal or La Rochefoucauld, for example, are made in the name of truth. The deepest appeal of maxims and of plagiarism seems to lie elsewhere. Lautréamont opposes "sentiments" to "the analysis of sentiments." The former "express happiness, bring smiles," and are dependent on space and duration; the latter is independent of space and duration, "expresses happiness, all personality apart [toute personnalité mise à part]. With feelings, everything is uncertainty." With the analysis of feelings, everything "is certainty. [Such analysis] is the expression of that happiness which results at a given moment from knowing restraint in the midst of good and evil passions." The predominance of analysis will institute a major change in the hierarchy of literary genres: "Tragedies, poems, elegies will no longer prevail. The coldness of the maxim will prevail!"

The perfection of the maxim thus seems to be analogous to the perfection of being purified of the stain of existence. The maxim is the product of that happy moment Lautréamont speaks of when, in the midst of its good or bad passions, the self manages to leap out of its own history into a verbal ordering of its history. A literature of maxims is the literature of absolutely secure sublimations; it has transcended the dialectical confusions of "virtues" and "vices," and, as Lautréamont puts it in a remarkable sequence, analysis "uses its calm to dissolve the description of those passions in a principle which circulates through the pages: the non-existence of evil." The reality of evil depends on opposition or conflict, on the possibility of destructive negation. In the maxim, opposition and negation no longer destroy; they have been reduced, or rather raised, to the status of aspects of composition. And purely compositional negation merely contributes to verbal plenitude; an analytic maxim is not less "full" because it contains a negation.

I spoke at the beginning of this chapter of the extraordinary literary self-consciousness of *Les Chants de Maldoror*. And we saw how the bookishness of that work seems to intensify the imagination of metamorphosis in Ducasse-Lautréamont-Maldoror. In the *Poésies*, we see the opposite effect of a total absorption in literature. Superficially, metamorphosis still seems possible, but it is no longer present as a phenomenon of being; we now have it only in the degraded form of deliberately inaccurate plagiarism. The writer floats among other writers' maxims, making new maxims from old ones, and therefore helping to propagate a potentially monstrous family of literary formulas. And in spite of all the transformations to which Lautréamont submits other writers' maxims, he is right to assert the antagonism between maxims and metamorphoses. Each maxim is perfectly self-contained. It has no capacity for becoming another maxim; it can simply be *juxtaposed* with other maxims with which there is no reason for it to be consistent. Lautréamont's maxims frequently contradict one another, and many of them make no logical sense at all. But, as the *Poésies* illustrate, the structural coherence of a sentence doesn't depend on the coherence of the thought it expresses. And whereas in *Maldoror* the arbitrary aspect of verbal combinations (*b* doesn't have to be like *a* in order to be compared to it) inspired adventures in new forms of being, this same aspect of language inspires nothing more than a mocking formal virtuosity in the *Poésies*.

Blanchot has pointed out the similarity between Lautréamont's stated aim in the *Poésies* and Valéry's poetic ambitions: "to raise poetry to a science of maxims, to unite it to the supreme banality or impersonal principle which animates the theorem." But the *excessive* solemnity with which Lautréamont pursues this goal makes him less solemn than either Valéry or Blanchot. The transformation of experience into maxims satisfies a desire for life as a closed structure, but perhaps because of its very removal from life, the maxim can resemble a philosophical sneer. Indeed, the potential for mockery in the maxim is so evident in the contradictory and often senseless maxims of the *Poésies* that the maxim itself is perhaps finally destroyed. For we can't help but see that the condition which allows for this superior mockery is the cretinization of language. Poetic impersonality in the *Poésies* is equivalent to madly ordered blabber. Lautréamont's extraordinary aptitude for violence never leaves him: there is something explosive even in his retreat into a literature of serene banality.

Nevertheless, it would be a mistake to underestimate the appeal of the literary and ontological ideal which the *Poésies* both ridicules and aspires to. An impersonal literature of anonymously conceived maxims is a seductive alternative to a self victimized by its own potential for metamorphoses. The curious sort of wandering which both Lautréamont and Emily Brontë seem finally tempted to choose is an escape from the wandering of the self among its many alien identities. It is the autonomous wandering of a literature divorced from any personal authorship, the triumph of a genre over the individual practice of a genre, and consequently the triumphant exclusion of disruptive desire from self-contained and petrified form.

CHAPTER EIGHT

Rimbaud's Simplicity

RIMBAUD'S MOST REVOLUTIONARY ambition for poetry was to make it *mean* as little as possible. There is one persistent theme — or rather gesture — throughout his life: the gesture of repudiation. And it is a repudiation more radical than mere revolt; it has the abstract purity of a mental mechanism which unfailingly ejects anything that threatens to occupy the mind. Rimbaud's violent destructiveness — which has often been commented on — is only the most spectacular manifestation of a more eerie, perhaps even mindless repetition of "no." Rimbaud doesn't merely reject certain modes of life and of art against which intelligible objections might be formulated; he repudiates whatever he risks *being*.

At the end of his childhood in Charleville, Rimbaud says "no" to the family, to the provinces, and to religion. In Paris, he says "no" to the literary world of the capital. As a writer, he says "no" to almost the entire history of literature. During the period of Voyance, he says "no" to society as it is, as well as to whatever he himself may be. The enigmatic "je est un autre" may be a formula which announces the self's separation from itself, the otherness of Rimbaud *to* Rimbaud. He is a European Christian, and he would repudiate Europe's Christian past. When he writes *Une Saison en enfer*, Rimbaud repudiates his own repudiations. Then, as a vagabond and later as an explorer and trader in Africa, Rimbaud says "no" to wandering and to adventurism by the fidelity with which he maintains contact with home and family in Charleville. In his desire to marry a European woman and settle down in Africa, he simultaneously repudiates Europe, his own homosexuality, and his past repudiations of the family and of institutionalized sexuality. And if we are to believe the story about his death-bed conversion, the dying Rimbaud even says "no" to a dismissal of religion perhaps best expressed in his casually blasphemous "Merde à Dieu!"

I want to study the Rimbaldian enterprise of negating meaning in poetry. The success of this enterprise depends on the poet's eliminating the traditional bases of interpretation in literature: not only literature's references to realities external to it, but also its elaborations of purely verbal structures of significance. The ideal Rimbaldian utterance would, I think, be wholly without mystery — nonreferential, nonrelational, and devoid of attitudes, feelings and tones. It would, most radically, imply the absence of any coherent and durable subjectivity. Literature would no longer reveal a self; rather, it would provide models of nonstructurable desires, of scenes of desire irreducible to a history of personality.

Rimbaud's extraordinary experiment can perhaps best be approached through a study of his water images. In "Après le déluge," the poet suggests that only a second flood will cleanse and renew the world. Water destroys, but in this prose poem from the *Illuminations*, the destruction is beneficent. The flood washes away everything Rimbaud hates in civilization, and it may also uncover a precious secret being withheld by a Queen-Sorceress. (As long as we don't possess this secret, life is only "un ennui.") The poet calls on a strikingly heterogeneous collection of objects, natural phenomena and human emotions to bring back the great Floods:

> Sourds, étang; — Ecume, roule sur le pont et par-dessus les bois; — draps noirs et orgues, — éclairs et tonnerre, — montez et roulez; — Eaux et tristesses, montez et relevez les Déluges.

> Gush forth, pond; — Foam, roll above the bridge and over the woods; — black palls and organs, — lightning and thunder, —

rise up and roll; — Waters and sorrows, rise up and release the Floods again.[1]

But, as we see in two other pieces from the *Illuminations*, "Nocturne vulgaire" and "Angoisse," the destructive process is not always an exhilarating one. The poet can feel, with anguish, that he is being "scourged through splashing waters," or tossed "on wounds" and "on racks, through the silence of the murderous waters and air," and on tortures which seem themselves to participate in a kind of liquidity in "their cruelly swelling silence [dans leur silence atrocement houleux]." Images of flooding thus lend themselves to a variety of situations and moods: the creatively destructive flooding of the world, or the poet's frightening immersion in violent waters, or, as in "Le Bateau ivre," an exhilarating surrender to the power of the sea. In "Après le déluge," the flood washes (and washes away) the world and allows it to begin again. In "Le Bateau ivre," Rimbaud imagines water not only as a condition for the appearance of "marvelous images," but also as the environment in which they are most likely to appear. Finally, "Angoisse" suggests that the cleansing waves can also serve a tortured and even masochistic imagination.

This apparent diversity can, however, be reduced to a single, if singularly complex, fantasy. Perhaps the flood provides Rimbaud with a displaced satisfaction of his legendary thirst. What, exactly, are the stages and the logic of this displacement? There is an astonishing passage in "Comédie de la soif" (from the *Derniers vers*), in which the *Moi* of the poem (to whom various sorts of drinks are offered) refuses to have anything more to do with

> ces boissons pures,
> Ces fleurs d'eau pour verres;
> Légendes ni figures
> Ne me désaltèrent;
>
> Chansonnier, ta filleule
> C'est ma soif si folle,
> Hydre intime sans gueules
> Qui mine et désole.

these pure drinks, these water-flowers for glasses; neither legends nor forms quench my thirst;

singer, your god-child is my thirst so mad, a mouthless intimate
hydra which consumes and ravages.

The poet's thirst — which seems to be both physical and esthetic
here — can no longer be sated by the very materials which provide
the inspiration for other poems in the *Derniers vers*: he rejects
legends and images or figures. And he seems to reject them because
his thirst itself is formless. It is like the many-headed hydra of
Lerna whose heads were both always there and never there since
they grew back as soon as they were cut off. But this mouthless,
intimate and mad thirst is curiously like the water which would ap-
pease it. It seems to eat away at him and erode his being, somewhat
as the flood of "Après le déluge" creates havoc in the world, or as
the rushing waters "scourge" the poet in "Nocturne vulgaire."
Finally, the hydra itself is an animal which lives in water. It's as if
the all-enveloping ambiance of the poet's thirst were the liquid
which it desperately needs. It wouldn't be enough merely to accept
the banal drinks which his family and friends offer him. Rather,
the frightening but also most profoundly desired satisfaction which
the poet dreams of is *to be liquefied*.

But to be liquefied is, of course, to be destroyed. As we've just
seen, Rimbaud's water images can serve what appear to be two
opposite functions: the Flood of "Après le déluge" washes the
world clean and allows it to present us once again with "marvelous
images," but water can also wash the poet away into anguishing
tortures. "Comédie de la soif" helps us to see the connection between the exalting dream and the frightening nightmare. The thirsty
Moi seems to prefer being destroyed to drinking, and destruction is
imagined as a merging with water. When the parents ask: "What
does man need? to drink," the *Moi* answers: "To die among bar-
barous rivers." Later in the poem, in refusing the wines and
absinthe proposed by his friends, the poet confesses:

> J'aime autant, mieux, même,
> Pourrir dans l'étang,
> Sous l'affreuse crème,
> Près des bois flottants.

I had as soon — rather, even — rot in the pond, beneath the
horrible scum, near the floating driftwood.

And his last wish is to die by being "condensed" into liquid:

> Mais fondre où fond ce nuage sans guide,
> — Oh! favorisé de ce qui est frais!
> Expirer en ces violettes humides
> Dont les aurores chargent les forêts?

But to dissolve where that wandering cloud is dissolving — Oh! favoured by what is cool! to expire in those damp violets with which the dawn weighs down the forests?[2]

What seem like the most somber possibilities in "Comédie de la soif" are expressed as desirable alternatives to the poem's other solutions to the poet's thirst. It would therefore be a simplification of this drama in Rimbaud's poetry to stop at any description of his being engulfed by water as a function of his masochistic imagination. "Comédie de la soif" helps us to see something crucial for the *Illuminations*: desire hallucinates the self into a scene in the external world. "What is drunkenness?" the *Moi* asks the friends who have invited him to drink wine and absinthe, and to ordinary drunkenness he opposes a scene in which both the self and nature swim, as it were, in new versions of being. The self "rots" in the pond, under a layer of thicker liquid (the "affreuse crème"), and the woods are set loose from their roots and "float" in this tableau of nightmarish (but wished for) metamorphoses. In the last stanza, to be "favoured by what is cool" is to have the privilege of being in a temperature where one will melt. Dawn condenses the mists of the night on violets, and by imagining his own death in the flowers' wetness, the poet makes himself part of the liquid floral weight borne by the forests at the first hour of the day.

Thus we see that there is a kind of washing from the outside which quenches thirst more than any banal act of drinking. More exactly, the thirsty poet's excited imagination doesn't settle for the "realistic" satisfaction of drinking; it evokes floods, or the poet's being buffeted by strong waves, or the "drunken boat's" enthusiastic descent into the unexplored seas, or, finally, the transformation of the poet himself into water. Thirst, paradoxically, is satisfied by a bath — but the bath must of course have the magic quality of dissolving that which it washes, of condensing the thirsty self into the water it longs for.

Thirst can provide us with an especially instructive model of desire in general. The activities by which an infant seeks to replace the painful lack of liquid by a pleasurable presence of liquid may, for example, include crying and swallowing. The body works with a logic which requires no logical thought: if the satisfaction which the thirsty infant desires was procured through the act of swallowing, then swallowing in itself may be the sufficient condition for the return of satisfaction. The infant's cries and the contraction of his throat muscles are already inventive ways to express and struggle against a painful lack. The activity of desire, while it may be inconceivable without a kind of knowledge or memory of satisfaction, is therefore always more than a reproduced memory. The absence of satisfaction excites the organism into imaginative activities. In the case of the thirsty infant, he invents a complex form of metonymic logic by which he "postulates" a necessary connection between warm milk flowing into his mouth, throat and stomach, and the swallowing which was, so to speak, contiguous with that process.

When we move to the mental representations of desire, the hallucinatory quality of desire is even more pronounced — or at least more obvious. The fundamental condition for desire is an absence or a lack, but desire is never only an absence. It is accompanied by activities designed to satisfy desire, and these activities already constitute in themselves a certain satisfaction of desire. In the excitement which accompanies the irritating lack in desire, we produce mental scenes which — in the masturbatory mode of desire — we may even confuse with the events in the world capable of fulfilling our wish. If the thirsty adult is generally a nonfantasizing seeker of real water, in his past he experienced thirst as hallucinatory drinking. In fact, as a fundamental desire of an organism which has not yet differentiated between the self and the world, thirst was probably the most powerful producer of fantasies in his life. It can, consequently, be thought of as the model of all future fantasies in which the principal activities of satisfaction will be mainly mental. Fantasy is central to desire, even though, in the economy of desire's interplay with the world, we must learn to reduce the role of fantasy in the pursuit of our satisfactions. And desiring fantasies are inventive elaborations of remembered satisfactions. We never exactly reproduce the latter; in the excitement of desire, we pick out associative material from our entire past and *re-create* the past satisfaction. Desire makes fiction of reality. With the generous gluttony of all intense desires, our hallucinated re-enactments of remembered pleasures are an improvement upon those pleasures whose absence initiates desire.

Rimbaud's water images suggest the essential nature of this improvement. The flood provides him with the visual satisfaction of an unlimited flow of water. It displaces the thirst of his own body onto the world's body, and a vision of universal inundation objectifies and satisfies an otherwise hopeless desire for wholly liquefied being. This displacement of water from the inside of the body to the world would seem to be, in spite of the grandiose vision of the flood, a weakening of the pleasure originally desired. The need for liquid is sublimated into a visual fantasy; a painful sensation is relieved by raising it to the level of a more imaginative — and more easily satisfied — desire. Incapable of hallucinating all the water his own body needs, Rimbaud puts his thirst at a certain distance from himself — in the world — and he then satisfies his displaced thirst by flooding the world. But, as we can see from "Comédie de la soif," what may seem like a compromise with urgent bodily desire is in fact a technique for metamorphosing the self into the desired objects. The poet would coerce the world into becoming an excited version of his desires. The self would *be* the objects which occupy consciousness. In a sense, then, a total invasion of the world by interpretive fantasy is equivalent to the elimination of the difference between the world and fantasy. The world becomes what the self desires, and, at the extreme, the triumph of desiring fantasy is a denial of the role of fantasy in desire. Desire, instead of merely characterizing the self, would accurately describe the world.

Several factors work against this project of defantasizing desire. To begin with, the very images through which we discover the project partially defeat it. In the last few pages, I have, after all, been translating Rimbaldian floods into a complex fantasy (or a desiring complex). That is, it has been possible, through interpretation, to reinstate the division between the self and the world; I have been looking at the scenes of Rimbaud's poetry as signs of Rimbaud's subjectivity. In part, this has been possible because Rimbaud's water images have the interpretive suggestiveness of dream images. Like dream images, they seem both to express certain thoughts and to be the result of a mental operation on these thoughts. We might remember that Freud seeks a method for interpreting dreams in order to get at the unconscious "dream-thought," which he conceives of as a wish capable of being expressed in the rational terms of conscious thought. The desires in dreams, however primitive their content may be, can be rationally formulated; they may indeed exist *as* a verbal idea in the unconscious. But, according to Freud, desires can be satisfied in dreams only because of the regressive mode in which they are expressed. The "dream-work" transforms the thought into a scene; dreams express desires in the *form* in which we experienced them before we were able to express them verbally — that is, as visual hallucinations. In one sense, the work of interpretation is not exactly a working "back" but rather, at least as far as form goes, a working "forward" — from consciousness as scenes to consciousness as verbally articulated thoughts. And this is the case because the only *problem* in dreams is a formal one. We must restate the desires in dreams in a more advanced code of consciousness, that is, in language. In a similar way, Rimbaud's flood scenes can be devisualized or, so to speak, interpreted "forward." In "Après le déluge," the poem seems to express a "poem-thought" (equivalent to a "dream-thought") which we might define as a wish to destroy the world and the self. ("Le Bateau ivre" expresses a similar wish.) The ambiguity of this desire in Rimbaud is suggested by an image which is itself appropriately ambiguous. The flood can merely wash away and destroy; in this respect, it corresponds to nothing more than a movement of pure negation. But water also washes clean, allows for new beginnings; and in this respect, we see that it expresses the Rimbaldian equivalence between annihilation and constantly renewed creation.

In one sense, it doesn't matter very much if our interpretation is right or wrong. What matters is that we haven't been coerced out of all interpretive ingenuity; we can make psychological sense out of the poet's hallucinated vision of the world. This is not only because of the psychological suggestiveness of Rimbaud's flood images (especially in conjunction with his thirst); we are also encouraged to restate water scenes as desiring complexes because of the frequency with which they appear in Rimbaud's poetry. The mere fact of repetition points to an obsessive affective pattern. Water images give a thematic continuity to Rimbaud's work. While they express a wish for universal destruction, the very repetition of that wish guarantees a durable stability to the desiring self. A discontinuous succession of "marvelous images" is balanced and somewhat subverted in Rimbaud by the constant re-presentation of the thirst, drinking and flooding motifs. The absolutely new scenes are made somewhat familiar by the reappearance, within them, of the conditions imagined as necessary in order to produce new scenes. The desire to wash away whatever *is* becomes, paradoxically, a stable and permanent element in Rimbaud's work.[3] Pictorialized consciousness can perhaps never be a total negation of the history of consciousness.

Now the opposition between scene and history or story is a crucial one in Rimbaud. The triumph of the former depends on the elimination of history, or at least on the irrelevance of any stories one might tell about the poet or his poetry. From this point of view, the major contrast in Rimbaud's work is between *Une Saison en enfer* and some of the *Illuminations*. The *Saison* is a desperate and confused surrender to the inevitability of both personal and cultural history. The very repudiation of the past is an act which *gives* a significant past to Rimbaud. It's difficult to know exactly what significance should be given to that "history of one of [Rimbaud's] follies," but the explicit intention of the *Saison* is nonetheless to explain and confess the dangerous ambitions which plunged Rimbaud into "hell." Story will never be entirely eliminated from Rimbaud's poetry, but from the early poems to the *Illuminations* we can trace a movement from an almost novelistic type of poetic narrative to theatrical scenes of fragmentary and discontinuous desires. And pure theatricality would, ideally, resist all interpretive efforts (all *critical* narratives).

Rimbaud moves toward the inexplicable scene. The poetry of pure designation which he will occasionally succeed in producing in the *Illuminations* implies the rejection of values which have generally been exalted in Western thought: depth, complexity, ambiguity, psychological richness. But in *Une Saison en enfer*, Rimbaud's repudiations of his past are made in a language which undermines the effectiveness of the repudiations themselves. The impossibility of escape from Europe (". . . I see," Rimbaud writes, "that my discomforts come from not having realized soon enough that we are in the West") is poignantly illustrated, in the *Saison*, by the profoundly European way in which Rimbaud speaks of his efforts at escape. Suzanne Bernard, commenting on the *Saison*'s famous last line ("[and I will be able] *to possess truth in one soul and one body*"), reminds us "how much importance Rimbaud always attached to this pursuit of *truth*, in spite of his efforts to escape from reality." But it is precisely Rimbaud's commitment to the distinction between "lies" and "truth" which condemns this stage of his negations to confusion and failure. Rimbaud uses the same terms to describe his "season in hell" *and* to evoke a future which we are meant to think of as different from this rebellious past. Truth, freedom, purity, God, reason, salvation: the principal motifs of the *Saison* are the fundamental categories of Western thought, and Rimbaud, at this stage, seems hopelessly imprisoned in them. He notes in "L'Impossible" that his mind is "asleep," and he goes on to write: "If it were always wide awake from this moment on, we'd soon come to the truth, which perhaps surrounds us with its angels weeping!" Instead of dismissing the myth of absolute truth, Rimbaud merely suggests that he was looking for truth in the wrong place.

Even more: a plausible case can be made for a certain *psychological* truth about Rimbaud himself. I'm not thinking merely of the recurrent water images which bizarrely construct a stable identity for the poet from the very repetition of his desire for universal destruction and self-negation. A more specific affective content can be given to Rimbaud's gestures of repudiation. Henry Miller and Yves Bonnefoy have emphasized the catastrophic nature of that posture of uncompromising negativity which Rimbaud sought to maintain. They both see Rimbaud's probable inability to trust his mother's love as a crucial factor in his chimerical dream of giving birth to himself. Only a continuously new world and a continuously new self would liberate Rimbaud from an attachment which he perhaps felt was *broken from the beginning*. The fractured, discontinuous self is the paradoxical solution to the lack of connection between the child and his mother. Unloved, Rimbaud, as Bonnefoy suggests, makes a virtue of *willing* the absence of love, of turning against himself and submitting self-hatred to a kind of alchemy from which it would emerge as the power to replace the discarded self with constantly new selves. But "being dispossessed of love," as Bonnefoy puts it, "deprives Rimbaud of [a] possible communion with what is." And this break between Rimbaud and the world is far from having only the happy result of helping him to escape from the petrifying structures which the world would impose on the self. It also leads to a merely different sort of structural rigidity — of which the *Saison* is the major example — in which experience is immediately classified within a system of antagonistic abstractions, or of what Bonnefoy calls "dangerous dualities" between what is and what is not.

But a criticism in search of psychological themes, with its postulation of a coherent and durable intentionality, is profoundly anti-Rimbaldian. It would be foolish to claim that Rimbaud successfully escapes from the premises of this criticism, but they are nonetheless a violation of his most original project.[4] We have only to return briefly to Rimbaud's thirst and to his images of water to see this. Water erodes. If, as I mentioned before, one of the ways in which the flood serves thirst is to make objects drinkable by breaking them up into softer, liquefied parts, this effect of water can also be taken as an important ontological clue. As a result of the flood, or of the agitated movements of the sea, things are broken up into distinct parts which float away from one another; the world becomes a mass of disconnected debris. But we have seen that the poet imagines *himself* being engulfed by water, even melting into the dew scattered on the flowers of entire forests. And this is nothing less than the imagination of personality itself becoming partial, disconnected impulses. The self would have no history; it would be a succession of unrelated desires.

In the "Lettre du Voyant," "Car JE est un autre" is immediately followed by: "Si le cuivre s'éveille clairon, il n'y a rien de sa faute." ("If brass wakes up a trumpet, it's not its fault.") We find another version of this in a letter to Georges Izambard written just before the more famous one to Paul Demeny: "JE est un autre. Tant pis pour le bois qui se trouve violon. . . ." ("*I* is someone else. So much the worse for the wood if it find itself a violin. . . .") The idea of the "I" as "another" is illustrated by images of sudden metamorphoses, of inexplicable leaps from one identity to another. One substance merely "is" or "finds itself" or "awakens" as another substance. (In "Ce qu'on dit au poète à propos de fleurs," we have something similar in the astonishing injunction to poets: "Trouve des Fleurs qui soient des chaises!") These examples can be taken as an assertion of identity within differences, or of abrupt metamorphoses, and they should remind us of *Les Chants de Maldoror* and of *Wuthering Heights*. But the most radical prose poems of the *Illuminations* don't exactly propose the sameness of different objects, or a sudden change of identity in objects. Rather, they frequently propose no connection at all between two scenes or among the various elements of a single scene. Metamorphosis and identity within difference are mysteries of being; in his most original poetic activity, Rimbaud, in a sense, proposes no ontological mystery at all. He gives us a scene; then it is as if the scene were washed away; and a new scene makes its appearance. The rhythm of consciousness which Proust's narrator finds so anguishing — no continuity, just the death of one mental state followed by the birth of another — is, for Rimbaud, the ideal rhythm of a consciousness which admits as its only continuity an incessant self-negation. The discontinuity of personality is mysterious only from the point of view of a commitment to or a yearning for what Proust calls "an individual, identical and permanent self." The partial, often unconnected selves represented by free-floating desires are frightening as long as we take this unified and stable self to be the natural structure of psychic life. But the mystery disappears once we rid ourselves, as I think Rimbaud tried to do, of this bias in favor of structured personality. The *Illuminations* are Rimbaud's attempt to *be* a purely *present* consciousness — one whose scenes have no past and seem defiantly to refuse the promise of any future.

Water washes away *and* creates debris. I emphasize this once again because it would, after all, be possible to conceive of coherently unified states of consciousness being washed away and then replaced by other coherently unified states of consciousness. The discontinuity would be from one state to another, but each state could, theoretically, constitute the model for a structured personality. But the erosive flood doesn't exactly transform the world and the mind into clean slates; it creates a kind of geographical havoc, and throws together fragments which "don't belong together," and makes momentary compositions (instantly decomposed) out of the most disparate elements. Several of the scenes in the *Illuminations* have those characteristics which in fact can already be found in some of Rimbaud's early poems: abstractions behave like concrete objects, attributes are raised to the status of substances, a divorce takes place between words and the things which they usually designate.

As we move dizzyingly back and forth between "the highest crests" and the "ravines" or "old craters" of "Villes," we find that

> Sur les passerelles de l'abîme et les toits des auberges l'ardeur du ciel pavoise les mâts. L'écroulement des apothéoses rejoint les champs des hauteurs où les centauresses séraphiques évoluent parmi les avalanches.

> On footbridges of the abyss and roofs of the inns the fire of the sky adorns the masts with flags. The collapse of apotheoses overtakes the fields of the hilltops where seraphic centauresses move among the avalanches.

And later, in the same piece: "Toutes les légendes évoluent et les élans se ruent dans les bourgs." ("All legends move and enthusiasms rush through the towns.") The carriage which the poet enters in "Nocturne vulgaire" has "un défaut en haut de la glace de droite" ("a blemish at the top of the window on the right") in which "tournoient les blêmes figures lunaires, feuilles, seins. — Un vert et un bleu très foncés envahissent l'image" ("swirl pale lunar figures, leaves, breasts. — A very deep green and blue invade the image"). In the world of "Barbare," there are "les formes, les sueurs, les chevelures et les yeux, flottant" ("the forms, the sweats, the heads of hair and the eyes, floating").

In speaking of this floating, unanchored quality of objects (or attributes or concepts) in Rimbaud's visions, Etiemble and Gauclère refer to a world without relationships, one in which each thing is enclosed within itself and "freed from the sociability with which we endow even material objects. . . ." The existence of forms, sweats, heads of hair, and eyes no longer depends on "any condition which is external to their essence." This is a perceptive critical remark, but is the reference to "essence" necessary? It seems to me that the floating a-sociability of Rimbaud's fragmented world excludes *all* sytems of definition, whether they be systems which define things through their relations to other things or whether they assume that each thing has a separate, unique essence which its relations may obscure. The *Illuminations* point toward a revolutionized consciousness precisely to the extent that Rimbaud substitutes fragmented vision for any conceptualizing definitions at all. The floating eyes and heads of hair, and, in the same poem, the "feminine voice" which has arrived at "the bottom of the volcanoes and the arctic grottoes" but which designates no feminine presence which might be its source, express a mind which has, as it were, broken up its contents into meaningless pieces. At the very most, those pieces are merely *available* for new relations or new essences. But nothing even suggests that such new significances are anticipated. In the passages I've just quoted, abstractions, sounds and even sweats (miraculously separated from the skin which sweats) have all been equalized as mere appearances in consciousness. Distinctions of mental levels, of categories of thought, of ontological states have all been washed away and we have photographs of the mind as a sea of debris promiscuously and insignificantly thrown together.

As an ideal limit toward which this poetic enterprise aspires, there would perhaps be nothing more than a succession of unrelated, briefly illuminated scenes. Rimbaud's poetry would be the description of that "succession psychologique de coupes de frises, de bandes atmosphériques et d'accidences géologiques" ("psychological series of sections of friezes, of atmospheric bands and of geological cracks") which the "watcher" of "Veillées" sees on the wall in front of him: "Rêve intense et rapide de groupes sentimentaux avec des êtres de tous les caractères parmi toutes les apparences." ("Intense and swift dream of sentimental groups with beings of all qualities among all semblances.") The rapidity with which these "slices" of vision follow one another is crucial: no one scene would last long enough for it to accumulate meanings or to establish priority over any other scene. The universality of these illuminations, far from heightening their significance, would indicate merely the undiscriminating, promiscuous nature of the appetitive imagination which produces them. If vision includes everything all at once ("beings of all qualities among all semblances"), how can it — or the eye (and the "I") which is having these visions — be characterized? There is, then, a curious equivalence between the mind as all appearances and the mind as a heterogeneous collection of partial impulses. The recording poet must of course proceed, in time, from one image to another; it is the very incompleteness or incoherence of each image which both isolates it from other images and makes the series theoretically endless. The partial self is like the universal self in that neither can be constituted as a distinctive, structured personality. Rimbaud doesn't construct a mental or a physical universe; he merely accumulates evidence of a deconstructed, flood-devastated world. In a universe of fragments, there are no longer the *limited totalities* which are necessary for any classification of being.

In Rimbaud, the poetic imagination tends to become a slide-projector which ejects each slide almost at the very instant it is lighted up. Perhaps the most innovative pieces of the *Illuminations* are those in which scenes seem to be merely piled up in an apparently random order. Formally, the model for this type of poetry is given to us in "Enfance III" and "IV." The third section simply enumerates unrelated scenes; each one-sentence paragraph contains a word-picture introduced by "Il y a." For example: "Il y a une horloge qui ne sonne pas. . . . Il y a une cathédrale qui descend et un lac qui monte." ("There is a clock that does not strike. . . . There is a cathedral that descends and a lake that rises.") In the fourth section, the poet moves among various identities. The first three short paragraphs begin with "Je suis" (the fourth is introduced by the more tentative "Je serais"), and there doesn't seem to be any connection between the different selves which he is assertively trying out:

> Je suis le saint, en prière sur la terrasse. . . .
> Je suis le savant au fauteuil sombre.
>
> Je serais bien l'enfant abandonné sur la jetée partie à la haute mer,
> le petit valet suivant l'allée dont le front touche le ciel.
>
> I am the saint, at prayer on the terrace. . . .
> I am the scholar in the dark armchair.
>
> I could well be the child abandoned on the jetty washed away to the high sea, the little valet following the lane whose brow touches the sky.

Thus Rimbaud enumerates some of the images and personae of childhood. The variety of sequences to "Il y a" and to "Je suis" in "Enfance" signifies an at least temporary suspension of any one particularly absorbing personality, and a return to the child's greedy availability to multiple scenes and multiple roles.

Two references to a forest as the general setting for all the scenes do give a certain unity to the third section of "Enfance," and both the fragmentary nature of the scenes and the identification of the poet with his visions are somewhat qualified by explicit references to someone watching the scenes and even entering into a relation with them. The poet is not merely — even momentarily — "a clock that does not strike"; he is also a separate presence, and he designates each scene ("Il y a") and even takes part in a couple of them. As in several other pieces in the *Illuminations*, the pure exteriority of vision seems to be qualified by a suggestion of the poet's participation in the vision. In the last paragraph of "Mystique," the narrator ambiguously enters a scene (from nature or from art?) in which, until then, he had existed only as a neutrally descriptive voice. Part of the fantastic tableau now "descends" near someone ready to be submerged in a kind of bath of cosmic fragrance: "La douceur fleurie des étoiles et du ciel et du reste descend en face du talus, comme un panier, — contre notre face, et fait l'abîme fleurant et bleu là-dessous." ("The flowery softness of the stars and of the sky and of the rest descends opposite the bank, like a basket, — against our face, and makes the abyss sweet smelling and blue below.") Similarly, "I" makes a sudden and mysteriously dramatic appearance at the end of "Being Beauteous." In "Aube," we move in the opposite direction, from the use of "I" throughout the poem to a single objectification of the self in the next to the last sentence: "L'aube et l'enfant tombèrent au bas du bois." ("Dawn and the child [fell at] the bottom of the wood.") When the self participates in the poem's entire "story," the illumination reminds us of a dream — as in "Nocturne vulgaire." It would be tempting to say that the desiring imagination in Rimbaud almost never completely eliminates an image of itself as the subject of desire. Total self-projection into the world is somewhat compromised by the self's distinct presence in the scenes which it has summoned into being. The narrator comes upon himself as an actor in the pictures he describes. He thereby defeats his most ambitious wish, but it could of course also be said that he thereby saves himself from a schizophrenic failure to distinguish *at all* between the self and the alien forms into which it has been projected.

But the participating self is in fact nothing more than *one element* in each illumination. That is, in Rimbaud the act of narration is never an occasion for the assertion of a controlling, or of a unifying and unified, personality. It is of course through the narrative voice that such assertions are implicitly made in realistic fiction. The heterogeneity and the hallucinatory qualities of novelistic vision are qualified by a narrative presence somewhat removed from the fictional scene, a presence identical to itself from the beginning to the end of the novel. From the continuity of tone in the narrative voice, we naturally (and rightly) infer psychological consistency; that voice refers to and is supported by a *person* unaffected by the accidents of his story (of history). Even when narrative point of view is entrusted to a character who undergoes profound moral changes during the course of the events being narrated (as in James's *The Ambassadors* or Gide's *L'Immoraliste*), such characters' psychic unity and intelligibility are rarely menaced by their apparent crises of being. And even the hallucinatory fragmentariness of Balzac is "redeemed" by the organizing authority of an always recognizable narrative voice. The disconnected, the accidental and the fragmentary are absorbed into a voice which is itself a guarantee of psychic wholeness and stability. Thus the realistic novelist can give us his disjointed fantasies as an accurate report on the external world, *and* he can separate himself, *qua* reporter, from a spectacle which might threaten his psychic unity.

The Rimbaldian narrator enjoys no such special privilege. He is either a neutrally descriptive function (and his characterless neutrality is in no way affected by the fantastic content of the scenes he describes), or he enters these scenes as *part* of the "illumination." In neither case does he claim for himself the special status of a fully constituted personality unaffected by the visions he evokes. In other words, there is no psychic totality in the *Illuminations* which might gather up the fragments of vision into an *individual's* point of view. The self in each illumination (as in some of our dreams) is all over and in no one particular place. And I find a special significance in this respect in those poems in which the narrator, so to speak, almost doesn't appear. In "Being Beauteous" and in "Mystique," the "I" and the "we" enter the poem only toward the end of the poem — not at all as unifying presences, but as mere additions to the scenes. The first person has no particular ontological distinction. It indicates merely another mode of appearance, and, far from guaranteeing the scene's homogeneity, it merely joins the already heterogeneous debris of the *Illuminations'* visions.

But language is of course a structured system, and as such — even without being explicitly psychological — it is inherently antagonistic to mental life as discontinuous, hallucinated and random identifications with the external world. The poetic illumination must pass through or "cross" language, but it must also dismiss a medium which both serves it and subverts its value. It should therefore "stay" in language as briefly as possible. Thus the rapid succession of heterogeneous scenes, and also what seems to be an effort to make a single verbal sequence so impenetrably dense that the reader can "understand" it only as fragmented bits of vision. In the one case, Rimbaud moves quickly — as in "Enfance," or the second half of "Phrases," or the first section of "Jeunesse" — from one distinct scene to the next. In the latter case, he gluts a narrative unit so that it is difficult either to settle on a dominant sense, or to arrange the various elements of sense in a structured hierarchy of significance.

There is, for example, this paragraph from "Barbare":

> Les brasiers, pleuvant aux rafales de givre, — Douceurs! — les feux à la pluie du vent de diamants jetée par le coeur terrestre éternellement carbonisé pour nous. — O monde!

> Blazing coals, raining in squalls of hoarfrost, — Delights! — fires in the rain of the wind of diamonds, rain hurled down by the earthly heart eternally carbonized for us. — O world!

The first visual juxtaposition — blazing coals in a rain of hoarfrost — is taken up again (after the mysterious exclamation "Delights!") in a more extended but hardly more intelligible fashion. The extension of the image turns out to be an extraordinary condensation, and only by somehow managing to grasp all the words at once, instead of reading them one after the other, can we hope to make a single scene out of such different elements. Fires are in a rain which itself is constituted by a wind made up of diamonds; and it is this burning, windy, diamond-filled rain which is being thrown up by the earth's heart which — in a sudden and radically new idea — is spoken of as eternally on fire for us. The peculiarity of the images, the number of things we have to see at once, the unexpected indication that it is raining up rather than down, and the final wrenching of our attention from the rain to the heart of the earth which a mysterious intentionality keeps burning for us: such dizzying equivalences and movements are contained within a single verbal sequence devoid of pauses. Strictly speaking, we should only run ahead from "fires" to "for us," and Rimbaud's syntax remains just regular enough so that verbal sequence in itself doesn't justify our stopping before the end of the paragraph.

We have an entirely different type of obscurity or difficulty in the *Illuminations* from what we find in Mallarmé. The latter's original syntax forces us constantly to *stop* reading. An unprecedented word order makes us ponder over the materiality of the words themselves, and any meaning we may come up with will be inseparable from the physical arrangement of the words. For it is precisely in the originality with which words have been placed in relation to one another that we immediately recognize the poetic specificity of Mallarmé's language. Syntax becomes a principal sign of the distance between poetry and ordinary language; it *is* the poetic message, at least to the extent that this message is an act of verbal positioning. Nothing could be more different from what we have been looking at in Rimbaud. He advertises a mocking indifference to *all* possibilities of verbal sequence merely by the way in which he gluts an ordinary verbal sequence, packs it almost to the point of exploding it, giving hardly any formal indication of the strain to which he is subjecting it. Word order — and ultimately language itself — is, implicitly, a trivial irrelevance compared to the agitated visions which words deceptively appear to carry with such ease. Rimbaud dismisses language by his indifference to the possibility of making it literally coincide with the visions of his poetry. This is exactly the opposite of what Paul de Man has aptly defined as Mallarmé's aim: the equivalence of the semantic dimension of words with their status as "objects." Ideally, the language of the *Illuminations* would perhaps be so ordinary as to be expendable. The passage I quoted a moment ago from "Barbare" does of course succeed in carrying several visual messages, but it is so inadequate to the violent originality of these visions that we can only be exasperated at having to read a succession of words in order to *see* the illuminated spaces of a wordless mind and a wordless world. It is as if Rimbaud would make us disgusted with linearity by a stubborn fidelity to it. He forces us to recognize the incompatibility of simultaneity with any form of temporal succession. What makes the *Illuminations* obscure is not (as it would be in poems by Mallarmé) the opacity of new verbal arrangements, but rather the very superfluity of Rimbaud's language. An inadequate vehicle both carries the illumination and blocks our perception of it.

There is a structural play in the *Illuminations* which perhaps indicates both Rimbaud's sense of the inevitability of patterns and his determination to undermine them. In Rimbaud's early poems, compositional order takes fairly obvious and conventional forms. Some narrative idea usually provides the unifying framework within which Rimbaud explores visionary resources to which any narrative unity is intrinsically irrelevant. "Le Bateau ivre," for example, is a dazzling inventory of hallucinatory images, but their potentially disruptive effect on our mental habits is checked by the rigorously logical progression of the poem from the boat's enthusiastic departure for the uncharted seas, to its description of its wanderings among the marvels of the "Poem of the Sea," to the final statement which seems to announce the double impossibility of the boat's continuing its exhausting adventures and of its returning to ordinary commercial routines. The ambiguities of meaning at the end of the poem don't affect this stable narrative line, which allows us to give at least a structural intelligibility to some of the poem's most mysterious images.

Structural coherence certainly doesn't disappear from the *Illuminations*, although it has now become a more complicated affair. In "Barbare," for example, a complex system of repetitions provides a sort of orchestral continuity to what François Ruchon has called "a fugue in red and white." We might recall that "Barbare" also contains the references to floating forms, sweats, eyes and hair, as well as to a sourceless feminine voice which has simply "arrived" at the bottom of volcanoes and arctic grottoes. A world of floating debris and, as we saw a moment ago, of complex pictures which must be seen all at once, but which — in language — can't be seen all at once, is contained within one of the most rigorously structured poems of the *Illuminations*. In another prose poem, "Métropolitain," the visions of each paragraph are characterized by a summarizing exclamation at the end of the paragraph (for example, "The city!," "The battle!," "the countryside") which both makes the paragraph intelligible and reductively unifies a diversified enumeration of scenes. The reader's need for order is routed only to be (too easily) satisfied later on. Thus "The battle!" follows another of those packed sentences which makes sense only if we see it all at once:

> Du désert de bitume fuient droit en déroute avec les nappes de brumes échelonnées en bandes affreuses au ciel qui se recourbe, se recule et descend formé de la plus sinistre fumée noire que puisse faire l'Océan en deuil, les casques, les roues, les barques, les croupes. — La bataille!

> From the asphalt desert there flee straight ahead in rout with sheets of fog echeloned in hideous bands on the sky that bends, recoils and sinks, formed of the most sinister black smoke which the Ocean in mourning can produce, helmets, wheels, barges, rumps. — The battle!

Before we are allowed to know *what* is fleeing, the poet describes both how it is fleeing ("straight ahead in rout") and the atmosphere in which this subjectless fleeing is taking place (not only the sheet of fog, but also the moving, smoke-filled sky on which the hideous layers of fog are laid out). In another paragraph, the indication "the sky" at the end is pitifully inadequate to a summary of roads, flowers, aristocracies, ancient music, closed inns, princesses and stars:

> Des routes bordées de grilles et de murs, contenant à peine leurs bosquets, et les atroces fleurs qu'on appellerait coeurs et soeurs, Damas damnant de longueur, — possessions de féeriques aristocraties ultra-Rhénanes, Japonaises, Guaranies, propres encore à recevoir la musique des anciens, — et il y a des auberges qui pour toujours n'ouvrent déjà plus; — il y a des princesses, et, si tu n'es pas trop accablé, l'étude des astres, — le ciel.

> Roads bordered by railings and walls, scarcely restraining their thickets, and the dreadful flowers one might call hearts and sisters, Damascus damning with dullness, — possessions of fairy-tale aristocracies from beyond the Rhine, Japanese, Guaranian, still fit to receive the music of the ancients, — and there are some inns which forevermore already no longer open; — there are princesses, and, if you're not too overwhelmed, the study of the stars, — the sky.

The dash is the punctuation mark best suited for such frenetically diverse evocations. What is set off by dashes is merely added to the rest; it doesn't necessarily have the illustrative value of what follows a colon, the subordinate value of a phrase within commas, or the frequently qualifying effect of a parenthetical expression. Dashes raise the weird possibility of a monstrously long and incoherent sentence which would, however, not have violated the fundamental conditions of sentence-making. They are the anti-structural luxury of sentence structure. In analogous fashion, the particular elements of Rimbaud's visions work against the coherent structures recognizable in almost all the *Illuminations*. Or rather, the relation between the two is one of play, subversion, and yet also of compromise. For if the final noun of each paragraph of "Métropolitain" provides only a mock unity for what has been evoked in each paragraph, it is nevertheless a compositional gesture which encourages us to believe at least a little in unity and coherence. The latter are, after all, seriously threatened in the paragraph we have just looked at: threatened not only by the heterogeneity and the chaotic universality of flowers, inns, and aristocracies from all over the world, but also by the probable substitution, in "coeurs et soeurs, Damas damnant de longueur," of sound-sense for meaning-sense. Such sound repetitions can of course create another type of unity of coherence (of which the poems of the *Derniers vers* are striking examples), but in "Métropolitain" they advertise the poet's availability to the random inspiration, his willingness to let us see the fragmentary nature of what the concluding word of each paragraph feebly claims to summarize.

In the *Illuminations*, Rimbaud works toward a type of poetry which would be at once utterly simple and utterly impenetrable. It would be descriptive without being mimetic or nostalgic. The imminent reality of the world which Rimbaud describes in the *Illuminations* is guaranteed by nothing more than the appetitive energy of a desiring imagination. Desire no longer responsible to memory: this chimerical formula perhaps best characterizes the goal of Rimbaud's Voyance. And it is a goal to which poetry and language are ultimately irrelevant. In his subversion of a psychology of origins (of historical causes, or thematic centers of the self), Rimbaud, unlike Proust, even rejects the aid of what might be called the ontological elusiveness of metaphor. The Proustian hero loses

himself in the multiple versions of himself scattered along the surfaces of his narrative. Self-repetition becomes self-diffusion; thanks
to the astonishing number of peripheral connections which Marcel
discovers as he recomposes his life, it becomes impossible to locate
a reliable center for his composition or his life. But composition for
Rimbaud is merely the accidental necessity for the transmission of
vision. The *Illuminations* aim for a nonconceptual and a nonverbal
immediacy. Rimbaud's scenes would dismiss the vehicle which
transmits them, the structural frame within which they are inevitably
placed and betrayed.

And yet the process of structural framing is central to the *Illuminations*. Rimbaud's most effective — and seemingly paradoxical —
strategy for escaping from the structured sublimations of art is to
present the scenes of illuminated consciousness as carefully composed artefacts. The prose poems of the *Illuminations* are frequently
reminders of other arts — especially of the theater and of painting.
The importance of painterly notations and of theatrical decors in the
Illuminations has often been noted. The fabulous atmosphere of
Rimbaud's visions is, for example, heightened by Rimbaud's emphasis on their theatrical nature: they are often presented as acts
or episodes in some extravagant "play" of the imagination. (Drugs
may have an influence in determining this predilection for scenic
effects: Albert Py, in his commentary on the *Illuminations*, reminds
us that Michaux speaks of a "theatricalizing of thought" under the
effect of hashish.) As for the allusions to painting, the very title
of Rimbaud's volume is of course significant. Verlaine emphasized
this aspect of the work when he wrote, in his preface to the 1866
edition, that the word "illuminations" is English "et veut dire
gravures colorées — coloured plates." While this has often been
taken as an invitation to minimize or even neglect the Voyance side
of the *Illuminations* (they are "merely" verbal paintings, descriptive
rather than metaphysical), it seems to me that the superficially more
banal sense of "illuminations" is consistent with what I have been
defining as Rimbaud's most extravagant ambitions. Both the
theatrical scene and the verbal engraving work toward the same
goal: a radical simplification of consciousness through the pictorial-
ization of consciousness. These appeals to art, while they might
seem to defeat an anti-structural enterprise, in fact operate as a safe-
guard against the conceptualizing power of language. Written

poetry is reduced almost to the status of stage directions in the textual version of a play, or of catalog descriptions of paintings. The framing process immobilizes vision within a strictly delimited area of illumination, and it therefore prevents us, as it were, from going outside the framed picture to pick up elements usually associated with the illuminated fragments — elements which might help us to transform the fragments into a totality. It's true that we move from one part of a picture to another in Rimbaud's hallucinatory descriptions, but this is of course unavoidable in any linear verbal text. The illumination *should* be seen entirely, and at once; our eyes should immediately grasp the entire picture. Through the frequently meticulous framing of his scenes, Rimbaud works against our tendency to wander visually. For this visual wandering usually operates as a powerful aid to our impulse to find intelligible structures in what we see. In *Discours, figures,* Jean-François Lyotard speaks of the "prejudice" of "mobility," of "the *movement* of the eye which, in running over the field [of vision] constructs it in order to *recognize* it, and thus rejects everything which is not immediately identifiable." The immobilized eye, on the other hand, seizes "the fundamental imbalance of the visual field," its "essential heterogeneity." The wandering eye absorbs peripheral objects into a structured and distinct vision; the motionless eye leaves intact the "vast peripheral fringe of curved space" which surrounds "the very small zone of distinct vision."[5] In Rimbaud, a radical heterogeneity has invaded the entire visual field; the "zone of distinct vision" itself resists being conceptualized and thereby being made recognizable. And a language which frequently seems to have only the modest function of designating the positions of things on a painted canvas or a stage imprisons us within a sharply defined scenic frame. The immobilized eye is forced to accept the (constantly renewed) finality of Rimbaud's fragmented universe.

To what extent does a revolutionized consciousness such as that induced by Rimbaud offer a model for cultural revolution? It's clear that Rimbaud thought of the two as going together. In the "Lettre du voyant," he speaks of the poet of the future as defining "the amount of the unknown awakening in the universal soul in his own time: he would produce more than the [formula] of his thought or the [annotation] *of his march towards Progress!* An enormity who has become [the norm] absorbed by everyone, he would really be a *multiplier of progress!*" Rimbaud's violent negativity could be thought of in terms of the wish to "give more" than the "formula" of his own being, to collectivize the self so that it may speak what he calls, in the same letter to Demeny, "a universal language."

In looking at the strategies of Rimbaud's self-negation, we have also been made aware of its inevitable limitations. The metaphorical flood is responsible for extraordinary devastations and dislocations, but it never wholly destroys the poet's habitual ways of structuring experience. Thematic continuities define a persistent psychological pattern in Rimbaud, a pattern in which we recognize a certain affective identity. Also, the poet's past is both repudiated and tantalizingly referred to; much of his work seems merely to be disguising its origins rather than making origins authentically irrelevant. Finally, the very composition of Rimbaud's verse and prose poems — and perhaps especially the sound patterns — impose verbal continuities and structure on an only partially fragmented consciousness. On the other hand, it's difficult to see how the project of continuous self-negation, were it to be successful, could lead to anything but what Henry Miller calls a *"living* suicide." What basis can there be for social regeneration if the only continuity allowed for in time is the repetition of saying "no"? Rimbaud seems to have wanted to do away with his own personality as a historical self and to make of this the basis of a universal revolution. But if consciousness is simplified to the point of never having any history at all (no continuities, no structures, no meanings), the very notion of its being a vehicle for universal "progress" is of course an absurd one. *Is* there a way of imagining certain recognizable orders of thought and perception which, however, will not merely reintroduce the individual and his idiosyncratic history into the universal enterprise of redefining human possibilities?

Rimbaud himself implicitly proposes an answer to this question by experimenting — especially in the *Illuminations* — with purely scenic versions of the self. The theatricalized self is, in a certain sense, a depersonalized self. While it does have thematic continuities which point unmistakably to an individual history, these continuities don't exactly constitute a person. They do little more than give a certain intelligibility to an otherwise discontinuous succession of fragmented images of the world. They define what may be obsessive visual preferences, but, far from structuring an entire personality, these visual preferences or motifs give us merely the traces, the marks inscribed on the world by what might be called a partial self. I mean partial in two senses: the recurrent designs reveal those pictures to which Rimbaud's desiring imagination is partial, and they also constitute coherent but fragmentary psychological units within the entire sequence of illuminated scenes. The recurrence of a certain type of design doesn't make it continuous with the elements surrounding it; certain structures are repeated, but their repetition doesn't necessarily create any structural relations between them and other pictures in the series. As a result, it's difficult to get beyond the pictures themselves to some significant statement about personality, even when the pictures obviously have some privileged significance.

In the theatricalized self, the scene is final. There is no "text" of personality behind it or prior to it from which we might demonstrate that it derives. (Artaud, as we shall see, makes an analogous point when he argues against the priority of the written text over the theatrical scene. The physical reality of theater is dissipated when it is treated as a mere derivation of a nonscenic, more conceptualized form of expression.) The self of the *Illuminations is* its floating, fragmented images. What Rimbaud's theatricalizing bias eliminates is the sort of continuity — the psychological inferences — provided by a reflective subjectivity. Scenic finality means that no reflection about the scenes can reduce them to a general significance. And since that general significance would be a total personality, we can also say that the scenic self (or, more properly, scenic selves) is depersonalized: the scenes don't "add up" to a personality. No *view of* the self enjoys the ontological privilege of unifying the multiple versions of being which desire incessantly produces.[6]

It is this subversion of the subjective self which provides the basis for a contact between the poet's revolutionized consciousness and a potentially revolutionary society. By refusing to tell *stories* about himself, the poet seems to be trying to escape from the sort of individuality which coincides exactly with a particular individual's history. Ideally, the most "characteristic" aspects of Rimbaud's visions would be characteristic not so much of Rimbaud the individual as of a certain region of Being in which Rimbaud partially participates. This is the kind of individuality which Gilles Deleuze finds in Proust: the individuality of a point of view embodied in but not dependent on the existence of an individual person. Instead of giving us information about the particular circumstances which may biographically account for the nature of Rimbaud's hallucinated vision, each of the *Illuminations* merely proposes a certain vision of the world as a legitimate *consequence* of numerous and vastly different personal histories. It eschews the psychologically circumstantial for a psychologically neutralized scene in which we may all find pictorial fragments of our own desiring imaginations. A kind of crooked transversal ray lights up slices of a universe laid to waste and re-created by a consciousness flooded with desire. And we are implicitly asked to entertain the strangest juxtapositions not in order to reconstitute a single man's total vision of the world, but rather in order to test our own potentiality for imagining new versions of reality. To what extent do the *Illuminations* tempt us into a richly productive discontinuity of desire, into a daring indifference to pre-established orders of desire and pre-established notions of how much "distortion" reality will tolerate on the part of our insistent desires? These are perhaps the most serious questions to ask about Rimbaud's work, and he helps us both to ask and to answer them by the energetic generosity with which he proposes *himself* to us as the variegated scenes of a new theater in which we may recognize some of our own unsuspected capacities for the "production" of our desires in the world.

Such recognitions depend, as I've said, on a certain depersonalization of desire, and, at the extreme, the theatricalized self of the *Illuminations* is an anonymous self. Rimbaud creates a kind of common space in which the desiring fantasies of different individuals may meet or at least touch peripherally, and the theatrical scene provides the artistic form perhaps best suited to this community of depersonalized fantasies. The potential anonymity of art seems always to have interested Rimbaud. Indeed, Yves Bonnefoy has made an argument for the "vieillerie poétique" of the *Derniers vers* as an esthetic strategy designed to erase what Bonnefoy calls "the problems of a person." The "artless rhythms" and "silly refrains" of popular old songs, children's books and signboards, circus backdrops and operas, Church Latin and erotic books full of spelling mistakes: the inspirations for the *Derniers vers*, as Rimbaud enumerates them in the *Saison*, suggest a view of art as a heterogeneous scrapbook, an impersonal and even haphazard collection of images and words from everywhere. But the poems of the *Dernier vers* point to an intensely personal drama. The musicality of Rimbaud's poems serves both to disguise the content of this drama and to compensate for the psychological obscurity of the poems by offering us intricate but coherent and analyzable structures of sound.

I think that in the *Illuminations* Rimbaud seeks to replace the linguistic opacity of the *Derniers vers* with linguistic transparency. Far from serving as a protective screen between us and the poet's secret psychological complexity, language in the *Illuminations* would be obliterated by the very luminosity of the pictures which language evokes. And the anonymous heterogeneity aimed for in the *Derniers vers* is achieved much more successfully in the *Illuminations* than in earlier poems. For the theatricalization of the self and its desires implies a certain preference for the most public versions of the self — versions in which the authorship of a scene becomes problematic or simply uninteresting. Thus the importance of those fabulous cities which Rimbaud invites us to explore in the *Illuminations*; or of traveling circuses, and of glamorously mysterious hotels and villas; or of the dizzying views of extraordinary natural landscapes. And these scenes are "made up" in the gaudiest hues. Our vision is dazzled by blazing fires and multicolored minerals. Everything is designed — as in a spectacularly vulgar circus number — to fascinate our eyes, to make it impossible for us to turn our glutted vision away from the hypnotic scene. These cineramic hallucinations attain a certain impersonality by the frankly excessive and improbable nature of the spectacle. It is as if we had all thrown something into these scenes in order to make them as inclusive and also as gaudily rich as possible. And so theatricalized desire in the *Illuminations*, while its remote "source" may be in a single poet's highly idiosyncratic psychology, takes on the aspect of an authentic community project.

The collectivization of desire is an ambition of modern theater. It means the expression of desire in purely scenic terms, and the use of the theatrical scene as a place in which individual histories can be disregarded or overcome and an entire community can both recognize and participate in the production of its most radically inventive wishes. Drama lacks what most strongly supports the ideal of individual personality in other literary forms: that incessant *voice* which, in poetry, prose fiction and the essay, never stops implying the presence of a stable and structured self as the center to which the world always returns and from which it receives its own re-assuringly stable designs. The self implicit in most literature is an ordered and ordering presence; what we "hear" in listening to its voice is a guarantee of wholeness, of totality, and therefore a nega-tion of the fragmentariness which that voice may even be explicitly documenting (but which it can't accept as final). We can therefore fully appreciate the revolutionary possibilities of Rimbaud's work only by turning away from his poetry and considering some modern theatrical adventures. In art, the theater is a privileged arena for testing the viability of a fragmented *and* collectivized self. It can enact modes of escape from the ideology of a full and fully struc-tured human character. But the theatricalized self is also the arena for a cruelty unmediated by any self-reflexiveness. Desire entirely transformed into scenes has escaped from the perhaps necessary judgment to which I referred a moment ago: a rational voice which makes a continuous narrative of our lives and to which pure spec-tacle is always — and perhaps rightly — suspect. Some scenes of desire from erotic literature may lead us to qualify whatever ex-hilaration we may feel at the prospect of desublimated desire and the deconstruction of personality. Both the desirability and the very possibility of such deconstructions are spectacularly put into question by the rites of devastation to which sexual theater initiates us.

CHAPTER NINE

Artaud, Defecation and Birth

PERHAPS THE MOST FUNDAMENTAL aspect of theatrical reform in the twentieth century has been the devaluation of the written theatrical text. And of course the figure most intimately connected with this project is Antonin Artaud. "We must be done with this superstition of texts and of *written* poetry," Artaud declared in 1933.[1] What is "this superstition of texts"? The text is the most respectable aspect of theatrical performance; it is, we might say, the strictly mental component of theater. The literary text qualifies the physical confrontations of theater (confrontations among actors as well as the spectator's erotic attachment to the actors); it is a reminder that physical presence is not indispensable to the "essence" of theater. Significantly, Artaud connects the tyranny of the text with the tyranny of the abstract. To repudiate the domination of theater by literature is to reaffirm the physical immediacy of the theater. And the primacy of the physical means that even the language of the theater must be different from the language of literature.

Balinese theater was for Artaud the revelation of a theatrical language in which words would be only one element, and not even the most important. In the angular poses of the Balinese actors, in the strange rhythms of their guttural sounds, in their grimaces and calculated muscular spasms, in the mysterious fusions of their voices with the sounds of musical instruments, in the "dance" of the geometrical robes which transform the Balinese players into "animated hieroglyphics," Artaud discovers "the meaning of a new physical language with its basis in signs and no longer in words." The physical elements of Western theater are intended to realize a literary text; they serve that text; essentially, they illustrate and decorate it. The secondary importance of actual performance in Western theater reinforces our traditional sense of the inferiority of the concrete to the abstract: the former carries meaning only to the extent that it reveals the latter. The abstraction is the gold nugget to be removed from the impure ore of concrete reality. What Artaud finds most astonishing in Balinese theater, on the other hand, "is this revealing aspect of matter which seems to be suddenly dispersed into signs in order to teach us the metaphysical identity of the concrete and the abstract." The physical elements of theater don't need the support of a text in order to be read as meaningful signs. What we must learn to read in the theater is not the "parent" text from which each production is derived, but rather the irreducible and immediately perceived language of movement, sounds, shapes and colors.

The devaluation of the literary text is a subversion of character structures. Psychology in the theater depends on the subordination of theater to literature or, more fundamentally, to verbal language. Linguistic structures inspire and cooperate intimately with psychological structures. Perhaps the most striking example in all literature of an attempt to bypass both types of structure can be found in Rimbaud. In his effort to reduce or simplify himself to a series of discontinuous, fragmented scenes — scenes of the external world which wholly objectify the desiring imagination — Rimbaud develops a suspicion of language itself. And, as we have seen in the preceding chapter, this impatience with language is the sign of Rimbaud's impatience with his own being. His radical negativity involves a continuous self-repudiation; no present moment is to be responsible to any past moment. Rimbaldian freedom implies a chimerical escape from any self-repetitions at all. And if the self is to be entirely without depth or historical references, its mode of expression must be a succession of nonstructurable visual "illuminations." Thus, unlike *Une Saison en Enfer*, in which language tells a story, and unlike the *Derniers vers*, where complex musical structures both conceal the poet's inner secrets and yet teasingly confirm their reality, the *Illuminations* are Rimbaud's effort to make language transparent to the hallucinated scene. It is as if he had realized that the particular attention which poetic language usually requires of us inevitably becomes a lesson in the strategies by which language constructs a coherent fiction. And coherent fictions undermine the project of constant self-repudiation: they imply duration, stability and repetition. Therefore, in order to escape from the temptation of structured coherence in the self, Rimbaud must also escape from his interest in the principal instrument of all sense-making operations — that is, his interest in language. The *Illuminations* are an attempt to depoeticize language, to deprive it of any poetic opacity and to reduce it to the status of an uninteresting, barely noticeable prosaic vehicle which would never infect the visions it carries with its own (undesirable) orders.

There is a striking parallelism between Artaud's theatrical manifestos and the program for poetry (and for being) implicit in Rimbaud's *Illuminations*. Far from suggesting that the physical language of theater should convey the same type of message as the literary text, Artaud emphasizes that to end the supremacy of words is to bring about a radical change in the nature of theatrical sense. To be done with literary masterpieces is to be done with psychology in the theater. "The domain of the theater is not psychological, but plastic and physical. . . ." Now theater is also metaphysical for Artaud, and what he means by a theatrical metaphysic is another question. It's one that his own productions never answered satisfactorily, and in his writings — especially in *Le Théâtre et son double* — the metaphysic of the concrete is often discussed vaguely, and at times it even seems to include notions from the very systems of abstraction which Artaud is apparently rejecting. (I'm thinking especially of his attempt to convince his readers that the violent theatrical gesture is also a "disinterested" gesture, as well as of his favorable view of spectacles which produce sublimation.) But in the present discussion we can limit ourselves to what I take to be Artaud's more authentic, and also more complexly ambiguous, gesture of rejection. Jacques Derrida has said that Artaud wants to abolish repetition. This is as fundamental a project in Artaud as it is in Rimbaud. First of all, the subordination of theater to the literary text makes of theater a mere repetition of literature. Secondly, the supremacy of verbal language is also the supremacy of a code which depends on repetition for its coherence.[2] Finally, Artaud's rejection of psychological theater is the natural corollary of his attack on logical discourse and on literary textuality. Psychological theater dramatizes self-repetitions which provide the thematic foundations for a coherently structured personality.

But Artaud's hostility to repetition makes him vulnerable to a type of analysis which exposes the thematic continuities of his own life. Part of the inescapable absurdity of the wish to abolish repetition is that the very persistence of that wish, and its various modulations, subvert the content of Artaud's project: he continuously repeats the project of abolishing repetitions. And we can be more psychologically specific about this enterprise. The central theme of Artaud's life, as Derrida has brilliantly shown, is a horror of all derivation. The inferior status of theatrical performance in Europe is the result of theater being considered as merely derived from literature. It is never entirely present to itself; it is always a reminder of its absent and more prestigious source. But this view of the relation between performance and text could be thought of as a sublimated version of Artaud's more visceral revolt against his own derivation from his parents. To be born is to be derived; thus Artaud's extraordinary insistence that his birth was a mistake. For example, Artaud wrote to Henri Parisot on September 7, 1945: "I didn't go to the Tarahumaras to look for Jesus Christ but rather for myself, Mr. Antonin Artaud, born September 4, 1896 in Marseille, 4, rue du Jardin des Plantes, from a uterus I had no need of and which I never had any need of even before, because that's no way to be born, when you're copulated and masturbated nine months by the membrane, the shiny membrane which devours without teeth as the Upanishads say, and I know that I was born in a different way, from my works and not from a mother, but the Mother resolved to take me and you see the result in my life."

To be born is the most dramatic example of a substance falling away from itself. The common denominator of Artaud's views on theater, language and psychology, as well as of his rejection of God and his mad claim that he owes his existence to no one but himself, is his revulsion at the phenomenon of dropping. To drop away from a source is to be derived from that source, and derivation is the mode of repetition which Artaud abhors. But it is as if he saw all repetitions as examples of derivation. It is therefore only in doing away with repetition itself that Artaud can hope both to correct the "mistake" of his birth and (like Rimbaud) to succeed in making the present give birth to itself in freeing it from any responsibility to the past.

In Artaud, the revolutionizing of the self implicit in this project is pursued with psychotic panic; and in that panic Artaud makes explicit the terrifying fantasies about the body which inform both his plans for a "theater of cruelty" and his repudiation of birth. These fantasies can be exceptionally useful in helping us to see what is at stake in perhaps all attempts to simplify character to de-sublimated, discontinuous scenes of the desiring imagination. "The anus is always terror," Artaud writes in a letter from the asylum at Rodez in which he attacks the "fecality" in Lewis Carroll's *Jabberwocky* as being that of "an English snob, who makes little curls of the obscene in himself as if he were applying curling-tongs to ringlets." *Jabberwocky* is soulless because it is without authentic obscenity: ". . . I refuse to admit that one can lose any excrement without acutely suffering from the simultaneous loss of one's soul, and there is no soul in *Jabberwocky*." From his early letters to Jacques Rivière to the hallucinating messages from Rodez, the constant theme of Artaud's anguish is a terrified fantasy of a dropping away of the self. To Rivière, he complains of "une véritable déperdition," of "a central caving in of the soul, . . . a kind of erosion . . . of thought." At Rodez, twenty years later, the connection between this spiritual erosion and loss of the soul through the anus will be made explicit. What is the logic of this connection? Why is the anus terror?

We may consider the excremental process and birth as the most appropriate physical models for all ontological reflection about individuality, self-repetition and death. ". . . Caca is the matter of the soul. . . ." Artaud profoundly writes from Rodez. Given Artaud's terror of the anus and his revulsion with birth, this astonishing formula is, I think, a condensed way of affirming that excremental droppings are inevitably — and, in one sense, rightly — associated with that "dropping away" from the mother which marks the birth of an individual soul. The connection between the two is by no means only a "sick" confusion between two fundamentally different biological operations. It's obvious that in its pathological form, a fantasy equivalence of birth with defecation involves confusing the vagina and the anus and a live infant with fecal matter. But the very real analogies between the two phenomena are perhaps more interesting. Giving birth and moving one's bowels are both concrete illustrations of that "miracle" — which in fact is a commonplace in the evolutionary scale from the unicellular organism to man — by which one substance becomes two substances. In both processes, being separates from itself.

Now in birth what is separated from the parent organism is new life; in defecation, it is of course merely waste, matter which the body can neither destroy nor use. The latter process, while it in fact demonstrates both the living economy of the body and the indestructibility of matter, comes nonetheless to be interpreted (especially in the child's fantasies) as a daily manifestation of our bodies' tendency to die. It is as if the body were continuously evacuating part of itself, transforming its living cells into dead waste. Artaud remains faithful to the child's view of fecal matter as a loss of life, as evidence of the mysterious amputation of its own living substance on the part of the body. In this fantasy the feces are the visible, externalized form of the body's death while we are still alive. But to be separated from the mother's body is also a form of death. Birth "condemns" us to individual life, and therefore to death; the beginning of a new life is of course also the promise of a new death. The crude physical analogies between birth and defecation — they are both, as it were, evacuations from below — are therefore reinforced by another, more essential, similarity: both evacuations seem to announce death. It is, very precisely, the "falling away" from another self which, by giving us individual life, made death inevitable. And in defecation the live body appears to illustrate its affinity with death throughout life. Thus, to the extent that it is the nature of an individual soul to have the awesome privilege of an individual death, the fate of the soul is prefigured in the body's daily "condemnation" of a part of its own contents as unusable waste. In a sense, the matter of the soul is indeed "caca," and the anus is, conversely, a principle of spiritual terror: to feel the body's waste pass through the anus and to see that waste is to witness a decomposition (a separation of matter from life) to which another passing through or dropping away originally and irrevocably doomed us.

But of course birth dooms us to death *in time*, and the fantasy identification of birth with death implies an indifference to the time *between* the two. Perhaps only a passionate interest in the "unfolding" of our lives' time can soften the shock of that falling away from the self which is intimately connected with death in both defecation and birth. In effect, we might say that Artaud, in his panic, would abolish all temporal processes, and this has important consequences for his revolutionary vision of the theater. To understand this, we should look at some other aspects of birth and of the anus as terror. For birth and defecation are instructive not merely about individuality and death; they also throw light on self-repetition and character formation in time. Birth is the fundamental example in human experience of self-repetition as productive of new being. The infant's parents have reproduced themselves in another individual. The unresolvable paradox of birth lies in this equivalence between self-reproduction and absolute difference. Thus birth is the model of all temporal processes which simultaneously establish continuities and discontinuities. It is the major human experience of difference within repetition, of a repetition which does not simply reproduce the same. On the one hand, birth is the model of all recurrences which make it possible for us to see intelligible structures in the world; all sense-making activity depends on the perception of repetition (or of parallelism and analogy). On the other hand, birth initiates us into the world of diversified forms.

Among the latter, we might include the forms of an individual character. The diversified coherence of a particular psychological history consists, precisely, in self-repetitions subverted and enriched by self-betrayals. And there are, of course, possibilities of terror in this process. There is, first of all, the terror of *mere* repetition, of that monotonous, timeless tick-tack of personality which, as we have seen, obsesses Gudrun in Lawrence's *Women in Love*. There is also the potential terror of having to recognize the self in a form alien to the self. In one sense, both the infant and fecal matter defy us to recognize ourselves in a foreign substance. And the history of personality includes numerous shocks of similar (non)recognitions. In literature, *A la Recherche du temps perdu* is the most exhaustive document we have of a man's incredulity in the face of what he himself becomes. The most mysterious crises for Proust's narrator are those moments when he can't find himself in the present, when he perceives no repetitions but only difference. Finally, there is the terror of loss — a terror which can be located both on the side of what has reproduced itself and on the side of what has been reproduced. In birth, defecation and the history of personality, the parent organism dissipates its contents merely by allowing them to be manifested in external forms. The mother literally loses a part of herself in the child; we throw away some of what the body has been containing in the excremental process; and in the time of an individual life, the self is lost (it spends itself) among the multiple alien circumstances in which it enacts and dissipates its history. If we consider loss from the point of view of what has been born, we see that the infant suffers the loss of its origin; and, in the history of personality, each new gesture creates another difference, however minute, which separates us irremediably from the permanently identical self which we might have preserved only by refusing any *performed* repetition at all, by refusing time itself.

It is this terror at the separation of the self from itself which we find in Artaud. The anus and birth are subjects of terror, but, if we accept the logic of what I've just been saying, so is the very time of an individual life. The cruel lesson which birth, defecation and an individual history teaches us is that I am never entirely present to myself. As Derrida says, repetition makes a present moment less fully present to itself. Part of what is in the present was already in the past, and therefore the present is, so to speak, partly somewhere (sometime) else. I too am always somewhere else, and all repetition is evidence of my being elsewhere. There are always spaces (physical and temporal) between a present gesture and the gesture it refers to. But there are no gestures from which all the others are derived; every moment in my life sends me to other moments. And, to the extent that I yearn to find an underived origin, I can only suffer from this experience of never being anything but a derived self, one whose differences are inseparable from its repetitions, in short a self always dropping away from — what?

The answer to this question obviously depends on our views concerning the final term (or the origin . . .) of our myths about origin. It seems likely that the prenatal experience of living in the mother's body lays the basis for the illusion of perfect presence. The notion of a transcendent being whose nature is wholly concentrated in its unchangeable presence is perhaps the most intellectually rarefied consequence of the prenatal confusion of our milieu with our being. We never wholly rid ourselves of this confusion; or, more precisely, we keep a nostalgia for a world in which being would everywhere always be equally present to itself. Instead, the self finds that it is at a distance from the world which nonetheless contains it. It is neither identical to the world nor is it clearly distinct from it; rather, it is always in the intervals between two fictions, the fiction of a world from which the self is absent and that of the self as a center without an environment, or as a fixed, nondisseminated presence. The physical separation of the infant from the parent in birth is the most spectacular evidence we are given of the space between the self and the world as well as between the self and its own history.[3] Artaud's most urgent need is to abolish these spaces, to save the self from any extensions or, to use a Derridean term, any dissemination which would scatter and destroy presence. Artaud's ideal, in Derrida's striking phrase, is a "Corps-propre-debout-sans-déchet." Without "déchet" (waste or residue): nothing must fall away from the body. But since the very shape of the body includes a certain falling away from itself, Artaud lives in terror of "the articulated body," of anatomical extensions which decentralize our physical being. And we can now see the most profound logic of Artaud's mistrust of verbal language: words articulate the self, they substitute a system of spaced repetitions and differences for pure presence. (Beckett pursues the same chimerical ideal. The "characters" in the novelistic trilogy move toward silence, immobility and even, in *L'Innommable*, a body reduced to — or perfected in — the shape of a ball with no extensions at all.)

Psychology is the attempt to systematize the self's losses of pure presence. It considers all behavior from the point of view of other behavior; the psychological interpretation of repetition and difference assumes the derived nature of all human activity. The anti-psychological bias of Artaud's program for the theater is therefore a logical and crucial aspect of his passionate antipathy toward all derivation. It's true that Artaud's rebellion, as Derrida has shown, is ambiguous and even self-defeating. Artaud rejects a "metaphysics of difference" which argues for the ontological inferiority of the phenomenal world by referring that world back to an underived cause which alone enjoys the privilege of full, nonreferential presence. But he keeps the cult of presence. Instead of recognizing that to abolish transcendence is also to lose the hope of *any* self-contained, "nondisseminated" presence in the universe, Artaud transfers the locus of perfect presence from a metaphysical reality to the phenomenal world itself, indeed to his own body (the "Corps-propre-debout-sans-déchet"). And to his thought; in one of the texts of *L'Ombilic des limbes*, Artaud spells out his notion of what thought should be: ". . . for me thinking is something other than not being completely dead, it means connecting up with oneself at every moment, it means that we never stop feeling ourselves in our inner being, in the unformulated mass of life, in the substance of our reality, it means not feeling any essential hole in ourselves, any vital absence, it means always feeling our thought equal to our thought." Nevertheless, as far as the consequences for theatrical theory and practice are concerned, this displacement of perfect presence is enormously important. Since in the theater the dramatic text plays the part of the source from which dramatic performance is derived, to abolish the "superstition of texts" is the first requirement of the theater of cruelty. To do away with psychological theater is just as necessary: the presence of the theater's multiple physical realities has been violated by our habit of translating dramatic performance into the psychology from which it presumably derives. Theatrical shapes and movements have been the mere "déchet," the "droppings," of abstract psychological and moral truths.

To shift the emphasis in theater from the textual to the scenic implies a redefinition of character and desire which would be as radical as that proposed by the *Illuminations*. Although Artaud never discusses his ideas in the terms I'm now using, his theatrical program is nonetheless an attack on the very bases of psychological intelligibility in our culture. The notion of a structured, unified character is inseparable from the phenomenon of derivation (and from a willingness to accept that phenomenon). In any coherent psychological portrait, the unity of personality depends on interrelated traits which are stabilized by their positions in a hierarchical structure. There are dominant traits and there are subordinate traits; certain aspects of personality are derived from other aspects; the self's "extensions" into various activities both diversify and repeat character. This unifying, hierarchical logic of personality is easy enough to see in early psychologies of the humors or of dominant faculties. It is also present, in more sophisticated form, in the psychoanalytic classifications of character traits as derived from fixations on different bodily pleasures; and the same unifying logic governs the judgmental discriminations about behavior in, for example, the Freudian use of such labels as "symptoms" and "sublimations."

Now Artaud himself is not very instructive about the consequences of a rejection of psychological drama. This is partly because his theatrical practice (what there was of it) was less original than his speculations about theater, and perhaps also because his own entrapment in the ideology of presence would in any case have condemned him to a static, monumental type of theatrical event. In his tortured struggle with the presence-absence duality, Artaud seems to have been incapable of imagining a theatrical scene which would *neither* refer us to preexistent texts (or to an implicit psychological unity) *nor* merely transfer the cult of total presence from abstract sources behind the scenes to the physical elements of theater themselves. As we shall see in a moment in looking at some contemporary examples, it's possible to conceive of a nonpsychological and a nontextual theater in terms of a certain *inadequacy* between dramatic presence and dramatic significance. The significance, however, would be literally nowhere, neither in the theater nor out of it; its nature would be more a question of positioning than of content. That is, nothing would ever be designed to centralize (and capsulize) dramatic meaning for us. All the physical elements of theater would be both excessive and inadequate: either charged with energies untranslatable into sense, or de-emphasized in ways designed to make us constantly look elsewhere. And this decentralization of theatrical presence forces the spectator to abandon a fixed, fetishistic attention to actors' bodies which, it could be argued, has provided the principal erotic pleasure of traditional theater.

Repetition has various modes, but it is inconceivable that repetition itself be abolished. The mode which haunts Artaud, and which he tries so desperately to eliminate, both in the theater and in his own being, might be thought of as a vertical or transcendental repetition. Phenomena repeat the source from which they derive, and ontologically, the phenomenal world is inferior to its origins and causes.

Performance is subordinate to texts; behavior merely illustrates character. There are viable alternatives to this sort of repetition, but it would be difficult to overemphasize its powerful (if frightening) appeal. As I suggested earlier, the connection between individuality, death, and character formation on the one hand and, on the other, repetition as a falling away from an origin ideally present to itself would seem to be a biologically authenticated connection. Artaud profoundly saw that to reject derivation implies a "refusal" of birth (and of defecation). We *are* a dropping away from an origin which we relive, in fantasy, as wholly adequate to itself; and in the body's wastes, death seems to be produced and made immediately visible to the living. The psychology most natural to us undoubtedly involves us in thinking of visible behavior as proceeding from and illustrating profound character structures. And the successful throwing off of this psychology involves a kind of murder. Birth is a "falling" from above, and so, in a sense, is vertical derivation (the play is a "déchet" from the text, behavior a "déchet" from our nature). Vertical derivation is therefore biologically linked to having parents. For Artaud to escape from being a "dropping," he must deny his birth, "kill" his parents. A murder, Derrida writes, is always at the origin of cruelty — murder of the parent, of the all-powerful Logos behind the theatrical scene, and, of course, murder of God. Ultimately, only deocide restores the dignity of concreteness to the theater (and to all human experience), for "God's history is . . . the history of the Work as excrement."

Artaud, like Rimbaud, forces us to see the unavoidable connection between the deconstruction of character and violence. Theater is intrinsically cruel — although for reasons which have little to do with the vague notions of "necessity," "difficulty" and "appetite for life" with which Artaud watered down his intuitions about theatrical cruelty. The particular power of theater lies in its immediately scenic nature. While Rimbaud had always to struggle against the conceptualizing tendencies of language, a theatrical performance can return us at once to visual modes of self-definition. Theater is the ideal space in which a regression from the structured sublimations of character can be enacted. No human performance eliminates psychology; but theatrical performance can return us to a psychology of the concrete. In what sense is this return violent or cruel?

First of all, theater allows us momentarily to forget the distinction between the self and the world — a distinction based on the infant's painful recognition that the scenes of his desiring imagination are internal scenes. Desire is mental, and therefore abstract, and our capacity for abstraction depends on our having been forced to discriminate between sensory experience and the fantasies of desire. We can see the complicity of language with this learning process. The most elementary verbal grammar helps us to systematize these discriminations (I'm thinking, for example, of the distinctions among pronouns, as well as of the implicit opposition between concrete and abstract in the difference between the present tense and past and future tenses), and we of course use words to represent — to present once again — realities no longer or not yet present. Thus a nonverbal coincidence of the self with the world is replaced by verbal descriptions of both what we perceive and what we feel, by the transposition of pictorial desire into narrative fictions. Our fictions express, elaborate and disguise our desires; they sublimate desire.[4] Finally, we reflect on the nature of our fictive scenes and stories, and finding patterns, analogies, themes (in short, repetitions) in the history of our imagination, we are naturally led to view that history as the display of a coherent character. Desire, blocked in its naïve confusions with the world, repeats itself at different levels of mental activity. A single desire runs through various preferences (preferences for certain sexual activities, for certain styles in other people, for particular rhythms of behavior, for particular systems of thought). Repeated and sublimated, desire thus creates personality.

Theater can offer us the extraordinary luxury of briefly destroying this entire process. We can now see that the violence of the theater which Artaud proposes to us is not only a question of patricide (or matricide) and deocide. The theatrical scene that is not subordinated to a literary text can also brush aside the hard-earned knowledge of the world as more than a performing space for my own identity. Theater reobjectifies desire, and when its scenes coincide with those of the spectator's own desiring imagination, it is as if, for a moment, he had recovered the happy illusion that his desires literally possess the world. Furthermore, in an essentially nonverbal theater no longer retelling stories already told in literature, we may also enjoy a loss of the continuities which our verbal fictions have discovered in (or imposed on) our desires. Psychological continuity thrives on the frustration of desire; desire, duplicated and sublimated in ideals and mental faculties, organizes a self. The victims of this process are the fragmentary, the accidental, the peripheral, the discontinuous. The scenic finality of theater allows for the reinstatement of a heterogeneous multiplicity of desire. A mass of memories and fantasies no longer has to be sacrificed to the structural harmony of character. Theater is the privileged esthetic space for structurally unassimilable desires.

But the indulgence of those desires obviously entails certain brutalities. To re-emphasize the fragmentary and the discontinuous is to fracture, to wound, the self. We undermine a psychological unity which we no longer think of as an inescapable psychic fate but which has performed the far from negligible service of providing us with an identity in the world. Representations of discontinuous impulses express partial selves; the person is dismembered by the very fertility of its resources. And in our exuberant fusion with those scenes which offer themselves, literally, as the theater of our desires, we may also become more readily disposed to violate *any* otherness in the external world. Consciousness liberated from the restrictive continuities of character may also be consciousness abandoned to the brutal if illusory omnipotence of masturbatory fantasies. The deconstruction of character in contemporary theatrical experiments is a complex adventure. Desiring impulses no longer contained by conscience or by a sense of responsibility toward one's own coherence are perhaps even more ferocious than the vengeful desires sanctioned by conscience. Some of these experiments (I'm thinking especially of Robert Wilson, Joe Chaikin, Peter Brook and Charles Ludlam) have in fact found strategies to tame a desiring imagination which they also encourage us to cultivate. Our discussion of contemporary theaters of desire will have to include a close look at the consequences of all serious enterprises of psychic deconstruction. For among those consequences, we inevitably find, to some degree, the pornographic tyrannies intrinsic to all desire.

CHAPTER TEN

Theaters of Desire

(Joe Chaikin, Robert Wilson and others)

TO DISCUSS THE most adventuresome contemporary theater is, in one sense, merely to document the relevance of Artaud's ideas to actual theatrical performance. I don't mean to deny the significant differences between, say, Jerzy Grotowski's Polish Laboratory Theater and Joe Chaikin's Open Theater; nor do I mean to suggest that any of the men I have in mind thinks of himself as merely providing a performing arena for the program outlined in *Le Théâtre et son double*. Grotowski, for example, sharply rejects what he judges to be Artaud's mistaken notions about Oriental signs and their relevance to Western theater. Nonetheless, the most interesting recent theater could be thought of as a testing ground for those positions on literary texts, on language, and on psychology which I have just discussed in relation to Artaud. First, the text: contemporary theater has indeed done away with "the superstition of texts." This rejection of the literary text's hegemony has taken a variety of forms. At one extreme, in street theater, the prepared text is reduced to the most meager and general indications of a story line or scheme of action. What actually happens during a performance depends on the particular audience which happens to stop and watch the group; performance is largely an improvised response to the unpredictable responses of people in the streets. A similar format can of course also be used in a traditional theater space. Much of the Living Theater's production of *Paradise Now*, for example, consisted of exchanges between the company and the audience. To a large extent the interest of an evening at *Paradise Now* depended not on the actors but on the people who happened to be in the theater. Even in groups which encourage neither audience participation nor improvisation from the actors, we find a similarly casual attitude toward the constituted text. Joe Chaikin frequently had a writer working with the Open Theater, but the group's fundamental obligation was almost never to a writer's work. (Exceptions have been Chaikin's production of Beckett's *Endgame* and his more recent version of Chekhov's *The Seagull*.[1]) The writer supplies language and thematic continuity; he can initiate a dramatic development or provide a unifying structure for various aspects of the work. He has a kind of catalytic function. Whatever text the writer offers is viewed not as the object to be performed, but rather as a challenge to the group's inventive ingenuities as they work on each production.

Texts are thus reduced, literally, to the status of pre-texts: they are both simply that which precedes the group's creative work, and a convenient occasion for testing the group's theatrical resources. This can be the case even when a well-known text is used. Grotowski has performed Marlowe's *Doctor Faustus* and Calderón's *The Constant Prince*; Brook has played Shakespeare; and Richard Schechner has used Euripides' *The Bacchae*. But even when a production remains faithful to the language of a literary text, Grotowski, Brook and Schechner treat the text — to adopt a distinction proposed by John Cage — as material and not as a model. In spite of the obviously great difference between street theater and Grotowski's *The Constant Prince*, in both cases there are no texts that would give us an adequate idea of the actual theatrical events. There have, of course, always been important variations in the many productions of classical plays. But the most innovative contemporary theater has not been simply more imaginative in its readings of Euripides or Shakespeare. Rather, the productions using established texts have frequently been closer to street theater (where the text is practically nonexistent) than to other productions of the same texts. And this is because of a casual disregard for the traditional primacy of the text. Literature has become a theatrical resource rather than the primary source of theater. The distance between text and performance has become so great that the act of reading is, to an unprecedented degree, discredited as a substitute for (or even a complement to) the theatrical experience.

As with Artaud, the devaluation of the text in recent theater is also a devaluation of verbal language and, to the extent of its dependence on language, of psychological drama. The escape from personality entails (but is not necessarily achieved by) an escape from language. But what is there is escape *to?* Once again, Artaud provides us with an answer. As we saw earlier, Balinese theater helped Artaud to discover "the meaning of a new physical language with its basis in signs and no longer in words," and, consequently, the possibility of transforming actors from more or less complex persons into "animated hieroglyphics." The subtleties of language in traditional theater create a psychology of subtle abstractions. A major enterprise of contemporary theater has been, as it were, to re-code human presences so that they no longer signify character or personality.

At Persepolis, Peter Brook worked with a language invented by the poet Ted Hughes. Brook and Hughes offer a contemporary version of the Rousseauistic myth of an original language, now lost, which directly expressed human feelings and was universally understood. Like Rousseau, they have spoken of the history of speech as "a withering away of plenitude," a narrowing of tonal resources. Orghast would be an effort to return to "a common tonal consciousness, a language belonging below the levels where differences appear." One could criticize this aim as belonging to that cult of presence, of the perfect origin, which has produced precisely the derivative theater which Brook would like to reject. As Derrida has shown, the myth of origins, of plenitude at the source, pursues us everywhere, and Brook's yearning for the (unimaginable) time in the history of languages when differences didn't yet exist reminds us of Artaud's nostalgia for underived being. In both cases, a rejection of theater derived from literary texts is nonetheless accompanied by a longing for the fully present "text" (a language, a self, or a body) at the source of and uncontaminated by the differentiating processes of history. One can be skeptical of these naïve views of linguistic and ontological origins and still feel that Brook's attempts to get into "the physiology of speech" did involve an important change in the codes of meaning used in the theater. Orghast was part of an effort to exploit the musical rather than the semantic potentialities of vocal sounds; Brook and Hughes wanted a language that would have the expressiveness of physical movements rather than of conceptual thought.

Now Brook seems less interested in questioning basic assumptions about the nature of personality than in eliminating cultural differences which prevent universal communication. Consequently, he has perhaps felt less uncomfortable than other contemporary directors with classical texts, and his work involves a less radical retraining of our perceptual habits than that of Chaikin and of Robert Wilson. Brook's most daring experiments aim at simplification of expression; he wants to find the gestures, the sounds and the settings which can communicate emotions to anyone anywhere. On the one hand, the invented language used at Persepolis was a way of exploring new possibilities in the human voice; like the cries and grimaces of the inmates in *Marat/Sade*, these novel sounds may have suggested expressive resources unavailable to more familiar speech. On the other hand, the plot of *Orghast* (though most of the spectators were surely unable to follow it) suggests a wish to return to the most recognizable moral schemes of Western culture. Brook has a taste for allegorical modes of action which re-educate us in the most conventional means of structuring human behavior. A rather vague notion of levels of feeling common to all men has led Brook to search for a universal theatrical language. Theater would help us to find those centers of human conduct which cultural differences have obscured. Brook is therefore less interested than Wilson (or Charles Ludlam) in what has traditionally been considered as the accidental, the peripheral or the perverse in human nature, and his theatrical techniques, unlike Wilson's, don't encourage us to stop searching for centers of action and of meaning. The aspect of Brook's work most relevant to the purpose of our discussion is his attempt to find an audience. Brook's most radical theatrical act has perhaps been simply his moving around the world in search of a public.

The dismissal of literary texts and the experimentation with new languages have, most interestingly, been part of an investigation into human resources mostly neglected by traditional theater. Superficially, one might suppose that improvisation would play an important role in this project. But in fact what the actor will almost always improvise is merely a type of personality which has generally been rendered with more skill by the rejected literary texts. Brook has said that improvisation brings the actor to his own barriers; Artaud proclaimed that the actor should be denied all personal initiative; and Grotowski's notion of the actor making a total gift of himself involves having him follow a "score" of fixed details. A radical deconstruction of the self is anything but a "natural" enterprise. In the face of any threat to those psychic structures which imprison desire but which also make our impulses intelligible to us, our spontaneous reaction is to reconstruct the menaced self. Only the most arduous discipline and the most extreme artifice can loosen the bonds of our attachment to an ideology of self-repetitions and sublimations.

The connection between new sounds in the theater and psychological deconstruction has perhaps been most evident in some of the work of the Open Theater. I have in mind mainly *The Mutation Show* and *Nightwalk*, both of which could be thought of as experiments in metamorphosis. Chaikin's extraordinary group often seemed to be physically enacting the metamorphic imagination of which Lautréamont's *Les Chants de Maldoror* is perhaps the most spectacular literary expression. Chaikin's actors could produce the most extraordinary sounds, which were sometimes meant to remind us of animals (the birds in *Nightwalk* and the sheep in *The Serpent*) and at other times were *merely different* sounds referring to nothing beyond themselves and which were simply offered as testimony of unsuspected vocal resources. There were moments in *The Mutation Show* when several actors made their sounds together, and these indescribably strange orchestrations were models of sensually pleasing, relaxingly meaningless human concerts. The variety of rhythms, pitches and volumes were a unique example of peaceful disharmony. The insistent but unaggressive independence of each body's sounds was impressively different from the more familiar conflict of sounds when groups of people begin to speak at the same time. Chaikin has said that "the original impulse, in the Open Theater, was to get away from talking . . ."; his group would suggest ways "to liberate the sounds closed up in us." In *The Mutation Show*, it was as if each actor were intent merely on producing his or her vocal specialty; and the various physical wills being expressed in this agreeable cacophony seemed devoid of any intention to use the voice in order to violate or to destroy the uniqueness carried by other voices.

In their deliberate abdication of the human voice as an instrument for rational speech, Chaikin's actors, like Lautréamont's ontologically floating narrator, also extended the boundaries of their identity into the animal world and even into the world of sounds in inanimate nature. And the pleasures of mutation were being proposed in an implicit contrast to the comfort of personality. Instead of the psychological continuity and consistency which theater usually proposes, *The Mutation Show* gave us a succession of structurally unrelated sounds and movements with which a human body can constitute an exaltingly discontinuous history. Of course, the discontinuity had limits, and Chaikin has spoken of his work as an effort to find the theme of someone's rhythm. In *The Mutation Show*, the audience quickly learned to associate particular gestures and sounds with each actor; thematic continuity was established which did give a kind of personality to each player. But the themes constituted vocal predilections and particular physical aptitudes rather than a psychological unity. We saw in the *Illuminations* that certain scenes have a privileged status in Rimbaud's imagination. But they don't exactly cohere with other scenes, and the relation between scenes is frequently one of mere juxtaposition. The *Illuminations* seem to be aiming at nothing more than a fragmentary coherence, the coherence of partial selves. In the same way, the actors of the Open Theater frequently displayed a virtuosity of being which included the recognizable talents and tastes of particular bodies and imaginations. But those thematic repetitions never reduced the extraordinary range of each actor's performance to what Chaikin has called an "organized identity." The actor remained a succession of heterogeneous acts, a mutant who returned from time to time to already performed partial identities which gave to his entire performance certain thematic emphases.

In one of their most interesting and entertaining mutations, the actors of *The Mutation Show* showed us old photographs of themselves and each one recited a brief autobiographical sketch of his or her "real" life. A comparison with Schechner's decision in *Dionysius 69* to allow his actors' offstage personalities to intrude on their performances is instructive. The complicity of Schechner's imagination with all the moral and psychological clichés of the culture which he thinks of himself as subverting was confirmed by the seriousness with which we were expected to watch his actors "being themselves." Although training in the Living Theater seems to be much better than in Schechner's group, the Becks made the same mistake in *Paradise Now*. In both cases, the potential shock of new modes of theatrical performance was mostly destroyed by a fall into the familiar psychological and intellectual styles of actors who, as soon as they "became themselves," were simply exposed as a rather mediocre and probably uncomprehending audience to the most original parts of their own performances. The intrusion of the "natural" into theater is merely a concession to the culture which contemporary theater claims to contest. A director's choice is always between two modes of theatrical self-performance, never between art and nature. Improvisation is nothing more than the invasion of theater by discredited modes of self-performance. In Chaikin's *Mutation Show*, the actors' "real" identities were comical. And one laughed not because a long-haired, big-city experimental actor was advertising his superiority to the square-looking Midwestern adolescent in the photograph, but because different moments in the actor's "real" life were cleverly exposed as involving metamorphoses almost as bizarre as those being enacted during the rest of *The Mutation Show*. The unity of one's life outside the theater might be as problematic as the unity among the various roles assumed by each actor. All the players might be thought of as announcing that they were mutants onstage and offstage. The actors' biographies were neither mocked nor solemnly respected, and we could take those photographs from the past simply as further evidence of the versatility of being which the theatrical performance we were watching continuously demonstrated.

Such dismissals of "organized identity" in the theater also involve the disruption of familiar temporal organizations. Traditional theater moves toward climaxes. Like the realistic fiction I discussed in Chapter Two, it has beginnings, middles and endings. Dramatists often try to give the impression of beginning a play *in medias res*; but the casual, superficially fragmented first scenes of realistic theater are always well-constructed — if disguised — expositions,

that is, classical beginnings. And this temporal structure — again
as in realistic prose narratives — is inseparable from a certain moral
and psychological significance. Literature works toward *dénouements*, which should be taken literally: climaxes unravel knots (of
significance). Experience is shown to be meaningful, and its meanings can be uncovered. What we generally mean by a hero in classical literature (and in nineteenth-century fiction) is a figure who
comes to know the truth about himself. And this implies not only
that there are such truths to be known, but also that there is a
coherently structured self to contain them.

The fragmentation of personality in modern literature has gone
along with a breaking up of traditional time schemes. Schechner
aptly speaks of the "discontinuous, often bumpy structure" of modern theatrical productions; instead of a steady movement toward a
climax, we often have "an uneven series of gathering tensions."
Schechner has also made the useful distinction between the "moti-
vationally connected sequences" of traditional drama and what he
calls "the progression of action-blocks" in contemporary theater.
It is in the work not of Schechner himself, but rather in that of
Robert Wilson, that we see the most extreme manipulations of time
in the theater as well as some of the most interesting aspects of psychological deconstruction in art. None of the contemporary theater
I've mentioned can rival Wilson's productions for sheer spectacle. The
dozens of players in each work, the dizzying number of things going
on, the elaborate sets, the hundreds of costumes, the rich colors and
symphonies of variegated sounds make Wilson the Cecil B. DeMille
of the avant-garde. But Wilson's intentions as a grand entertainer
are, to say the least, ambiguous. His work — especially *The Life
and Times of Sigmund Freud* and *The Life and Times of Joseph
Stalin* — seems calculated to realize Lautréamont's intention of
"cretinizing" the artist's public. Each of the productions I've just
mentioned lasted twelve hours, from early in the evening to early
the next morning. And neither production was "about" Freud or
Stalin; most of the tableaux which constituted each work had no
discernible relation either to one another or to the "serious" topic
parodistically announced in the title.

Now during the twelve hours of *Freud* or *Stalin* we are obviously
not "moving anywhere" in the traditional sense of working through
complications that will in some way be resolved by the end of the

play. No one moment in Wilson's works seemed designed to be more dramatic or more significant than other moments. Wilson likes to repeat episodes or gestures and to have them played in slow motion, the effect of which is not to increase our awareness of dramatic significance, but rather to make us unable to locate any salient moments at all in a pleasingly or maddeningly drawn out movement or episode. The monstrous length of these works, and the fact that they were played all night not only drowned any potentially dramatic episode in a seemingly endless duration; our most elemental sense of time became confused and distorted. Wilson encouraged his audiences to sleep for a while every now and then, and dozing off a few times during the night naturally had a rather chaotic effect on our sense of the spectacle. We moved from waking time to the time of dreams, and then, without knowing how much we had missed, back to the theatrical performance. The juxtapositions of different modes of awareness of time, the temporal extensions, condensations and discontinuities destroyed our usual securities about the linear movement of time. Somewhat like Proust's narrator in the experiences described in the first pages of *A la Recherche du temps perdu*, we could find our knowledge of who and where we were upset by our disturbed sense of how much time had passed, of what time was, and of what kind of time we were in.

Wilson's work realizes that confusion between the subjective and the objective which we have encountered in the spectacular literary example of Rimbaud's *Illuminations*. More than any other theatrical artist I've mentioned, Wilson's hypnotic theater brilliantly succeeds in passing itself off not as a world to be reflected on, but as scenes indistinguishable from our fantasies. The tableaux in *The Life and Times of Joseph Stalin*, for example, without resembling the dreams we may have had while sleeping, are nonetheless a continuation of the *type* of relation between the self and the world which dreams exemplify. Temporally discontinuous, obsessively repetitive, indifferent to rationality and to the discursive or informational function of language, Wilson's tableaux, like our dreams, briefly transformed the world into the diversified scenes of a desiring imagination. In reality, the world is of course the field of numerous and conflicting desiring imaginations. And, because of these conflicts, we learn to subordinate our desires to an awareness of the difference between imagination and the world; we negotiate a workable compromise with the desires of others and with such inevitabilities as age and death. The irresponsible and exhilarating lesson of Wilson's theater, on the other hand, has frequently been that we don't have to *know* anything; we have only to be ready to enlarge our repertory of desirable spectacles. And if we are ready to do this, it is because we have also been pleasantly coerced into recognizing the superiority of Wilson's dream tableaux to those from which we may have just awakened. Wilson constructs and embellishes each scene with artistic resources obviously unavailable to the extremely ingenious but anxious and hurried imagination which makes our dreams. The unconscious has limited dramatic resources, because it can never "play" outside the history of a single individual's imagination. In the theater, the imaginations of several people contribute to a single spectacle, and this collectivization of desire both diversifies the scene of desire and protects us from the solipsistic brutalities of individual fantasies.

The sort of theater which Wilson has given us also lacks the complicity of dreams with the structured personality. Dreams are subject to interpretations, which means that they have a recognizable hierarchy of meaningfulness, as well as significant repetitions and affective centers. Wilson invites us to sleep, to dream, and to awake in order to lose ourselves in a spectacle which prolongs the dreamer's ignorance of the distinction between the world and the scene of his desires. But the theatricalized self in dreams, however disconnected the various elements of its scenes may be, can, in the time of interpretation, eventually be read in terms of fundamental desires. The strategy of dreams is to disguise, but by no means to eliminate, dominant obsessional structures. It's as if the choice of unconscious desires which make their way into dreams involved a certain politicizing of the unconscious. Freud spoke of representability as one of the conditions which must be fulfilled before a desire can be enacted in dreams. But representability for a mental "system" mediating between consciousness and the unconscious means emotional centrality and thematic coherence. Even when the scenes of a dream are richly varied, that variety doesn't represent the heterogeneity of unconscious desires. Rather, it expresses the syntax and the logic peculiar to the dream-work, which, for example, in its apparent discontinuities and neglect of cause-and-effect, creates an appearance of free-floating, nonthematized fantasy which interpretation quickly gets beyond. Psychoanalysis easily — and convincingly — finds governing patterns, or a dominant scheme of desire, in dreams. I think that such schemes *are* in dreams, and it is almost as if the unconscious were pandering to the demand for unity and centrality on the part of our rational thought. Individual desires appear to enter dreams on the condition that they can be related to other desires and integrated into larger psychic structures. Dreams are the result of a political compromise: the unconscious is allowed to cross the "boundary" in dream-consciousness provided that it fulfill certain residence requirements. From the host of our unconscious desires, a "happy few" are selected, disguised and represented in dreams at once alien to our most rationalistic views of ourselves and yet (as interpretation shows) compatible with the rational economy of consciousness.

During a performance of *The Life and Times of Joseph Stalin,* one awoke from the perennially significant dreams of individuals and entered a world where, as in the most original of Rimbaud's *Illuminations,* a scene appeared to be an insignificant collection of heterogeneous parts. And Wilson's spectacles are psychologically anonymous *because* they accumulate only specificities. His tableaux don't illustrate a personality; they give space to and orchestrate various scenes which have occupied the imagination of this man or this group. Sounds, gestures and costumes in Wilson's theater are particular and momentary concretions, and this sort of particularity could belong to anyone. It is not what we usually call a psychological particularity. It has nothing to contribute either to a portrait of individual personality or a myth about human nature. Unlike the objects and gestures of dreams, objects and gestures in Wilson's theater don't designate feelings hidden behind them. Furthermore, the anonymity of Wilson's theater makes it universally accessible. But the universality of his work is not that of dream-symbols (which is a universality of content and therefore contributes to theories of human nature). It is rather a performative universality: the range of scenic fantasies which his work presents is available to the human imagination in general merely as spectacles which might be performed. These spectacles are neither necessary nor significant; they merely illustrate some of the entertaining *uses* to which a discontinuous desiring imagination can put the "material" of the world.

Much of the contemporary theater I've discussed — and Wilson's more particularly — could be thought of as engaged in decentralizing the audience's attention. Numerous aspects of traditional theater work to centralize our attention. For example, no matter how cluttered the stage may become, we always know where the main action is. In scenes where several things are going on at the same time, dramatists and directors have never hesitated to use a variety of devices to keep our attention focused on the principal part of the scene. Also, the movement toward climaxes or *dénouements* could be thought of as a way of closing in, during the time of the drama, on its central significance. Among the characters in most plays, there are major figures and minor figures, those who are crucial to the central action and those who have only tangential relations to it. And a central character tends to move toward his own centrality, toward that part of himself which we will recognize as his dominant passion or his major virtue or error. The bias of centrality holds literary works together; it also holds together the self. A "person" is someone whose behavior, however complex, can be referred to a central consistency (a consistency powerful enough to tolerate some genuine inconsistency and even a little irrelevance).

One of the most effective strategies for undermining centrality in contemporary theater is Wilson's use of multiple actions occurring simultaneously. In *Stalin* and in *Freud*, we frequently are unable to see and hear everything going on at any one moment. To take examples from *The Life and Times of Joseph Stalin*, a runner crossing the back of the stage every few moments, someone else crawling like a serpent across the stage, the backs of the heads and shoulders of players lined up in front of the stage, who are themselves watching the rest of the action *and* performing little numbers of their own, the monologues, the songs, and the conspicuously elegant couple watching the play from their lighted box: at any one moment, several of these elements were competing for our attention. As a result, we were continually discovering that we were in the "wrong place" — or, more accurately, that there was no right place, or that there were always other places. Instead of discovering where to look most intently, we were constantly seeing things we hadn't noticed before. And it can't be said that these things distracted our attention, for there was nothing genuinely central from which our attention might be distracted. The action was always somewhere else, but not because we haven't yet reached the right place (the sacred depository of a central truth), but because nothing was ever "entirely" in one place.

But nothing is ever entirely anywhere. If we look intently at one part of a Wilson tableau, our attention is peripherally solicited by other parts of the tableau. Our eye may anxiously seek out the other elements in a scene which would help us to see each part of the scene in relation to a general scheme of significance. But we find only other fragments, and, in contrast to the usual effects of visual wandering, our moving around a field of vision doesn't help us to absorb its various elements into a single structured scene. The peripheral never lends itself to a centralizing process; centers turn out to be fictions which can be disposed of for the sake of the multiple dramatic fictions which Wilson is offering us. Wilson's theater teaches us that visual mobility doesn't necessarily reduce heterogeneity.[2] And this luxuriantly fragmented theatrical scene can serve as a model for the spectator's renunciation (however momentary) of his "organized identity" and for his enjoyment of multiple partial selves. With Wilson — and, in different ways, with the Open Theater, with Brook and with the Theater of the Ridiculous — theater becomes the laboratory for the recovery and even the fabrication of psychic diversity, of the heterogeneity of desire.[3]

CHAPTER ELEVEN

Persons in Pieces

THE ACHIEVEMENTS of the contemporary theater groups I've just spoken of will seem all the more impressive if we look more closely at the dangers inherent to an emphasis on the scenic nature of desire. We might say that the activity of desiring, in its purest form, involves an undisturbed use of the world as the theater for our fantasies. The theatricalization of desire is always a potential suppression of all otherness. The uninhibited play of desire has a logic which leads, ultimately, to the annihilation of the world. The ideal context for triumphant desire is masturbation, in which the world conjured up is responsible only to a personal formula for satisfaction. Melanie Klein emphasized the importance of masturbatory fantasies for the forms taken by children's play as well as by their later sublimations. In the work of Jean Genet, whose Kleinian insights matured far from the analytic couch, we see a striking confirmation of the continuities between the activity of desire, fantasies of omnipotence, and the artistic imagination.

The paradoxical nature of uncompromised desire is that it is simultaneously the experience of a lack and the experience of omnipotence: we yearn for what we don't have in fantasies which provide us with ideal (both perfect and insubstantial) possessions of what we don't have. Curiously, it is in his plays that Genet seems most conscious of the world as a scene of resistance to desire. In his prose narratives, he exposes most freely the extravagant ambitions of the theatricalized self. This is especially striking in what I take to be Genet's most ambitious work, *Pompes funèbres*. The book was inspired by the death of one of Genet's lovers, Jean D., a twenty-year-old Communist Resistance fighter shot down in 1944 on the barricades in Paris "by the bullet of a charming young collaborator."[1] The "avowed aim" of *Pompes funèbres* will be "to tell the glory of Jean D.," but, as Genet already confides on the second page, the work "perhaps has more unforeseeable secondary aims." Indeed, the "secondary aims" are the important ones, and they are also very complex. This tragic death turns out to be an enormous piece of good luck, and *Pompes funèbres*, instead of being a hymn of praise to Jean himself, will be a solemn, richly ornamented ceremony of *profit*, a ceremony almost of unashamed gratitude. It is a work in praise not of Jean, but of his death.

Genet discovers his love for Jean only now, a love exactly equivalent to the pain he feels at losing him. But is Jean really lost? Not at all; his death is the happy condition for a total possession. The loved one's presence no longer interferes with the lover's assimilation of him. Jean now exists nowhere except in Genet's imagination. And this internalization of the loved one is expressed in fantasies of eating him. The activity of mourning in *Pompes funèbres* is cannibalistic. Genet can now subject his lover to whatever forms may appeal to Genet's imagination: for example, a matchbox in his pocket, or a garbage pail lovingly covered with flowers bespattered with filth when the pail explodes. Dead, Jean has become raw material for literature, an image which can be digested into and metamorphosed by the writer's imaginative "system."

Even stranger is Genet's idolatry of Jean's murderers. Those "unforeseeable secondary aims" turn out to involve a celebration of Nazism. In part, Genet retrospectively wills Jean's death as a desperate strategy for dominating his pain; he makes his suffering more bearable by taking the responsibility for what has caused it. But this is a comparatively banal project. The anguish caused by Jean's death seems to disappear as Genet discovers the extraordinary opportunity for exaltation which that death offers him. *Pompes funèbres* largely consists of fantasies of sex among Nazis or between Nazis and French collaborators. By reveling in these fantasies, Genet excites himself into a sympathetic identification with Jean's murderers which obviously facilitates his cannibalistic appropriation of Jean. In the process, however, a more general significance is revealed: at the limit, the enjoyment of sexual *and* literary fantasies requires the annihilation of all humanity. The brutality of Genet's sexual fantasies suggests the masturbator's murderous intolerance of whatever spoils his exciting sexual inventions. The onanist is a rigorous novelistic plotter. He crudely dramatizes the self-projectiveness of all literary invention, and, primitively and melodramatically, he reveals the evil of love and of literature as a desire to coerce the world into being an exciting replica of the self.

That coercion is explicitly referred to in *Pompes funèbres* in the passages where Genet announces and prepares the fantasy-episodes about to be elaborated. His desires *need* certain incidents, and in the onanistic privacy of the literary imagination, Genet remakes the world so that these incidents can take place. (And his narrative frequently explains the fantasy-logic which requires particular events.) The glamour of Nazism in *Pompes funèbres* is its total destructiveness; the appeal of destruction is the space it clears for an existence made wholly imaginary. Evil is the totalitarian freedom of the imagination, a brutal violation of reality by fantasy. *Pompes funèbres* gives us a brilliantly reductive argument for the masturbatory, cannibalistic, evil nature of literature; it proposes a view of literature as the Hitlerism of the spirit.

Even more interestingly, the cult of Hitler in *Pompes funèbres* exposes the relation between the totalitarian project of omnipotence and the radical experience, in desire, of a lack. The displacement of purpose in the book — the gliding toward "unforeseeable secondary aims" — also involves a shifting from the desire to possess Jean to the desire to possess, in the sense of taking on, the beauty of both Jean and his murderers. The lack which Genet seems to become most acutely aware of as a result of Jean's death is his own lack of physical beauty and strength. Hitler's power is perhaps only a secondary reason for Genet's identification with him. What may fascinate him most in Hitler is that the dictator, like him, was small, weak and unattractive. And yet he managed to transform this lack of being into an explosive projection into the world of force, hugeness and physical glamour. How? What *Pompes funèbres* suggests is that by being sodomized by men stronger and more attractive than they, or by pushing their tongues as far as possible into those men's rectums, Hitler and Genet assimilate the substance of the other men's beauty. And this taking in of beauty (which, for Genet, appears to be the spiritual essence of sperm and excrement) is a necessary preliminary to the re-creation of the world in the image of one's desires.

In one of the book's most extraordinary passages, Hitler reflects on this double operation of assimilation and emission:

> Puny, ridiculous little fellow that I was, I emitted upon the world a power extracted from the pure, sheer beauty of athletes and hoodlums. . . . In the secrecy of my night I took upon myself [j'endossais] — the right way of putting it if one bears in mind the homage paid to my body [à mon dos: to my back] — the beauty of Gerard in particular and then that of all the lads in the Reich: the sailors with a girl's ribbon, the tank crews, the artillery-men, the aces of the Luftwaffe, and the beauty that my love had appropriated was retransmitted by my hands, by my poor puffy, ridiculous face, by my hoarse [voice filled with come] to the loveliest armies in the world. Carrying such a charge, which had come from them and returned to them, drunk with themselves and with me, what else could these youngsters do but go out and die?

Love is an "impounding" of someone else's desirable beauty. Hitler and Genet lack their own manhood; they open their mouths and their anuses in order to absorb the manhood of others. And the most original twist in this game of procuring one's identity through sex is the return of masculine strength and beauty to external reality. For Genet, the most fascinating side of Hitler is that he wasn't content merely to keep for himself the beauty of all his young German fighters. He "retransmitted" it to the world — more precisely to the source from which it came: "to the loveliest armies in the world." The crucial change is that the beauty of others is now Hitler's emission, or ejaculation, onto the world. It is in Hitler's throat (in his hoarse voice "filled with come") and in his rectum that his army's sperm acquires the power to change the world.

Pompes funèbres is full of betrayals and murders. Genet even suggests, in his description of German soldiers firing at their own images in a mirror, and also in his remark that Riton's betrayal of twenty-eight prisoners is primarily a betrayal of himself, that self-annihilation is the condition for omnipotence. The very insignificance of Hitler and of Genet facilitates their being reduced to nothing at all. Emptied of all being, they become magnetic voids which absorb the being of others and use that alien being as raw material for a godlike control over the nature of reality. Genet and his hero-dictator suffer from a fantastic ontological hunger. They both illustrate desire as a pure lack — as if it were devoid of all subjectivity and consisted only of images of a transfigured world. More exactly, their subjectivity seems to contain no awareness of the self as distinct from the world; self-awareness exercises no restraint on self-projection. If there is no self inside, or if it has been murdered, the "person" becomes an aptitude for total self-objectification. And absolute weakness is equivalent to absolute power: Genet "expresses himself" by the energy of his cannibalistic absorption of what is different from Genet. He is nothing; he dreams only of others. But his images of others dramatize fantasies of sexual power which are in fact the sign of Genet's own desiring imagination. The entire universe comes to be nothing more than a field of images and anecdotes for the representation of Genet's sense of his lack of power. Thus Genet re-creates the world as a dramatization of the powerful being he lacks. The empty self is the all-powerful self; unable to find himself anywhere, Genet is everywhere, and the world monotonously — and docilely — repeats what he wishes to be.

The price of Genet's fantastic power over reality is a parodistic simplification of reality. Being is nearly reduced to a few sodomitic poses, and Genet's narrow range of fantasy is ornamented rather than expanded by his surrealistic verbal fireworks. *Pompes funèbres* is at once complicated, gaudy and obvious. Sartre has insisted on Genet's need to essentialize existence. The latter seeks to petrify reality, to freeze the living into gestures and poses which express immutable essences. This indisputable intention in Genet is best understood as a consequence of the drama of empty yet omnipotent being which we have just looked at. It is the weakness of existence in Genet which accounts for his obsession with essence. He experiences himself so radically *as* a lack — as helpless desire — that he seems able to conceive of the living only as exaggeratedly stable presence. To exist for Genet is to make the theatrical gesture which will immediately create and publicize the self. "Quels gestes faire?" — this question is asked over and over again in Genet's work. The victorious ejaculation onto the world doesn't create any rich existential confusion. Rather, the streams of sperm (and, implicitly, of excrement) immediately settle into scenes which have the fixity and the stability of sculpture. It's as if Genet recognized that his power over reality could be guaranteed only if he severely limited his desiring imagination of reality. He tyrannically simplifies the world so that it may be entirely and repeatedly recognizable as the achievement of Genet's desire for physical power and beauty. Thus the directorial care with which each gesture is prepared and carried out: it will stand as a permanent sign of its author's creative omnipotence.

Given Genet's extraordinary and mad project, a certain cheapening of reality has to take place. The reduction of reality (its annihilation and the impoverished form in which it is reborn) is the necessary condition for the realization of Genet's ambitions. His work is therefore uninteresting from the point of view of psychological and moral subtlety or complexity, and fascinating in its diagrammatic perspective on desire as both a lack and a potential devastation of the world. *Pompes funèbres* is Genet's most impressive performance of self-annihilating and world-devouring power. Finally, however, the frozen tableaux of this autobiographical fiction are aerated, mobilized by Genet's occasional mockery of his own fantasies even as he celebrates his poverty-stricken autonomy. We have, for example, the funny fantasy of Hitler's sudden transformation from an active butch brute to the soft passive queen of Genet's universe, as well as Genet's fantasy of being dressed all in white for his marriage to Riton, "though with a decoration of large black crepe cabbage rosettes at each joint, at the elbows, the knees, the fingers, the ankles, the neck, the waist, the throat, the prick, and the anus. Would Riton accept me dressed that way and in a bedroom decked with irises?" Humor in *Pompes funèbres* provides the notes of a self-awareness otherwise absent from Genet's universe. It is the sign of a subjectivity not entirely absorbed into the violent and rather cheaply obscene images of a theatricalized self.

There is no such qualifying humor in "Pauline Réage's" *Histoire d'O* and in "Jean de Berg's" *L'Image*. *Histoire d'O* (like *Clarissa* and parts of *Justine*) places us inside the violated woman's mind. But, in spite of all the narrative introspection which this makes possible, the novel is essentially theatrical. Each of the sexual and sadistic acts of "Pauline Réage's" work is like an act or a scene in a play: it has been carefully prepared by a "director's" imagination, and the major episodes of *O* (O's initiation at Roissy, her ordeal at La Pérouse, the branding of Sir Stephen's initials on her buttocks) take place, as it were, in front of an audience. Sexual fantasy is primarily scenic. In *Pompes funèbres*, *Histoire d'O*, and *L'Image*, we are very much aware of a particular subjectivity "behind" the work; but this dominant self, unlike the self we hear in the narrative voice of a Balzacian or a Stendhalian narrator, expresses itself chiefly through scenic means and only rarely in the substance and tone of narrative reflection. The authorial self is almost entirely theatricalized, and narrative point of view either directs our attention to the processes of theatricalizing the self (in Genet), or is reduced to the status of stage directions intended to help us visualize each scene (in *L'Image*).

The interesting twist in *Histoire d'O* is that subjectivity has been made extremely important, but the subject whose experience we share has practically no responsibility at all for the story being told from her point of view. We are asked to be interested in a victimized consciousness. Of course, O's mind is "fancied up" with psychological and religious reflections which give to the book the customary novelistic movement between narrative and scene. Also, this exposure is one more "opening" of O: we penetrate her mind even more easily than her lovers penetrate her body. But to be in O's consciousness is, necessarily, to be fascinated by a far more important subjectivity, one which comes to us, as it comes to her, only through the scenarios she agrees to perform. Telling the story from O's point of view obviously gives to the novel its psychological density; it would also seem to protect O's lovers from any penetration at all.

O's lovers are of course not excluded from the acts performed for their benefit, but they can enjoy those acts without having to give any account of their enjoyment. O is told immediately after arriving at Roissy that she must never look her torturers and lovers in the face. This can be reformulated: the scene of desire (O) must never establish a relation with the desiring self (O's lovers). O must do nothing more than represent her lovers' desires. Early in the novel, she is given an extremely interesting lecture on the reason why she will be frequently whipped. It will be "less for our pleasure than for your enlightenment," the men at Roissy tell her. She will be tortured "less to make you suffer, scream, or shed tears than to make you feel, *through* this suffering, that you are not free but fettered, and to teach you that you are totally dedicated to something outside yourself." O must learn to do (ultimately, to think or to feel) nothing distinct from her lovers' wishes; she is to *be* the theater of their desires. She belongs to René's — and later to Sir Stephen's — imaginations, and in the novel they are characterized *in* her behavior. But in order to dramatize their desires, she must, in a sense, be unaware of them. She must perform but not observe; observation invites reflection, and reflection would be the sign of a subjectivity different from her lovers'. Thus it is possible, curiously enough, to consider *Histoire d'O* not from the point of view of O's psychology (which has been the main preoccupation of critical discussion of the novel), but rather from the perspective of the male lovers' psychology — a psychology at once hidden and totally exposed.

There are varying degrees of erotic power among the male masters in the novel, but essentially they all have the same identity. They can therefore watch each other's sexual prowess without envy or jealousy or desire. I propose to consider *Histoire d'O* as a kind of fantasy-blueprint of pure heterosexual desire, a mad dream of the "ideal" resolution (especially by men) of Oedipal conflicts. In this fantasized form, we might say that having successfully identified himself as a man, the post-Oedipal heterosexual male may no longer find any mystery of sexual identity in himself or in other men. They don't have to be thought about, and he himself doesn't have to be thought about.

It's significant, in this respect, that "Pauline Réage" manages to be convincing about René's nonsexual idolatry of Sir Stephen. I realize that there are what might be called technical reasons for the absence of any homosexual implications in René and Sir Stephen's friendship. Good erotic fiction (like most good traditional literature of any type) depends on a gradual escalation of our interest: we don't get the really exciting stuff right away, and the writer artfully builds up to the most inventive and potentially shocking sex. The relation between René and Sir Stephen is in one sense a compositional resource, to use a Jamesian term, which helps "Pauline Réage" to escalate "her" story. It is a convenient device for what amounts almost to a new beginning after one-third of the novel has been written. The imagination of sex and cruelty associated with René seems to have become exhausted, and a new character designates and perhaps helps to inspire a new register of sexual fantasy. Furthermore, one could also say that to introduce male homosexuality into O's story would involve a senseless change of audience midway through the novel. Erotic fiction is clearly intended for specific audiences, and we don't need elaborate psychological speculation to account for a calculated dismissal of a theme which would spoil the satisfactions offered in heterosexual pornography. And yet — doesn't the convention itself invite speculation? The fact that the main audience for heterosexual pornography is men doesn't adequately explain a consistent peculiarity: that male (but not female) homosexuality is taboo in this literature. And as far as compositional resources are concerned, Sir Stephen's nature can't be entirely absorbed into his function. Why did "Pauline Réage" choose this particular character (and his friendship with René) as a way of accelerating the erotic pace of her story?

Sir Stephen, considerably older than René, is like a father to O's first lover. But he is a father one is no longer jealous of. The Oedipal conflict has been resolved, and the son has renounced his own desires for the woman; René recognizes that O belongs first of all to Sir Stephen. The older man is no longer a rival; he is only an ideal. And the ideal appears to be worshiped without curiosity. O is forced to recognize that with Sir Stephen, René yields to a "vocation" as "servant or acolyte." The proof of this is "that he watched [guettait] Sir Stephen's face more closely than he did hers" at the very moment when O's own features are interestingly "immersed" in the sexual pleasure which Sir Stephen brutally offers her. But René, unlike a Proustian lover, isn't trying to penetrate the secret of someone else's mysteriously different "formula" for sexual excitement. He looks at Sir Stephen admiringly and gratefully: admiringly because of the older man's power over O (which René also has), and gratefully because Sir Stephen has "deigned to take pleasure in something [René] had given him."

This is the untroubled nonsexual adoration of an ideal version of the self. O realized, "Pauline Réage" writes, that ". . . through the medium of her body, shared between them, they attained something more mysterious and perhaps more acute, more intense than an amorous communion, the very conception of which was arduous but whose reality and force she could not deny." That union is, I think, a union with the same, and "Pauline Réage" profoundly suggests that this fascinated worship of an almost omnipotent version of one's own identity can make for a communion even "more acute" than the communion of sexual love. In a sense, René and Sir Stephen's heterosexuality depends on a "homosexuality" so profound that it can dispense with sexual desire. Between O and Sir Stephen, René obviously "prefers" Sir Stephen, but he prefers him as he would instinctively value his own life ahead of anyone else's life. Women are desired because they are different, but the stimulating lack in desire is perhaps no match for the ecstatically calm contemplation of one's own self, for a kind of self-effacement in the name of the self.

When we actually have homosexual desires in *Histoire d'O* — as in O's sexual interest in other women — "Pauline Réage" explicitly defines these desires as a form of self-love. O takes with other women the active, pursuing role which men take with her. She is overwhelmed at the signs of sexual pleasure on their faces, less, "Pauline Réage" adds, out of "amour-propre" than out of "admiration"; but the admiration is nonetheless for something she recognizes as belonging to herself. Homosexuality is, for O, a way of briefly leaving herself in order to observe herself. She becomes a man, as it were, in order to put some distance between her consciousness and her identity, and from this male perspective she sees herself as men see her. At a certain distance, she discovers the advantages of her difference from men: "The power she acknowledged that her girl friends held over her was at the same time a guarantee of her own power over men." As for the other women to whom O makes love, they are both all-important and insignificant. They are necessary in order for O to see herself, but precisely because O loves women in "the way one can be in love with one's own image," individual girls don't matter but only "girls as such, girls in general."

In the sexual universe of *Histoire d'O* a man's most intense joy is to watch the signs of another man enjoying the uncontrollable pleasure he gives to a woman, and the "heroine" of the novel is overwhelmed by the spectacle of other women being overwhelmed as men overwhelm her. Sex is the power to make someone else powerless, and the joy of sex is given by reflected images of that power. In half of humanity, the heterosexual characters of *O* find reflections of themselves; but in the other half there is a difference which has to be conquered, overwhelmed. Other people are either "all me," or "not at all me." From the man's point of view, the only way in which the woman can be reduced is not by a change in her identity, but rather by her *enslavement to the male version of her difference.*

To say that *Histoire d'O* is sexist is almost a charitable way of describing this elegantly narrated orgy of a (probably male) heterosexual imagination. It's as if the psychology of women were a kind of structural inference from the psychology of men. If the purest version of a man's nature is fantasized as the dangerously self-assertive father of the Oedipal stage, then the essence of the other sex, already castrated in the male imagination, is a readiness to give up the self. Women's nature, in this fantasy, is to enact the desiring fantasies of men. Only self-immolation gives to *O* her plenitude as a woman. Even the woman's homosexuality — which in Proust makes her hopelessly inaccessible to a man's imagination — is, in *Histoire d'O*, a way of extending male conquests. *O* may go to bed with women, as we saw a moment ago, in order to receive "a guarantee of her own power over men," but she willingly abdicates her power by making these women into gifts for her male masters. ". . . It seemed to O that the girls she caressed belonged by right to the man to whom she belonged, and that she was only present by proxy." *O* is the well-trained hunting dog who knocks down the game and brings it back to its master. One could hardly go further in the imagination of masculine power. Even in the secret caresses of two women, the man is there. He may know very little about the pleasures of these alien bodies, but he is always the cause of those pleasures. One of the women is standing in for him, and all female excitement is a tribute to a man's power to stimulate women into a passionate desire to sacrifice themselves to him.

The extraordinary brutality of this enterprise in *Histoire d'O* suggests a persistent and exasperating sense of the difference between triumphant fantasy and real otherness. It's as if the masculine imagination had already recognized the impossibility of realizing its dream of power. The scenes of absolute power over women in *Histoire d'O* contain signs of a rageful revenge against women for *not* enslaving themselves to men's version of their difference. And there are other hints of the difference never being completely vanquished or reduced. Significantly, the only thing O can't bring herself to do for Sir Stephen (and René had never asked her to do it) is to masturbate in front of him. Given everything O does agree to do, we might at first be puzzled by this unexpected — and misplaced? — reticence. But, in a sense, women are penetrated most profoundly by men when men can watch them experiencing a pleasure from which men are absent. They may think of men while masturbating, but then such thoughts are part of their nature as women; they are generated by the woman herself, not by a man's touch. Above all, the man doesn't see those thoughts; he sees only a physically different creature stimulate herself, and this scene of difference is uncontaminated by the familiar images of his own sexuality which he is forced to see when his body excites a woman's body. Beyond the fantasy of women's obedience to men's desires, there is a dream of women offering the spectacle of their autonomy to men. O is severely punished for refusing to do this, but she doesn't give in. (On the other hand, we might say that this refusal is compensated for by O's reluctance to masturbate even when she is alone. She occasionally caresses herself "furtively" when she is sleeping alone — "but she had never tried to carry it to a climax." Thus the woman is not quite allowed to play [with] herself. A man must be present in order for her to be stimulated, even if he is only vicariously present in the imagination of the active partner in female homosexuality.)

There is a more conclusive tribute to the slave's power in *Histoire d'O*. It is connected to O's pride, which seems to increase as her apparent degradation becomes more and more spectacular. O comes to hate her freedom, and "Pauline Réage" insists, in a rather

heavy-handed way, on the analogies between O's willing enslavement to her lovers and a nun's surrender to God. The self is a
burden which O is happy to be rid of; but, with a perversity familiar
to theologians and saints, O finds in the very loss of self an occasion
for self-glorification. "She considered herself fortunate to count
enough in [René's] eyes for him to derive pleasure from offending
her, as believers give thanks to God for humbling them." But the
religious reference here obscures a psychology of pride which is
exposed much more clearly in a later passage in the novel, one which
includes no allusions to God: "[O's] absolute certainty that when
[Sir Stephen] touched her, whether it was to fondle or flog her,
when he ordered her to do something it was solely because he
wanted to, her certainty that all he cared about was his own desire,
so overwhelmed and gratified O that each time she saw a new proof
of it, and often even when it merely occurred to her in thought,
a cape of fire, a burning breastplate extending from the shoulders
to the knees, descended upon her." What O has discovered is a
fundamental axiom of personal power: the only absolutely certain
sign of our desirability (of our power over others) is if others seek
to "touch" us without paying any attention at all to our own desires. Totally without human respect, Sir Stephen comes toward O
only because he desires her, and it is thus as if it were O's nature,
as it is God's nature, to inspire love. All our relations with other
people are determined, in varying degrees, by our imagination of
what they expect from us; "civilized" human contacts depend on
this readiness to accommodate desire to the ways in which other
people wish to be desired. But we condescend to such accommodations, and by generously taking other people into account, we obscure the signs of their intrinsic power to excite us into pursuing
them. Each time, however, that Sir Stephen approaches O, it is only
because he wants something from her, and therefore, in a curious
way, it is he who is enslaved to her capacity for producing desires
in him. In the same way that man's nature doesn't allow for an
authentic absence of love for God, it would seem that Sir Stephen
— as O joyfully recognizes — can no longer deprive himself of the
pleasure of beating her and sodomizing her. At the moment of a
spectacular male triumph — the reduction of women to passionately
willing performances of men's desires — the supremacy of women
is just as spectacularly asserted.

What might be taken as a sign of the male lover's invulnerability in O — the fact that while he demands obedience, he doesn't seem to need any confirmation of his specifically erotic power over his female slave — can therefore also be thought of as his inability to stop desiring his slave. Total security and total dependence bizarrely coincide: René and Sir Stephen take it for granted that women "belong" to them, but the infinite worth of the slave is advertised by the very attention which the master brings to the process of destroying her alien desires. Should this be used to suggest that "Pauline Réage" is, as "her" name asks us to believe, a woman? Given the complexity of the fantasies we have now reached, such a question should appear irrelevant. If we take the author to be a man, it can be said that he imagines both the elimination of the woman's otherness, and the anguishing persistence of her difference. If *Histoire d'O* was written by a woman, it can just as plausibly be said that a woman imagines both her surrender to a phallic God's brutal designs, and the subtle strategy by which her very self-abdication transforms every lash of the whip on her body into a tribute to her power to fascinate.

Histoire d'O exposes the cool and murderous reduction of otherness in a (mad) heterosexual theatricalization of desire. And the violence exposed in this impressive book is not the destructuring violence of the *Illuminations* or of the contemporary theater I discussed earlier. It is a violence which would simultaneously annihilate all differences and petrify each sex in its inconceivable difference. The hallucinatory scenes of Rimbaud proposed new juxtapositions to a world devastated by the "floods" of the poet's negating energies. The scenes of rape and torture in *O*, on the other hand — like the scenes of Genet's masturbatory fantasies, but without his qualifying humor — merely repeat, with increasing intensity, the single project of an already fixed identity. The fantasy of a securely immobilized sexual identity transforms half of the world (the other sex) into a source of terror — unless, as we see in *O*, others are hallucinated into a passionate willingness to "belong" to us, to be the property of our imagination.

The appearance of Sir Stephen in *Histoire d'O* is the signal of an escalation in the novel's ingenious brutalities. However, he also brings into the story a humanizing vulnerability. From the very beginning, O wants Sir Stephen to love her, and, even more strangely, she will *look at him* in order to spy on the signs of his desire and his love. Significantly, Sir Stephen's taking over from René is also accompanied by a new kind of introspective questioning in the narrative. Not only does O reflect more about the strange pride which her enslavement makes her feel; she also anxiously watches Sir Stephen in order to find out if he loves her, and she even wonders once if her lover's verbal brutality toward her isn't designed to make *him* suffer rather than her. This startling interpretive subtlety seems out of place in a work apparently dominated by nonreflective scenic versions of desire; it even announces another type of novel, the kind of Proustian fiction also pointed to by René's jealousy of Jacqueline late in the novel, his anguished effort to reach her "raison d'être," her "truth."

We might say that *Histoire d'O*, in spite of numerous scenes of sex, mostly illustrates what Freud calls in "Instincts and Their Vicissitudes" a first stage of "sadistic" fantasy. This is a nonerotic stage in which the desire to control or to master has not yet been attached to sexual pleasure. Sex in *Histoire d'O* primarily serves an asexual design. In one sense, Sir Stephen carries this design even further than René. When he announces that O must learn to separate obedience from love, he is reformulating the Freudian definition of a stage at which we might have a nonerotic imagination of the world's submission to our will. At the same time, however, Sir Stephen sexualizes the impulse to master and the impulse to be mastered. Unlike René, he strikes O himself, and it is suggested that his own equilibrium is shattered by the pleasure he enjoys while whipping her. We see him (as we never see René) as pale as O herself just before he beats her. And just after his initials are burned into her buttocks, O, before passing out, has a glimpse, "between two waves of darkness, of Sir Stephen's ghastly pale face."

It is at these moments that O sees Sir Stephen's love, and his love seems to include an identification with O's pain. Interestingly enough, this is the explanation of the erotic pleasure of sadism which Freud seems to be offering in "Instincts and Their Vicissitudes." In Freud's second stage, we abandon the object or person we wish to master and the impulse to control is turned in upon ourselves; when, in stage three, another person is again sought as an object, he takes over our original sadistic role, and because of the change in stage two in the aim of the instinct, we enjoy the masochistic satisfaction of being dominated by others. It is at the masochistic stage that we discover the possibility of pleasure in physical suffering: the sensation of pain produced by the use of another person to satisfy an aggressive impulse to exercise power over the self "extends [übergreifen] into sexual excitation" and the groundwork is thereby laid for masochistic sexuality (for finding pain pleasurable). As a result of this connection, the wish to dominate others is also sexualized, and we will sadistically enjoy their pain. We are erotically stimulated by someone else's pain because we identify with it, having already experienced pain as pleasure: that is, sadism is projected masochism.[2]

Nothing of the sort is suggested in René's cruelty in *Histoire d'O*, or indeed in Sir Stephen's *intended* cruelty. But "Pauline Réage" does invite us to entertain the possibility that Sir Stephen himself suffers in the torture he inflicts on O, and that his suffering is a perhaps masochistic function of his love for O. Sado-masochism has now become the sign of erotic excitement. But then the desire for O would no longer be a desire to master pure difference. It would now be a desire to experience erotic intensity *through* her suffering, which means that Sir Stephen's desire *for* O is also a desire to *be* O. In this erotic violence, the tragic separation between man and woman (which is the major subject of "Pauline Réage's" work) is somewhat reduced, since O and Sir Stephen's need for each other includes a partial exchange of identities. (Not only does O think that Sir Stephen says something cruel to her in order to suffer himself; in her spying on the signs of his desire, she also begins to behave like him.) And this entire enterprise depends on a certain reciprocity between the tortured performer and her sadistic public. The possibility of the player becoming the audience — and vice versa — blocks the annihilation of otherness toward which a more securely theatrical self nonreflectively aims.

Is it necessary to use such extreme examples as *Histoire d'O* in an argument about the return of desire to scenic modes of expression? More than any other kind of literary expression, sado-masochistic pornography teaches us that, potentially, desire can necessitate a ruthless intolerance of otherness. On the one hand, we can desire only what we lack, and what is therefore — at least at the moment of desire — different from ourselves. On the other hand, the fantasies which accompany desire are a rewriting of the world according to the terms of a particular desiring imagination. In a sense, desire is always a pseudo-lack; to the extent that a fantasy realizes the desire it expresses, there is already satisfaction in our longing, plenitude in our emptiness. Essentially, we would like the world to repeat our fantasies, to give us a satisfaction we have already given ourselves. Extreme erotic literature allows us to enjoy the illusion that this is possible. Sexual slavery gives a certain (deceptive) probability to the dream of the world as pure obedience, for — except for literal starvation, which could also inspire documents of cruel omnipotence — only our own sexual desires have taught us that human beings may be willing to renounce their independent wills for the sake of intensely pleasurable sensations. Because sexual excitement momentarily shatters the will and disintegrates the constructed self, it provides the most convincing situation for a portrayal, in literature, of one person gaining mastery over another person. But enslavement is revealing about the master's imagination of slavery's pleasure: he knows that the world can be enslaved because of his own esteem (or taste) for the excitements to which freedom is often sacrificed.

But this very shattering of the self in sex modifies the totalitarian designs inherent to all desire. Sex illustrates the breakdown of the totalitarian project in the very excitement which accompanies the carrying out of that project. The self is excited to the point of going to pieces at the very moment it triumphantly enacts its hegemony over the world. And so, as *Histoire d'O* instructively allows us to see, we can be "saved" (reintegrated to our lost selves) only by paying attention to the other person, by actively seeking to promote not just obedience to us, but also an interest in us — an interest in which we can find a reflection, intact, of our otherwise shattered identity. Only the violent confrontations we have been looking at immediately and explicitly teach us something about both the dangers of desires and the peculiar logic (of ecstasy) by which we must cultivate, rather than destroy, other people in order to recover from the disintegrating excitement into which they plunge us.

In "Jean de Berg's" *L'Image*, a male character — Jean — is invited to watch and to participate in the enslavement of a young girl, Anne, by her female lover, Claire. This invitation is preparatory to

Jean's taking with Claire the sadistic role that Claire has been taking with Anne. We are meant to understand that Claire and Anne are two versions of the same "character" or, more precisely, complementary versions of a single sexual identity. Claire sees an image of herself in Anne, and this image is the masochistic support of her sadism. *L'Image* gives us the "real" sadism which, as we have seen, is practically nonexistent in the master-slave relationships of *Histoire d'O*. "Jean de Berg" shows us both the sadist and the masochist experiencing erotic excitement as a direct result of physical pain. Anne gets wet, as Claire gleefully points out to Jean, at the very thought of being whipped. And, on the sadistic side, Jean notices Claire's "mounting excitement" as she becomes more and more brutal with Anne. Anne's "martyred buttocks" stimulate Jean, and he is sexually aroused by the young girl's "groans of agony" as Claire sticks long needles into her breasts and thighs. Indeed, in this climactic episode he becomes so excited that he pushes Claire aside in order to whip Anne on the breasts, "reveling in it," and finally raping her, "without any thought for her suffering, penetrating the half-dead body through its smallest opening."

Now the sadist responds as if his body were being stimulated erotically, but what stimulates him (or her) are someone else's sensations. Sadistic sexuality is by nature an abstract sexuality, an almost purely imaginative eroticism. Nonetheless, the sadist experiences intense pleasure as a result of someone else's pain. I think that this can be understood only if we come back to the Freudian suggestion that sadism is projected masochism. We can be excited by the pain of others because we have ourselves already experienced pain as sexually exciting. *L'Image* is an extraordinary dramatization of this argument. Claire's encouragement of Jean to treat Anne sadistically is her way of training him to treat *her* sadistically. The principal lesson of the book is that every sadist needs a master. If the pleasure of inflicting pain is, profoundly, the pleasure of experiencing it, then the sadist logically seeks someone else to relieve him of the exhausting responsibility of making a victim suffer in order to enjoy suffering himself. Jean is, so to speak, the most economical solution to Claire's masochism. Once he begins to beat her, she no longer has to beat Anne in order to enjoy pain, *and* she doesn't even have to keep both the sadistic and the masochistic roles internally. Jean takes over the duties of Claire's masochistic sadism (which was played out with Anne), as well as of an implied direct masochism (that is, the doubling of the self in which Claire would sexually excite herself by inflicting pain on herself).

Even more interestingly, *L'Image* suggests an identity between masochism and the desire to master someone else. In the Freudian scheme I've been referring to, the sado-masochistic complex enters the picture when we discover the erotic potentialities in our *renunciation* of the project of mastering others. And the crucial link between the impulse to master others and masochism seems to be a narcissism inherent to all sexuality. The self-shattering which takes place in sexual stimulation also reinforces the self. For while someone else may be necessary for our sexual pleasure, we can feel this pleasure only as a creation of our own body. In our sexual intensities, we are carried away, lost to ourselves (and this is that tribute to the other which we saw in Sir Stephen's desire for O), but in this very disintegration of the self a foundation is being laid for boundless self-love. Nothing is more astonishing to us than the capacity of our bodies to shatter us with pleasure, and so sexuality initiates self-fascination. The most pleasurable sex with another person, while it may obviously strengthen our attachment to that person, is also an overwhelming revelation of what our own body is capable of producing. And perhaps the body's most remarkable production is pleasure made from pain.

In *L'Image*, Jean is a mere instrument of female narcissism, in spite of the extraordinary profit he seems to derive from Claire's use of him. Claire frequently stares at Anne, with, Jean remarks, "what seemed to me to be either hatred, or the deepest passion." Claire's tenderness toward Anne is indistinguishable from her brutality. Indeed, her tenderness *is* her brutality, for in her monstrously cruel treatment of the girl she is paying tribute to her own body's capacity for the most extreme sensations. We might even say that Anne is nothing more than the literary device which externalizes Claire's narcissistic wonder at her body's production of masochistic pleasure. Claire's assumption of Anne's role with Jean at the end of the novel therefore coincides exactly with her total domination of him. Everything in the novel is a tribute to *her* body. Claire ends up in double control of Jean. First of all, he now needs her for his own pleasure — needs both her body and her slavish obedience. And secondly, she has made him into the servant of her own sensations:

her body, like Anne's, will be the tortured idol of their love, and even as she authorizes Jean to "beat her to death if it would amuse" him, she is preparing a ceremony of self-adoration, one in which both he and she will worship the miracle of her masochism.

However, this exercise in perfect control also confirms the problematic nature of the controlling figure's identity. There is a type of control which merely freezes the individual within a strictly defined sexual identity, and there are other controlling strategies which actually facilitate a kind of ontological floating. In *Histoire d'O*, we found a brilliantly executed example of the first type. René and, to a certain extent, Sir Stephen, want to reduce O to an obedient enactment of their own wills. Sex and physical torture provide the training-ground where this is accomplished, but their suitability as techniques of enslavement depends less on the uncontrollable pleasure they provide than on the self-humiliation in which sex and suffering educate the slave. O, unlike Anne in *L'Image*, is never excited by being whipped; and while we are told, for example, that René passionately loves to watch O being raped and beaten, it is only with Sir Stephen that we glimpse an occasional sign of the master being carried away by the pleasure of observing his victim's pain. O's lovers enslave her in order to do away with her differences; the *pleasure* they expect from this mastery is discreetly eluded, is, we might say, repressed from the novel.

"Pauline Réage" tells us that O's pleasure at her female partner's sexual pleasure is "so acute" as to turn her head, not because she identifies with the other woman's excitement at those moments, but because she thinks of the pleasure which her own excitement gives to men. The source of O's excitement is her effect on someone else (the absent man). In *Histoire d'O*, narcissism reinforces psychic rigidity. O's pride at the idea of how much pleasure she gives to men imprisons her in the feminine role which is the condition for her giving men pleasure. In *L'Image*, on the other hand, narcissism is the occasion of a kind of jumping out of the self. The torturers' excitement is an important pornographic element in the novel, and it is also an indication of their psychic mobility. The torturer identifies with the victim's sensations. Self-excitement is felt directly; it is not refracted, as in *O*, through someone else's pleasure at one's own sexual transports. Claire wants Jean to be present at the games of erotic torture that she plays with Anne, but it is not Jean's excitement which stimulates her; Claire is moved directly by the other self she finds in Anne. Narcissistic pleasure in *L'Image* shatters the ego shell which narcissism generally reinforces. Indeed, such pleasure already accomplishes the leap from one sexual identity to another which "Jean de Berg's" novel both achieves almost at once and suspensefully works up to.

Claire's absorption in Anne's masochistic suffering is a way of losing the self which imposes that suffering on Anne. And lesbianism, curiously enough, may make the ego shell especially fragile. Of course, if we consider Anne merely as an image of Claire, there is, from this interpretive perspective, only one woman in the novel, and therefore no real lesbianism. But the modestly realistic form which this self-projection takes — the two parts of the self have different names, different ages, different physical traits — authorizes a more literal reading of the story in terms of a sado-masochistic relation between two women. And, from this point of view, the consequence of a passion for sameness turns out to be an unanchored self. Seen in more conventional psychoanalytic terms, lesbianism (and homosexuality in general) would be an attempt to possess a fixed image of the self. The absorption in other people of the same sex would be the sign of an insecurity about one's "really" belonging to one's biological sex; the homosexual would find himself (would freeze himself) only in his or her possession of another man or woman (who would be the objectifying of a problematic self). What I'm suggesting, however, is that even if this represents an accurate (if partial) etiology of homosexuality, the consequences of homosexual desire may subvert its presumed purpose.

Narcissism in homosexuality may be, more than one usually suspects, of the self-shattering type. The homosexual inevitably loses some of the benefit, for the ego, of his or her partner's sexual excitement. For that very identification with the other which is implicit in a homosexual choice makes it difficult to create the distance at which one can take the other person's excitement as a tribute to one's own securely constituted and different self. Superficially, narcissism is perhaps the most visible characteristic of homosexual behavior. But its very visibility may be the sign of its absence as a sexual satisfaction. And, much more profoundly, homosexual self-absorption may be the desperate effort to resolve a grave doubt resulting from homosexual desire: *the doubt about which self to adore.* In *L'Image*, the excitement which Anne's excitement provokes in Claire seems to be entirely a sharing of the girl's masochistic sexuality. It is not the excitement of seeing her own appeal as a mistress reflected in Anne's willing enslavement. Claire, unlike the men in *Histoire d'O*, is not reinforced in her sadistic role by the spectacle of her victim's suffering. If sadism involves a masochistic identification with the victim, it's nonetheless true that in heterosexuality the difference of sex makes that identification somewhat more difficult. The heterosexual's narcissistic identification with his or her partner's pleasure is qualified by a sense of the partner's irreducible otherness. A man can't lose himself (the male sexuality he is enacting) in the woman's pleasure; his capacity for sexual differentiation is limited by a "realistic" sense of a biological difference which he will never be able to reduce. He is therefore perhaps more receptive to the sort of narcissism I've associated with *Histoire d'O*: not the thrill of self-shattering sensations, but a circuitous (and cool) self-admiration induced by the spectacle of a sexual transport which he can't share but which he has — most impressively — produced.

Would this be true of Jean in the heterosexual and sadomasochistic affair so spectacularly inaugurated in the final scene of *L'Image*? This question is unanswerable, but it brings us to a more fundamental question: who is Jean? He is the pseudonymous author of *L'Image* who is a "real" character in the novel. Jean, the character we are meant to believe in, is the nonexistent "Jean de Berg." The interest of such novelistic games is quickly exhausted, but in *L'Image* the indefinite status of Jean (and of "Jean de Berg") is, I think, a way of making a crucial point. Within the story, Jean is of course led by Claire; he is led to enslave her, but it's nonetheless she who writes the scenario and times its progress. That is, we have a peculiar situation in which a figure who is at once author, narrator and character is in fact only a manipulated audience. In a sense, "Jean de Berg" is a pseudonym for Claire, who is the author of *L'Image*. "Jean de Berg," however, does exist: he is each reader of the novel, and his real name changes each time someone else picks up the novel. *L'Image* thus presents with special clarity an important fact about all fictions by an essentially manipulated, passive narrator: they are told from the reader's point of view.

This is equivalent to saying that point of view in "Jean de Berg's" work is more theatrical than it is novelistic. Unlike *Histoire d'O*, *L'Image* has practically no narrative reflectiveness; Jean is never introspective in the way that O is. He merely describes scenes as if he were the spectator of a theatrical performance. (The dramatic form of the story is emphasized by the organization of its ten sections as scenic episodes.) By virtue of both his privileged voyeurism and his manipulated passivity, Jean could even be taken as an emblem of the audience in traditional theater. And, from this perspective, *L'Image* could also be thought of as a breaking down of the traditional separation between dramatic scene and audience. Jean joins the passion; the audience begins to act. On the one hand, the theatrical form of *L'Image* makes this merger especially striking. It's precisely in a work which has encouraged us to think in terms of the usual theatrical dichotomy between players and spectators that the spectator (and, by implication, the reader . . .) plunges into the action. On the other hand, Jean's joining in the performance could be thought of as a reaffirmation of the subverted distinction. There is no dialogue between him and the scene of desire; nor does he engage in any reflections about his relation to that scene. I realize that such exchanges would destroy the erotic power of this sort of novel, but my point is, precisely, that the appeal of erotic fiction depends on the ease with which it allows us unreflectively to theatricalize desire. The logic of erotic fantasy dictates the scenic form of *L'Image* (and, to a lesser degree, *Histoire d'O* and *Pompes funèbres*). And these works encourage us to believe that the scenes of desire can be enacted in the world. Sexual obedience is an exciting metaphor for a world constantly open to — always ready to be penetrated by — our desires.

In *L'Image*, the audience participates in the story by becoming a scene. It is, I think, for this reason that — in spite of the problematic nature of the characters' sexual identities which I discussed a moment ago — the substitution of Jean and Claire for Claire and Anne doesn't modify the violence of sex in *L'Image*. Jean (the internalized audience) is seduced into becoming part of the play and thereby exposing himself. All of Jean's cool estheticism (his passionless appreciation of elegant designs in scenes of torture) disappears when he finally loses control of himself and sodomizes the half-dead Anne. Claire shrewdly takes her cue from that transport of sadistic desire. The critical esthete has been transformed into a passionate player; the actor's training is now complete, and he is ready to relieve Claire of a role which has really been destined for him. The audience's protected isolation is thus destroyed in *L'Image*, but the audience is not asked to invent any part of the performance. Jean will presumably repeat with Claire what he has seen Claire do with Anne. The theatrical spectator gives up his passive, protected position in *L'Image*, but there is no suggestion that the physical violence of the performance will be modulated by, say, a passion for interpretation. That is, *L'Image* — which is after all a novel — fails to profit from what we might call the humanizing potentialities of novelistic form. Narrative reflection in fiction generally demonstrates the impossibility of separating action from reaction, a text from its interpretation. Human behavior is never "pure action"; it is always already a text actively engaged in some form of interpretive reflection. (In James's *The Ambassadors*, we even have a moral investigation of such reflection. Strether's observation of others *is* the main action of the novel; indeed, the text becomes a critical consideration of the desires which are brought into play by such observation.) *L'Image* keeps the clichéd opposition between spectacle and spectator intact: all the passion belongs to the former, all the observation belongs to the latter. The spectator joins the spectacle, but neither seems to be changed as a result of this union. In other words, *L'Image* sanctions a fundamental myth of our culture: the myth of a difference of nature between passion and intelligence, or between desire and interpretive fantasy, or, finally, between art and criticism.

The contemporary theater which I discussed in Chapter Ten has none of the violent pornography of *Histoire d'O* and *L'Image*, and yet even those theatrical experiments suggest a certain price to be paid for the concrete representation of a deconstructed self. Robert Wilson, for example, encourages us to "join the play" in a manner analogous to Claire's seduction of Jean in *L'Image*. The blurring of the boundaries between our own dreams and the dreamlike spectacles of an all-night marathon organized by Wilson makes the spectator's mode of perception resemble the mode of the performance he is watching. The "syntax" of his reaction to the spectacle comes to be identical to that of the spectacle itself, and he risks losing that distance between the spectator and the artistic performance which differentiates art from criticism just enough to introduce a dialogue or exchange into human experience. Perhaps the only "critical" response adequate to *The Life and Times of Joseph Stalin* is a willingness to abandon our commitment to any coherent identity, to the continuity and consistency of our desires. Much of the best contemporary theater seems to provoke in its audience an intense enjoyment of scenes referring to nothing beyond the physical elements which constitute them. Ideally, that enjoyment would be so intense that audiences would become anxious to make their own personalities de-signify, to substitute a sensual heterogeneity of being for psychological coherence. Understanding and judgment are irrelevant; we are asked to change our mode of being. The unrepressed scene of desire contains a tyrannical if implicit negation of other scenes. Repressed desires, on the other hand, whether they issue in symptoms or sublimations, are troubled desires, and, like all problematic versions of being, they indicate at least some recognition of other desires. The desublimated scene of desire entertains nothing but its own representation — as if it would replace the violence of conflict in life with the violence of annihilating self-absorptions.

If I have spoken at some length about contemporary theater, it is partly out of a sense that there may be something we wish to resist in this seductive retraining of the self. But it is of course also because I think this coercive enterprise is essentially beneficent, and that both an esthetic and an ethic of the fragmented self can be defended — even in a language which could never hope to perform that self. I have, from the very beginning of this book, been asking that we attempt to resist the appeal of that unity of personality assumed by all humanistic psychologies. My studies of Racine and of realistic fiction emphasized some of the ambiguities — moral duplicity, social timidity, suicidal melancholy — in the stage of psychic growth at which psychoanalysis locates the emergence of a truly individual and coherent self. (We also saw, even in Racine, the possibilities of self-creative rebellion in the archaic desiring impulses of the pre-Oedipal imagination.) The revolutionized consciousness which the second half of our study has been rather ambivalently moving toward (and moving around) may appear wholly alien to logical discourse. And yet it is, I think, only by allowing itself to be penetrated by logical argument that the theatricalized self can be saved from its own potential for a terroristic mode of desire.

The penetration of art by criticism already exists within art, for the latter is always a kind of interpretive discourse. All languages construct fictions — that is, interpretations of reality — and the difference between art and criticism is one of interpretive modes rather than one of ontological status. Art does not tell us the "truth" about the real any more than criticism tells us the "truth" about art. The interpretive activity naturally associated with criticism is intrinsic to all our mental operations. Desire is inseparable from fantasy — which is to say that the longing to repeat a remembered satisfaction includes a revised version of the satisfaction, an interpretive re-creation of an original (if unlocatable) pleasure. The differences among mental activities are differences of interpretive procedures. And once criticism stops fishing for the truth in art, it can engage in the only activity which demonstrates both its own specificity and its affinities with art. That is, criticism can openly assume its status as an interpretive fiction, and yet demonstrate that its particular brand of interpretation consists in the elucidation of the sense-making procedures in art. Criticism is an interpretive reflection on the modes of interpretation in art. And in assuming what I take to be its only essential difference from art, criticism can help us to see the problematic nature of its relation to art. For the very nature of the difference between the two designates the profound similarity between the two. The identity of art is in part *to be* criticism, just as the very identity of criticism subverts any secure identifications of criticism and allows for the unpredictable "sliding" of critical discourse into the grooves or modes of artistic discourse.

Indeed, some of the most interesting modern criticism — especially in France since Gaston Bachelard — has demonstrated that the more seriously criticism takes its official function of remaining faithful to the text, the more it resembles art. The most profound fidelity to the work of art is to imitate it: the critic follows his writer so closely that he begins to duplicate the latter's achievement. Or, to put it in another way, critical discourse begins to resemble the literature which is its object by drawing attention to itself. While criticism continues to lean on other texts, it also now seems to be making a claim for the esthetic appeal of its own procedures; the myth of criticism as a transparent explication of literature is abandoned. The critic may not only borrow some of the sense-making procedures which he rightly attributes to art (for example, the use of a metaphor to convey an interpretive judgment, or — in the case of Blanchot — an indulgence in paradoxical "argument"). He may also draw attention to the seductiveness of the most discursive or even rationalistic aspects of critical argument. The *play* of criticism becomes visible. And we discover that the pleasures of conceptual experimentation, of dismissible speculation, are the specific pleasures of critical form. Thus the critical text comes to have an opacity not unlike that which the poet's fascination with the materiality of words gives to poetic language. Critical argument has "shapes" or "gestures" perhaps as seductive as those of sculpture or dance. . . . We have moved toward a community of writers, and away from hierarchical distinctions among poets, novelists and critics.[3]

But however problematic the separate identities of criticism and art may become, to a certain extent the former will always undermine an art of the fragmentary and the discontinuous. Significantly, the criticism which, until now, has most successfully sought to duplicate the intimate "movements" in art is also committed to making visible the individualizing coherence of a writer's work. The studies of Georges Poulet and of Jean-Pierre Richard, for example, are subversive of traditional criticism in the sense that they ignore the latter's insistence on analytical detachment and certain kinds of judgment. But thematic criticism also reinforces the traditional esthetic criterion of an artistic unity based on a coherent "vision of the world." Nothing could be more alien to this "artistic" criticism than a fragmentary or a collective art — or, at the extreme, an art without authorship.[4]

But such art is probably alien to any effort at critical interpretation. What differentiates criticism from art is precisely an interpretive mode intent on sorting out persistent meanings or intentions, and on elucidating the structural sense of art. Criticism strains toward continuity, unity and centrality of argument. Confronted with the anonymous particularity of scenes from Rimbaud's *Illuminations* or Robert Wilson's theater, the critic perhaps can't help but seek out — or invent — a "self" whose unifying designs he finds, if not in the content of those scenes, then in the very enterprise of doing away with structurable content, of eliminating repetition. The theatricalized self brings us back to the scenic mode of desire, and therefore to a kind of art much more remote from criticism than, say, the comparatively discursive art of realistic fiction. Criticism reformulates scenic desire in terms of persistent intentions and unifying structures. However profound the critic's sympathy may be with the discontinuous, the fragmentary and the peripheral, his own enterprise is always an argument for the inescapable presence, and even the irresistible appeal, of the general design.

Nonetheless, art and criticism take place within a single field of interpretation, and consequently every critical act and every artistic performance are, potentially, reminders of the problematic nature of the critic's and the artist's identities. The potential for criticism in art and for art in criticism, can, I think, be a major force in the promotion of psychic mobility. And psychic mobility can rescue us from the tyrannical rigidities of both sublimated desire (petrified and disguised in character structures) and scenic desire. If I have, on the whole, been arguing for an art which mocks our faith in psychological coherence and in the civilizing value of sublimation, it is because I think that an imagination of the deconstructed, perhaps even demolished, self is the necessary point of departure for an authentically civilizing skepticism about the nature of our desires and the nature of our being. Scenic desire, as we have had ample occasion to see, lends itself all too easily to devastations of being. But in the literary universe of partial selves — inhabited by such different works as Rimbaud's *Illuminations* and "Jean de Berg's" *L'Image* — there is nonetheless a greater likelihood of movements *among* different forms of desire and of being than in a world of fixed character structures. For what we call character is also a partial self. Its appearance of completeness, of wholeness, may be nothing more than the illusion created by the *centralizing* of a partial self. Such centralization involves both the organization of our desires into psychic structures and the expulsion of nonstructurable desires. Character, in short, is also a piece of a person; it has the factitious coherence of all obsessions. Only the mobility of desublimated desires preserves the mobility of being itself. An exuberant indefinite-ness about our own identity can both preserve the heterogeneity of our desires and rescue us from the totalitarian insistence natural to all desire.

It would, however, be impossible to eliminate all fixed character structures. The theatrical self of the *Illuminations* or of a Robert Wilson extravaganza is a triumph for desublimated desire which can be sustained only in literature, and even then only momentarily. To live entirely without sublimation and psychic continuities is un-thinkable. And even in the imaginary, "irresponsible" spaces of literature, psychic coherence, as we have seen most dramatically in Rimbaud, inevitably reappears. But we might argue that even the structured self can enter that play of mobile desire without which any project of radical self-revision runs the risk of merely changing the mode in which the self seeks terroristically to impose its desires on the world. I have spoken of a problematic reflectiveness about our identity. There is the nonreflective psychic mobility of the scenic self; but a certain mobility of being can also be achieved by the sort of multiplicity of *verbal* self-interpretations which we find in Proust. For such reflectiveness to take place, the repression, repetition and sublimation of desire must have proceeded to a point at which the very notion of the self has become a coherent and rather elaborate fiction. It's true that such fictions tend to im-mobilize us in a single identity. But they must also be sustained in time, and the accidents of history happily subvert those sense-making impulses which would reduce history to the persistence of orders and systems.

To live in time is an apprenticeship in techniques for deflecting desire into activities and a personality which are socially viable. Literature is instructive in this respect: scenes of desire in literary works are surrounded by and submitted to *developments* which compromise but which also humanize desire. On the one hand, litera-ture hallucinates the world in order to accommodate desire. On the other hand, it illustrates the ways in which we learn, in time, to make what Melanie Klein called reparations to the world for our imaginary devastations of it. Literature thus makes a double argu-ment. It invites us to return to that variety of scenes of desire which is stifled by the interpretive tracing back of all desires to a single, continuous design in a supposed maturing of desire. The literary imagination reinstates the world of desiring fantasies as a world of reinvented, richly fragmented and diversified body-memories. But, at the same time, it also gives ample space to those processes by which we make a continuous *story* of our desires, processes which also teach us to give up the intensities of an infinitely desirable hallucinated world for the somewhat disappointing enjoyments of fulfilled desires.

Notes

Notes to "Murderous Lovers"

1.   Think, think, Cephissa, of that cruel night
which fell eternally for a whole people;
see Pyrrhus, his eyes flashing in the glare
of our burning palaces, who trampled his way
across my murdered brothers; see him enter,
well-smeared with blood, cheering the carnage on;
recall the victors' cries, recall the cries
of the dying, choked in fire, put to the sword;
and, crazed among those horrors, Andromache:
that is how Pyrrhus came into my view;
those are the glories with which he crowned himself;
there, indeed, is the husband you offer.

   This is George Dillon's translation in the University of Chicago Press edition of *Three Plays of Racine: Phèdre, Britannicus, Andromaque* (1961).

2. *L'Anti-Oedipe* (1972) was announced as the first volume of *Capitalisme et schizophrénie*. In 1975, Deleuze and Guattari published *Kafka/Pour une littérature mineure*.

3. Michel Foucault's forthcoming study of sexuality in Western civilization includes a persuasive consideration of both the epistemology and the therapeutic techniques of psychoanalysis as political strategies designed to reinforce social control of the individual's desires.

4. I'm thinking especially of the work of Jacques Lacan, Jean Laplanche, J.-B. Pontalis and Serge Leclair. The best English introduction to these important thinkers is the issue of *Yale French Studies* entitled *French Freud*, ed. Jeffrey Mehlman (No. 48).

Notes to Chapter One

1. (Paris, 1969.) Mauron's study was presented as a thesis to the University of Aix-Marseille, and was first published in 1957 by the *Annales* of the Faculté des Lettres of Aix.

2. It might seem more logical to say that Titus hesitates between Bérénice and Rome. Mauron is more or less forced to split Bérénice into two opposing forces, since the scheme is meant to illustrate the antagonistic appeals of two women in each case. We can, I think, object to this distortion and still agree with the general argument Mauron makes.

3. Mauron quotes the passage in Act Two, Scene Two, which begins:

> Depuis près de six mois, honteux, désespéré,
> Portant partout le trait dont je suis déchiré,
> Contre vous, contre moi vainement je m'éprouve.

> For six long months ashamed and in despair,
> Pierced by the shaft implanted in my side,
> I battle with myself, with you, in vain.

For the few quotations from Racine in this chapter, I use the Penguin Classics translation of John Cairncross for *Phèdre* and *Iphigénie*, and George Dillon's translation for *Britannicus* in *Three Plays of Racine: Phèdre, Britannicus, Andromaque*.

4. See, for example, *Sexuality and the Psychology of Love*, ed. Philip Rieff (New York, 1963), p. 191, and *New Introductory Lectures on*

Psychoanalysis, ed. and tr. James Strachey (New York, 1965), pp. 129–34.

5. Raymond Picard has brilliantly documented that success in *La Carrière de Jean Racine*.

6. I'm thinking of Clytemnestre's outrage at the thought of not being at the marriage ceremony to give her daughter away properly, and also of her irritation with that black sheep of the family, Helen of Troy, who has brought them only scandal and war. Roland Barthes, in *Sur Racine*, mentions the comically quarrelsome tone of certain scenes in *Iphigénie*; he also emphasizes the "prosaic" nature of relationships in the play, and the "intense family life" of *Iphigénie*.

7. Melanie Klein speaks of the uselessness of stimulating the child's ego development when the analyst is interested in discovering the child's problems. A diversity of games is unnecessary; all the material the analyst needs is already present in the child's behavior at the beginning of treatment. (See *The Psychoanalysis of Children*, tr. Alix Strachey [New York, 1969], pp. 114–15).

8. Appropriately, this will be the last time I mention Astyanax. His indeterminate "presence" is scattered throughout this book, disseminated in forms as various as Proust's metaphorical imagination, the Stendhalian hero's improvised monologues, a Robert Wilson tableau, and, in *Histoire d'O*, Sir Stephen's ghastly pale face just after his initials are burned into O's buttocks. . . .

(I suppose I should add that the Astyanax I've referred to is definitely not the child in the ancient version of the story who is hurled by the Greeks from the walls of Troy. Racine's Astyanax will live.)

Notes to Chapter Two

1. Barthes' 1955 review of Robbe-Grillet's *Le Voyeur* is reprinted as "Littérature littérale" in the *Essais critiques*. Poirier's review of Pynchon was in the March 3, 1973, issue of the *Saturday Review of the Arts*.

2. Frank Kermode has studied, in *The Sense of an Ending*, the "paradigms of apocalypse" in Western culture, the "coherent patterns which, by the provision of an end, make possible a satisfying consonance with the origins and with the middle."

3. In this connection, see Robert Alter's *Partial Magic: The Novel as a Self-Conscious Genre* (University of California Press, 1975).

4. This is true of those great novels which Richard Chase attempted to exonerate from such criticism by calling them romances. These works, as the unfortunate destinies of Huck Finn and Deerslayer show, eventually submit to the pressures that belong to the realistic novel. This point has been eloquently made by Richard Poirier in *A World Elsewhere*.

5. For example, in the Dickensian figures of Turkey and Nippers, but not in the hero of Melville's "Bartleby, the Scrivener."

6. Translations from Balzac are my own.

7. The Proust quotations are from the Random House Moncrieff-Blossom translation. For some very suggestive remarks about the role of desire in Proust, see Eléonore M. Zimmermann, "Le rôle de Swann et de la société dans l'acte de création proustien," *Studi francesi* (No. 45, 1971).

8. For a more detailed version of the ideas in this paragraph, see Chapter Four of *Balzac to Beckett*.

Notes to Chapter Three

1. The translations in this chapter are my own, although I have consulted and found helpful both the Lowell Bair translation in the Bantam Books edition of *Madame Bovary* which I edited, and the Norton Critical Edition, edited with a substantially new translation by Paul de Man, based on the version by Eleanor Marx Aveling.

2. See Genette, "Silences de Flaubert," *Figures* (Paris, 1966), and Rousset, "*Madame Bovary* ou le 'livre sur rien.' Un aspect de l'art du roman chez Flaubert: le point de vue," *Forme et signification/Essais sur les structures littéraires de Corneille à Claudel* (Paris, 1962).

Notes to Chapter Four

1. All the translations from Stendhal are my own.

2. This should be qualified. Julien cries when he learns of his father's death, and Lucien suffers from a "burning remorse for not feeling any friendship or tenderness for his father." The nice fathers in Stendhal (in *Lucien Leuwen* and *Armance*) can be respected; the hero can't love them.

3. I rely on some concepts of Melanie Klein here. Stendhal's work not only dramatizes the most familiar Freudian version of Oedipal structures, it is also a striking literary confirmation of those pre-Oedipal fantasies most impressively elaborated by Karl Abraham, Klein and W. Ronald Fairbairn.

4. I have in mind Stendhal's famous comparison of politics in a novel to a pistol shot in the middle of a concert.

Notes to Chapter Six

1. This should of course be distinguished from nonidentical repetition, that is, from repetition which makes possible our historical perception of difference. I will speak further on of this second type of repetition in Lawrence; we have already glanced at an example of it in Proust. In Chapter Nine, we will be considering Artaud's horror of all derivation as a desperate effort to remove repetition entirely from life. For a philosophical discussion of these questions, see Gilles Deleuze, *Différence et répétition*.

2. "Singleness" is also a positive term in Lawrence. I'll return to this later.

3. Kate Millett quotes this passage in her acute if frequently coarse and misleading denunciation of Lawrence in *Sexual Politics*. She also speaks of what she calls Lawrence's considerable inhibition and strong negative feelings about female sexuality.

4. The arguments over anal sex in Lawrence were recently taken up again, in lively fashion, in two issues of *Novel: A Forum on Fiction*. See Mark Spilka, "Lawrence Up-Tight," *Novel*, IV (1971), and "Critical Exchange," *Novel*, V (1971).

5. A rationale, such as it is, for Lawrence's analogies between parts of the body and aspects of the psyche is presented in his two essays, "Psychoanalysis and the Unconscious" and "Fantasia of the Unconscious."

6. The situation is all the more ironic in that Lawrence was anxious to distinguish between what he calls in "Pornography and Obscenity" the "creative flow" of "the sex functions" and the flow "towards

dissolution, de-creation" in "the excrementory functions." The two sets of functions are, he writes, "utterly different in direction."

7. For an intelligent attempt to establish these distinctions with some clarity, see the chapter on *Women in Love* in George H. Ford, *Double Measure: A Study of the Novels and Stories of D. H. Lawrence.*

8. Chapter Two on "Realism and the Fear of Desire" presents a more elaborate argument about the politics of realism in the nineteenth-century novel.

Notes to Chapter Seven

1. The quotations from Lautréamont in this chapter come from the Guy Wernham translation of his work, first published by New Directions in 1943.

2. We should also note that the actual process of self-transformation is suggested in Lautréamont's work: Maldoror *becomes* a shark or a swan. Cathy, on the other hand, says that she *is* Heathcliff. Strictly speaking, there are no leaps of being in *Wuthering Heights*. Cathy, so to speak, already is Heathcliff before or rather without leaving herself. The possibility of metamorphosis in the self is presented as an identity between two different selves. The relation between Cathy and Heathcliff is somewhat like the relation between the two terms of a "beau comme" comparison in Lautréamont — to the extent, that is, that we succeed in keeping in mind the first term in spite of our enormous leap away from it. Emily Brontë's heroine is not only capable of a radical self-distancing, she also insists on the *presence* of the distant self. Or, to put this in another way, the imagination of metamorphosis in *Wuthering Heights* doesn't produce only differences; difference itself is also mysteriously presented as sameness.

3. In "Conflicting Impulses in *Wuthering Heights*," *Nineteenth-Century Fiction*, XVII (June 1962).

4. The family should perhaps more properly be used as a biological model of difference within repetition. But in *Wuthering Heights* it is one of the two elements in a fantasy which melodramatically polarizes pure otherness (Heathcliff) in opposition to a self always identical to itself (in familial self-repetitions). But of course what the parent (re)produces in the child is a *different self*. I'll be returning to the question of birth within another discussion of repetition and difference in Chapter Nine on Artaud.

Notes to Chapter Eight

1. For *Une Saison en enfer* and the *Illuminations*, I have used Enid Rhodes Peschel's recent translation (New York, 1973). For Rimbaud's letters and for his verse, Oliver Bernard's "plain prose translations," as he calls them, are decent enough, and I have therefore used his Penguin edition of *Rimbaud* for those pieces not in Peschel.

2. Passages from "Le Bateau ivre" which are thematically similar to the ones I discuss from "Comédie de la soif" inevitably come to mind:

> L'eau verte pénétra ma coque de sapin
> Et des taches de vins bleus et des vomissures
> Me lava, dispersant gouvernail et grappin.

. . . the green water penetrated my pinewood hull and washed me clean of the splashes of blue wine and vomit, carrying away both rudder and anchor.

and:

> Ô que ma quille éclate! Ô que j'aille à la mer!
>
> Si je désire une eau d'Europe, c'est la flache
> Noire et froide où vers le crépuscule embaumé
> Un enfant accroupi plein de tristesses, lâche
> Un bateau frêle comme un papillon de mai.

O let my keel split! O let me sink to the bottom!

If there is one water in Europe I want, it is the black cold pool
where into the scented twilight a child squatting full of sadness
launches a boat as fragile as a butterfly in May.

3. We might have chosen other thematically significant imagery in
   Rimbaud. For example, there are all the mists or clouds which
   dissolve, or through which the poet glimpses the principal scene in
   several poems of the *Illuminations*. When mists don't condense,
   Rimbaud sees through them; and this becomes generalized into a
   visual theme of seeing things not only through mists, but through any
   intermediate and framing object.

4. We should, however, note that two of the best studies of Rimbaud
   are "thematic" in precisely the sense which, I think, is ultimately
   discredited by the *Illuminations*; Jacques Rivière's *Rimbaud*, and
   Jean-Pierre Richard's essay "Rimbaud ou la poésie du devenir," in
   Poésie et profondeur.

5. When we look at some contemporary theatrical experiments in Chapter
   Ten — especially at the theater of Robert Wilson — we will, however,
   find tactics designed to make the spectators' eyes wander as part of a
   more general strategy of dramatizing the heterogeneity of desire.

6. Gilles Deleuze makes remarks similar to these in *Proust et les signes*.
   I think they are much more applicable to Rimbaud than to Proust;
   the latter never gives up the project of finding an invariable self
   which would "totalize" and give sense to all the self's desires — even
   though Proust's own work implicitly dismisses that project.

Notes to Chapter Nine

1. All the translations from Artaud are my own.

2. *Any* code is of course unthinkable without repetition. In a sense, Artaud's project is obviously absurd, but the devaluation of verbal language has important consequences for the theater. Repetition can't be abolished, but the psychology supported by rational discourse can be replaced by a purely scenic psychology already pointed to in the *Illuminations*.

3. Birth is the origin of derivation in an individual's life, although this is obviously not the same thing as saying that it is the origin of Artaud's traumatized interpretation of birth. The (hypothetical) origins of an obsession inevitably get lost in our enactments of it. Artaud's horror of being born may, after all, be the retroactive effect on his memory of birth of a view of defecation as a loss of self. But such causal origins are in fact impossible to locate. Artaud's hatred of derivation and repetition exists nowhere apart from his performances of that hatred; there is no unperformed source from which all versions of the theme proceed.

4. They may also be meant to seduce reality into conforming to desire. Our very willingness to admit the fictive status of our stories about the world suggests a wish to strike a bargain with the world. More secretly, we hope that fiction will have an energy sufficient to transform the world and thus return us to that harmony between desire and reality which would make fictional narratives obsolescent. . . .

Notes to Chapter Ten

1. Chaikin's Open Theater is now disbanded. In 1975, he directed *A Fable*, with the collaboration of Jean-Claude Van Itallie (as writer) and Richard Peaslee (as composer). In 1976, Chaikin returned to acting in a production of *Woyzeck*.

2. For an example of heterogeneity as a result of *im*mobility, see my discussion of Rimbaud's technique of framing the scenes of the *Illuminations* (Chapter Eight, pp. 252–53). There is a stimulating discussion of the relation between visual mobility or immobility and the heterogeneity of our visual field in Jean-François Lyotard's *Discours, figures* (see especially pp. 156–57).

3. The theater I've been considering in this chapter can also help us to redefine our erotic relation to the theatrical scene. I think that in traditional drama, all the factors which tend to focus our attention on central meanings also encourage a fetishistic attention to the actors' bodies. Theatrical voyeurism is the sexualizing of our centralizing impulse. The sensual appeal of visual mobility, on the other hand, helps to defeat this fetishistic attachment to parts of the theatrical scene — an attachment which parodies but is also faithful to those centralizing impulses which produce "character" and impoverish desire.

Notes to Chapter Eleven

1. I have used the English translations of the three French works I discuss in detail in this chapter: Bernard Frechtman's version of *Funeral Rites*, Sabine d'Estrée's translation for *Story of O*, and Patsy Southgate's translation of *The Image* (all published by Grove Press).

2. The date of Freud's essay is 1915. My summary of Freud's argument is inspired by Jean Laplanche's brilliant discussion of "Instincts and Their Vicissitudes" in Chapter Five of *Vie et mort en psychanalyse* (now available in an excellent translation by Jeffrey Mehlman [Baltimore, 1976]). In Laplanche's phrasing of the primacy of masochism: "The masochistic fantasy is fundamental, whereas the sadistic fantasy implies an identification with the suffering object; it is within the suffering position that the enjoyment [la jouissance] lies." The "extension" of pain into sexual excitement may depend on a notion of sexuality itself as the product of any shattering (pleasant or unpleasant) of the self's equilibrium. Laplanche takes the position that "a fantasy, the introjection of the object, is a perturbation [ébranlement] and, in its essence (whether its 'content' be pleasant or unpleasant), a generator of auto-erotic exitation." The obscure — and crucial — point of course concerns the genesis of sexuality, and Laplanche's argument of this point would require a much longer theoretical discussion (to which I hope to return in another work). In Freud's 1924 essay, "The Economic Problem in Masochism," the views expressed in "Instincts and Their Vicissitudes" are reformulated in the light of the "death instinct" put forward in *Beyond the Pleasure Principle*.

3. In one of the most stimulating passages of *S/Z*, Roland Barthes suggests that we stop considering literature and painting from within "une réflexion hiérarchique." Barthes asks: "Why not renounce the plurality of 'arts,' in order to affirm more effectively the plurality of 'texts'?" (p. 62). The best example of seductively artistic criticism I know is Lawrence's *Studies in Classic American Literature*.

4. When Deleuze and Derrida talk about literary works, they are (unlike Poulet, Richard and Starobinski) interested in "partial selves," self-fragmentations and more or less successful enterprises in the subversion of a cult of psychic totality and full psychic presence. But the critical essays in which this interest is expressed are themselves closer to a traditionally discursive, analytically detached criticism which the now rather old-fashioned work of Richard and of Poulet had in fact moved beyond. The mode of critical writing was more radically new in critics who sought out traditional values in literature (a coherent intentionality) than in the writers who have most effectively contested those values (in a discursive mode derived from them . . .). But Derrida's latest work — *Glas* — is a fascinating attempt to move toward authentically new shapes of "critical" discourse.

I should also add that there is, as we saw in our study of James, an extremity of critical discourse which is also depersonalized, inexpressive of any self at all. But we must distinguish between the anonymous *particularities* of the *Illuminations* and the anonymity occasionally reached by criticism: the latter is the result of verbal speculation, of a surrender to the appeals of abstract design in language.

Index